RADICAL WOMEN IN LATIN AMERICA

RADICAL WOMEN IN LATIN AMERICA

LEFT | AND | RIGHT

WITHDRAWN

EDITED BY **VICTORIA GONZÁLEZ** AND **KAREN KAMPWIRTH**

THE PENNSYLVANIA STATE UNIVERSITY PRESS | UNIVERSITY PARK, PENNSYLVANIA

Columbia FLI Partnership
HQ1236.5 L37 R33 2001

Library of Congress Cataloging-in-Publication Data

Radical women in Latin America : left and right /
edited by Victoria González and Karen Kampwirth.
p.   cm.
Includes bibliographical references and index.
ISBN 0-271-02100-4 (cloth : acid-free paper)
ISBN 0-271-02101-2 (paper : acid-free paper)
1.Women radicals—Latin America. 2. Women
political activists—Latin America. 3. Feminists—Latin
America. I. González, Victoria, 1969–
II. Kampwirth, Karen, 1964–

HQ1236.5.L37 R33 2001
305.42'098—dc21
                                                00-057131

                          •

CONTENTS

ACKNOWLEDGMENTS

Many people made this project possible. Victoria would like to thank her mother, Kathy Hoyt, her aunt, V.A., Gerardo Sevilla, Karen Kampwirth, Jane Slaughter, Jeff Gould, Peter Guardino, Muriel Nazzari, Arlene Díaz, Soili Buska, Eugenia Rodríguez, Ivania Paladino, Circles Robinson, Pilar Bezanilla, Julie Cummings, Turid Hagene, Jennifer Guglielmo, Jesse Méndez, Eloisa Méndez, Claire Kinsley, Lisa Zimmerman, Sharon Rogers, Kitty Madden, Oscar Rivera, Bayardo González, Paula González, Ben Rigberg, Dean Kotlowski, Gerónima Ubeda, Dora Ubeda, Celina Gallardo, Engel Ortega, Diana Pritchard, Mariano Vargas, Barbara Seitz, Guillermo Martínez, Patricia Elvir, Saul Arana, Silvia Torres, Margarita Vannini, Miguel Angel Herrera, Frances Kinloch, and the staffs at the Archivo Nacional and the Grupo Venancia in Matagalpa. For their financial assistance, she thanks Indiana University's History Department and Center for Latin American and Caribbean Studies, the Institute for the Study of World Politics, the American Association of University Women, Oberlin College, and the National Hispanic Scholarship Fund.

Karen would like to thank María Dolores Alvarez, Silvia Carrazco, Laura Enríquez, Victoria González, Anne Larson, Marcos Membreño, Duane Oldfield, Elena Quiñónez and the entire Quiñónez Cajina family, Eric Selbin, Millie Thayer, and Tom Walker. Thanks are also due to Knox College for its generosity in providing the faculty research grants that made this possible.

Both of us would like to thank the contributors to the book and all the people who generously agreed to be interviewed. The Latin American Studies Association (LASA) provided the opportunity to present earlier versions of almost all the chapters in this book at two panels of the 1998 LASA meeting. The staff at Puntos de Encuentro in Managua graciously allowed us to present a version of our research for this book as part of the Universidad de las Mujeres series in July 1998 and provided the photo for the cover of the book. We thank all the people who have commented on the chapters in this book, especially Elisabeth Friedman and Elizabeth Hutchison. Finally, a special thanks to Amy Bank and Ana Criquillón, the matchmakers without whom this book would never have been written.

Victoria González
Karen Kampwirth

INTRODUCTION

The last three decades of the twentieth century witnessed a boom in writings about Latin American women, particularly about women on the left of the political spectrum. Yet the involvement of women in right-wing political movements has been largely ignored, much to the detriment of a more nuanced understanding of women and politics in Latin America. In this multidisciplinary collection of essays, we provide a new perspective as we consider—in a single volume—women's political activities and alliances on the left *and* the right.

Why is it important to study women on the right? And what can we learn from jointly addressing their experiences and those of leftist women? Studying women on the right is crucial to understanding the development of dictatorship and authoritarianism in Latin America. Moreover, the stories of both right- and left-wing women challenge traditional portrayals of men as inherently violent and women as inherently peaceful. They also force us to confront once again the fact that there is no automatic sisterhood among women, even among those of the same class and ethnicity. On the other hand, by addressing the lives of women on the left and the right simultaneously, we understand the many similarities that unite women, even across immense political divides.

The women whose experiences we document in this volume can be considered *radical* for several different reasons. Radicalism, for us, is defined by both tactics and goals. Clearly, the women who joined armed struggles made radical choices in their lives, choices only a minority of women have made throughout history. And regardless of whether they embraced violence as a political option, all these women settled on political paths that took them beyond electoral politics. They chose a variety of methods (violence, nonpartisanship, dictatorship, and authoritarianism) to deal directly with the roots of the problems they saw in society. Radical women tended to use unconventional tactics so as to transform, rather than merely reform, their societies.

Although it is fairly easy to categorize the radical activists in this volume as leftist or rightist, it is somewhat harder to come up with definitions of "right" and "left" that are applicable to all of twentieth-century Latin America. The difficulties with terminology arise because there is no monolithic left or right and because meanings change over time and place. We do think, however, that the terms have been and continue to be meaningful, and that basic distinctions between the left and the right can and must be drawn.

The *right* has been characterized by anticommunism, opposition to class struggle, and the favoring of hierarchical survival strategies like patron-clientelism. Moreover, those on the right are generally opposed to the imposition of equality by the state and are in favor of individual justice. The *left* has been characterized primarily by its call for social justice and its strong stance in favor of state intervention to promote social and economic equality. Historically, most on the left have supported class struggle.

It is important to note in this context that the right, like the left, is dynamic, and it often stands for change. Additionally, the right—or the left, depending on the country and the particular historical moment—is sometimes at the center and not at the margins of the political spectrum. Thus, although the women in this book are radicals, they are not necessarily extremists. Women have played crucial roles on the left and the right throughout Latin America. Shortly, we will present an overview and analysis of those roles, but we would like to begin with an overview of nineteenth- and twentieth-century Latin American political history for those readers who are not already familiar with the region.

A Brief Review of Latin American Political History

The bloody wars for independence that took place in much of Latin America in the first two decades of the nineteenth century—and the political vacuum that followed independence—had long-lasting consequences. One of these was the development of *caudillismo,* a social system based upon the mutual dependence and loyalty of a strong man (a *caudillo*) and his followers and sustained by patron-client relations and violence or the threat of violence. Many of Latin America's well-known nineteenth-century political leaders (Santa Anna in Mexico, Rosas in Argentina, Bolivar in Colombia) were *caudillos.*

Another legacy of the wars for independence was the split between liberals and conservatives among the political elite. Early nineteenth-century liberals favored the continuation of the Bourbon reforms implemented by the Spanish crown before independence, reforms that sought to restrict the power of the Catholic Church and implement freer trade and a more modern administration of the colonies. In contrast, conservatives in Latin America advocated authoritarian, centralized government (and sometimes monarchy), greater economic regulation, and special Church privileges.

Throughout the late nineteenth and early twentieth centuries, liberals, in general, advocated limited representative democracy, decentralized governments, and reduced economic regulation, as well as the separation of church and state. Major differences between liberals and conservatives thus revolved around two particular issues: the extent to which trade should be regulated and, most important, the roles of the Catholic Church and the military in post-independence society. Liberals favored a secular state and were against special privileges for members of the clergy and the military. Specifically, they tended to feel that the Catholic Church stood in the way of progress, competed with the state for loyalty, and had too much economic and political power. Conservatives, on the other hand, wanted to maintain social order: for them, the military and the Church were tools for social control.

In spite of the clear disagreements between liberals and conservatives, the conflict between these two groups was sometimes more about who would hold power than about their salient political differences. But wars between liberals and conservatives did take place, sometimes with devastating consequences for the recently independent countries. In a few extreme cases, like that of Nicaragua during the 1850s, the conflict between the liberal and conservative parties led to foreign intervention. William Walker, a U.S. mercenary invited by the Liberals to help defeat the Conservatives, unexpectedly took over the nation and declared himself president. Although Walker was soon defeated by his former Liberal allies, his presence in Nicaragua discredited the Liberal party, preventing it from rising to power until the late nineteenth century. Elsewhere in Latin America, liberals were able to gain power by the middle of the nineteenth century, leading to the creation of secular, laissez-faire, liberal states. The main contradiction in these societies was that liberals sought to modernize political and economic structures without addressing the underlying inequalities in society, a contradiction that led to the rise of "first wave" feminism in Latin America and leftist organizing in general. Secular societies needed secular teachers, and feminism sprouted throughout Latin America among the first generations of public school instructors, who tended to favor increased educational opportunities for women. In addition, feminists supported female suffrage in the late nineteenth and early twentieth centuries, although most Latin American women would not gain the vote until the 1940s and 1950s. These two issues would characterize first wave feminism, which was inevitably middle-class in character.

Other than perhaps the political parties themselves, no institution has had as much influence on politics in Latin America as the Catholic Church. The Church's role dates back to its participation in the colonial period that began more than five hundred years ago. Colonialism allowed Europeans to get access to the labor, land, and other resources of the New World. At the same time, colonialism provided the Catholic Church with an opportunity to convert millions of indigenous people. This spiritual justification for colonialism meant that the hierarchy of the Church was often slow to criticize the mass murder and economic exploitation inherent in the colonial project.

In general, the colonial alliance between temporal and spiritual power held fast through the twentieth century. The Catholic Church often promoted the idea that "the meek shall inherit the earth," interpreting that phrase to mean that those who meekly accepted social inequalities in this life would be rewarded in the next. Church leaders were particularly hesitant to address gender inequality, since such inequality was directly endorsed by the Vatican: sacraments could be carried out by men and men alone. Instead, women were to be content with the roles of mother and intermediary, imitating Mary, the mother of Jesus.

Yet the alliance between the Church and the authoritarian state was not the only tradition that could be traced back to the colonial period. At times, lower-level clergy—including priests like Bartolomé de las Casas of Mexico and Antonio Valdivieso of Nicaragua—harshly criticized worldly inequalities, especially the abuse of indigenous people. That tradition of identification with the poorest and least advantaged would find its expression, beginning in the late 1960s, in liberation theology. Liberation theologians encouraged Catholics (organized in small groups known as *base communities*) to evaluate daily life in the light of the Bible. And just as God had called on Moses to lead the Jews out of their oppression in Egypt, God called on Moses' successors in the twentieth century to lead their people out of oppression.

But just what it meant to lead people out of oppression was disputed, since there were many ways in which to contest authoritarianism and inequality. In the twentieth century, armed struggle was one common strategy that succeeded in overthrowing authoritarian regimes in four countries

(Mexico in 1917, Bolivia in 1952, Cuba in 1959, and Nicaragua in 1979); scores of other guerrilla movements failed to seize the state.

While some found social inequality to be so entrenched that they resorted to arms, many more Latin Americans contested inequality through peaceful means. Throughout the twentieth century, labor unions (both urban and, to a lesser extent, rural) gave disadvantaged people a chance to improve their working conditions. In many countries, labor unions gained access to the state in alliance with populist political parties (such as Mexico's PRI, Argentina's Peronist party, and Peru's APRA), but that access often came at the cost of incorporation into a hierarchical structure and deradicalizing economic demands. Whatever the balance of benefits and costs, there is no doubt that Latin American union activists, like guerrillas, were often highly oriented toward the state.

Many women became politicized through protests against the state during the periods when dictatorships ruled a number of South American countries (Argentina, Brazil, Chile, Uruguay from the 1960s through the 1980s) and Central American countries (El Salvador, Guatemala, Nicaragua from the 1930s through the 1980s). Citizens of all the countries analyzed in this book experienced periods of dictatorship during the twentieth century; however, the nature of the dictatorships varied, as did the responses of women to those dictatorships.

The South American military dictatorships arose in societies that were among the most industrialized, urbanized, developed, and democratic[1] in Latin America. Those dictatorships, often called *bureaucratic authoritarian regimes,* were typically justified by their proponents as a solution to the messiness and even anarchy inherent in democracy. And so, in the three South American countries studied in this book, tens of thousands were tortured and killed by the military dictators in the name of order.

Many women created new organizations in response to the South American dictatorships, and some women could build on skills they had gained from participating in party or union politics during earlier democratic periods. Left-wing women organized in two main ways: they either organized human rights groups to demand both an end to state violence and the return of their "disappeared" children, or they formed cost-of-living groups to pro-

---

1. This is not to imply that those countries were perfectly democratic up until the military coups that ushered in the bureaucratic authoritarian regimes. But—compared to many other countries in Latin America—these countries had been characterized by more consistent democratic rule over the course of the twentieth century. This was especially true for Chile and Uruguay.

test the negative impact of the dictatorships on their ability to feed their families. Those women's groups were often the first organizations to dare to challenge the power of the military, thus playing a critical role in the beginning of the transition to democracy. Right-wing women, as we will show in this book, also participated politically during the time of the South American dictatorships, supporting the military's efforts to pacify what it saw as unruly societies.

In contrast, the Central American dictators ruled over societies that were among the most agrarian, rural, and underdeveloped in Latin America. They were societies that had experienced only short and highly compromised periods of electoral democracy in the twentieth century, and their rulers could be called traditional dictators. That is, they often ruled in the name of a few individuals or families and they did not tend to justify their rule as a temporary break within an otherwise democratic history.

In response to those highly entrenched dictatorships, left-wing women in Central America often responded in kind: they joined guerrilla movements and took up arms, hoping to overthrow the dictatorships and transform their societies. Many other left-wing women in Central America (as in South America) engaged in human rights or cost-of-living activism. Yet the Central American activists were not necessarily the same as the South American activists. Even members of those unarmed groups tended to sympathize with the goals of the guerrillas, if not always with their tactics. Right-wing women were also active in Central American politics, as we will show, sometimes rising to positions of power within the dictatorships and sometimes directly confronting left-wing women activists.

In the late twentieth century, during the transitions to democracy in both Central and South America, a number of social movements emerged that would have a different relationship to political parties and the state than earlier movements had had. Many activists began to question the state-oriented model of social movement politics that had characterized most activism over the twentieth century; that questioning led to the rise of what have been called "new social movements."

The new social movements were diverse and promoted a variety of causes, including indigenous rights, black people's rights, women's rights, gay and lesbian rights, neighborhood improvement, and environmental protection. Unlike movements in western Europe and North America that have also been labeled "new," these movements were deeply concerned with questions of class, largely because economic inequality and poverty remained far more brutal in Latin America than in the north. Moreover (and again unlike their northern counterparts), the new social movements of Latin America retained some orientation toward the state, in part because the state was still the best source of badly needed resources. But in contrast with the economically oriented and state-focused guerrilla and labor activists who preceded them, new social movement activists tended to view inequality as a complex phenomenon with dimensions that were private as well as public.

So while traditional demands like redistribution remained, new ones, such as sexual freedom, were added to the agenda. By the last decade of the twentieth century, many of the new social movements had institutionalized into nongovernmental organizations (or NGOs), often with the support of foreign funders. As with the previous twists and turns of Latin American politics, this new development was complicated: the growth of NGOs created opportunities for long-term advocacy at the same time that it created new resentments, since many lacked access to the funding that made NGOs possible.

An Overview of the Book

The essays in this volume focus on six countries (Nicaragua, El Salvador, Guatemala, Argentina, Brazil, and Chile) in which women have played a prominent role in radical public politics. In order to highlight the fact that there is no single experience or interpretation of politics in any country, the book includes more than one essay on Nicaragua, El Salvador, Brazil, and Chile. The first part of the book focuses on Central America.

In Chapter 1, Victoria González analyzes how an early-twentieth-century feminist movement metamorphosed, by the 1950s, into a nonfeminist right-wing Somocista women's movement; her reading challenges traditional portrayals of Nicaraguan women as having only recently awakened to politics and feminism.[2] González argues that many women backed the Somoza family and its right-wing Liberal Party between 1936 and 1979 in exchange for suffrage and increased educational and economic opportunities. This chapter examines some of the limits and complexities of women's support for the Somozas and shows that concerns about female sexuality and women's

2. See Helen Collinson, ed., *Women and Revolution in Nicaragua* (London: Zed Books, 1990). See also Benjamin Keen, *A History of Latin America* (Boston: Houghton Mifflin, 1996), and Anna M. Fernández Poncela, "Nicaraguan Women: Legal, Political, and Social Spaces," in *Gender Politics in Latin America: Debates in Theory and Practice,* ed. Elizabeth Dore (New York: Monthly Review Press, 1997).

proper roles in society were central to the development of the anti-Somocista movement.

In Chapter 2, Karen Kampwirth compares the Sandinista revolutionary guerrillas of the 1970s who overthrew the Somoza dictatorship to the counterrevolutionary ("Contra") guerrillas of the 1980s who sought to overthrow the Sandinista government. This chapter addresses the socioeconomic and ideological factors that made it possible for women in these two groups to become armed combatants as well as the personal reasons that contributed to their decisions. Additionally, Kampwirth examines the experiences of these groups, observing differences and commonalities, and she considers the ways in which participation in a guerrilla movement affected women's later lives. She notes in conclusion that Sandinista women were more likely than Contra women to become involved in later struggles for gender equality.

María Teresa Blandón gives us a feminist activist's account of developments in the Nicaraguan women's movement at the end of the 1990s in Chapter 3. Blandón addresses the formation in 1996 of the National Coalition of Women, an organization that brought women from the left and the right together in order to press for feminist demands. The construction of an autonomous women's movement that values diversity and promotes radical change is what made the coalition—the most heterogeneous political experiment to date—possible. It marks the first time that Sandinista women, autonomous feminists, and right-wing women have come together and agreed upon a common (albeit limited) agenda.

Together, the first three essays fill a significant gap in the literature on twentieth-century Nicaraguan women. They help explain, from a gendered perspective, the most important political developments in that country over the last hundred years: the rise and fall of the Somozas (1936–79) and the Sandinistas (1979–90) as well as the re-emergence of the feminist movement in the 1990s after it was co-opted by the Somozas in the 1950s.

The three essays that deal with El Salvador analyze the emergence of second wave feminism from a number of angles. In Chapter 4, Patricia Hipsher examines the leftist origins of second wave feminism and the ways in which this legacy has affected coalition building between left- and right-wing women. Hipsher concludes that the relationship between the revolutionary left and feminism became a major obstacle not only for the formation of an autonomous feminist movement but also for coalition building across political lines. In spite of the existing difficulties, feminists and women on the right have been able to find common ground on the issues of domestic violence, child support, and women's participation in politics. Issues like abortion or free trade zone reforms, however, which deal with sexual morality or class, demonstrate that there are some irreconcilable differences between these two groups.

Kelley Ready, in Chapter 5, considers the ways in which feminists reconstructed fatherhood and motherhood in postwar neoliberal El Salvador. In coalition with right-wing women activists, feminists succeeded in passing legislation that requires candidates for elected positions to get legal clearance certifying that they do not owe child support payments. Obligating men to be financially responsible for their offspring did not challenge the neoliberal state's economic agenda, because it did not require state funds. However, it did involve a rethinking of the social roles of women and men—the ultimate goal of feminist organizations like the Women for Dignity and Life (Las Dignas), which founded the Association of Mothers Seeking Child Support (AMD).

In Chapter 6, Ilja Luciak focuses on Guatemala, drawing comparisons between that country, El Salvador, and Nicaragua. He examines women's participation in the revolutionary movements and analyzes the steps made toward gender equality in the period after the peace accords, concluding that the participation of women in the Guatemalan guerrilla army was much more limited than that of women in El Salvador's FMLN (Farabundo Martí National Liberation Front) or even in Nicaragua's FSLN (Sandinista National Liberation Front). Nonetheless, women's rights were specifically addressed in the 1996 Guatemalan peace agreements—more than in the 1992 Salvadoran peace accords. The Guatemalan peace agreements responded to a greater feminist influence for a number of reasons, including pressure from Guatemalan women's groups within the Assembly of Civil Society, the impact of feminist scholarship like that of Maxine Molyneux, and international factors such as the emergence of significant feminist movements elsewhere in Central America in the 1990s and the United Nations Conference on Women held in Beijing in 1995. In spite of this increased societal awareness, Luciak contends that gender equality will flourish in the URNG (Guatemalan National Revolutionary Unity) only if it succeeds in the difficult endeavor of making the transition from a guerrilla coalition to a political party.

The second part of this volume deals with South American women. In Chapter 7, Sandra McGee Deutsch examines women's participation in extreme right-wing organizations in Argentina, Brazil, and Chile from 1900 to 1940. Upper- and middle-class women joined these groups as an extension of their activities in the Church. They saw their mission as one of spreading patriotism, morality, and bourgeois notions of femininity, often overtly rejecting femin*ism* despite the fact that some of their goals overlapped those of feminists. Through their activism, they also honed their skills and developed a greater sense of autonomy. Their participation in the extreme right reveals the peaceful and class-conciliatory side of violent movements.

Liesl Haas analyzes the relationship between the women's movement and the Workers' Party (PT) in Brazil in Chapter 8. She discusses the ideological and historical similarities between the women's movement and the Workers' Party, the position of feminists within the PT, and the extent to which feminism has influenced the philosophy of the party. Haas suggests that in the period following the transition to democracy, the PT made a greater effort to promote female candidates and incorporate women into politics than other parties did. However, the power held by labor unions and the Catholic Church constrained feminist change within the PT. Haas concludes that in spite of these limitations, the links between social movements and political parties can contribute to more democratic representation in Brazil.

In Chapter 9, Lisa Baldez examines nonpartisanship as a strategy used by women on both the left and the right in Chile. She considers two organizations: Feminine Power mobilized against Salvador Allende in the 1970s, and Women for Life was formed in 1983 to oppose the military government of Augusto Pinochet. Baldez argues that female party leaders in both instances adopted nonpartisanship in order to respond to a genuinely felt moral crisis and to tap strategically into conventional norms governing women's roles. Despite the fact that the women of Feminine Power pointedly rejected feminist goals and the members of Women for Life actively embraced those goals, both groups mobilized on the basis of their identities as women. This chapter contends that when women mobilize as political outsiders they forward their own gendered version of antipolitics.

Margaret Power argues, in Chapter 10, that between 1973 and 1988 the Chilean military government promoted women's roles as mothers and that right-wing women largely accepted that discourse. Within a greater "politics of antipolitics" context, women were portrayed as apolitical—and the military, too, projected an apolitical image. Right-wing women explicitly rejected feminism; yet, through their discourse, many of them implicitly espoused feminist ideas and demands. The reassertion of the political party system in the late 1980s revealed many of the contradictions inherent in the position of right-wing women. Attempts by Lucía Hiriart to create a pro-Pinochet women's movement failed, as many right-wing women embraced the return to politics (and chose not to be in an organization led by Pinochet's wife).

As a result of the plebiscite opening, right-wing women no longer identified exclusively as mothers; they were now citizens as well.

Four Themes

This book illuminates four interrelated themes: (1) the relationship of the political left and right to organized feminism; (2) the extent of women's autonomy from political parties, guerrilla movements, and other male-dominated organizations; (3) the possibilities for coalition building between left- and right-wing women; and (4) how and why women justify their political actions through maternalist discourses.

Theme 1: Feminism

The theme of feminism is so central to this book that it figures in every one of the chapters, as the above chapter summaries suggest. What did feminism mean for the women who are discussed in the following pages? Did it mean the same thing for radicals of the left and the right? Did they identify with a feminist project or did they reject it? And what was that project, anyway?

A single definition of feminism is elusive: meanings shifted over the course of the twentieth century and from country to country. Even in a single country, at a given point in time, individuals did not always mean the same thing when they spoke of "feminism." Nonetheless, shifting definitions do not mean that the word was meaningless. Far from it: in most (if not all) Latin American countries, the word *feminism* was used throughout the course of the twentieth century, and in many cases, its usage dates back to the late nineteenth century.[3] The passion that has often accompanied defenses of feminism—or attacks upon it—indicates just how important the concept is for understanding life in Latin America.

That passion was clear in an essay directed at the more than six hundred women who attended two "Feminist Congresses" held on the Yucatán pen-

3. María del Carmen Feijoo and Mónica Gogna, "Women in the Transition to Democracy," in *Women and Social Change in Latin America,* ed. Elizabeth Jelin (London: Zed Books, 1990), 80; Francesca Miller, *Latin American Women and the Search for Social Justice* (Hanover: University Press of New England, 1991), 35; and Gina Vargas, "El futuro desde la perspectiva de las mujeres," in *500 años de patriarcado en el nuevo mundo,* ed. Clara Leyla Alfonso (Santo Domingo, República Dominicana: Red Entre Mujeres, un Diálogo Sur-Norte/Centro de Investigación para la Acción Femenina [CIPAF], 1993), 142.

insula in Mexico in 1916.[4] Julio Hernández, the essayist, opened with a question: "Is feminism, as it is understood today by Mexican women, really a natural and physiological function, or is it an amoral and purely pathological state?" He then promised the reader that he would study the question "with a serenity of spirit that will no doubt calm our beautiful compatriots from the peninsula."[5]

Hernández considered all the differences between men and women and then, like many other leftists in Latin America, argued that one of those differences made the feminist project highly dangerous. While men show "notable tendencies toward the emancipation of their ideas," women are "still in their theological infancy," and therefore are controlled by the priests, who are not even truly Mexican but Roman. If women continue to be so loyal to the Roman Catholic Church, Hernández wrote, "they will continue, as they are up until this point, as the eternal slaves of error and of its worldly promoters, and as a result, as the irreconcilable enemies of the Fatherland."[6]

He recommended, then, that participants in national congresses not waste their time discussing "if they should be voting participants in the electoral struggles, or if they will play an active role in the government." Instead, their time would be better spent with "serious" questions like "What measures should they employ to free women from the clergy[?] . . . What measures should they employ so that women succeed in conquering husbands who can love them for their whole lives? . . . What measures should they employ so that there are no more celibate men in the Republic?"[7]

Ignoring the advice of men like Hernández, Latin American feminists of the first several decades of the twentieth century fought for a series of social reforms, including the extension of the vote to women. They argued that a better society might be constructed by enfranchising women and through reforms such as protecting working mothers and abolishing prostitution and alcoholism.[8] Some feminists also demanded sex education and equal pay for equal work.

4. On those Congresses, see Ana Lau and Carmen Ramos, *Mujeres y revolución, 1900–1917* (Mexico City: Instituto Nacional de Estudios Históricos de la Revolución Mexicana, 1993), 55–60.

5. Julio Hernández, "El feminismo y la educación: La mujer debe colaborar a la creación de la patria" (1916), in *Mujeres y revolución,* by Lau and Ramos, 145.

6. Ibid., 147–48.

7. Ibid., 148–49.

8. Miller, *Latin American Women,* 97; Virginia Mora Carvajal, "Mujeres e historia en América Latina: En busca de una identidad de género," in *Entre silencios y voces: Género e historia en América Central (1750–1990),* ed. Eugenia Rodríguez Sáenz (San José, Costa Rica: Centro Nacional para el Desarrollo de la Mujer y la Familia, 1997), 5.

But the battle over suffrage was to be a longer one for Latin American feminists than for their counterparts in the north; the arguments of men like Hernández were very influential within the Latin American left. Fearing that enfranchising women would empower the Church and other conservative sectors, liberals and leftists were highly resistant to women's pleas for the right to vote. (When women finally did get the vote,[9] it was often because conservative politicians granted it to them, thinking that women's votes would strengthen the right.[10])

Despite the eventual successes of the early feminist movement, the class background of its members was an impediment to the development of a broad-based movement. In a region that was—and still is—deeply divided by class and ethnic differences, feminists, who tended to be middle-class and well-educated, could not (or would not) reach out to the majority of less privileged women.[11] Those who did concern themselves with improving the lives of poor and working-class women tended to adopt paternalistic attitudes. In the end, the first wave of Latin American feminism—due to its small size, middle-class character, and to the authoritarian conditions under which women often won the right to vote—was nearly forgotten by second wave feminist activists. This was an unfortunate occurrence, because it played into the myth, promoted by some on the left and on the right, that the late-twentieth-century struggle for women's rights was a foreign imposition.

After women were granted the right to vote, the first wave of Latin American feminism largely ebbed away. When feminism rose again, beginning in the 1960s and 1970s, it would have a somewhat different class character and a new set of demands. As in the United States, second wave feminism in Latin America arose out of what was called the "new left."[12] New left activists in both regions shared a vision of a more egalitarian world and a commitment to promote that world through organized protest. But—again in both regions—those egalitarian values tended to be left at the doorway when activists returned home at night. Many male leaders, and a number of female

9. Ecuadoran women were the earliest to be enfranchised in Latin America; they won the vote in 1929. Paraguayan women were the latest to be enfranchised (1961). For a list of women's suffrage enactment dates for Latin American countries, see Miller, *Latin American Women,* 96.

10. Ibid., 97.

11. Mora Carvajal, "Mujeres e historia," 5.

12. Miller, *Latin American Women,* 203; Nancy Saporta Sternbach, Marysa Navarro-Aranguren, Patricia Chuchryk, and Sonia E. Alvarez, "Feminisms in Latin America: From Bogotá to San Bernardo," in *The Making of Social Movements in Latin America,* ed. Arturo Escobar and Sonia E. Alvarez (Boulder, Colo.: Westview Press, 1993), 211.

leaders, were unwilling to extend their egalitarianism to relations between men and women. The rhetoric of equality, democracy, and revolution stood opposed to the reality of unchallenged gender inequality, and this contradiction gave birth to second wave feminism.

For all the similarities in the origins of second wave feminism in North, South, and Central America, there were differences. In the United States, movements like those for civil rights and against the Vietnam War prevailed, but the Latin American new left was characterized by movements with a sharper awareness of class: economic survival groups, radical Catholic Church organizations, and guerrilla movements. Not surprisingly, Latin America—a region characterized by greater poverty and inequality than the United States and a tradition of thinking in class terms—produced a new left, and a second wave of feminism, in which the struggle against class inequality was integral to theory and practice.[13] While they often broke formally with the leftist organizations through which they had first been politicized, "Latin American feminists retained a commitment to radical change in social relations of production—as well as reproduction—while continuing to struggle against sexism within the Left. That is, although feminism in many countries broke with the Left organizationally, it did not fully do so ideologically."[14]

The high degree of class consciousness that characterizes second wave feminism in Latin America is a strength; feminist movements in the north, by comparison, have struggled to incorporate issues of class into their agendas. At the same time, the more holistic nature of Latin American feminism is sometimes an impediment to coalition building. Right-wing women who might identify with some of the positions of feminist activists—such as opposition to domestic violence or support for pay equity—are often unwilling to ally with feminists because they see them as threatening their class interests.

Another difference between the second waves of feminism in Latin America and North America is that for many Latin Americans, the feminist movement and the women's movement were not synonymous. This distinction was due, in part, to the way in which women entered politics in the region. In Latin America, many groups involved in issues that were not directly related to gender equality—for example, those opposing state violence

    13. Norma Stoltz Chinchilla, "Marxism, Feminism, and the Struggle for Democracy in Latin America," in *The Making of Social Movements in Latin America*, ed. Escobar and Alvarez, 46.
    14. Sternbach et al., "Feminisms in Latin America," 211.

or demanding public health care—were nonetheless predominantly or entirely made up of women.[15]

Activists in women's groups that fought gender inequality (and academics who wrote about them) often distinguished between their work and that of other organized women by naming their sort of organizing "feminist" and the other "feminine"[16] or by labeling their groups "feminist organizations" and the others "women's organizations."[17] Some drew a distinction between activism in defense of *strategic* gender interests and activism in defense of *practical* gender interests.[18] These three sets of labels were roughly synonymous, setting strategies that directly confronted gender inequality apart from those that did not directly confront it (either because the activists were reluctant to take the risk of doing so or because they had other goals).[19]

A final distinction—one made between work with a feminist perspective and work with a gender perspective—did not parallel the other three sets of categories. A feminist perspective was one that analyzed gender relations and challenged inequalities between men and women; the focus of a gender perspective, however, was not always clear. The term was generally used, from the 1980s onward, by women who wished to identify with the struggle

15. See, for example, Ingo Bultmann, Michaela Hellman, Klaus Meschkat, and Jorge Rojas, eds., *Democracia sin movimiento social? Sindicatos, organizaciones vecinales y movimiento de mujeres en Chile y Mexico* (Caracas: Editorial Nueva Sociedad, 1995); Dore, ed., *Gender Politics in Latin America*; Jo Fisher, *Out of the Shadows: Women, Resistance, and Politics in South America* (London: Latin American Bureau, 1993); Jane S. Jaquette, ed., *The Women's Movement in Latin America: Participation and Democracy* (Boulder, Colo.: Westview Press, 1994); Jelin, ed., *Women and Social Change in Latin America*; and Sarah A. Radcliffe and Sallie Westwood, eds., *Viva: Women and Popular Protest in Latin America* (New York: Routledge, 1993).

16. Sonia E. Alvarez, *Engendering Democracy in Brazil: Women's Movements in Transition Politics* (Princeton: Princeton University Press, 1990), 10, 24–26.

17. Adriana Santa Cruz, "Los movimientos de mujeres: Una perspectiva latinoamericana," in *Y hasta cuando esperaremos mandan-dirun-dirun-dan: Mujer y poder en América Latina* (Caracas: Editorial Nueva Sociedad, 1989), 46; Virginia Vargas, prologue to *Hacer política desde las mujeres,* by Mujeres por la Dignidad y la Vida (San Salvador: Doble G Impresores, 1993), 9.

18. Mujeres por la Dignidad y la Vida, *Hacer política desde las mujeres,* 70; Maxine Molyneux, "Mobilization Without Emancipation? Women's Interests, the State, and Revolution," in *Transition and Development: Problems of Third World Socialism,* ed. Richard Fagen, Carmen Diana Deere, and José Luis Caraggio (New York: Monthly Review Press, 1986), 283–86; Mercedes Olivera, "Práctica feminista en el movimiento zapatista de liberación nacional," in *Chiapas, y las mujeres, que?* ed. Rosa Rojas, vol. 2 (Mexico City: Editorial La Correa Feminista, 1995), 177.

19. For a discussion of the debate among feminist academics over the usefulness of these categories, see Karen Kampwirth, "Feminism, Antifeminism, and Electoral Politics in Postwar Nicaragua and El Salvador," *Political Science Quarterly* 113, no. 2 (1998), 259–60.

against gender inequality but did not wish to identify with organized feminists, whom they portrayed as being against men. *Gender theory* was thus a softer version of feminist theory, in their minds. Organized feminists sometimes explained that those who worked from a feminist perspective analyzed and acted against gender inequality and that those who used a gender perspective wished to analyze gender inequality without doing anything about it.

Clearly there was a certain hostility inherent in these characterizations of other women. And not all the women who were ambivalent about the feminist movement agreed with one another. Two very different groups of women distanced themselves from feminism and the feminist label by embracing the gender perspective; the first group did so out of class concerns, while the second group preferred the term for political reasons.

In Latin America, feminism has often been associated with the middle class. For the most part, this association was accurate during the first wave and the early days of the second wave. But the characterization became much less true as many women who were initially mobilized in defense of class and family interests—in the guerrilla wars in Central America and in the struggles against the military dictatorships in South America—came to identify with the feminist project. Even so, as the twentieth century reached its end, many leftist working-class women whose activism fit the definitions we have presented of *feminist* work nonetheless preferred that it be called *gender* work.

The second group that rejected the term *feminist perspective* in favor of the euphemistic *gender perspective* did so for reasons that were rooted in the leftist origins of second wave feminism. Women who identified with the right—and who thought that their careers within right-wing political parties or the business world were limited by sexism—were in a serious bind. On the one hand, their strategic gender consciousness might have led them to seek out (or at least identify with) women who worked for greater gender equality—in other words, the feminists. Yet, as right-wingers, they could not ally with those left-wing women without violating their political identities in some ways. Starting in the 1980s, these women pursued a strategy that would allow them to escape this dilemma: they would repudiate feminism while asserting their commitment to a gender perspective. So, ironically, the gender perspective was defended both by working-class women who thought that the feminists were not sufficiently concerned about ending class inequality and by right-wing women who thought that the feminists were too concerned about ending class inequality.

It was probably inevitable that far more women who called themselves feminist would be linked to the left than to the right, both for the historical reasons we have discussed and for ideological reasons. As feminists fought inequality in gender relations, they were more likely to be affiliated with those who opposed inequality in other aspects of life, like class relations or ethnic relations. It was difficult (though hardly impossible) for a right-wing woman to identify with many aspects of feminism; the liberal model of feminism dominant in the United States—with its emphasis on legal rather than structural change—was far less prominent in Latin America.

Theme 2: Autonomy ~ important aspect

If to gain autonomy in a personal sense is to become an adult, to make independent decisions, to control one's own money, and to speak for oneself, then autonomy in an organizational sense is somewhat similar. As members of the Dignas, a group of autonomous feminists in El Salvador, wrote, "movement autonomy is understood as the capacity to define, in a sovereign way, [the movement's] own objectives and ways of struggling and to make demands that it considers important and current for women and for the whole society."[20]

One of the many things that right-wing and left-wing women who worked for gender equality had in common was precisely the struggle for autonomy. Hence, autonomy—independence from political parties and guerrilla organizations—is the second theme that runs through the majority of the chapters in this book. Victoria González shows how the women of the Somoza dictatorship (1936–79) constantly negotiated the balance between loyalty to the Somoza regime and personal autonomy for themselves within the Nationalist Liberal Party. In her chapter, María Teresa Blandón argues that the National Women's Coalition in Nicaragua would not have been possible if not for the autonomy that many Nicaraguan feminists had won from the Sandinista Front by the late 1990s.

Patricia Hipsher argues that second wave Salvadoran feminism is an unintended legacy of the guerrilla war of the 1980s—yet the legacy of the war has also impeded the movement in its efforts to wrest autonomy from the former guerrilla parties, reduce internal sectarianism, and forge coalitions with right-wing women. And Ilja Luciak evaluates the ongoing tensions around the issue of autonomy for the women of Guatemala's guerrilla coali-

20. Mujeres por la Dignidad y la Vida, *Hacer política desde las mujeres,* 109.

tion, comparing those experiences with the longer autonomy battles that have been waged by female guerrillas in El Salvador and Nicaragua.

Sandra McGee Deutsch explores right-wing women's activism in Argentina, Brazil, and Chile during the first four decades of the twentieth century. While right-wing men usually succeeded in incorporating women into their groups as helpmates rather than leaders, the women who took up those positions often enjoyed some personal autonomy through their participation—to the point that they sometimes came to support women's suffrage and moderate feminism. Liesl Haas considers the relationship between feminism and the Brazilian Workers' Party (PT), finding that while the PT was more sympathetic to questions of women's autonomy and gender equality than other parties were, in the mid-1990s, significant barriers to women's participation in the PT remained. Finally, Lisa Baldez suggests that Chilean right- and left-wing women have not demanded autonomy from political parties precisely because they organized by claiming to be inherently apolitical and therefore not in need of autonomy.

Why did the issue of autonomy dominate Latin American feminist debates in the last two decades of the twentieth century? When Latin American feminists demanded autonomy, what did they have in mind, and why did they want it? What were the costs of seeking autonomy? What about the costs of actually *getting* autonomy?

The same process that indirectly created second wave feminism—the mobilization of women within struggles against right-wing authoritarian governments in Central and South America—also led many women to desire autonomy; the left-wing organizations through which they had developed their political ideas and learned organizing skills were, all too often, uninterested in (or even hostile to) their concerns about gender inequality. If relations between men and women were even on the agenda, they were put off until a later date, a date that never seemed to arrive. And the predominance of the vanguard model of politics—in which a central party knowingly guides the actions of its members—made internal debate difficult and pushed many to seek autonomy.

The issue of autonomy was not confined to the left, however. Right-wing women often found themselves in a parallel situation, as they tended to hold subordinate positions within their organizations, organizations that saw gender inequality as natural and unchangeable—and thus often did not even promise that equality between men and women would be a goal. While right-wing women have been far less likely than left-wing women to seek autonomy formally, their efforts to open up spaces for women within their organizations have been part of the process that has permitted coalitions of left- and right-wing women to form around common issues.

In countries like El Salvador, the quest for autonomy was not easy. The vast majority of the women's organizations that existed in the years following the end of the war in 1992 had been founded by one of the five guerrilla groups during the war. The leaders of those guerrilla movements (converted into political parties following the war) often felt betrayed by the members of "their" women's organizations and they let them know it. As the Dignas noted, "those who hold power do not give it up spontaneously or generously."[21]

Feminists found themselves confronting old allies, and the personal and political costs of seeking autonomy were often high. Still, according to the strongest advocates of autonomy, it was only by asserting independence from old allies that groups could negotiate as equals rather than dependents.[22] Had those groups chosen not to seek autonomy, deciding instead to work for women's equality within the old structures, they might have found themselves—and their goals—forever subordinated. Yet too strong a commitment to an independent feminist identity without a willingness to compromise could force feminists to run the risk "of remaining weak [and] isolated."[23]

A further dilemma was that a successful battle for one form of autonomy, such as independence from a political party, often left other forms of dependence intact or even exacerbated them. Institutions such as the state, the Church, labor unions, and international agencies sometimes took on new importance as providers of funds and political support, support that might come with strings attached. Ultimately, there was no such thing as complete autonomy; it had to be negotiated and renegotiated with each new alliance.

The issue of autonomy was at the root of a heated debate that dominated the seventh feminist Encuentro in Chile in 1996 and that continued, to a much lesser extent, at the eighth feminist Encuentro in the Dominican Republic in 1999. At the Chilean Encuentro a group of self-described "autonomous" women, mainly South Americans, criticized other feminists for

21. Ibid., 110.
22. Ibid., 111.
23. Virginia Guzmán, *Los azarosos años 80: Aciertos y desencuentros del movimiento de mujeres en Latinoamérica y el Caribe* (Lima: Red Entre Mujeres, Diálogo Sur-Norte, 1994), 13. For an excellent analysis of the politics of autonomy, see Maruja Barrig, "The Difficult Equilibrium Between Bread and Roses: Women's Organizations and Democracy in Peru," in *The Women's Movement in Latin America*, ed. Jaquette, 159–73.

having been co-opted and "institutionalized" into governmental or nongovernmental organizations and for having lost their earlier radicalism.

This division between the autonomous and the institutionalized might have appeared to be another manifestation of an issue that had occupied Latin American feminists for decades, but it was actually more complex. Some women, like the Nicaraguans and Salvadorans who had waged heated battles for autonomy from the guerrillas and the left-wing political parties, found that at the Encuentro they were lumped into the category of the institutionalized. This was quite ironic, since it was because of their successful battles for autonomy that they had the political space necessary to found feminist nongovernmental organizations. So those women were autonomous within the context of their own countries but not autonomous according to those who dominated the Chilean Encuentro. Clearly the autonomous women of the Chilean Encuentro had hit upon a sensitive issue and a real problem: the dangers of dependence on outsiders. But any blanket refusal to accept outside funding ran the risk of reducing Latin American feminism to a movement of middle- and upper-class women, a situation much like that of the decades of the first wave, when those who founded organizations and attended conferences were the few who could cover expenses out of their own pocketbooks.[24]

By the end of the twentieth century, many Latin American women were working for gender equality from a variety of spaces, including formally autonomous feminist organizations, women's secretariats in the political parties and unions, neighborhood improvement associations, human rights groups, and women's clinics. Not all of them embraced the feminist label or the agenda implied by that label; perhaps even fewer were interested in formal autonomy. But that multiplicity of organizing techniques was, in many ways, a strength that contributed to making the women's movement "the strongest social movement" in Latin America.[25]

The impressive organizing capacity of women's rights activists was dem-

24. Lisa Baldez, Kelley Ready, and Millie Thayer, email communications with author, March 2000; Silvia Carrazco, conversation with author, July 1998; documents at "Sobre el VIII Encuentro Feminista de América Latina y el Caribe" (http://www.nodo50.org/mujeresred/VIIIencuentro. html) and "Realizado en la República Dominicana: VIII Encuentro Feminista Latinoamericano y del Caribe," *La Jornada,* 3 January 2000 (http://www.jornada.unam.mx/2000/ene00/000103/ articulos.htm); and Sonia E. Alvarez, "Latin American Feminisms 'Go Global': Trends of the 1990s and Challenges for the New Millennium," in *Cultures of Politics, Politics of Cultures: Revisioning Latin American Social Movements,* ed. Sonia E. Alvarez, Evelina Dagnino, and Arturo Escobar (Boulder, Colo.: Westview Press, 1998), 293–324. On the first several Encuentros, see Sternbach et al., "Feminisms in Latin America."

25. Red Entre Mujeres, "Presentación," in *Los azarosos años 80,* ed. Guzmán, 9.

onstrated when, as part of the preparations for the fourth global women's conference in Beijing, United Nations officials tried to unilaterally impose a coordinator for each region. When a woman was chosen to coordinate the Latin American delegations without even consulting members of regional organizations and networks, activists from across the region launched "a lightning action." In the words of one of those activists, in less than a week, "we sent hundreds of faxes to the UN demanding that this woman be replaced by a woman from the movement, and we were successful. . . . That gave us, from the beginning, great legitimacy before the UN and before the other regions and global networks since [Latin America] was the only region that obtained that change. That also marked us, from the beginning, with a movement 'style' and a degree of rebellion that were expressed at many other points during the whole process."[26] The organizational capacity and rebelliousness of the Latin American women's movement, developed over decades of confrontations with armed opponents and skeptical allies, were resources that women's movement activists brought with them when they took on a new challenge: building coalitions with women of the right, many of whom had been on the opposite side of bloody battles only a few years before.

Theme 3: Coalition Building Across Political Lines

Coalition building across political lines is the most unusual of all the themes in this book, one that has been given almost no attention in the existing literature on women's organizing in the region. In fact, coalition building across political lines was so unusual that the theme does not appear, except implicitly,[27] in the majority of the chapters in this book. Over the course of the twentieth century, very few women's organizations dared to cross the left/right divide. The same history that made Latin American women's organizing especially class-conscious and political in orientation also made coalition building more difficult than it might have been in other regions. Yet the possibility of women's rights coalitions that cross partisan lines is so intriguing that it could hardly be left out of a comparative collection on left- and

26. Virginia Vargas Valente, "Disputando el espacio global: El movimiento de mujeres y la IV Conferencia Mundial de Beijing," *Nueva Sociedad* 141 (January-February 1996), 45.

27. We say that the theme of coalitions appears implicitly because all the chapters trace the evolution of radical women's organizing on either the left or right or both. A careful reader will note how these histories created opportunities for coalition building or, more often, how they impeded the formation of coalitions that would cross lines of class and politics.

right-wing women. Karen Kampwirth concludes Chapter 2 by considering a number of efforts to build coalitions between the women of the left-wing Sandinista Front and the women of the right-wing Contras in Nicaragua. In Chapter 3, María Teresa Blandón evaluates the National Women's Coalition in Nicaragua, a coalition that was formed by women from almost all points on the political spectrum[28] to promote their shared interest in greater gender equality.

In Chapter 4, Patricia Hipsher analyzes the historical impediments to coalition building across the left/right divide in El Salvador, and she considers the cases in which feminist activists and female representatives to Congress have joined forces to highlight the issues of domestic violence, responsible paternity, and political quotas for women. In Chapter 5, Kelley Ready provides an in-depth analysis of one of these cases in El Salvador: the successful coalitional effort to require, by law, that elected officials prove that they have taken economic responsibility for their children before being allowed to take office.

We should not be surprised that such coalitions were few and far between in twentieth-century Latin America. In fact, coalition building is always a difficult undertaking; even coalitions between groups of women with similar political perspectives and goals are often impeded by the struggle over resources,[29] a particularly serious issue in a region characterized by significant poverty. Building coalitions between women who do not share many goals is, obviously, far more difficult. Yet it is not impossible, due to one of the basic tenets of feminist thought: gender interests should not be conflated with class or other sorts of interests.

Although we do not think that the claim that gender interests are independent from other sorts of interests is particularly controversial, the existing political language does not reflect that reality. We are stuck with a one-dimensional model of politics—a straight line from left to right—that has no space for right-wing women who embrace a gender perspective, opposing sexual inequality while ignoring or supporting inequality of other sorts. An examination of coalitions between right- and left-wing women in favor of their shared gender interests suggests that we need a far more nuanced model, one that would capture all the dimensions of real people's engagement in politics.

28. The coalition included feminists, women's movement activists, Contras, Sandinistas, Liberal party activists, and centrists; that is, women from all across the political spectrum, except those who had openly identified with the Somoza dictatorship.

29. Barrig, "Difficult Equilibrium," 168.

Theme 4: Maternalism

The relationship between women, motherhood, and political participation in Latin America has been analyzed primarily in the context of two specific historical developments: the rise of feminism in the late nineteenth and early twentieth centuries, and the creation of "mothers' groups" in the mid- to late twentieth century. It is largely accepted that first wave feminists in Latin America, like first wave feminists in some parts of Europe, stressed and embraced motherhood. Francesca Miller, a pioneer in the study of the history of feminism in Latin America, has stated, "In the Latin American context, the feminine is cherished, the womanly—the ability to bear and raise children, to nurture a family—is celebrated. Rather than reject their socially defined roles as mothers, as wives, Latin American feminists may be understood as women acting to protest laws and conditions which threaten their ability to fulfill that role. Moreover, there is an explicit spiritual or moral content to the declarations of Latin American feminists which has strong parallels with feminist thought as it developed in Catholic Europe."[30]

K. Lynn Stoner and Asunción Lavrin also argue that first wave Latin American feminists, unlike feminists in the United States and England, have had a relatively conflict-free relationship to motherhood. Stoner notes that in Cuba, first wave "feminism was pro women, pro family, pro motherhood, and pro children."[31] And in her study on Argentina, Chile, and Uruguay, Lavrin makes a similar point: "It is not surprising that Southern Cone feminists opted for a feminism that would fit into their social milieu and be acceptable to other women as well as to the men who held the reins of power. Feminism oriented toward motherhood was more than a strategy to win favorable legislation, it was an essential component of their cultural heritage: a tune that feminists not only knew how to play but wished to play."[32] The ties between motherhood and women's activism, then, appear to be long-standing in Latin America, dating back at least to the nineteenth century.[33] However, these

30. Miller, *Latin American Women*, 74.

31. K. Lynn Stoner, *From the House to the Streets: The Cuban Woman's Movement for Legal Reform, 1898–1940* (Durham: Duke University Press, 1991), 7.

32. Asunción Lavrin, *Women, Feminism, and Social Change in Argentina, Chile, and Uruguay, 1890–1940* (Lincoln: University of Nebraska Press, 1995), 38.

33. For additional works on maternalism and feminism, see Susan K. Besse, *Restructuring Patriarchy: The Modernization of Gender Inequality in Brazil, 1914–1940* (Chapel Hill: The University of North Carolina Press, 1996); Donna Guy, "The Politics of Pan-American Cooperation: Maternalist Feminism and the Child Rights Movement, 1913–1960," *Gender and History* 10, no. 3 (1998): 449–69; and June E. Hahner, *Emancipating the Female Sex: The Struggle for Women's Rights in Brazil, 1850–1940* (Durham: Duke University Press, 1990).

early links could withstand additional scrutiny. Most important, the relation-ship between mothers and politics has not yet been completely disentangled from stereotypical views of Latin American women, images epitomized by the concept of *"marianismo."*[34]

Although some studies on first wave feminism have accepted maternal discourses at face value, the contradictory effects of using motherhood to justify women's engagement in politics are obvious. Lavrin notes that "[s]ince gender typing can be a double-edged sword, in politics it reinforced the stereotype of women's biological image that confined them to specific areas of public life."[35] By stressing women's biological capabilities, the rheto-ric of motherhood can place limits on the incorporation of women into cer-tain aspects of political life, even as it opens up some other political spaces.

The liberating and the restricting aspects of using motherhood as a springboard into politics have been closely examined by those trying to ex-plain the phenomenon of mothers' movements during the second half of the twentieth century.[36] The complexities of maternal politics are also ad-dressed by the authors in this volume as they analyze women's involvement as mothers on the left and the right. Victoria González discusses some of the reasons that anti-Somocista women resorted to maternalist discourses to justify their involvement in politics while most Somocista women did not. Karen Kampwirth addresses the irony present in Contra women's use of the

34. In 1973, Evelyn P. Stevens argued that *marianismo* was "the cult of feminine spiritual superiority, which teaches that women are semidivine, morally superior to and spiritually stronger than men." Stevens maintained that *marianismo* was Latin American women's re-sponse to *machismo,* which she defined as the "cult of virility." According to Stevens, Latin American women have been able and willing to gain power only through their roles as mothers and the manipulation of their male kin, i.e., through *marianismo.* See Evelyn P. Stevens, "Mari-anismo: The Other Face of Machismo," in *Confronting Change, Challenging Tradition: Women in Latin American History,* ed. Gertrude Yeager (Wilmington, Del.: Scholarly Resources, 1994), 4, 9.

35. Lavrin, *Women, Feminism, and Social Change,* 13.

36. For more on mothers' movements—and on women's participation as mothers in so-cial movements and politics in general—see Elsa Chaney, *Supermadre: Women in Politics in Latin America* (Austin: University of Texas Press, 1979); Marguerite Guzmán Bouvard, *Revolu-tionizing Motherhood: The Mothers of the Plaza de Mayo* (Wilmington, Del.: Scholarly Re-sources, 1994); Tessa Cubitt and Helen Greenslade, "Public and Private Spheres: The End of Dichotomy," in *Gender Politics in Latin America,* ed. Dore; Nikki Craske, *Women and Politics in Latin America* (New Brunswick: Rutgers University Press, 1999); Fisher, *Out of the Shadows;* Karen Kampwirth, "The Mother of the Nicaraguans: Doña Violeta and the UNO's Gender Agenda," *Latin American Perspectives* 23, no. 1 (1996): 67–86; Jennifer Schirmer, "The Seeking of Truth and the Gendering of Consciousness: The CoMadres of El Salvador and the CONAVI-GUA Widows of Guatemala," in *Viva,* ed. Radcliffe and Westwood; and Lynn Stephen, *Women and Social Movements in Latin America: Power from Below* (Austin: University of Texas Press, 1997).

rhetoric of motherhood, given that many of those who joined the guerrillas did not have sons of military age. She concludes that "[t]he language of maternalism is useful even when women's motivations are not strictly maternal, since it is the language of everyday experience, and since it is so malleable."[37]

Maternal discourse is indeed malleable and quite compatible with other discourses. It easily complemented the Chilean rhetoric of nonpartisanship discussed by Lisa Baldez and right-wing Argentine bourgeois notions of femininity discussed by Sandra McGee Deutsch. The malleability of mother politics also has its limits, however. As Margaret Power points out, right-wing Chilean women's political identities did not rest solely on their roles as mothers, a fact which became clear as the 1988 plebiscite drew near. In addition to their roles as mothers, female activists wanted to be citizens engaged in traditional party politics.

Although the exaltation of mothers and motherhood is often associated with the right, it has also been a characteristic of the traditional left and of some feminists. *Maternalism,* defined in this context as the use of motherhood to justify political activism, cuts across the political spectrum. Undoubtedly, thousands (if not millions) of women throughout history have become politicized through motherhood. They have expanded their concern for their own children to a concern for other people's children, a phenomenon celebrated by some scholars.[38] But there are problems with it. As Kathleen Blee points out: "there is no simple relationship between motherhood and politics. . . . If motherhood has broadened the political horizons of some women, in other cases it has promoted a very narrow and exclusive identity for women as guardians of their racial, social class, or national identities and futures."[39] Blee goes on to warn us that "[m]otherhood can generate racist and reactionary political attitudes and actions."[40] Given these findings, we believe that we must carefully avoid romanticizing maternal politics while taking into account the fact that most women are indeed mothers.

The comparative study of rightist and leftist women in Latin America adds a great deal to our understanding of politics in the region. Furthermore, the

---

37. See Kampwirth, this volume, 96.

38. See, for example, Alexis Jetter, Annelise Orleck, and Diana Taylor, eds., *The Politics of Motherhood: Activist Voices from Left to Right* (Hanover: University Press of New England, 1997), 18, 357.

39. Kathleen Blee, "Mothers in Race-Hate Movements," in *The Politics of Motherhood,* ed. Jetter, Orleck, and Taylor, 249.

40. Ibid.

comparison of two major subregions—Central America and South America—further clarifies the varied political opportunities and constraints that have shaped female activism in Latin America as a whole. Logically, since national politics in the two subregions have differed significantly, women in those subregions faced different challenges as they sought to organize politically.

We cannot explain crucial political transitions (such as the rise and fall of the Sandinistas in Nicaragua or the demise of the military dictatorships in Argentina, Chile, and Brazil) without considering women's roles on both sides of the political divide. Studies like these also help paint a more complex—and therefore more realistic—picture of Latin American women's lives. Finally, the examination of rightist women's experiences in politics challenges an academic tendency to deny racist, anti-Semitic, and classist women an active role in Latin American history while paying attention to the activities of their male counterparts. We need a full accounting of women's participation in public politics, and the record must include reprehensible acts as well as laudable ones. Until women's capacity for antidemocratic activism is accepted and understood, women will not be seen as fully human.

BIBLIOGRAPHY

Alvarez, Sonia E. *Engendering Democracy in Brazil: Women's Movements in Transition Politics.* Princeton: Princeton University Press, 1990.
———. "Latin American Feminisms 'Go Global': Trends of the 1990s and Challenges for the New Millennium." In *Cultures of Politics, Politics of Cultures: Re-visioning Latin American Social Movements,* edited by Sonia E. Alvarez, Evelina Dagnino, and Arturo Escobar. Boulder, Colo.: Westview Press, 1998.
Barrig, Maruja. "The Difficult Equilibrium Between Bread and Roses: Women's Organizations and Democracy in Peru." In *The Women's Movement in Latin America: Participation and Democracy,* edited by Jane S. Jaquette. Boulder, Colo.: Westview Press, 1994.
Besse, Susan K. *Restructuring Patriarchy: The Modernization of Gender Inequality in Brazil, 1914–1940.* Chapel Hill: The University of North Carolina Press, 1996.
Blee, Kathleen. "Mothers in Race-Hate Movements." In *The Politics of Motherhood: Activist Voices from Left to Right,* edited by Alexis Jetter, Annelise Orleck, and Diana Taylor. Hanover: University Press of New England, 1997.
Bultmann, Ingo, Michaela Hellman, Klaus Meschkat, and Jorge Rojas, eds. *Democracia sin movimiento social? Sindicatos, organizaciones vecinales y movimiento de mujeres en Chile y Mexico.* Caracas: Editorial Nueva Sociedad, 1995.
Chaney, Elsa. *Supermadre: Women in Politics in Latin America.* Austin: University of Texas Press, 1979.
Chinchilla, Norma Stoltz. "Marxism, Feminism, and the Struggle for Democracy in Latin America." In *The Making of Social Movements in Latin America,* edited by Arturo Escobar and Sonia E. Alvarez. Boulder, Colo.: Westview Press, 1992.

Collinson, Helen, ed. *Women and Revolution in Nicaragua*. London: Zed Books, 1990.

Craske, Nikki. *Women and Politics in Latin America*. New Brunswick: Rutgers University Press, 1999.

Cubitt, Tessa, and Helen Greenslade. "Public and Private Spheres: The End of Dichotomy." In *Gender Politics in Latin America: Debates in Theory and Practice,* edited by Elizabeth Dore. New York: Monthly Review Press, 1997.

Dore, Elizabeth, ed. *Gender Politics in Latin America: Debates in Theory and Practice.* New York: Monthly Review Press, 1997.

Feijoo, María del Carmen, and Mónica Gogna. "Women in the Transition to Democracy." In *Women and Social Change in Latin America,* edited by Elizabeth Jelin. London: Zed Books, 1990.

Fernández Poncela, Anna M. "Nicaraguan Women: Legal, Political, and Social Spaces." In *Gender Politics in Latin America: Debates in Theory and Practice,* edited by Elizabeth Dore. New York: Monthly Review Press, 1997.

Fisher, Jo. *Out of the Shadows: Women, Resistance, and Politics in South America.* London: Latin American Bureau, 1993.

Guy, Donna. "The Politics of Pan-American Cooperation: Maternalist Feminism and the Child Rights Movement, 1913–1960." *Gender and History* 10, no. 3 (1998): 449–69.

Guzmán, Virginia. *Los azarosos años 80: Aciertos y desencuentros del movimiento de mujeres en Latinoamérica y el Caribe.* Lima: Red Entre Mujeres, Diálogo Sur-Norte, 1994.

Guzmán Bouvard, Marguerite. *Revolutionizing Motherhood: The Mothers of the Plaza de Mayo.* Wilmington, Del.: Scholarly Resources, 1994.

Hahner, June E. *Emancipating the Female Sex: The Struggle for Women's Rights in Brazil, 1850–1940.* Durham: Duke University Press, 1990.

Hernández, Julio. "El feminismo y la educación: La mujer debe colaborar a la creación de la patria" (1916). In *Mujeres y revolución, 1900–1917,* by Ana Lau and Carmen Ramos. Mexico City: Instituto Nacional de Estudios Históricos de la Revolución Mexicana, 1993.

Jaquette, Jane S., ed. *The Women's Movement in Latin America: Participation and Democracy.* Boulder, Colo.: Westview Press, 1994.

Jelin, Elizabeth, ed. *Women and Social Change in Latin America.* London: Zed Books, 1990.

Jetter, Alexis, Annelise Orleck, and Diana Taylor, eds. *The Politics of Motherhood: Activist Voices from Left to Right.* Hanover: University Press of New England, 1997.

Kampwirth, Karen. "The Mother of the Nicaraguans: Doña Violeta and the UNO's Gender Agenda." *Latin American Perspectives* 23, no. 1 (1996): 67–86.

———. "Feminism, Antifeminism, and Electoral Politics in Postwar Nicaragua and El Salvador." *Political Science Quarterly* 113, no. 2 (1998): 259–79.

Keen, Benjamin. *A History of Latin America.* Boston: Houghton Mifflin, 1996.

Lau, Ana, and Carmen Ramos. *Mujeres y revolución, 1900–1917.* Mexico City: Instituto Nacional de Estudios Históricos de la Revolución Mexicana, 1993.

Lavrin, Asunción. *Women, Feminism, and Social Change in Argentina, Chile, and Uruguay, 1890–1940.* Lincoln: University of Nebraska Press, 1995.

Miller, Francesca. *Latin American Women and the Search for Social Justice.* Hanover: University Press of New England, 1991.

Molyneux, Maxine. "Mobilization Without Emancipation? Women's Interests, the

State, and Revolution." In *Transition and Development: Problems of Third World Socialism*, edited by Richard Fagen, Carmen Diana Deere, and José Luis Caraggio. New York: Monthly Review Press, 1986.

Mora Carvajal, Virginia. "Mujeres e historia en América Latina: En busca de una identidad de género." In *Entre silencios y voces: Género e historia en América Central (1750–1990)*, edited by Eugenia Rodríguez Sáenz. San José, Costa Rica: Centro Nacional para el Desarrollo de la Mujer y la Familia, 1997.

Mujeres por la Dignidad y la Vida (Dignas). *Hacer política desde las mujeres*. San Salvador: Doble G Impresores, 1993.

Olivera, Mercedes. "Práctica feminista en el movimiento zapatista de liberación nacional." In *Chiapas, y las mujeres, que?* edited by Rosa Rojas. Vol. 2. Mexico City: Editorial La Correa Feminista, 1995.

Radcliffe, Sarah A., and Sallie Westwood, eds. *Viva: Women and Popular Protest in Latin America*. New York: Routledge, 1993.

Red Entre Mujeres. "Presentación." In *Los azarosos años 80: Aciertos y desencuentros del movimiento de mujeres en Latinoamérica y el Caribe*, edited by Virginia Guzmán. Lima: Red Entre Mujeres, Diálogo Sur-Norte, 1994.

Santa Cruz, Adriana. "Los movimientos de mujeres: Una perspectiva latinoamericana." In *Y hasta cuando esperaremos mandan-dirun-dirun-dan: Mujer y poder en América Latina*, edited by Alberto Koschützke. Caracas: Editorial Nueva Sociedad, 1989.

Schirmer, Jennifer. "The Seeking of Truth and the Gendering of Consciousness: The CoMadres of El Salvador and the CONAVIGUA Widows of Guatemala." In *Viva: Women and Popular Protest in Latin America*, edited by Sarah A. Radcliffe and Sallie Westwood. London: Routledge, 1993.

Stephen, Lynn. *Women and Social Movements in Latin America: Power from Below*. Austin: University of Texas Press, 1997.

Sternbach, Nancy Saporta, Marysa Navarro-Aranguren, Patricia Chuchryk, and Sonia E. Alvarez. "Feminisms in Latin America: From Bogotá to San Bernardo." In *The Making of Social Movements in Latin America*, edited by Arturo Escobar and Sonia E. Alvarez. Boulder, Colo.: Westview Press, 1992.

Stevens, Evelyn P. "Marianismo: The Other Face of Machismo." In *Confronting Change, Challenging Tradition: Women in Latin American History*, edited by Gertrude Yeager. Wilmington, Del.: Scholarly Resources, 1994.

Stoner, K. Lynn. *From the House to the Streets: The Cuban Woman's Movement for Legal Reform, 1898–1940*. Durham: Duke University Press, 1991.

Vargas, Gina. "El futuro desde la perspectiva de las mujeres." In *500 años de patriarcado en el nuevo mundo*, edited by Clara Leyla Alfonso. Santo Domingo, República Dominicana: Red Entre Mujeres, un Diálogo Sur-Norte/Centro de Investigación para la Acción Femenina (CIPAF), 1993.

Vargas, Virginia. Prologue to *Hacer política desde las mujeres*, by Mujeres por la Dignidad y la Vida (Dignas). San Salvador: Doble G Impresores, 1993.

Vargas Valente, Virginia. "Disputando el espacio global: El movimiento de mujeres y la IV Conferencia Mundial de Beijing." *Nueva Sociedad* 141 (January–February 1996): 43–53.

PART I

Radical Women in
Central America

CHRONOLOGY OF NICARAGUA

1927–33 Nationalist leader Augusto C. Sandino fights against U.S. intervention.

1932 Women petition for the right to vote in U.S.-supervised elections. The U.S. military command denies women the right to vote.

1933 U.S. Marines withdraw from Nicaragua. Sandino agrees to a truce.

1934 Anastasio Somoza García, head of the National Guard created by the U.S. Marines, assassinates Sandino.

1936 Anastasio Somoza García comes to power as the result of a coup d'état.

1939 Women petition unsuccessfully for the right to vote.

1944 Massive demonstrations take place against the Somoza administration.

1955 Women win the vote. The Feminine Wing of the Somozas' Nationalist Liberal Party is formed under the direction of Somocista attorney Olga Núñez de Saballos.

1956 Rigoberto López Pérez assassinates Anastasio Somoza García. Repression against the population increases in the aftermath of Somoza's death.

1957 Women vote for the first time in presidential elections. Luis Somoza Debayle, son of Anastasio Somoza García, is elected president.

1961 Carlos Fonseca, Tomás Borge, and Silvio Mayorga form the FSLN (Sandinista National Liberation Front).

1962 Josefa Toledo de Aguerri, Nicaragua's foremost feminist, dies.

1963 Presidential election takes place. René Schick, the Somocista candidate, becomes president.

1963 The Organization of Democratic Women is founded under the auspices of the Nicaraguan Socialist Party.

1966 René Schick dies. Anastasio Somoza Debayle is elected
president.

1966 The FSLN creates the Patriotic Alliance of Nicaraguan Women,
under the direction of peasant activist Gladys Baez.

1972 An earthquake devastates Managua.

1977 Sandinista women organize against the dictatorship through
AMPRONAC, the Association of Women Confronting National
Problems.

1978 Anti-Somocista leader Pedro Joaquín Chamorro is
assassinated.

19 July 1979 Popular insurrection led by the FSLN triumphs against
Somoza.

1979 AMPRONAC turns into AMNLAE, the Luisa Amanda Espinoza
Nicaraguan Women's Association.

1982–89 A counterrevolutionary (Contra) war is waged against the
Sandinista Revolution with the full support of the U.S.
government.

1983 AMNLAE begins working with mothers of Sandinista
combatants, heroes, and martyrs.

1990 The FSLN loses the election to Violeta Barrios de Chamorro,
widow of Pedro Joaquín Chamorro and head of the anti-
Sandinista UNO (National Opposition Union) coalition.
Barrios de Chamorro becomes the first woman president in
Central America.

1990–92 Intense debates take place within the Nicaraguan women's
movement regarding AMNLAE's lack of autonomy from the
FSLN.

1992 The Nicaraguan Women's Conference—"Diverse but
United"—takes place with the participation of more than
eight hundred women. This is the largest nonpartisan
women's gathering in the nation's history.

1996 The National Coalition of Women is formed, uniting women
on the left and the right to press for a common agenda.

1996 Right-wing Liberal Party candidate Arnoldo Alemán wins
presidential election.

1998 Zoilamérica Narváez, stepdaughter of former FSLN president
Daniel Ortega, publicly accuses her adoptive father of raping
her.

CHRONOLOGY OF EL SALVADOR

1921–22 Working-class women protest against the Meléndez administration, demanding the release of political prisoners.

1930 The Communist Party of El Salvador (PCS) is formed.

1931 General Maximiliano Hernández Martínez ousts president-elect Arturo Araujo.

1932 PCS leader Farabundo Martí leads unsuccessful revolt against Hernández Martínez. Martí is publicly executed, thirty thousand peasants are assassinated, and the PCS is outlawed. Women's Committees support the popular uprising led by Martí.

1938 Women's right to vote is recognized by the Constitution.

1944 The Association of Democratic Women (AMD) and the Women's Democratic Front (FDF) are formed.

1945 The Salvadoran Women's League is formed.

1950 Women are able to vote.

1957 Rosa Ochoa becomes a cofounder of the Sisterhood (Fraternity) of Salvadoran Women, an association that has links to the Communist Party. It is disbanded in 1969 due to political persecution. Many participants in this organization later join ANDES, the predominantly female teachers' union. Others regroup in AMPES, the Association of Progressive Women of El Salvador, which has ties to the Communist Party.

1961 The Christian Democratic Party is formed.

1969 The "Soccer War" between El Salvador and Honduras takes place, taking several thousand lives and leaving one hundred thousand Salvadorans homeless.

1972 José Napoleón Duarte, the Christian Democratic Party candidate, wins the presidential election, but the electoral commission hands the presidency over to Colonel Arturo Armando Molina.

1975 The Association of Progressive Women of El Salvador (AMPES) is formed.

1977   Monsignor Oscar Arnulfo Romero becomes Archbishop of El
Salvador. The Committee of Mothers of Political Prisoners
(CoMadres), the Committee for the Liberty of Political Prisoners
and the Disappeared, and a Feminine Front are formed. General
Carlos Humberto Romero becomes president.

1978   The Association of Market Vendors and Workers (AUTRAMES) is
formed. The Association of Women in El Salvador (AMES) is
formed.

1979   Over six hundred political killings take place. The first military
junta is formed. The United States increases military aid.

1980   Archbishop Romero protests death squad killings. He is
murdered while saying Mass. Four U.S. churchwomen are raped
and killed. The United States cuts off military aid to the
Salvadoran government. The Farabundo Martí National Liberation
Front (FMLN) is formed to coordinate guerrilla movement. The
FMLN includes the PCS, which forms the Armed Forces of
Liberation (FAL) in 1980, the Popular Liberation Forces (FPL), and
the People's Revolutionary Army (ERP). The Lil Milagro Ramírez
Association of Women for Democracy is formed.

1981   Ronald Reagan takes office as president of the United States and
resumes military aid. Right-wing extremist Roberto D'Abuisson
forms the Nationalist Republican Alliance (ARENA). FMLN
launches "final offensive." The Unitary Committee of Salvadoran
Women (CUMS) is formed.

1983   The Association of Salvadoran Women (ASMUSA) and the
Organization of Salvadoran Women for Peace (ORMUSA) are
formed.

1984   The Reagan administration supports winning presidential
candidate Duarte against ARENA's D'Abuisson.

1987   AMES becomes part of the Salvadoran Women's Union (UMS), a
coalition of the five revolutionary women's associations
associated with the FMLN. A new generation of partisan women's
organizations is formed. This new generation includes Women
for Dignity and Life (Las Dignas) and the Mélida Anaya Montes
Women's Movement (MAM).

1989   Alfredo Cristiani, the right-wing ARENA candidate, wins the
presidential election. FMLN launches offensive. The government
retaliates with aerial bombings. Six Jesuit priests are assassinated
by the army.

1990   The United Nations sponsors peace talks between the FMLN and
the government.

1992   The ARENA administration and the FMLN sign a peace
agreement. The FMLN disarms its forces.

1993   The U.N.-sponsored Truth Commission finds that 85 percent of
the nine thousand human rights abuses investigated and 95
percent of the killings that took place in the 1970s and 1980s
were committed by government-supported death squads and the
military.[1]

1994   The FMLN is the country's second strongest political force in the
presidential election won by Armando Calderón Sol of the ARENA
party.

1996   Female representatives in the Legislative Assembly create the
Women's Political Party Forum, a nonpartisan women's coalition.
A law against domestic violence is approved.

1997   Legislative Assembly passes a bill requiring that all political
candidates get clearance certifying that they are not in arrears for
child support payments.

---

1. Benjamin Keen, *A History of Latin America* (Boston: Houghton Mifflin, 1996), 479.

CHRONOLOGY OF GUATEMALA

1931 Rightist General Jorge Ubico comes to power.

1944 Dictator Ubico resigns amidst popular protests. The Guatemalan Women's Alliance is formed. It is dissolved by the government in 1954.

1945 Civilian Juan José Arévalo is elected president.

1947 First Interamerican Women's Congress takes place. Women from nineteen nations attend.

1950 Colonel Jacobo Arbenz becomes president.

1952 The Guatemalan Labor Party is legalized. Arbenz initiates an agrarian reform that is resisted by the United Fruit Company and the U.S. government.

1954 Carlos Castillo Armas overthrows Jacobo Arbenz with the assistance of the CIA. From then on, Guatemala is governed by military or military-dominated regimes. Under these regimes, extreme right-wing groups of self-appointed vigilantes, including the Secret Anti-Communist Army (ESA) and the White Hand, torture and murder those suspected of leftist involvement.

1963 The Revolutionary Armed Forces (FAR) is formed.

1966 The army embarks on a counterinsurgency campaign against the guerrillas in the countryside. In response, guerrillas concentrate their attacks on the capital.

1968 U.S. Ambassador John Gordon Mein is assassinated.

1972 The Guerrilla Army of the Poor (EGP) is formed.

1979 The Revolutionary Organization of People in Arms (ORPA) is formed.

1980 A group from Quiche takes over the Spanish Embassy in protest against the government. The government burns the building and the demonstrators.

1980   The National Union of Guatemalan Women is formed. That same year, the feminist Alaide Foppa is disappeared. Foppa's daughter is a leader of the Guerrilla Army of the Poor.

1982   Four leftist organizations—the Guerrilla Army of the Poor, the Revolutionary Armed Forces, the Revolutionary Organization of People in Arms, and the Guatemalan Workers' Party (PGT)—join together to form the Guatemalan National Revolutionary Unity (URNG). General Efraín Ríos Montt comes to power through a coup. Under Ríos Montt, over seventy thousand deaths take place in the countryside.

Early 1980s   The National Coordinator of Widows of Guatemala (CONAVIGUA) is formed.

1983   President Efraín Ríos Montt is deposed by General Humberto Mejía Victores.

1985   Christian Democratic Party candidate Vinicio Cerezo wins presidential election.

1986   Council of Maya Women is formed.

1987   The Office of Human Rights Ombudsman is formed, but Cerezo is criticized for not investigating human rights abuses.

1988   Group of Guatemalan Women (CGM) is formed.

1990   Jorge Serrano wins presidential election in coalition with the Christian Democratic Party. He recognizes Belize as an independent state.

1991   Women in Action is formed.

1992   Rigoberta Menchú, a Maya activist, wins a Nobel Peace Prize. The National Commission on Women is formed.

1993   Serrano conducts an "autogolpe," a coup against his own administration. He then is forced to flee the country. Congress names Human Rights Ombudsman Ramiro De León Carpio as Serrano's replacement.

1995   Center-right National Advancement Party (PAN) candidate Alvaro Arzú is elected president.

1996   The URNG and the Guatemalan government sign a peace accord. The United Nations Mission for Human Rights Verification in Guatemala (MINUGUA) supervises the implementation of the accord. The URNG agrees to demobilize its military forces. Almost three thousand combatants (80 percent of whom are indigenous people) are demobilized.

1999   First meeting of female URNG militants takes place.

2000   Alfonso Portillo, from the extreme right-wing party
Guatemalan Republican Front (FRG, founded by Ríos Montt in
1998), wins the presidential election.

1 | Somocista Women, Right-Wing Politics, and Feminism in Nicaragua, 1936–1979

Victoria González

In 1979, Nicaraguan women overwhelmingly supported the leftist Sandinista revolution that brought an end to forty-three years of right-wing Somoza dictatorship. More than two decades later, Nicaragua has the strongest women's movement in Central America. These facts led scholars to maintain that women in Nicaragua first organized politically on the left and that their political and feminist awakening occurred recently—within the last twenty years.[1] I propose an alternative understanding of Nicaraguan women's history.

Nicaraguan women have been politically active for generations,[2] and as early as 1837, in fact, there had been an interest in eliminating the tyranny of male domination. This interest grew into full-fledged campaigns for woman suffrage and access to education for women in the 1880s. By the 1920s a small, urban, predominantly middle-class group of Nicaraguan women began to call itself "feminist." Nicaragua boasted a vibrant feminist movement in the 1920s, '30s, and '40s.[3] In the decades that followed, however, early twen-

An earlier version of this chapter appeared in Eugenia Rodríguez Sáenz, ed., *Entre silencios y voces: Género e historia en América Central (1750–1990)* (San José, Costa Rica: Centro Nacional para el Desarrollo de la Mujer y Familia, 1997). This research was funded with a Dissertation Fellowship from the American Association of University Women, a grant from the Institute for the Study of World Politics, and a Foreign Language Area Studies (FLAS) Fellowship.

1. See Helen Collinson, ed., *Women and Revolution in Nicaragua* (London: Zed Books, 1990). See also Benjamin Keen, *A History of Latin America* (Boston: Houghton Mifflin, 1996).

2. My conclusions are based on archival research and oral interviews with two dozen Somocista women and dozens of anti-Somocista activists. Pseudonyms are used to protect the informants. All interviews were conducted in the U.S. and Nicaragua between 1994 and 2000.

3. For more information on the history of feminism in Nicaragua, see Victoria González, "Josefa Toledo de Aguerri (1866–1962) and the Forgotten History of Nicaraguan Feminism, 1821–1955" (master's thesis, University of New Mexico, 1996). See also David Whisnant, *Rascally Signs in Sacred Places: The Politics of Culture in Nicaragua* (Chapel Hill: The University of North Carolina Press, 1995), 407–13.

tieth-century feminism in Nicaragua was erased from the nation's historical memory. A new generation of women appropriated the feminist movement, transforming it into a partisan, pro-Somoza, nonfeminist women's movement. By 1957, the year women first had the opportunity to vote, the Somozas took all the credit for woman suffrage, ignoring feminist contributions to that struggle.

Thousands upon thousands of women voluntarily supported the Somozas and their right-wing Nationalist Liberal Party (PLN) between 1936 and 1979.[4] These women self-identified as supporters of the Somozas and the Liberal Party. As a group, they were nominally Catholic, middle- and working-class urban women who lived on the country's Pacific Coast and Central Highlands.[5] The first generation of Somocista women was impressive, for it was a generation of firsts: it included the nation's first female attorneys, the first female mayors, and so forth. This group of women, born in the 1920s, also included a large number of public school teachers. Many were unmarried.[6]

Somocista women as a whole backed the Somoza family and its Liberal Party in exchange for suffrage and increased political, educational, and economic opportunities. They backed the Somozas' clientelistic system in part because they received goods, services, and (most important) jobs in exchange for their votes and political support. Many were also attracted to the Somozas' populist leadership style, their anticommunism, their economic policies, and the Liberal Party's long-standing position in favor of women's secular education and woman suffrage—a position very much at odds with the Conservative anti-Somocista tradition, but typical among Liberals throughout Latin America.[7] Somocista women, however, were never a homogeneous group, not even politically, and they were certainly not naive. Most did not support every action the Somozas took. And they supported patron-clientelism as long as they considered it to be a fair exchange. In the mid-

4. The many women who were forced to vote for the Somozas and participate in pro-Somoza activities were not Somocistas.
5. My research focuses only on the Pacific Coast and Central Highlands. The history of the Atlantic Coast follows a different course.
6. Most of the Somocista women I interviewed were of this generation.
7. For more on Liberal reforms in Nicaragua, see Elizabeth Dore, "The Holy Family: Imagined Households in Latin America," in *Gender Politics in Latin America: Debates in Theory and Practice,* ed. Dore (New York: Monthly Review Press, 1997). See also Teresa Cobo del Arco, *Politicas de género durante el liberalismó: Nicaragua 1893–1909* (Managua: UCA, 2000). For more on Liberalism and gender throughout Latin America, see Elizabeth Dore and Maxine Molyneux, eds., *Hidden Histories of Gender and the State in Latin America* (Durham: Duke University Press, 2000). See also Francesca Miller, *Latin American Women and the Search for Social Justice* (Hanover: University Press of New England, 1991).

1970s, once they felt that the system was falling apart, some Somocista women became Sandinista supporters.

Although Somocista women worked hard to secure increased access to employment, education, and public office for women, they were not feminists. Their primary concern was the well-being of their male-dominated party. Women's issues always took second place. In this respect, Somocista women shared a great deal with Sandinista women. Additionally, they shared a lack of organizational autonomy within their parties.[8] Both groups were originally mobilized from above, within women's sections of their parties. Somocistas were organized in the Ala Femenina del Partido Liberal Nacionalista (the Feminine Wing of the Nationalist Liberal Party). Sandinistas were organized in AMPRONAC (Asociación de Mujeres ante la Problematica Nacional) in the late 1970s and then in AMNLAE (Asociación de Mujeres Nicaragüenses Luisa Amanda Espinoza) in the 1980s and 1990s. To make this comparison between Somocista and Sandinista women is heresy in many Sandinista and pro-Sandinista circles, for FSLN (Sandinista National Liberation Front) members and sympathizers find it hard to admit similarities between themselves and supporters of a bloody dictatorship. Just as controversial is my contention that maternalism (the exaltation of motherhood promoted as policy by many right-wing governments), which played a crucial role in anti-Somocista women's mobilization, played a relatively minor one in Somocista women's activism.

The disappearance, jailing, and assassination of thousands of young people by the Somozas' National Guard forced anti-Somocista women to organize as mothers.[9] Anti-Somocista women adopted a maternalist discourse rarely seen among Somocista activists. Surprisingly, perhaps, the Somozas—unlike other right-wing regimes—did not emphasize women's roles as mothers as the only appropriate ones for women.[10] Nonetheless, Somocista women did

8. For more on Sandinista women's lack of autonomy during the 1980s, see Anna M. Fernández Poncela, "Nicaraguan Women: Legal, Political, and Social Spaces," in *Gender Politics in Latin America*, ed. Dore. See also Margaret Randall, *Sandino's Daughters Revisited: Feminism in Nicaragua* (New Brunswick: Rutgers University Press, 1994).

9. See Suzanne Baker, "Gender Ideologies and Social Change in Revolutionary Nicaragua" (Ph.D. diss., Boston University, 1995); Patricia Chuchryk, "Women in the Revolution," in *Revolution and Counterrevolution*, ed. Thomas W. Walker (Boulder, Colo.: Westview Press, 1991); and Susan Ramírez-Horton, "The Role of Women in the Nicaraguan Revolution," in *Nicaragua in Revolution*, ed. Thomas W. Walker (New York: Praeger, 1982).

10. For more on right-wing regimes and maternalism in Chile, Argentina, and Brazil, see the essays by Margaret Power and Sandra McGee Deutsch in this volume. For more on right-wing regimes and maternalism in Europe, see Claudia Koonz, *Mothers in the Fatherland: Women, the Family, and Nazi Politics* (New York: St. Martin's Press, 1987), and Victoria de Grazia, *How Fascism Ruled Women: Italy, 1922–1945* (Berkeley and Los Angeles: University of California Press, 1992).

sometimes mobilize as mothers, especially in their fight against communism, suggesting that maternalism acquires greater importance in the context of war or when there is a possibility of war. Another instance in which maternalism prevailed within Somocismo was in the discourse of individual working women looking for jobs or economic assistance within the clientelistic system. It was precisely in order to fulfill their roles as female heads of households that some working-class women supported the dictatorship, hoping to advance economically in exchange for their pro-Somoza votes.[11]

To the dismay of many Conservatives,[12] the Somozas mobilized women politically and economically, incorporating them into the modern Nicaraguan state through state employment. Although statistics vary depending on the study, there was a gradual increase in the percentage of women employed outside the home between the 1950s and the 1970s. According to Gary Ruchwarger, in 1950 women constituted 14 percent of the economically active population. This percentage climbed to 21.9 percent in 1970,[13] reflecting a significant increase in the number of professional women. A study conducted in 1974 by the business school INCAE (Instituto Centroamericano de Administración de Empresas) revealed that women represented 47 percent of the professional/technical sector in the urban zones of Masaya and León. In these same cities, 39 percent of the employers and administrators and 70 percent of the workers in commerce and sales were female.[14] Forty-three percent of the economically active population in these two cities was made up of women, the same percentage reflected at the national level among the urban population.[15] This increase in women's labor force participation—primarily the increase in the professional and technical fields—was surely related to the enlargement of the Nicaraguan middle class, which went from being 11 percent of the population in 1960 to 15 percent in 1975.[16]

11. Nicaragua, like other Latin American countries, has had a large number of female-headed households throughout the last two centuries. See Dore, "The Holy Family."

12. Conservatives like Francisco Palma Martínez complained in the 1940s, "Now woman looks for a job and finds one. . . . Work is a disgrace for woman. When she works she rebels against her parents." See Francisco Palma Martínez, *El siglo de los topos: Crítica y enseñanza en plan de ciencia: Filosofía del sexo, psicología, sociología, eugenesia, religión y arte* (León: Editorial La Patria, n.d.), 66. Unless otherwise noted, all translations are my own. For more on Conservative perspectives on gender, see Whisnant, *Rascally Signs,* 395, 397.

13. Gary Ruchwarger, *People in Power: Forging a Grassroots Democracy in Nicaragua* (South Hadley, Mass.: Bergin and Garvey, 1987), 199.

14. Paula Diebold de Cruz and Mayra Pasos de Rappacioli, *Report on the Role of Women in the Economic Development of Nicaragua* (Managua: USAID, 1975), 66.

15. Ibid., 65, 66.

16. Amalia Chamorro, "Estado y hegemonía durante el somocismo," in *Economía y sociedad en la construcción del estado en Nicaragua,* ed. Alberto Lanuza, Juan Luis Vázquez, Amaru Barahona, and Amalia Chamorro (San José, Costa Rica: ICAP, 1983), 254.

Like most of the world, Nicaragua had experienced an economic depression during the 1930s; by the late 1940s and early 1950s, however, an economic upturn was evident. There was another downswing in the mid-1950s followed by an upsurge in the 1960s. Statistics indicate that many among the upper and middle classes benefited from these growth-recession cycles,[17] leading to the increase of the nation's middle class. By the mid-1970s, however, the Nicaraguan economy had begun a downward turn, taking its toll on the entire population and particularly on women. Although there are discrepancies in the figures regarding urban unemployment, it appears to have been higher among women than men during the last years of the dictatorship. The 1974 census indicates that the percentage of unemployed urban men was 6.4 percent, compared to 7.2 percent of women.[18] Increasing unemployment and the general crisis that engulfed the country in 1978 and 1979 did not diminish the faith of those women who even today claim to be Somocistas and who, with pride, proclaim that under the Somozas, "we all made up the Liberal Party."[19] But it did make even the most firm supporters of the regime admit that the last Somoza "might have gone too far."[20]

While the state sector was expanding, the Somozas had been able to offer women jobs as state employees (positions as teachers, nurses, pharmacists, judges, lawyers, secretaries, receptionists, telegraph and telephone operators, bank tellers, social workers, day care workers, dietitians, laboratory technicians, cooks, cleaning personnel in public buildings, and the like). When the economy suffered, women's participation in formal economic sectors was curtailed. The Somozas nonetheless had mobilized women across different economic sectors, some of which grew during hard economic times. In addition to making a special effort to target teachers and professionals, the Somozas made an effort to mobilize the largely female market sellers and prostitutes. Members of these two groups would support the regime over the long term. The figure of the prostitute, in fact, came to symbolize the moral corruption of the dictatorship for those on the left. Brothels were among the first buildings to be destroyed during the Sandinista revolution in 1979, and dozens of prostitutes were jailed, to be eventually "rehabilitated" by the Sandinista state.[21] The political mobilization of these

17. See John Booth, *The End and the Beginning: The Nicaraguan Revolution*, 2d ed. (Boulder, Colo.: Westview Press, 1985), 63, 65, 78. For evidence of middle-class economic prosperity in the 1950s, see also Knut Walter, "Del protectorado a la revolución," in *Encuentros con la historia*, ed. Margarita Vannini (Managua: IHN-UCA, 1995), 351.

18. Diebold de Cruz and Pasos de Rappacioli, *Report*, 66.

19. Antonia Rodríguez [pseud.], interview by author.

20. Interviews with several Somocista women.

21. See *La prostitución en Nicaragua* (Managua: Programa de Rehabilitación del INSSBI, 1980).

"women of ill repute" and the Somozas' institutionalization of prostitution for the economic gain of their National Guard[22] left anti-Somocistas in Nicaragua equating *all* Somocista women's activism with prostitution.[23] Two additional factors caused the Somoza period to be remembered—even today—as one of extreme sexual chaos and corruption, one in which the Somozas' female supporters are supposed to have been particularly corrupt. The opposition was outraged by the state-sponsored sexual violence against anti-Somocista women—and the personal role male members of the Somoza family played in the sexual torture of their victims[24]—as well as the incorporation of urban women into the labor force.

Pedro Joaquín Chamorro, the vocal opposition leader assassinated by the Somozas in 1978, described the Somoza period as "the total inversion of the moral values of Nicaraguan life: prostitutes against mothers, alcohol against civic duty, blackmail against honesty, lowlifes against citizenry."[25] The triumph of mothers against prostitutes was the situation Nicaragua faced in 1979. But what about the right-wing traditions so many Nicaraguan women had embraced over the course of the century? Had these simply disappeared? Knowledge of these traditions can help explain why so many women voted against the Sandinistas in 1990, why so many voted in favor of a right-wing Liberal candidate in 1996, and why the dictatorship lasted so long in the first place. The examination of sexual politics under the dictatorship is also crucial to our understanding of more recent political developments in Nicaragua. The fact that the Somoza years are characterized today as ones of sexual disorder is a political victory for the FSLN and the Conservative Party, the Somozas' official opposition, for it means that the official Somocista discourse which portrayed the regime as orderly did not prevail. Ironically, how-

22. Ibid. See also Collinson, ed., *Women and Revolution*, 69; A. Chamorro, "Estado y hegemonía," 271; and Jeffrey L. Gould, *To Lead as Equals: Rural Protest and Political Consciousness in Chinandega, Nicaragua, 1912–1979* (Chapel Hill: The University of North Carolina Press, 1990), 169.

23. This assertion is based on dozens of interviews with Sandinistas and Somocista activists. See also Pedro Joaquín Chamorro, *Estirpe sangrienta: Los Somoza* (Managua: Ediciones el Pez y la Serpiente, 1978), 160, and Viktor Morales Henriquez, *De Mrs. Hanna a la Dinorah: Principio y fin de la dictadura somocista: Historia de medio siglo de corrupción* (Managua?: n.p., 1980?).

24. Two cases of sexual violence against women drew a great deal of international attention and criticism. The first was the rape of Doris María Tijerino, jailed by the Somozas in 1969. The second was the rape of a Peace Corps volunteer by a National Guard soldier in 1979. See Denis Lynn Daly Heyck, *Life Stories of the Nicaraguan Revolution* (London: Routledge, 1990), 64–67, and Katherine Hoyt, *Thirty Years of Memories: Dictatorship, Revolution, and Nicaragua Solidarity* (Washington, D.C.: Nicaragua Network Education Fund, 1996), 62.

25. P. Chamorro, *Estirpe sangrienta,* 163.

Sandinista

ever, the image of sexual chaos under the Somozas was popularized precisely because it reinforced already-established societal restrictions (upheld by a significant sector of anti-Somocistas) against women in public. The condemnation of women in public prevalent among Conservatives helps explain the way in which Violeta Barrios de Chamorro justified her presidency (1990–96). She was heir to the Conservative Party's tradition, which extolled women's maternal and domestic roles in society. Therefore, she had to justify her participation in politics through maternalist rhetoric, proclaiming to be "the Mother of the Nicaraguans."[26] Doña Violeta was rectifying not only ten years of Sandinista gender policies but also the previous forty-three years of Liberal Somocista ones, many of which did not coincide with Conservative views on women.

The links between dictatorship and prostitution affected not only the Somozas' Conservative opposition; they also had a profound effect on the Sandinistas' gender policies. The FSLN leadership wasted no time in banning prostitution, doing so in the first few months after the triumph of the revolution. As Helen Collinson notes, "for the Sandinistas, prostitution epitomized all the wrongs of the Somoza regime."[27] Clearly, then, the FSLN fashioned its policies on gender in direct response to the Somozas' corruption; the revolutionary "New Man" was not to engage in the sexual degradation of women (a characteristic of Somocista masculinity). Against this backdrop, it is not surprising that many Sandinistas in the 1990s defended former Sandinista President Daniel Ortega against accusations of rape and incest made by his stepdaughter, Zoilamérica Narváez. For many FSLN supporters, what Narváez claims Ortega did was unimaginable, because similar abuse had taken place under the Somozas and it was not supposed to occur under the Sandinistas.

Unlike Somocista women under the dictatorship, during the 1980s, Sandinista women as a group were spared the embarrassment and shame of supporting political figures accused of unthinkable sexual crimes. This changed abruptly in 1998, once Narváez's accusations were made public. In spite of this unexpected turn of events in Nicaraguan history, which underscores the similarities between the Somoza dictatorship and the Sandinista revolution, important differences between the experiences of Somocista and Sandinista women must be stressed. Somocista women defended a regime

26. For more on Barrios de Chamorro's maternal image, see Karen Kampwirth, "The Mother of the Nicaraguans: Doña Violeta and the UNO's Gender Agenda," *Latin American Perspectives* 23, no. 1 (1996): 67–86.

27. Collinson, ed., *Women and Revolution,* 69.

that systematically oppressed women through state-sponsored prostitution rings and the rape of female prisoners. The FSLN was not accused of such things. And although both Somocista and Sandinista women were treated as public women (sexually loose women) by their enemies for assuming public political and economic roles in society, there is one other crucial difference in their mobilization, beyond the obvious political differences: the mobilization of Sandinista women, and their struggle for autonomy from the FSLN, eventually led to the emergence of a "second wave" of feminism in Nicaragua. By comparison, the mobilization of Somocista women and their acceptance of their dependent status effectively co-opted Nicaragua's first wave of feminism and delayed the re-emergence of feminism in the second half of the twentieth century.

Organizationally, this chapter consists of three parts. The first traces the mid-twentieth-century transition from feminism to a Somocista women's movement. The second addresses the Somocista women's movement.[28] And the third sheds light on the relationship between sex and politics during the Somozas' regime. Because of its importance, I discuss in depth the Ala Femenina's role in erasing feminism from Nicaraguan history. I also address the role the Ala played in upholding the dictatorship. The working-class leader Nicolasa Sevilla—an alleged prostitute and madam—was a major figure among Somocista women; therefore, her contributions to the regime are also explored here. The chapter concludes by taking us back to the topics of maternalism, prostitution, and Somocista sexual politics.

The Transition from an Independent Feminist Movement to a Liberal Discourse on Women's Rights

A wide variety of independent[29] women's organizations existed in Nicaragua during the first half of the twentieth century. Those groups working specifically on women's rights tended to sympathize with liberalism, for, unlike the Conservative Party, the Liberal Party had promised as early as 1916 to endorse woman suffrage.[30] Feminist groups were especially eager to cooperate

28. Many Somocista women's groups made up what I am calling the "Somocista women's movement." However, I deal only with the Ala Femenina, the largest, most prominent, and most political of these groups.

29. By "independent," I mean that they were not directly tied to political parties, the state, or the Catholic Church.

30. *El 93: Diario político y de variedades,* 1 September 1916.

with Liberal politicians in enacting suffrage and the other political change upon which both Liberals and feminists seemed to agree easily: women's increased access to higher education. Although women failed to obtain the vote under the U.S.-supervised 1932 elections, due to the guerrilla war being waged against Augusto C. Sandino,[31] the mid-1930s were a particularly hopeful period for feminists. At that time the newly installed Somoza administration seemed receptive to feminist concerns. Anastasio Somoza García's wife, Salvadora Debayle, belonged to many women's organizations. Moreover, she and her family were personally acquainted with Josefa Toledo de Aguerri (1866–1962), the most well-known feminist and suffragist of the time.[32] The First Lady's father, the medical doctor Luis H. Debayle (1865–1938), had shared a strong friendship with Toledo de Aguerri based on their mutual devotion to the arts and their service to the poor.[33] Perhaps due to this longstanding friendship, feminists received encouragement from the extended Somoza family even before Somoza García's ascent to power. In 1933, Nicaragua's Acting Minister to the United States, Luis Manuel Debayle (Luis H. Debayle's son), gave a speech to a group of Woman Party members in the United States. Debayle noted: "The feminists in Nicaragua claim that, inasmuch as the Constitution does not mention sex as a qualification or hindrance to citizenship and its prerogatives, the custom which has excluded women from the vote, and in general, from the right to hold office, has no fundamental basis." Debayle also stressed the following point to his audience: "The country that has not given its women the opportunities afforded to its men advances very slowly towards the goal of the perfect state, and the hope of every nation lies in its recognition of this fact."[34]

Statements like these indicate that individuals in the Nicaraguan government were aware of feminists' demands and open to their suggestions in the early 1930s. Most important, the awareness continued throughout the decade. A few years after Debayle's speech, in 1937, Toledo de Aguerri was the

31. The U.S. Marines waged a counterinsurgency war against the anti-imperialist leader Augusto C. Sandino from 1927 through 1933. The Marines withdrew in 1933 after failing to defeat Sandino, who was murdered in 1934 on Anastasio Somoza García's orders. The 1932 election was won by Liberal Juan Bautista Sacasa, who was then deposed in 1936 by Somoza García.

32. See Josefa Toledo de Aguerri, *Educación y feminismo: Sobre enseñanza: Artículos varios (Reproducciones)* (Managua: Talleres Nacionales de Imprenta y Encuadernación, 1940), 57–62.

33. Jorge Eduardo Arellano, *Heroes sin fusil: 140 nicaragüenses sobresalientes* (Managua: Editorial Hispamer, 1998), 267, 268.

34. Luis Manuel Debayle, "The Status of Women in Nicaragua," *Mid-Pacific Magazine* 45, no. 3 (1933), 238, 237.

keynote speaker at a cultural event organized in honor of Somoza García and his wife. Since the First Lady was the honorary president of LIMDI y Cruzada (the International League of Iberian and Hispanic American Women and the Nicaraguan Women's Crusade), one of the many feminist organizations in which Toledo de Aguerri participated, the keynote address was appropriately about feminism.

In her presentation, Toledo de Aguerri carefully explained LIMDI y Cruzada's feminist objectives:

> **1st—*To create schools*** . . . [including] technical schools, so that women can support themselves, [and] literacy schools for peasant women, who make up the majority of the country.
> **2nd—*The social and political liberation of woman.*** Practical schooling in the social and political duties of citizenship, for without a voice and a vote [women] cannot offer their social and political cooperation.
> **3rd—*National autonomy.*** We inherited from our ancestors a Nation [*Patria*] we must conserve and defend.
> **4th—**[*To foster*] Intellectual Culture through conferences on the Sciences, the Arts and Literature, to give woman a greater understanding, so as to demand from her greater responsibility.[35]

Two years later, erroneously believing that the climate favored change, Josefa Toledo de Aguerri was involved in presenting one of many petitions before Nicaragua's Constitutional Assembly, this time urging the Somoza government to make good on its promise to grant women the vote: "[The Nicaraguan woman] hopes with confidence that the President of the Republic, General A. Somoza, will fulfill the promise he made in his Governing Program [*Programa de Gobierno*]. He understands that one must govern with the acquiescence of the entire country, not only with a certain part of it."[36]

Knowing the highest levels of government were well aware of their goals, and thinking they had weighty support within the Somocista regime, the tactics used by feminists in this suffrage drive were different from those used in earlier campaigns. Though men in the previous century had tended to speak on behalf of women, that certainly was not the case in 1939. In the "Feminist Petition to the Constitutional [Assembly] Demanding Woman's

35. Toledo de Aguerri, *Educación y feminismo*, 28, 29.
36. Ibid., 25.

Rights as Citizen of the Republic" drafted by Toledo de Aguerri, women spoke quite forcefully on their own behalf:

> In the name of justice and reason we, a group of Nicaraguan women, have come as representatives of the country's women, to ask that you faithfully interpret our way of thinking and feeling with regards to our rights as citizens of the Republic. . . .
> We ask that the . . . Nicaraguan woman [have] the right to:
> a)—"The same political treatment as man."
> b)—"The enjoyment of equality in civil matters."
> c)—"The widest opportunities and protection in the workplace," and
> d)—"The greatest protection as mothers."
>
> THESE DEMANDS ARE MADE BY:
>
> The poor woman . . . the middle-class woman . . . the intellectual and wealthy woman . . .[37]

Many independent feminist women's groups were involved in drafting this petition. Among the organizations were LIMDI y Cruzada, the Nicaraguan International League for Peace and Freedom Delegation, the First Feminine Pan-American Education League, the Inter-American Committee on Women, and the Working Women's Cultural Center.[38] After this attempt failed to win the vote for women, Josefa Toledo de Aguerri and her generation of feminists started to disappear from Somocista propaganda and public view; they were eventually replaced with a watered-down Somocista version of "feminism" and women's rights.

National and international events contributed to the defeat of woman suffrage in the 1930s. As noted earlier, U.S. intervention postponed women's attempt to secure the vote in 1932. According to the *New York Times,* Clark Howell Woodward, the U.S. admiral in charge of supervising elections in Nicaragua that year, formally denied suffrage to women, suggesting that feminists should submit their request at a later (and more convenient) time: "Admiral C. H. Woodward of the United States Navy, Chairman of the Election Mission, in a letter . . . to Señora María A. Gomez, a feminist leader in Managua, announced that while he was in sympathy with her proposal that women [be] permitted to vote he could not accede to her request that they

37. Ibid., 21, 24.
38. Ibid., 25.

be allowed to do so in the November elections. He advised Señora Gomez to present the project of permitting women's suffrage to the next Congress."[39] The widespread conflict between secular liberalism and Catholicism present throughout Latin America also had a negative effect on the struggle for woman suffrage. The Catholic Church actively organized women during the 1930s and 1940s in organizations like the Juventud Obrera Catolica (JOC).[40] Since the Catholic Church was allied with the Conservative Party, Liberals feared that the majority of women, if given a chance, would vote for Conservative candidates. That was exactly the reasoning the Liberal Assembly delegate Guillermo Sevilla Sacasa gave for his anti-suffrage vote in 1939. Although he conceded that feminists had had a long history of independent activism, he believed that most women would be manipulated by their confessors into voting against their own interests. In his speech before the Assembly, Sevilla Sacasa stated:

> The feminist current is felt everywhere. It races, throbs . . . throughout the Universe. . . . As I . . . contemplate the panorama offered by the Nicaraguan population . . . I see that a group of brave women rises proudly above the general feminine mass. . . . Any one of these women is . . . worth more than a hundred men . . . and could exercise suffrage better . . . than most men.
> [B]ut unfortunately . . . the Nicaraguan woman, in general terms . . . is not fit [*capacitada*] to vote. . . . She is not fit precisely because our woman lacks philosophical and religious independence . . . [o]ur woman becomes transformed and loses all independence when she kneels before a priest in the confession booth, or when she . . . listens to the words of a Bishop. . . . A Minister of the Church . . . can do what he wants at that moment with our woman.[41]

In spite of Sevilla Sacasa's refusal to support woman suffrage in 1939, in 1944 the Liberal Party once again "declared [itself] in favor of . . . woman suffrage."[42] Then, in 1945, "Deputy Roberto González presented a bill in the House of Deputies to grant women equal rights with men to vote in national

39. "Nicaraguan Women Lose: Plea to Be Allowed to Vote in November Elections is Rejected," *New York Times*, 27 September 1932, 12.

40. Josefina Arnesto, interview by author, Matagalpa, Nicaragua, 12 July 1995.

41. Guillermo Sevilla Sacasa, *La mujer nicaragüense ante el derecho a sufragar: Por que me opuse a que se le concediera: La verdad sobre mi actitud en la constituyente* (Managua: Talleres Gráficos Perez, 1939), 5, 6.

42. "Nicaragua Liberals Act: Convention Favors Presidential Re-election and Woman Suffrage," *New York Times*, 11 January 1944, 5.

and local elections."[43] Although the bill was defeated, woman suffrage continued to be brought up as an issue in legislative sessions. The 1950 Constitution was "criticized by leading Nicaraguan women inasmuch as suffrage rights would not be exercised until [the] 1964 [election]. Some women [petitioned] Congress for reconsideration of the article and immediate suffrage."[44]

Women's petitions did not bring about immediate suffrage in 1950, but two small victories were won. First, the Conservative Party decided to support woman suffrage publicly at that time.[45] Second, "a resolution was approved that would permit the Congress, by a two-thirds majority vote, to extend the franchise to women when it saw fit."[46] With bipartisan support, suffrage was only five years away, although women would not actually vote in national elections until 1957.

By the early 1950s, once the Somoza family had established itself comfortably in power, feminists were hardly mentioned in the official rhetoric, although an active feminist movement in Nicaragua continued to exist at least until the end of the decade. Between the mid-1950s and 1979 the primary women the Somozas acknowledged as contributing to the advancement of women in Nicaragua were the members of the Ala Femenina. In praise of the organization's efforts on behalf of his 1957 electoral campaign, Luis Somoza called the Ala not the wings of the party, but its breast [*la pechuga*], the most savory part of a chicken.[47] Luis Somoza's brother, Anastasio Somoza Debayle—the third and last Somoza to hold power—also gave perpetual praise to the "dynamic . . . women affiliated with the Nationalist Liberal Party."[48]

In the 1960s and 1970s the term *feminism* was rarely employed; when it *was* used, it was applied by Ala members to themselves or to—of all people—Anastasio Somoza Debayle.[49] "Tachito," as he was often called, also came close to calling himself a feminist. As he campaigned for president throughout Nicaragua in 1966, he mentioned women's rights in most of his

43. "Women's Vote Bill in Nicaragua," *New York Times,* 9 May 1945, 14.
44. "Nicaraguan Women Seek Vote," *New York Times,* 17 August 1950, 17.
45. Ibid.
46. "Nicaraguan Women Not to Vote," *New York Times,* 2 September 1950, 6.
47. Rodríguez, interview.
48. *Hacia la meta . . . Mensajes políticos del Gral. Anastasio Somoza Debayle, Presidente Constitucional de Nicaragua 1967–1972 ante la gran convención del Partido Liberal Nacionalista, durante su campaña electoral y toma de posesión* (Managua: Imprenta Nacional, 1968), 14.
49. *Corona fúnebre en recuerdo de la Doctora Olga Núñez de Saballos: Primer aniversario de su muerte* (Managua: Imprenta Nacional, 12 September 1972), 66.

speeches. In fact, he took credit, on behalf of his family and the Nationalist Liberal Party, for "incorporating into political life [the nation's] most beloved being . . . the Nicaraguan woman."[50] Somoza repeatedly pointed out that the PLN was "the party which [had given] women equality before the law."[51]

What Somoza and Ala members failed to mention was the feminist contribution to the struggle for woman suffrage. Ironically, the Ala's Secretary, journalist Lucrecia Noguera Carazo, did mention feminist Josefa Toledo de Aguerri in her writings, but only as a "prestigious educator" who had held "great meaning for the cultural life of the Nicaraguan woman."[52] The Ala's impact in forging an alternative interpretation of history was such that its founder, Olga Núñez de Saballos (1920–71), erroneously came to be known as "the first woman to occupy a public post during this century, as Cultural Attaché at the Nicaraguan Embassy in Washington."[53] This belief became popular even though Núñez de Saballos and Toledo de Aguerri had known each other in the 1950s, and it was clear the latter had earlier governmental experience. (Toledo de Aguerri had been named General Director of Public Instruction in 1924 and was part of the first group of women to enter officially into the world of government. Before her, in 1922, María de Ibarra, stationed in Detroit, had been the first woman to be named Consul to the United States. And in 1924, Juana Molina de Fromen, Toledo de Aguerri's friend, was named Assistant Secretary of Public Instruction.)[54]

The Ala Femenina del Partido Liberal: Objectives and Achievements

Olga Núñez de Saballos, Nicaragua's first female attorney, founded the Feminine Wing of the Somozas' Nationalist Liberal Party in 1955. The Ala Femenina was created to meet the needs of the PLN as well as those of Nicaragua's first generation of university-educated liberal women. On the one hand, the Ala displaced, appropriated, and/or co-opted previously independent (often

---

50. *Hacia la meta . . .*, 14.
51. Ibid., 145.
52. Lucrecia Noguera Carazo, *Evolución cultural y política de la mujer nicaragüense* (Managua: n.p., 1974), 7.
53. Ibid., 12.
54. See Julio C. Hernández, "Puntos culminantes del primer congreso pedagogico nicaragüense," *Semanario el digesto* 1, no. 38 (22 September 1951), and Debayle, "The Status of Women in Nicaragua," 238.

feminist) women's organizations in order for the Party to exercise direct control over women—now possible voters. On the other hand, the Ala opened up for Liberal women a sanctioned political space—albeit a limited one—in which to maneuver and become involved in electoral politics as voters. In other words, the Ala was created to deal with a new factor in party politics: woman suffrage. Significantly, the PLN popularized the creation of "feminine wings" within male-dominated parties. The pattern became well established during the dictatorship and continues up to this day.[55]

Through the creation of a state-sponsored countrywide network of women, the Ala Femenina helped create a popular Somocista discourse in Nicaragua. In stressing this point, I am building on historian Jeffrey L. Gould's arguments on Somocista populism. Unlike most interpreters of the regime, Gould contends that "the Somozas [during the early part of their administration] created a populist political style that combined an anti-oligarchic discourse with appeals to the working masses. . . . Workers and peasants largely accepted the Somozas' variant of populism and its corresponding rules of the game, but at the same time, they shaped and transformed Somocista populism."[56]

The Somozas clearly made a strong appeal for support to Nicaragua's female population. The dictatorship promoted limited women's rights in exchange for women's votes and political backing. Moreover, it attempted to control the rules of the game through co-optation and appropriation. Like workers, however, women as a group were also able to "shape and transform" the populist Somocista discourse and make it their own.

The Ala's Electoral Work

Although the Somozas maintained themselves in power through a dictatorship, they held periodic elections, which had great symbolic value for Somocistas in spite of their fraudulent nature. Women played a central role in these elections. Since the Ala was charged with mobilizing women in support of the regime, a great part of its activism centered on electoral campaigns.

55. As early as 1935, the Partido Trabajador Nicaragüense had organized socialist women in the Frente Obrero Femenino. See Armando Amador, *Un siglo de lucha de los trabajadores de Nicaragua* (Managua: UCA, 1992), 94. During the 1960s and 1970s, Conservative women were organized in the Frente Femenino Conservador. See Amelia Borge de Sotomayor, *La condición legal de la mujer y su situación de hecho: Compilación y analisis de leyes que discriminan a la mujer* (Medford, Mass.: Tufts University, 1975), 15. Sandinista women were organized in AMPRONAC in the 1970s and in AMNLAE from the 1980s onward.

56. Gould, *To Lead as Equals*, 293.

The Ala participated actively and creatively in the 1957, 1963, 1967, and 1974 presidential campaigns, specifically targeting female voters through its political propaganda. In 1956, for example, a song was composed by and for *"señoritas liberales."* These were its lyrics:

> Soon we will vote
> soon we will vote
> and Somoza will win . . .
>
> *compañeras* let's vote
> *compañeras* let's vote . . .
>
> With God's blessing
> With God's blessing
> we will win the elections
> with the Boogie-Woogie SO
> with the Boogie-Woogie MO
> with the Boogie-Woogie ZA . . .[57]

Somocista women's votes for Luis Somoza, the winning candidate in the 1957 election, symbolically honored the memory of Anastasio Somoza García, the patriarch who had allowed them to become full citizens. On a more immediate level, however, Somocista women were swayed by the thirty-three-year-old agricultural engineer's personality and appearance. In the eyes of Antonia Rodríguez, a former Ala member, Luis Somoza was "a very cultured, very sensitive man, who was open to poor people and very open to the public. He was handsome, light-skinned, good looking, elegant. . . . He would ask [Ala members] 'where are my *pechugas?*' and we would all run to embrace him."[58]

After Luis Somoza completed his six-year term, Nicaragua held its first secret ballot elections in 1963. René Schick Gutiérrez, the Somocista candidate, was elected but died in office. A presidential election was held again in 1967, and the third and youngest Somoza won by an impressive margin. According to author Bernard Diederich, "Somoza declared he had received 480,162 of the reportedly 652,244 votes cast. The majority of votes were cast by women."[59]

57. "Boogie-Woogie Somoza," *Nicaragua: Patria arte cultura,* no. 9 (February 1956).
58. Rodríguez, interview.
59. Bernard Diederich, *Somoza and the Legacy of U.S. Involvement in Central America* (New York: E. P. Dutton, 1981), 82.

During the 1974 elections, the Ala celebrated its nineteenth birthday by providing the Somozas with 60 to 67 percent of their electoral votes.[60] These figures proved, in the eyes of journalist (and cofounder of the Ala) Lucrecia Noguera Carazo, that the Ala had become a "powerful" group.[61] According to another Ala cofounder, teacher Mary Coco Maltez de Callejas, the wings of the Liberal party had turned into its "backbone."[62] Without a doubt, the Ala occupied a privileged position within the dictatorship. By successfully fostering women's support for the Somoza regime, the Ala helped legitimize elections compromised by allegations of fraud.[63]

Ala members, however, were not just seeking votes for the Somozas. They sought support for their own political aspirations as well. By 1975, Liberal women (most of them affiliated with the Ala) held a wide variety of posts within the Somoza administration and within the Somocista Nationalist Liberal Party (PLN). Twelve percent of the PLN's Convention Representatives were women (by comparison, women made up only 5 percent of the Conservative Party's Convention Representatives).[64] At that time there were also thirteen female mayors, one female senator, one female Vice-Minister of the National District (Managua), one female Vice-Minister of Public Education, one female Chief of Commerce, one female President of the Junta Nacional de Asistencia y Previsión Social (the equivalent of a Social Security and Welfare Department), and eleven female local judges.[65]

The Ala: Its Members and Organizational Structure

In part, the Ala's success was due to its member recruitment tactics and its organizational structure. The members of its inner circle tended to be personally hand-picked by the organization's leaders (thus assuring a middleclass professional makeup). Antonia Rodríguez, for instance, recalls that Olga Núñez de Saballos, the Ala's founder, personally invited her to attend Ala meetings. Rodríguez, a health care professional, was recruited in the mid-

---

60. Noguera Carazo, *Evolución cultural,* 16.
61. Ibid., 15.
62. *Corona funebre,* 69.
63. For allegations of fraud, see *Nicaragua: Election Factbook* (Washington, D.C.: Institute for the Comparative Study of Political Systems, a division of Operations and Policy Research, Inc., 1967). See also George A. Bowdler and Patrick Cotter, *Voter Participation in Central America, 1954–1981: An Exploration* (Washington, D.C.: University Press of America, 1982), 64.
64. Borge de Sotomayor, *La condición legal de la mujer,* 3, 4.
65. For a longer list of women who occupied government positions in 1975, see ibid., 16, 17.

1960s, soon after she arrived in Managua from her hometown outside the capital. Being invited to join such a prestigious organization was an honor for Rodríguez, who was tired of the limits that a small town placed on professional middle-class women. Ala membership gave her the respect she sought as a woman, a professional, and a Liberal. In the Ala, Rodríguez found a ready-made set of friends, mentors, and colleagues. The connections she made in the organization have lasted her a lifetime, helping her (and her friends and relatives) obtain employment and other material benefits. Equally important, the Ala helped Rodríguez adjust to life in the capital, incorporating her directly into the center of Liberal political life. Through the Ala Rodríguez came to be personally acquainted with dozens of high-level female and male politicians who could assist her in times of need. Like other Ala members, Rodríguez attended, co-planned, and co-organized Ala meetings and pro-Somoza rallies. And Rodríguez provided the Managua Ala office with her insider's knowledge of the politics of her hometown, thus helping the organization devise campaign strategies appropriate for the region.[66]

Organizationally, the Ala resembled a pyramid. At the highest level, the Ala responded to the orders given by two men: the President of the Republic and the Nationalist Liberal Party Chair. The second level of command was made up of the Ala's National Directorate (Directiva Nacional). This select group included a president, a vice-president, a secretary, a treasurer, and representatives (vocales) from the country's different provinces (departamentos).[67] The Ala chapters present in each one of Nicaragua's sixteen departamentos were responsible to the National Directorate. Subordinated to these regional chapters were 134 municipio or county-level Ala affiliates.[68] At the bottom of the pyramid were the "Liberal Women Committees" present in electoral precincts (cantones) throughout the nation.[69] Although elections were held within the Ala, high-level posts tended to be occupied for life. The Ala, like the Somoza regime, was hierarchical, nondemocratic, and authoritarian. And again like the Somoza administration, the Ala was accused of imposing official candidates on local communities and of bribing voters.[70] Through their participation in the Ala, women did not learn "democracy" but a hierarchical conceptualization of politics. Although Ala members incorporated working-class women as well as women from regions outside the

66. Rodríguez, interview.
67. Ibid.
68. Borge de Sotomayor, La condición legal de la mujer, 14.
69. Ibid.
70. Alejandra Flores [pseud.], interview by author.

capital into their organizational pyramid, only urban, middle-class professional members participated in national decision-making processes. In short, the Ala simultaneously reinforced a class hierarchy among women within its own structure and within society at large *and* stressed the importance of local identities for its own gain, as it helped bolster the political and bureaucratic primacy of the capital.

From 1955 through 1971, the Ala was centered around the figure of its founder and president, attorney Olga Núñez de Saballos. This period constituted the Ala's golden age. During that time Ala members became intoxicated with Somocismo and Somocista rhetoric. They believed the dictatorship when it told them time after time that women were integral to Somocismo and the Nationalist Liberal Party. In the eyes of Ala women, the PLN had proven itself by giving women the vote. From their perspective, it would continue opening the doors of opportunity for them. Most important, perhaps, Somocista women wanted to make Somocismo their own, a process the regime encouraged since it did not threaten the dictatorship's existence.

"La Nicolasa"

The role women in the Ala played cannot be properly understood unless Nicolasa Sevilla's support for the Somoza regime is also taken into account. While the Ala tried to channel middle-class women's political participation into "proper" and acceptable expressions, "la Nicolasa" symbolized the unrestrained manifestation of lower-class women's political passion. While the Ala was charged with tactfully gaining women's support for the Somozas, Sevilla and her followers, both men and women, heckled, tormented, humiliated, and attacked those who refused to be swayed by "polite" tactics. Because she was a woman, one willing to engage personally in violent acts, Sevilla (during her early years of political activism) was most effective at intimidating other women, particularly those who belonged to the middle and upper classes. The primary targets of Sevilla's "*turbas,*" or gangs—as they were called by their detractors—initially were the wives, sisters, and daughters of politicians who opposed Somoza. From the 1940s onward, whenever "the wives of [anti-Somocista] ministers protested in public, Nicolasa would make them run."[71] Although there are no claims that she ever killed anyone personally, with her bare hands, rumor has it that Sevilla always carried a gun

71. Rodríguez, interview.

in her purse.[72] Most significantly, she was invariably accompanied by several armed male bodyguards.[73] Nicolasa Sevilla's political life, most of which centered in the capital, spanned almost the entire dictatorship. She supported the first, second, and third Somoza. Imprisoned by the Sandinistas in 1979, she was eventually released by FSLN Comandante Tomás Borge because of her advanced age.[74]

Sevilla's personal life is the subject of great debate. Among Sandinistas, she is remembered as a "former prostitute and intimate friend of Somoza García," one who caused the jailing and death of many anti-Somoza activists.[75] Josefa Ortega, a Sandinista woman who knew Sevilla's son, best summarizes the Sandinista perspective on Sevilla: "Nicolasa was a bad woman."[76] The recollections of Somocistas are more nuanced. Antonia Rodríguez remembers that Sevilla had a child with Liberal attorney and former Vice-President Enoc Aguado in the 1930s or 1940s. After her relationship with Aguado ended, Sevilla "lived with other men," eventually marrying Eugenio Solorzano, a founder of AMROC (the Association of Retired Military Officers, Workers and Peasants of Nicaragua) and high-level administrator of the National District (the city of Managua). Her husband's position helped Sevilla come into contact with the people her enemies would later call "thugs": garbage collectors, street sweepers, slaughterhouse employees, and other city workers whom she recruited to vote for the Somozas.[77]

Today, some Nicaraguans remember Sevilla as the president of AMROC.[78] This was not the case. Sevilla was actually the founder and leader of the Somocista Popular Fronts, anti-Communist gangs made up of urban working-class men in their twenties and thirties, some of them members of the Somocista youth organization, the Juventud Somocista.[79] In the eyes of its opponents, Sevilla's Somocista Popular Fronts functioned as a paramilitary terrorist organization[80] and might have in fact been related to the Mano Blanca, a government-supported anti-Sandinista clandestine terrorist group that emerged in the late 1970s.[81] Regardless of whether the latter allegation

72. Rafael Suárez [pseud.], interview by author.

73. Ibid.

74. Tomás Borge, interview by author, New York City, 18 March 1997.

75. Morales Henríquez, *De Mrs. Hanna a la Dinorah*, 74; Josefa Ortega [pseud.], interview by author.

76. Ortega, interview.

77. Rodríguez, interview.

78. Suárez, interview; Mario Vega [pseud.], personal conversation with author.

79. "Luctuosa," *Ala Femenina* 1, no. 2 (1955), 47.

80. See *Nicaragua: Election Factbook*, 16.

81. Suárez, interview.

is true, there is no doubt that Sevilla wielded great power among her followers at the grassroots level and instilled fear among the population at large.

In addition to her privileged position within working-class Somocismo, Sevilla held a special place within the middle and upper echelons of the dictatorship. She participated in electoral campaigns, published articles in Somocista newspapers, and had a say in the government's upper circles. According to Antonia Rodríguez, "there was a Sevilla representative in every electoral district."[82] She was also "given the run of two pro-government newspapers," in which she "vilified Managua society."[83] Moreover, Sevilla "could go to any Ministry and the secretary there could not tell her to wait. Her power was extraordinary."[84]

Most important, perhaps, Sevilla was perceived as being always at the president's side: "wherever Somoza went, there she went."[85] William Krehm, a *Time* reporter who witnessed Sevilla's activism firsthand in the 1940s, notes that Sevilla, the "skinny, blue-eyed . . . owner of a cut-rate brothel"[86] indeed "became a pillar of the regime."[87] How exactly Sevilla came to wield so much power remains unclear.

According to Antonia Rodríguez, "leaders are not born, they are made. Somoza [García] saw something in [Sevilla] and knew it would benefit him to have her on his side. . . . She was like attorney Olga Núñez de Saballos, but in a different realm. She made her own organization. But as I said, she was not upper-class, she was of the people."[88] And according to Reina Zambrano, a well-known anti-Somocista activist who had many confrontations with Sevilla, "la Nicolasa" became a Somoza supporter because Enoc Aguado, a high-level Liberal politician who rebelled against Somoza, had refused to marry her. Aguado, the founder of the Independent Liberal Party or PLI, turned against Somoza in the 1940s. It is rumored that Somoza later poisoned him on Sevilla's request.[89]

Personal encounters like those Zambrano, Rodríguez, and Krehm had with Sevilla and her followers helped turn "la Nicolasa" into a legendary figure, one of national and international proportions. Because she became

82. Rodríguez, interview.
83. William Krehm, "Call All Trulls," *Time,* 7 August 1944, 38.
84. Rodríguez, interview.
85. Suárez, interview.
86. Krehm, "Call All Trulls," 38.
87. Quoted in Gregorio Selser, *Nicaragua de Walker a Somoza* (Mexico City: Mex Sur Editorial S.A., 1984), 250.
88. Rodríguez, interview.
89. Reina Zambrano [pseud.], interview by author.

so controversial, it is often hard to separate fact from fiction in the stories told about her. Nonetheless, certain events did take place and deserve special notice, especially actions Sevilla took in 1944 and 1962.

By most accounts, Sevilla first gained national and international attention in 1944. Sources agree that on 29 June of that year, an anti-Somoza protest taking place in Managua was met by a counterprotest led by Sevilla. Both groups were made up of women. However, the anti-Somocista forces were made up of middle-class women, and the pro-Somoza faction was working-class.[90] According to the conservative newspaper *La Prensa,* Sevilla's followers were "a rabble of market vendors and women of ill-repute."[91] William Krehm's article "Call All Trulls" presents a detailed description of events. According to Krehm,

> a procession of dignified, black-clad . . . elderly mothers, respectable wives and daughters . . . [were] protest[ing] the mass arrest of more than 600 opponents of Dictator Anastasio Somoza . . . [when] [o]ut of the Managua slums rushed mobs of prostitutes. They pressed around the horrified women and girls, slapped them, spat at them. Male relatives came to the rescue [and] dispersed the screaming trulls. Then, from an official Government auto jumped . . . Nicolasa Sevilla. . . . Threatening the older women with a knife, she spluttered filth at the prettier girls. . . . [T]he harlotry then receded into the slums. But the President invited Nicolasa to the Palace, called her his "very good friend," and introduced her to outraged callers.[92]

Later that year, according to Krehm, Sevilla "invaded the Chamber of Deputies and slapped a speaker."[93]

Confronting anti-Somocistas inside governmental buildings would come to be one of Sevilla's trademarks. The tactic was seemingly supported by the Somozas themselves, for similar events took place years later. Author Bernard Diederich recalls how, in 1962,

> an anti-Somoza crowd entered the Congress Building to protest [a law under consideration]. They were expected. Waiting for them was a gang of eighty government thugs headed by Nicolasa Sevilla,

90. Rodríguez, interview. See also Diederich, *Somoza;* Selser, *Nicaragua de Walker a Somoza;* and Krehm, "Call All Trulls."
91. Cited in Knut Walter, *The Regime of Anastasio Somoza, 1936–1956* (Chapel Hill: The University of North Carolina Press, 1993), 131.
92. Krehm, "Call All Trulls," 38.
93. Ibid.

a tough-looking woman who commanded the Somoza male street gangs in Managua. When the demonstrators cried "Liberty" and "The Somozas must go" they were met with knives and sticks. Some of Nicolasa's boys even drew pistols and fired into the crowd. When the half-hour melee ended and the demonstrators had retreated, there were no dead, but there were thirty-five wounded, including "la Nicolasa" who had been hit on the head by a chair. The congressmen continued their session and passed the new broadcast law in the presence of the National Guard, guns drawn.[94]

Attorney Miriam Argüello, the most prominent female activist in the Conservative Party, was present on that occasion and notes: "I remember having been there that day, when the Congress was going to discuss what came to be called the 'Black Code,' a law against freedom of the press. We decided, those of us in the opposition, in the Conservative Party, to go to Congress on the day of the debate, to protest that law. So we went. When we got there, Nicolasa came in with her gangs, armed with sticks. Guns went off, people were injured."[95]

On another occasion, Sevilla and her followers attacked Radio Mundial and savagely beat its owner, Manuel Arana, and the journalist Joaquín Absalom Pastora, among others.[96] Sevilla would also routinely undress anti-Somocista women in the street, throw sand in their eyes, and shout insults at them.[97] The opposition newspaper La Prensa noted that "she ha[d] no respect for age or political affiliation, for she has even insulted the daughters of Liberals who collaborate with the Somozas."[98] The latter accusation was verified by Somocista women in interviews I conducted. Marta García, a middle-class founder of the Ala, noted: "Nicolasa was sincere about her work. She did it thinking she was doing a great job." Her legacy was "to have made people enthusiastic, but she caused the government [and middle-class Liberal women] conflicts. Nicolasa would call [Ala members] 'the intellectuals.' She gave us a hard time at first because she was jealous. She didn't like us, she attacked us a lot. We were a little scared of her."[99]

In spite of the immense class conflicts within the Somocista women's

---

94. Diederich, Somoza, 71.
95. Miriam Argüello, interview by author, Managua, 29 November 1997.
96. Evelia Matamoros [pseud.], interview by author.
97. "La Nicolasa Sevilla es la mejor propaganda para la oposición," La Prensa, 11 July 1944, 1, 4.
98. Ibid.
99. Marta García [pseud.], interview by author.

movement, evident in the testimony of García and many other informants, women of different social classes worked together on behalf of the regime. And ironically, in spite of the fear that "la Nicolasa" provoked in middle-class Somocista women, Ala members benefited from Sevilla's bad reputation. The inevitable comparison with "la Nicolasa" helped women like Marta García appear to be more reasonable and less "public" than the Somocista women of the popular forces.

As these brief yet detailed accounts suggest, Sevilla's followers changed over the course of twenty years. In the 1940s, she led mostly working-class women; by the 1960s, her constituency included many working-class men. Two related factors might have led to this change. First, Sevilla became part of the Somoza establishment. Her new position must have required a new image, one not tarnished by the presence of working-class women of "ill-repute." Second, Sevilla's association with AMROC gave her access to a different sector of the population and to a certain amount of wealth. Sevilla obviously took advantage of her position to mobilize men of the popular classes. In fact, she sometimes even bought their support.[100]

Although Sevilla's followers might have changed throughout the decades, her endorsement of the Somoza family never seemed to flounder. For over thirty years she dressed in red, the color of Liberalism in Nicaragua.[101] In the early 1980s Sevilla was still considered feisty and someone to be reckoned with. According to Antonia Rodríguez, Sevilla constantly harassed her Sandinista jailers. Gray-haired and aged, "la Nicolasa" taunted them by pledging her unending support for the Nationalist Liberal Party, until they eventually freed her from jail.[102]

Mothers and Prostitutes

In general, middle-class Somocista women, even if they were mothers, did not participate in Somocismo to better fulfill their domestic roles. Their attraction to the regime was mainly fueled by their new political identity as citizens and their new economic identity as state employees, although they used maternalist discourse to obtain the support of working women and to mobilize them politically. Marta García recalls that "we would tell [poor

compare to sandinista

100. Suárez, interview.
101. Rodríguez, interview.
102. Ibid.

women] that they should vote for their future and for the future of their children; we especially lifted up the hopes single mothers had for their children."[103]

As a group, female Somocista leaders of different class backgrounds did not personally subscribe to maternalism, even though they resorted to maternalist discourse to strike a chord among their followers and society at large. For the most part, women leaders saw themselves as genderless and believed that they had earned their leadership role through hard work that went beyond voting and marching in the streets. Like some men, some female Somocista leaders seemed to look down upon women who identified primarily as mothers and/or used motherhood as a springboard for political activism. Thus, I find no prominent Somocista mothers' groups within the Somocista women's movement, although poor women did use the language of motherhood to bargain, on an individual basis, with the dictators for their share of the clientelistic pyramid. The following letter was written to Anastasio Somoza Debayle in 1962:

Very esteemed Sir:

I am a humble woman who earns a living with a small clothing store on the sidewalk of the Central Market. I ardently ask for your help . . . because you truly have a good heart towards poor people, for my poverty is due to my husband's illness and at the same time to a robbery. . . . I am in a very sorry economic state, I have to feed four children and buy medicines for my husband. . . .
I wish to inform you that I am the daughter of . . . an Eastern Market Somocista Committee President and I am a Somocista Liberal . . . I also cooperate with the Ala Femenina in the propaganda for my party.[104]

This situation constitutes the essence of clientelism, in which favors are exchanged between unequal individuals, creating an asymmetrical power relationship.[105] Although women in general have had less access than men to clientelistic pyramids,[106] in the case of Nicaragua under the Somozas, women occupied a central place in the system; even so, they rarely bargained collec-

103. García, interview.
104. Año 1961–1962. Fondo Presidencial. Sección Secretaría Privada. Ref.: Correspondencia Particular. Caja # 772. Archivo Nacional, Palacio Nacional, Managua.
105. Nikki Craske, *Women and Politics in Latin America* (New Brunswick: Rutgers University Press, 1999), 29.
106. Ibid.

tively as mothers. Somocista women did organize as mothers, though, in their fight against communism. A telegram sent to Somoza in 1969 by nine Diriamba women exemplifies this position: "Recognizing that it is our obligation to defend our interests, we are sending to you our message of solidarity. We are simply MOTHERS. . . . We have observed how other countries in the American [continent] have fallen under the yoke of communism, but we feel sure and confident as Nicaraguans that we have a firm government that will help us to unmask [communism's] skillful costumes and lies. As mothers, we thank you for your effort and work."[107]

It is possible that maternalist sentiment surfaced primarily among those women who did not consider themselves to be politicians and who in fact identified primarily as mothers. Additionally, it seems that women resorted to maternalist discourse when faced with armed conflict or the possibility of war. This was precisely the case of anti-Somocista women. Since the Somozas jailed and/or disappeared thousands of young men and women, the mothers of these activists were, of necessity, politicized as mothers.

The picture is more complicated, however, since male Conservative anti-Somocista activists seemed to believe that women's mobilization was acceptable only when it was an extension of the traditional mother/wife role. Thus, because Somocista women were mobilized in a variety of ways, because the Somozas institutionalized prostitution for their economic gain, and because prostitutes played a political role in the dictatorship, Conservative anti-Somocistas considered Somocista women as a group to be loose women, i.e., prostitutes. Pedro Joaquín Chamorro, a leading critic of the Somozas, best summed up this position (but he was by no means the only one to take it). Recalling a time he and others were arrested in the 1950s, Chamorro noted,

> we were given to . . . a gang paid by the Somozas to spit at us and throw rocks at us.
> The crowd was led by a woman called Nicolasa Sevilla, whose history has stained Nicaraguan politics. She was furious and shouted the most obscene utterances imaginable.
> She had really been sent to "block" the entrance of our relatives. . . . It was the old trick used by Somoza since 1944, when he paid a large number of prostitutes to throw themselves at the mothers and wives of those who were imprisoned at the time, as they walked clad in black through the streets of Managua. In [Somoza's] attitude then, and in his sons' attitude now, there was a dichotomy upon

107. *Novedades,* 18 August 1969, 7.

which the regime established itself: immorality on the one hand, and terror on the other. It was the total inversion of the moral values of Nicaraguan life: prostitutes against mothers, alcohol against civic duty, blackmail against honesty, lowlifes against citizenry.[108]

Under the Somoza dictatorship, the female Somocista prostitute who sold her body to a regime supported by the United States—the "María de los Guardias" popularized in song by world-renowned Nicaraguan musician Carlos Mejía Godoy—became an entrenched symbol in political and popular discourse, and the links between barracks and brothels were strengthened at every level. In fact, between 1927 and 1955, prostitution came to be officially regulated by the police and the brand-new U.S.-sponsored National Guard. According to critics of regulation, the U.S. military presence in Managua during the late 1920s brought about the proliferation of prostitution and sexually transmitted diseases, the backdrop for the regulatory legislation of 1927[109] that forced prostitutes to register as such and to report on a weekly basis for gynecological exams. Women who did not register and did not submit to medical exams were to be arrested and fined by the Prophylactic Police, the National Police, or the National Guard.

The regulation of prostitution ended in 1955, with the passage of punitive measures against those involved in prostitution.[110] Nonetheless, prostitution continued to flourish—for the law was applied selectively, primarily against non-Somocistas involved in the trade and those who operated clandestinely, without paying the required bribes, as was the case of Sonia Rocha from the province of León. In 1962, Rocha wrote the following letter to the Secretary of the Presidency:

Honorable Dr. Ramiro Sacasa Guerrero,

From the beginning I have been a Liberal and a fervent Somocista and I have even had fights defending the cause. I am a poor woman who receives assistance from no one and with my sewing, washing and ironing I manage through life. To make matters worse, I had two operations three months ago and due to this I am now in debt; but what has aggravated my situation the most is the following: [Fernando] Agüero supporters, to damage me, have bad-mouthed me

108. P. Chamorro, *Estirpe sangrienta,* 162, 163.

109. E. Mendieta, "Evolución de la legislación nicaragüense sobre la prostitución," *Pensamiento y sociedad* (n.d.), 18.

110. Ibid., 35.

to the Departmental Commander of the G.N. [National Guard] and even on the radio, saying that I traffic with women of bad conduct in my home. The National Guard has arrested me three times and I have had to spend on an attorney and fines almost four hundred cordobas, which I am paying in installments. What really happened is that sometimes society [male] friends, among them doctors, have begged me to let them meet with young women in my home and I have agreed to such pleas; but in light of what has happened, I no longer allow such visits.

Now that I have explained what has occurred, I beg you to talk to the appropriate person, so that I will not be bothered again. . . . I hope you are kind enough to respond to me by telegram.[111]

As can be seen from this letter, by the 1960s the National Guard had taken firm control of the prostitution industry. Regarding the Guard's role in prostitution, Helen Collinson writes, "In Somoza's days . . . prostitution . . . flourished under the patronage of the regime itself; Somoza's National Guard were also deeply implicated. 'The brothel owners used to give the Guardia a cut,' explains an ex-prostitute from the port of Corinto. 'If the prostitutes managed to escape, the Guardia would seek them out and return them to the owners.' "[112]

Sometimes the administration of brothels was even more direct, for some members of the National Guard were owners of their own centers of prostitution.[113] According to Gregorio Selser, "General Gustavo Montiel, with the participation of high-ranking National Guard officials, retired and active, administrate[d] high-class prostitution motels in the outskirts of Managua . . . in association with Pro-Batista Cubans."[114] The income generated from prostitution was an integral part of the dictatorship's internal dynamics. Selser contends that

the highest officials were implicated in the business of prostitution motels. . . . Through this web they had indirect access to income, and they were supported by the tolerance and the authorizing wink which emanated from the supreme power. . . . National Guard members stole and engaged in extortion because the government paid

111. Año 1962. Fondo Presidencial. Sección Secretaría Presidencial. Ref.: Miscelaneo. Caja # 773. Archivo Nacional, Palacio Nacional, Managua.

112. Collinson, ed., *Women and Revolution,* 69.

113. Ibid., 70.

114. Selser, *Nicaragua de Walker a Somoza,* 267.

them poorly; the government underpaid guards in order to induce them to criminal activities. [Crime] automatically associated thieves and extortionists with their tolerating superiors. Therefore, guards had to be the first defenders of the system through which they obtained their pitiful legal salaries and their extra income, which was not legal, but was accepted at all levels.[115]

Prostitution clearly played a crucial economic role within Somocismo. But why did Nicolasa Sevilla, a semi-illiterate former prostitute and madam, gain such visibility within a right-wing regime? Although socially marginalized, prostitutes appear to have occupied a key place in the nation's political discourse and in politics itself, becoming an integral part of Nicaragua's imaginary and body politic. During the 1920s, when the U.S. Marines had ordered the destruction of Juan Bautista Sacasa's and Augusto Cesar Sandino's arms, a group of "patriotic prostitutes"[116] supported Sandino's struggle against U.S. intervention:

What Sacasa and his general could not or did not do, was done by a group of public women in the [Puerto Cabezas] port.
The patriotism of these women could be felt in the strength of their feelings and they considered it their duty to assist Sandino and his men in the task of saving the Nicaraguan arms from the actions of the invaders. Led by Sandino, each one of them brought out from under her clothes a double-barrel rifle and as much ammunition as she was able to carry. This is how Sandino found himself in the early hours of the next morning with a good number of rifles and more than seven thousand cartridges.[117]

The figure of the prostitute is a particularly useful one in politics due to its malleability. Without a doubt, concerns over U.S. occupation and its consequences have been valid, as was the opposition to the Somoza dictatorship. In this context, however, the actions of "good" anti-imperialist prostitutes become nothing more than a way to question the manhood of "sellouts" like Sacasa, while the actions of "bad" Somocista prostitutes be-

115. Ibid., 269.
116. Donna Guy uses this term in *Sex and Danger in Buenos Aires: Prostitution, Family, and Nation in Argentina* (Lincoln: University of Nebraska Press, 1990), 207.
117. Xavier Campos Ponce, *Sandino: Biografía de un héroe* (Mexico City: EDAMEX, 1979), 38, 39.

come a Nicaraguan version of the Malinche story,[118] in which women are simultaneously pitied and blamed for the downfall of their people. Letters like the one written by Sonia Rocha, however, demonstrate that Somocista women involved in prostitution were not simply victims of or accomplices in the regime's immorality. Although they occupied a vulnerable position in society and were victims of their political enemies and the National Guard of their own party, they also had a voice and believed they had rights. Their situation was quite complex—and must be recognized and documented as such.

Sexual Order, Sexual Disorder, and Resistance

Where anti-Somocistas saw sexual and familial chaos, some Somocista women saw a source of sexual and familial order in their lives, even though the Somozas did not proclaim to be upholding a strict moral code (as other right-wing movements have done). As might be expected, Somocista women sometimes attributed to the Somozas a paternal role. More unusual is the fact that some women asked the Somozas to intervene personally in their marital disputes. The portrayal of the Somozas as "fathers of the poor"—a portrayal they promoted and embraced—was quite popular. Yolanda Herrera wrote in a letter to Luis Somoza: "when your dear father died [in 1956] I went to visit you at the Worker's Hall [Casa del Obrero] and at the [National] Palace. His death pained me as if he had been my father."[119] In another letter to Luis Somoza, Mercedes Sotelo declared, "Sir, you are my refuge and my father. I have no one else to confide in, please forgive this trouble I am causing you. I hope to be consoled by you."[120] On another occasion Carmen Salazar wrote, "You are like a father to me and that is why I feel a need to tell you what is happening to me."[121] As historian Sandra McGee Deutsch has noted for Juan Domingo Perón in Argentina, the emphasis on a dictator's paternal

118. Malintzin Tenepal, an Indian woman, supposedly became Hernán Cortés's lover and translator, helping him to conquer Mexico. The word "Malinchista" is used today in Mexico and Nicaragua to denote a traitor or sell-out.
119. Pseudonym. Año 1961–1962. Fondo Presidencial. Sección Secretaría Privada. Ref: Correspondencia Particular. Caja # 772. Archivo Nacional, Palacio Nacional, Managua.
120. Pseudonym. Año 1960–1962. Fondo Presidencial. Sección Secretaría Privada. Ref: Correspondencia Particular. Caja # 773. Archivo Nacional, Palacio Nacional, Managua.
121. Pseudonym. Año 1960–1962. Fondo Presidencial. Sección Secretaría Privada. Ref: Correspondencia Miscelanea. Caja # 773. Archivo Nacional, Palacio Nacional, Managua.

qualities limits the autonomy and power of the working classes.[122] But the excessive deference might also convey resistance,[123] especially when praise was followed by requests for goods and services or when Somoza García was compared to Jesus Christ, as in the following letter written by Eva Telica to Luis Somoza in 1957: "today and always it is our duty to be all together, all of us women, so that General Somoza's fruit be blessed among all of us women we must go forward with our triumphant march and shout Long Live God our Father in heaven and General Somoza look after his angels, who left us the angel of peace, and the guardian angel for the happiness and tranquility of our Nicaragua."[124]

Somocista women also approached the Somozas in order to receive help with their marital problems. In particular, wives of military men looked to the Somozas to regulate their sexual lives and punish their cheating husbands. These wives expected the Somozas to control the sexual excesses of their military personnel, but the end results were not always completely satisfactory. In the case of Aurora Balladares, the Somozas gave her wayward husband an ultimatum. To Balladares's dismay, the high-ranking member of the military chose his lover over her! Balladares, a political leader in her own right who never remarried, is still grateful to the Somozas for their emotional support during such difficult times and for the fair treatment she received in Somocista politics even though she obtained a divorce.[125]

On another occasion, Nadia Otero wrote to the Secretary of the Presidency asking for help in regard to her husband's infidelity:

Dear Dr:

David has become involved with a bad woman . . . who has almost succeeded in destroying my home, after taking what he could be giving to us. I have terrible reports about her and I am desperate, for she gets him drunk and takes his money and then he has none left for us.

I write all of this to you because I know how good you are and how Catholic and as a result you will understand that the destruction of

122. Sandra McGee Deutsch, "Gender and Sociopolitical Change in Twentieth-Century Latin America," *Hispanic American Historical Review* 71, no. 2 (1991), 279.

123. Jeffrey L. Gould, *To Die in This Way: Nicaraguan Indians and the Myth of Mestizaje, 1880–1965* (Durham: Duke University Press, 1998), 79.

124. Pseudonym. Año 1957. Fondo Presidencial. Sección Partido Liberal Secretaría Privada. Referencia P. Liberal (Ala Femenina), Asignatura 295. Archivo Nacional, Palacio Nacional, Managua.

125. Aurora Balladares [pseud.], interview by author.

a marriage where there are children is a crime. I don't understand what has happened to David, I think that woman has given him something to forget his obligations as a father, not to mention those of a husband. . . . In short, I cannot force him to love me, only to give me child support.[126]

Ramiro Sacasa Guerrero, Secretary to the President, answered Otero's letter, but this was probably not the response she had hoped for:

Since you tell me you do not want David to know that you told me about the situation you are in, I am unable to help you with this matter, for any action on my part would enable him to know that you have told me, since he knows I am not a psychic and have no other way of finding out about these things.

I think you and your children are the ones who, proceeding with ability and tactfulness, can reconquer David. The woman you mentioned has no moral authority to come between you and David, and I do not think that David would ever allow her to occupy that position, nor do I think she would seek it, for the information I have reveals that she is not satisfied with the support of only one [male] friend.

Hoping that the light of harmony, which is the basis for happiness, will shine again soon in your home . . . I greet you with affection.[127]

As in other right-wing movements in diverse parts of the world, such as the Ku Klux Klan in the United States, the Somocista government represented a last resort for women like Nadia Otero who were desperate due to their poverty and to the abuse they received at the hands of their husbands.[128] Obviously, the hope and comfort that the dictatorship provided for some women does not change the terrible legacy of the Somozas. But it does help explain its long-lasting appeal.

---

126. Pseudonym. Año 1962. Fondo Presidencial. Sección Secretaría Privada. Ref: M = Miscelaneo. Caja # 773. Archivo Nacional, Palacio Nacional, Managua.

127. Año 1962. Fondo Presidencial. Sección Secretaría Privada. Ref: M = Miscelaneo. Caja # 773. Archivo Nacional, Palacio Nacional, Managua.

128. For more on women and the Ku Klux Klan, see Kathleen M. Blee, *Women of the Klan: Racism and Gender in the 1920s* (Berkeley and Los Angeles: University of California Press, 1991), and Nancy MacLean, *Behind the Mask of Chivalry: The Making of the Second Ku Klux Klan* (Oxford: Oxford University Press, 1994).

Conclusion

Through the Ala, a nonfeminist organization that supported women's political rights but did not threaten the status quo, the Somozas appropriated feminism. After the 1950s, the dictatorship claimed that it alone was responsible for the advancements made in women's status. Somocista Liberalism became synonymous with a populist discourse on women's rights. As a result, the term *feminism* disappeared almost completely from public use in Nicaragua and did not reappear until after 1979.

In part, the purpose of the Ala was to put a kinder face on Somocismo, one that would appeal to middle-class Liberal women. In this, the Ala succeeded for over twenty years. The Ala helped legitimize the regime, giving it a credibility it sorely needed. But the Ala was more than a tool the Somozas used for gaining women's votes. Through their participation in the Ala, middle-class Liberal women were able to make Somocismo their own and become incorporated more fully into the traditionally male world of politics. The middle-class respectability of the Ala, however, depended on the continuous stereotyping of the Ala's counterpart: working-class women activists. In spite of the incredible discrimination they faced in politics, women of the popular classes were also drawn to Somocismo. Nicolasa Sevilla, among others, came to wield a great degree of power within the dictatorship. Like middle-class women of the Ala, she was also able to define Somocismo on her own terms.

As a whole, the Somozas' policy toward women was simple and clear-cut: women would gain basic rights, like the vote, full access to the universities, state employment, and some government positions, in exchange for supporting the dictatorship. What would unite Somocista women of different social classes was their new function as citizens in a Liberal republic and workers in a patron-clientelistic state. When suffrage declined in importance during the 1970s due to the increased militarization of politics, commonalities among Somocista women also decreased. As corruption, repression, and unemployment increased within the last Somoza administration, the importance of women's citizenship and women's work diminished, leading some Somocista women to support the Sandinistas.

During the Somoza regime a combination of factors led women on the left to be mobilized as mothers and wives while women on the right were considered prostitutes by their enemies. In part, it was the dictatorship's political mobilization of prostitutes like Nicolasa Sevilla and the promotion of prostitution for economic gain that led the opposition to condemn female

Somocista sexuality. Just as crucial, however, was the fact that Somocista women broke with traditional mores by not using maternalist language to justify their public political and economic activities. The presence of these right-wing women in public was threatening to many Conservative anti-Somocistas, and as a result, Somocista women's activism was dismissed with centuries-old tactics that stressed women's sexual corruption. Since anti-Somocista women claimed that they had no choice but to rebel against the dictatorship, their activism was deemed acceptable by their male counterparts. It would take decades, though, for anti-Somocista women to create a different paradigm for their relationship to politics—a paradigm still under construction.

Clearly, Somocista women played a key role within the dictatorship, as important as that played by men, for they helped determine the path that Nicaragua took between 1936 and 1979. For this reason, they deserve a prominent place in Nicaraguan history. Additionally, their voices complicate traditional dichotomies that portray women as inherently good and peaceful (or as sexually corrupt) and men as inherently bad and violent. The study of Somocista women, then, is about gender and politics. However, it is also about identity, how people choose to remember their past, who gets to write a nation's history, and whose story gets told. In Nicaragua today, many argue that documenting Somocista women's experiences is akin to legitimizing the dictatorship. Many anti-Somocista activists feel that women who supported the abuses committed by the Somozas lost the right to have a history and that their existence needs to be erased from the nation's memory. Additionally, some activists for women's rights feel that only "good" things done by women should be told, and that if Somocista women's stories are to be recorded, these women should be portrayed as having been manipulated by the regime. Such strong feelings demonstrate that the Somocista past continues to haunt Nicaragua in obvious and not-so-obvious ways; we may well benefit from understanding the legacy of Somocista women. But what exactly is that legacy? At a speech taking place during a recent Sandinista Party Congress, a female foreign observer asked a rank-and-file male participant who the fiery Sandinista female speaker was. The man responded, "I think her name is Nicolasa something or other." Not surprisingly, the woman's name was *not* Nicolasa (hardly any women are named Nicolasa in today's Nicaragua).[129] What is important to stress is that in this man's subconscious, it seemed that women in politics were automatically Nicolasas, i.e., prosti-

129. Katherine Hoyt, personal conversation, Washington, D.C., 20 December 1997.

tutes. This anecdote shows quite clearly that Nicaraguan women—on the left and on the right—stand in the shadow of their Somocista foremothers. What Nicaraguans make of this remains to be seen.

Meanwhile, Somocista women's experiences can help expand scholarly understandings of the role gender plays in right-wing politics, leading us toward comparative analyses of women's political activism. For instance, the Nicaraguan case can lead us to ask why right-wing movements in other parts of the world mobilized women as mothers while the Somozas mobilized women as voters and workers. Additionally, the study of Somocista women complicates one of the primary goals of both feminist activism and women's history, which is to give women a voice. Listening to right-wing women's stories challenges historians to expand the boundaries of women's history while forcing all of us to recognize the nuances of human experience.

BIBLIOGRAPHY

PRIMARY SOURCES

Archives

Archivo Nacional, Palacio Nacional, Managua.

Newspapers

El 93: Diario político y de variedades (León)
Nicaragua: Patria arte cultura (Managua)
Novedades (Managua)
La Prensa (Managua)
The New York Times

Interviews and Personal Conversations

Argüello, Miriam. Interview by author. Managua, 29 November 1997.
Arnesto, Josefina. Interview by author. Matagalpa, 12 July 1995.
Balladares, Aurora [pseud.]. Interview by author.
Borge, Tomás. Interview by author. New York City, 18 March 1997.
Flores, Alejandra [pseud.] Interview by author.
García, Marta [pseud.]. Interview by author.
Hoyt, Katherine. Personal conversation with author. Washington, D.C., 20 December 1997.
Matamoros, Evelia [pseud.]. Interview by author.
Ortega, Josefa [pseud.]. Interview by author.
Rodríguez, Antonia [pseud.]. Interview by author.
Suárez, Rafael [pseud.]. Interview by author.
Vega, Mario [pseud.]. Personal conversation with author.
Zambrano, Reina [pseud.]. Interview by author.

Other Primary Sources

Borge de Sotomayor, Amelia. *La condición legal de la mujer y su situación de hecho: Compilación y analisis de leyes que discriminan a la mujer.* Medford, Mass.: Tufts University, 1975.

Chamorro, Pedro Joaquín. *Estirpe sangrienta: Los Somoza.* Managua: Ediciones el Pez y la Serpiente, 1978.

Corona funebre en recuerdo de la Doctora Olga Núñez de Saballos: Primer aniversario de su muerte. Managua: Imprenta Nacional, 12 September 1972.

Debayle, Luis Manuel. "The Status of Women in Nicaragua." *Mid-Pacific Magazine* (Honolulu) 45, no. 3 (1933): 237–39.

Diebold de Cruz, Paula, and Mayra Pasos de Rappacioli. *Report on the Role of Women in the Economic Development of Nicaragua.* Managua: USAID, 1975.

Hacia la meta . . . Mensajes políticos del Gral. Anastasio Somoza Debayle, Presidente Constitucional de Nicaragua 1967–1972 ante la gran convención del Partido Liberal Nacionalista, durante su campaña electoral y toma de posesión. Managua: Imprenta Nacional, 1968.

Hernández, Julio C. "Puntos culminantes del primer congreso pedagogico nicaragüense." *Semanario el digesto* (Managua) 1, no. 38 (22 September 1951).

Krehm, William. "Call All Trulls." *Time,* 7 August 1944, 38.

La prostitución en Nicaragua. Managua: Programa de Rehabilitación del INSSBI, 1980.

"Luctuosa." *Ala Femenina* 1, no. 2 (1955), 47.

Mendieta, E. "Evolución de la legislación nicaragüense sobre la prostitución." *Pensamiento y sociedad* (Managua) (n.d.): 13–36.

Nicaragua: Election Factbook. Washington, D.C.: Institute for the Comparative Study of Political Systems, a division of Operations and Policy Research, Inc., 1967.

Noguera Carazo, Lucrecia. *Evolución cultural y política de la mujer nicaragüense.* Managua: n.p., 1974.

Palma Martínez, Francisco. *El siglo de los topos: Crítica y enseñanza en plan de ciencia: Filosofía del sexo, psicología, sociología, eugenesia, religión y arte.* León: Editorial La Patria, n.d.

Sevilla Sacasa, Guillermo. *La mujer nicaragüense ante el derecho a sufragar: Por que me opuse a que se le concediera: La verdad sobre mi actitud en la constituyente.* Managua: Talleres Gráficos Perez, 1939.

Toledo de Aguerri, Josefa. *Educación y feminismo: Sobre enseñanza: Articulos varios. (Reproducciones.)* Managua: Talleres Nacionales de Imprenta y Encuadernación, 1940.

SECONDARY SOURCES

Amador, Armando. *Un siglo de lucha de los trabajadores de Nicaragua.* Managua: UCA, 1992.

Arellano, Jorge Eduardo. *Heroes sin fusil: 140 nicaragüenses sobresalientes.* Managua: Editorial Hispamer, 1998.

Baker, Suzanne. "Gender Ideologies and Social Change in Revolutionary Nicaragua." Ph.D. diss., Boston University, 1995.

Blee, Kathleen M. *Women of the Klan: Racism and Gender in the 1920s.* Berkeley and Los Angeles: University of California Press, 1991.

Booth, John. *The End and the Beginning: The Nicaraguan Revolution*. 2d ed. Boulder, Colo.: Westview Press, 1985.

Bowdler, George A., and Patrick Cotter. *Voter Participation in Central America, 1954–1981: An Exploration*. Washington, D.C.: University Press of America, 1982.

Campos Ponce, Xavier. *Sandino: Biografía de un héroe*. Mexico City: EDAMEX, 1979.

Chamorro, Amalia. "Estado y hegemonía durante el somocismo." In *Economía y sociedad en la construcción del estado en Nicaragua*, edited by Alberto Lanuza, Juan Luis Vázquez, Amaru Barahona, and Amalia Chamorro. San José, Costa Rica: ICAP, 1983.

Chuchryk, Patricia. "Women in the Revolution." In *Revolution and Counterrevolution*, edited by Thomas W. Walker. Boulder, Colo.: Westview Press, 1991.

Cobo del Arco, Teresa. *Politicas de género durante el liberalismó: Nicaragua 1893–1909*. Managua: UCA, 2000.

Collinson, Helen, ed. *Women and Revolution in Nicaragua*. London: Zed Books, 1990.

Craske, Nikki. *Women and Politics in Latin America*. New Brunswick: Rutgers University Press, 1999.

De Grazia, Victoria. *How Fascism Ruled Women: Italy, 1922–1945*. Berkeley and Los Angeles: University of California Press, 1992.

Diederich, Bernard. *Somoza and the Legacy of U.S. Involvement in Central America*. New York: E. P. Dutton, 1981.

Dore, Elizabeth. "The Holy Family: Imagined Households in Latin America." In *Gender Politics in Latin America: Debates in Theory and Practice*, edited by Elizabeth Dore. New York: Monthly Review Press, 1997.

———, ed. *Gender Politics in Latin America: Debates in Theory and Practice*. New York: Monthly Review Press, 1997.

Dore, Elizabeth, and Maxine Molyneux, eds. *Hidden Histories of Gender and the State in Latin America*. Durham: Duke University Press, 2000.

Fernández Poncela, Anna M. "Nicaraguan Women: Legal, Political, and Social Spaces." In *Gender Politics in Latin America: Debates in Theory and Practice*, edited by Elizabeth Dore. New York: Monthly Review Press, 1997.

González, Victoria. "Josefa Toledo de Aguerri (1866–1962) and the Forgotten History of Nicaraguan Feminism, 1821–1955." Master's thesis, University of New Mexico, 1996.

———. "Mujeres somocistas: 'La pechuga' y el corazón de la dictadura nicaragüense (1936–1979)." In *Entre silencios y voces: Género e historia en América Central (1750–1990)*, edited by Eugenia Rodríguez Sáenz. San José, Costa Rica: Centro Nacional para el Desarrollo de la Mujer y la Familia, 1997.

Gould, Jeffrey L. *To Lead as Equals: Rural Protest and Political Consciousness in Chinandega, Nicaragua, 1912–1979*. Chapel Hill: The University of North Carolina Press, 1990.

———. *To Die in This Way: Nicaraguan Indians and the Myth of Mestizaje, 1880–1965*. Durham: Duke University Press, 1998.

Guy, Donna. *Sex and Danger in Buenos Aires: Prostitution, Family, and Nation in Argentina*. Lincoln: University of Nebraska Press, 1990.

Heyck, Denis Lynn Daly. *Life Stories of the Nicaraguan Revolution*. London: Routledge, 1990.

Hoyt, Katherine. *Thirty Years of Memories: Dictatorship, Revolution, and Nicaragua Solidarity*. Washington, D.C.: Nicaragua Network Education Fund, 1996.

Kampwirth, Karen. "The Mother of the Nicaraguans: Doña Violeta and the UNO's Gender Agenda." *Latin American Perspectives* 23, no. 1 (1996): 67–86.

Keen, Benjamin. *A History of Latin America.* Boston: Houghton Mifflin, 1996.

Koonz, Claudia. *Mothers in the Fatherland: Women, the Family, and Nazi Politics.* New York: St. Martin's Press, 1987.

MacLean, Nancy. *Behind the Mask of Chivalry: The Making of the Second Ku Klux Klan.* Oxford: Oxford University Press, 1994.

McGee Deutsch, Sandra. "Gender and Sociopolitical Change in Twentieth-Century Latin America." *Hispanic American Historical Review* 71, no. 2 (1991): 259–306.

Miller, Francesca. *Latin American Women and the Search for Social Justice.* Hanover: University Press of New England, 1991.

Morales Henríquez, Viktor. *De Mrs. Hanna a la Dinorah: Principio y fin de la dictadura somocista: Historia de medio siglo de corrupción.* [Managua?]: n.p., [1980?].

Ramírez-Horton, Susan. "The Role of Women in the Nicaraguan Revolution." In *Nicaragua in Revolution,* edited by Thomas W. Walker. New York: Praeger, 1982.

Randall, Margaret. *Sandino's Daughters Revisited: Feminism in Nicaragua.* New Brunswick: Rutgers University Press, 1994.

Rodríguez Sáenz, Eugenia, ed. *Entre silencios y voces: Género e historia en América Central (1750–1990).* San José, Costa Rica: Centro Nacional para el Desarrollo de la Mujer y Familia, 1997.

Ruchwarger, Gary. *People in Power: Forging a Grassroots Democracy in Nicaragua.* South Hadley, Mass.: Bergin and Garvey, 1987.

Selser, Gregorio. *Nicaragua de Walker a Somoza.* Mexico City: Mex Sur Editorial S.A., 1984.

Vannini, Margarita, ed. *Encuentros con la historia.* Managua: IHN-UCA, 1995.

Walter, Knut. *The Regime of Anastasio Somoza, 1936–1956.* Chapel Hill: The University of North Carolina Press, 1993.

———. "Del protectorado a la revolución." In *Encuentros con la historia,* edited by Margarita Vannini. Managua: IHN-UCA, 1995.

Whisnant, David. *Rascally Signs in Sacred Places: The Politics of Culture in Nicaragua.* Chapel Hill: The University of North Carolina Press, 1995.

2 | Women in the Armed Struggles in Nicaragua
Sandinistas and Contras Compared

Karen Kampwirth

During the second half of the twentieth century, Nicaragua saw more than its fair share of guerrilla movements on both the left and the right. Extreme conditions—dictatorship, vicious poverty, foreign intervention—often engendered extreme solutions. And women were active participants in the search for solutions in Nicaragua. In the case of the Sandinista guerrilla movement of the 1960s and 1970s that would eventually topple the Somoza dictatorship, the role of women is well known. Various authors have estimated that 30 percent of the combatants (and significant numbers of guerrilla leaders) were women,[1] although one review of the records of deaths in combat suggested that only 6.6 percent of Sandinista combatants were women.[2]

In contrast, the presence of women within the Contras[3]—the right-wing guerrillas who attempted to overthrow the Sandinistas in the 1980s—has been consistently ignored in the literature on the Contras[4] and in the litera-

1. Helen Collinson, ed., *Women and Revolution in Nicaragua* (London: Zed Books, 1990), 154; Patricia Flynn, "Women Challenge the Myth," in *Revolution in Central America,* ed. Stanford Central America Action Network (Boulder, Colo.: Westview Press, 1983), 416; Linda L. Reif, "Women in Latin American Guerrilla Movements: A Comparative Perspective," *Comparative Politics* 18, no. 2 (1986), 158; Timothy Wickham-Crowley, *Guerrillas and Revolution in Latin America* (Princeton: Princeton University Press, 1992), 21.

2. Carlos Vilas, *The Sandinista Revolution: National Liberation and Social Transformation in Central America* (New York: Monthly Review Press, 1986), 108–9.

3. I will refer to them as Contras in this article, as that is the term that is most familiar to readers in the United States. The people I interviewed usually referred to themselves as belonging to the Resistance, although they also called themselves Contras.

4. See, for example, Shirley Christian, *Nicaragua: Revolution in the Family* (New York: Vintage Books, 1986); CIAV/OEA (Comisión Internacional de Apoyo y Verificación de la Organización de Estados Americanos), "Cuadros estadísticos del proceso de desmovilización y repatriación en Nicaragua," Managua, July 1991, unpublished document; Orlando Núñez, Gloria

ture on women in Nicaraguan politics.[5] Nonetheless, women did participate in the Contra struggle as combatants; in addition, they took on a wide range of support roles, including those of messenger, radio operator, paramedic, and cook. One Contra commander estimated that about 10 percent of those who died in the struggle were women,[6] while another claimed that 15.6 percent of the combatants were women.[7] A third source suggested that women constituted 7 percent of the Contra combatants.[8] Women's representation within the ranks of Contra support workers was considerably larger; at least 39 percent of those who demobilized at the war's end in 1990 were women.[9]

What kinds of women[10] became involved in these movements, and what

Cardenal, Amanda Lorío, Sonia Agurto, Juan Morales, Javier Pasquier, Javier Matus, and Rubén Pasos, *La guerra y el campesinado en Nicaragua* (Managua: Editorial Ciencias Sociales, 1998); R. Pardo-Maurer, *The Contras, 1980–1989: A Special Kind of Politics* (New York: Praeger, 1990); and Thomas W. Walker, ed., *Reagan Versus the Sandinistas: The Undeclared War on Nicaragua* (Boulder, Colo.: Westview Press, 1987). Partial exceptions to the tendency to ignore the role of women in the Contra movement are Alejandro Bendaña, *Una tragedia campesina: Testimonios de la resistencia* (Managua: COMPANIC, 1991); Christopher Dickey, *With the Contras: A Reporter in the Wilds of Nicaragua* (New York: Simon and Schuster, 1987); Jaime Morales Carazo, *La contra* (Mexico City: Editorial Planeta, 1989); and Zoilamérica Ortega, *Desmovilizados de la guerra en la construcción de la paz en Nicaragua* (Managua: Imprimatur Artes Gráficas, 1996).

5. See, for example, Ada Julia Brenes, Ivania Lovo, Olga Luz Restrepo, Sylvia Saakes, and Flor de María Zúniga, *La mujer nicaragüense en los años 80* (Managua: Ediciones Nicarao, 1991); Collinson, ed., *Women and Revolution;* Clara Murguialday, *Nicaragua, revolución y feminismo* (Madrid: Editorial Revolución, 1990); and Margaret Randall, *Sandino's Daughters Revisited: Feminism in Nicaragua* (New Brunswick: Rutgers University Press, 1994) and *Gathering Rage: The Failure of Twentieth-Century Revolutions to Develop a Feminist Agenda* (New York: Monthly Review Press, 1992).

6. Justo Pastor Palacios ("Comandante Indio") told me that 1,120 women and more than 10,000 men died fighting with the Contras (interview by author, Managua, 30 July 1998).

7. Elida María Galeano ("Comandante Chaparra") told me that the Contra army comprised 22,413 combatants, of whom 3,500 were women (interview by author, Managua, 9 July 1998).

8. Timothy Brown, "Women Unfit for Combat? Au Contraire!" *Wall Street Journal*, 30 September 1997, A22.

9. According to one source, 39 percent of the demobilized were women (Ortega, *Desmovilizados de la guerra,* 19). But it is likely that the actual numbers of demobilized women were higher. Ilja Luciak suggested that the figure of 39 percent probably reflects a mistake in calculating the demobilization data: in the data he has, the sum total of all female relatives, with the exception of daughters, results in a figure of 39 percent. However, the figure is 59.55 percent when daughters are included (personal communication to author, 4 November 1998).

10. Many of the findings of this chapter—regarding the sorts of women who became guerrillas and their reasons for doing so—probably apply to men as well. I am confident that this is true regarding the structural factors that I will identify, given that considerable research has already been done on social structures and Nicaraguan guerrillas (much of which is cited in this chapter). But I am far less confident that my findings regarding the role of preexisting networks and personal factors also apply to men, since to find out, someone would have to do extensive interviews with male guerrillas on their personal experiences going back to childhood,

were their motivations? Why did one set of women join a radical left-wing movement and, a few years later, another set join a radical right-wing movement? How did both groups of women manage to break the constraints of their traditional roles so as to enter the armed struggles of the 1960s, 1970s, and 1980s? Once women were involved in a guerrilla movement, how were they treated by men in the movement? A central component of the mystique of guerrilla struggle is its radical egalitarianism; to what extent did reality live up to the myth?

This chapter focuses on the experiences of the women who joined guerrilla movements, rather than on international factors, but that does not mean that I am unaware of the international context that shaped counterrevolutionary politics. Without a doubt, the Reagan administration's massive involvement in funding the movement—and even in organizing it—meant that the Contras were much greater in numbers and destructiveness than they would have been otherwise.[11] But at the same time, most of the people who joined the Contras were motivated by grievances that were not solely created by the Reagan administration.[12] In this chapter I will consider the reasons for women's participation in the Contra and Sandinista movements, based on the personal accounts of some of those women.

The research for this chapter included interviews with forty-five women: twenty-four were active in the guerrilla struggle against Somoza and still identified as leftists, in one way or another, at the time of the interviews. Eighteen were active in the guerrilla struggle against the Sandinistas, and three were active in both the anti-Somoza and anti-Sandinista movements. They all lived in the Managua area at the time of the interviews (1991, 1997, and 1998),

---

interviews that (as far as I know) have not yet been done. That would be a really interesting direction for new research, which would be most effectively carried out by male researchers.

11. As the war neared its end in 1988, fifty-eight thousand people—out of a population of a little over three million—had been killed. Carlos Vilas, *Between Earthquakes and Volcanoes: Market, State, and the Revolutions in Central America* (New York: Monthly Review Press, 1995), 138; also see Edgar Chamorro, *Packaging the Contras: A Case of CIA Disinformation,* Monograph Series no. 2 (New York: Institute for Media Analysis, 1987); Christian Smith, *Resisting Reagan: The U.S. Central America Peace Movement* (Chicago: University of Chicago Press, 1996); Walker, *Reagan Versus the Sandinistas.*

12. Nonetheless, the Reagan administration was responsible for creating some of the conditions that pushed people into the Contra movement. Six of the twenty-one Contras I interviewed mentioned opposition to the draft as one of the major reasons for joining the counterrevolutionaries, even though the draft had not existed until Contra attacks began. Similarly, Christopher Dickey notes that few of those who would become Contras "had thought of becoming contras before the spring of 1982. Many of them said they had little to complain about from the Sandinistas until the [Contras'] March 14 blowing of the bridges provoked the state of emergency" (Dickey, *With the Contras,* 142).

though the majority grew up in other parts of Nicaragua and later migrated to the capital.

As is perhaps inevitable, my samples were skewed in particular ways. Every one of the former Sandinistas was active in the women's movement at the time of the interviews, while only two of the former Contras were involved in the women's movement (and they had both been involved in the struggle against the Somoza dictatorship). This certainly does not mean that all Sandinista guerrillas went on to become feminists.[13] But the difference in my samples is not a simple methodological error: there were hundreds, perhaps thousands, of women who were first mobilized through the Sandinista struggle in the 1960s and 1970s and who went on to organize for gender equality in the 1980s and 1990s. In contrast, I could find no former Contras (except those who had once been anti-Somocistas) who were active in the movement for gender equality in the late 1990s.

Responding to the Structural Crisis

The rise of left- and right-wing guerrilla groups, and the roles of women within those groups, can be partially explained by considering social and economic structures. Halfway through the Somoza dynasty, Nicaragua began to change in ways that allowed many women to choose radical solutions to their problems, to throw in their lot with the Sandinistas in the 1960s and 1970s.

That structural transformation also helps explain the rise of the Contras, though in a less direct way. After taking power in 1979, the Sandinistas responded to the Somozas' legacy of economic inequality in ways that sometimes encroached upon local communities and markets. Those policies disturbed certain sectors of the rural population, including some rural women, and led to the formation of the Contra movement.

Starting in the mid-twentieth century, a series of socioeconomic changes occurred as Nicaragua (like other countries in the region) became more tightly linked to the global economy. During the course of the Somoza re-

13. The reason that the Sandinistas I interviewed were all people who had become women's movement activists is because I did those interviews as part of the research for a book on the rise of organized feminism as an unintended outcome of left-wing guerrilla struggle (Karen Kampwirth, *Revolution in the Real World: Women and Guerrilla Movements in Latin America* [University Park: The Pennsylvania State University Press, forthcoming]).

gime, Nicaragua was characterized by a progressively more unequal distribution of resources as peasants were pushed off their land to make room for agro-export production. So many poor farmers were driven away from their land that by 1978, shortly before the overthrow of Somoza, more than "three quarters of the economically active population engaged in agriculture could be classified as landless or land poor."[14]

Increased landlessness had the effect of putting downward pressure on wages, especially as the main cash crops—cotton and coffee—were not very labor intensive, except during the harvest. Many who had formerly been middle peasants, working as subsistence farmers on small plots of land, found that they had become poor peasants (with less than enough land for bare subsistence) or rural proletarians (with no land at all), forced to compete for jobs on the plantations of large landowners.

While the supply of newly landless workers increased, the demand for workers remained largely fixed, leading to a fall in wages. To make things worse, food prices rose at the same time; as land was concentrated and converted to cash crop production, less land was dedicated to food production, ending Nicaragua's self-sufficiency in food.[15] Squeezed between rising food prices and declining job opportunities, most rural dwellers did not have enough income to cover even their minimal nutritional requirements.[16] But despite the growing misery of the majority, in macroeconomic terms, Nicaragua was a success story. As Carlos Vilas put it, "One of the most sustained runs of capitalist growth in the entire post-war [World War II] period generated some of the period's most widespread and brutal impoverishment. In other words, it was not the *failure* of capitalist development that provided the economic ingredient for revolution—it was its success."[17]

Individual families responded to the structural crisis in various ways. One response to increasing misery in the countryside was for more women to

14. T. David Mason, "Women's Participation in Central American Revolutions," *Comparative Political Studies* 25, no. 1 (1992), 68. In Nicaragua, agriculture plays a very significant role in the economy and therefore in politics, though that role diminished over the period of time under consideration here. While 62 percent of the economically active population worked in agriculture in 1960, that percentage had dropped to 39 percent in 1980, immediately following the fall of Somoza. John Booth, *The End and the Beginning: The Nicaraguan Revolution*, 2d ed. (Boulder, Colo.: Westview Press, 1985), 148.

15. Laura J. Enríquez, *Harvesting Change: Labor and Agrarian Reform in Nicaragua, 1979–1990* (Chapel Hill: The University of North Carolina Press, 1991), 46.

16. Laura J. Enríquez, *Agrarian Reform and Class Consciousness in Nicaragua* (Gainesville: University of Florida Press, 1997), 62–63.

17. Vilas, *Between Earthquakes and Volcanoes*, 66.

enter the labor force.[18] Another solution was for some members of the family to migrate (either to other rural areas, to urban areas, or less often, abroad) in search of work.[19] But too often, men's migration forced more women to seek paid employment. Often men left in search of work but never returned. While the abandonment of women was hardly a new feature of family life in Nicaragua, households headed by single mothers became quite common as the twentieth century wore on. By 1978, an estimated one-third to one-half of all families were headed by single females.[20]

Such households were particularly vulnerable economically. Since there were fewer economic opportunities for women than for men in the countryside, women made up a significant proportion of the hundreds of thousands who migrated to the cities during the second half of the twentieth century.[21]

18. In 1950, women constituted only 14 percent of the economically active population but, by 1977, they constituted 29 percent of the [formal] labor force, and a much larger percentage of the informal sector (Mason, "Women's Participation," 74).

19. Migrating to the cities in search of work was so common that between 1950 and 1980 the population of the capital, Managua, grew from 110,000 to 662,000, an increase of 507 percent (Vilas, *Between Earthquakes and Volcanoes,* 59). While only 15 percent of the population lived in cities in 1950, 54 percent were city dwellers by 1980 (Enríquez, *Agrarian Reform and Class Consciousness,* 182).

20. Good data on family structures is difficult to come by in Nicaragua, particularly if one is interested in tracing change over time. Three of five studies conducted between 1950 and 1975 found that about a quarter of all households were headed by single females. The other two studies reached different conclusions. Reynaldo Antonio Tefel's 1972 study of poor urban households found that 48 percent were headed by single women, and the Banco de Vivienda de Nicaragua's 1975 study found that only 10.4 percent of households in the study were headed by single women. These studies are reviewed in Paula Diebold de Cruz and Mayra Pasos de Rappacioli, *Report on the Role of Women in the Economic Development of Nicaragua* (Managua: USAID, 1975), 12. Another compilation of three sources estimated that one-third to one-half of households were headed by single females by 1978 (Mason, "Women's Participation," 76). A third review of two later studies found similar figures: according to a 1987 study, 24.3 percent of households were headed by women, and a 1993 study put the number at 28 percent. Both the 1987 and 1993 studies found that rates of single-female-headed households were higher in urban areas: 30.3 percent and 37 percent, respectively (María Angélica Fauné, *Mujeres y familias centroamericanas: Principales problemas y tendencias,* vol. 3 [San José, Costa Rica: Litografía e Imprenta LIL S.A., 1995], 92). A fourth review of studies that were not cited in the first three reviews also found high rates of single-female-headed households nationwide, and even higher rates in Managua: about 50 percent—according to a 1970 study—and 60 percent according to a 1984 source (Beth Stephens, "Changes in the Laws Governing the Parent-Child Relationship in Post-Revolutionary Nicaragua," *Hastings International and Comparative Law Review* 12, no 1 [1988], 139). All of these studies found that rates of female-headed households in Nicaragua were high nationwide and even higher in the urban areas, and they may have shown an increase over time, though some of the variation was probably due to class differences in the samples.

21. This inequality in employment opportunities—men having greater opportunities to work in rural agriculture, women having greater opportunities to find work in urban domestic service—was a long-term trend in Nicaragua, a trend that helps explain the gender imbalance

Through migration, thousands of girls and women had the opportunity to compare their lives with those of other people in other parts of the country. This comparison often was a radicalizing experience, one that women might collectively act upon in the relative freedom of the cities.

Structural changes, then—the concentration of land, breakup of households, urbanization, and large-scale entrance of women into the labor force—had an impact on participation in the guerrilla struggle. Large numbers of the newly landless were open to mobilization by a group like the Sandinista Front for National Liberation (Frente Sandinista de Liberación Nacional, or FSLN), which offered political and economic solutions to their problems.[22] And not only do these socioeconomic factors help explain the high levels of participation in the guerrilla movement: they also help explain the high levels of *female* participation. The disruption of family life and the massive entrance of women into the workforce, both indirectly caused by land concentration, started many women on a path of community participation that eventually led to participation in the guerrilla struggle. This was the case not only for older women but also for their daughters.

For Emilia,[23] the absence of male authority figures and the experience of migration from the countryside to the city allowed her mother—and her—to participate in revolutionary organizations in the 1970s.

> Mom raised me until I was ten years old. She washed, ironed, and took care of chickens and pigs to sell. Then my Mom separated from my Dad and I had to work as a maid. I lived where I worked. . . . My bosses were organized with the guerrilla army. . . . One began to hear about Sandino's guerrillas. They told me that perhaps some day all of you can cease to be maids.[24]

For a rural woman, like Emilia's mother, the loss of a husband's support created an economic crisis that could only be resolved at a very high cost. Because she was already working for income, the only way to survive was to

---

between urban and rural dwellers. That imbalance became less acute over time, though it did not cease to exist during the second half of the Somoza dictatorship. In 1950, 44.2 percent of urban dwellers were men, while 55.8 percent were women; in 1960, 46 percent were men, while 54 percent were women; in 1970, 47.1 percent were men, while 52.9 percent were women; and in 1980, the year after Anastasio Somoza was overthrown, 47.9 percent were men while 52.1 percent were women (figures from Ana Isabel García and Enrique Gomáriz, *Mujeres centroamericanas* [San José, Costa Rica: FLACSO, 1989], 360; also see Mason, "Women's Participation," 76).

22. Booth, *The End and the Beginning,* 85; Mason, "Women's Participation," 72.

23. Emilia's name is a pseudonym, as are all first-name identifications.

24. Emilia, interview by author, Managua, 27 January 1997.

send her young children to work. For Emilia herself, entering the workforce did not immediately create organizing opportunities, despite the fact that her bosses were themselves organized in the guerrilla struggle. But hearing of "Sandino's guerrillas" did plant the idea of organizing. After she migrated, Emilia would act on that thought.

> In 1972 we came to live here in Ciudad Sandino. My Mom was the first to organize. Later she started to integrate me. At that time [Maryknoll sister] Maura Clarke came and with her we started to organize ourselves directly. Maura was a very revolutionary *compañera* despite the fact that she was a nun. There were ten women more or less. . . . We were charged 20 cordobas for water. So we started to go out into the street. We said 10 yes, 20 no. Light also: 15 yes, 20 no. . . . The majority of the women were very timid, they didn't want to leave their houses on account of their husbands . . . [in contrast] the majority of us were single women. I had already been married and I had separated from him; I had a daughter. We lived with my Mom and a sister. . . . That was the beginning of the struggle and we already were starting to talk more deeply as women, about women's rights. Around 1978 we gave the organization a name: AM-PRONAC.[25] It was already a national organization.[26]

The economic crisis that drove Emilia's family to migrate did not disappear with their arrival in Ciudad Sandino. But things were different in some ways: organizing was easier.

In part that was because the Church, through Sister Maura Clarke, supported women's organizing. That organizing was not very radical; the call was merely for lowering the price of basic services. And it was hardly feminist, if feminist organizing is organizing that directly challenges gendered power relations. Nonetheless, it was a threat to many, and men often dealt with that threat by forbidding their women to participate. So the women who organized through the Church were not drawn from all sectors: they were mainly single women—those who were most economically desperate but most personally free.

> At that time I was already a worker. We organized in the factory, we would bring flyers to the factory. They said to me, [Emilia,] they are going to kill you, they are going to imprison you. But I didn't pay

25. AMPRONAC stood for Asociación de Mujeres Ante la Problematica Nacional.
26. Emilia, interview.

much attention. Around 1978, once at a convention in Carazo, a Sandinista convention, some reporters arrived from *La Prensa.* They didn't let them in but a reporter took a picture of me. . . . When I arrived at work, my boss called me and he showed me the photo and he said, what were you doing there? He said, look, if I see you there again, I will have you arrested. . . . The next day the National Guard arrived at my workplace and didn't pull anyone out. At 3:00 that afternoon we left. Another *compañero* got off his bus and there they were waiting for him. He was in prison for three months. You couldn't recognize him when he got out, he was all swollen. And they kept a watch on my house.[27]

Emilia's work was risky, without a doubt, but the same sexism that made it hard for women to organize also gave a certain degree of protection to female activists. While her fellow worker, a man, was captured and tortured for three months, she was not. Her house was watched by the police, but even though she was also involved in revolutionary organizing, she was not seen as equally threatening.[28] The Somoza government's sexism left women like Emilia relatively free to organize in ways that would help bring down the Somozas.

Structures and the Counterrevolution

The counterrevolutionary movement of the 1980s also was a response to the structural transformation that began in the mid-twentieth century, but it was a dramatically different response; the women involved differed somewhat from those who joined the Sandinista movement. In my interviews, Contra women tended to fit into two separate categories: either they were urban

27. Ibid.
28. My claim is not that women were immune from the Somoza dictatorship's violence; however, in comparison to men, women were somewhat less likely to be targeted by the regime. In other countries, women have also often found themselves somewhat freer than men to join in opposition politics, due to the myth of women as inherently apolitical and harmless. See, for example, Sonia E. Alvarez, *Engendering Democracy in Brazil* (Princeton: Princeton University Press, 1990); Jane S. Jaquette, ed., *The Women's Movement in Latin America: Participation and Democracy* (Boulder, Colo.: Westview Press, 1994); Kristi Long, *We All Fought for Freedom: Women in Poland's Solidarity Movement* (Boulder, Colo.: Westview Press, 1996); Reif, "Women in Latin American Guerrilla Movements"; and Georgina Waylen, "Women and Democratization: Conceptualizing Gender Relations in Transition Politics," *World Politics* (March 1994): 327–54.

women with ties to the Somozas, or they were rural women who moved to the Managua area after 1990 with no significant family ties to Somocismo.[29] Women in the first category had received personal benefits from the Somozas. Understandably, they were unhappy because their political patrons had been overturned, and in some cases, because they had been imprisoned and tortured by the Sandinistas in the first years of the revolution. These women were all of urban origin—and they were older.[30] People like them, with close ties to the Somoza regime, represented a minority within my sample (seven out of twenty-one), despite the fact that my sample probably over-represents urban Contras (since I conducted all my interviews in the Managua area). Within the Contra coalition as a whole, urban former Somocistas were also in the minority, although they were disproportionally represented at the highest levels of Contra leadership.[31]

The second category of women that I interviewed had little[32] or nothing to do with the Somoza regime. They were generally poor rural dwellers, apparently the very people by and for whom the revolution had been made. But they (and their families) had generally not experienced Somocismo in the same way as the families of the women who supported the Sandinista movement had. While they were also poor, they were usually middle peasants (those with enough land for subsistence, and possibly some surplus). In contrast, poor peasants (those with less than enough land for bare subsis-

29. A few women in my sample did not fit perfectly into either the urban/Somocista or rural/non-Somocista categories. Two women, both born in 1945, were of urban origin with no ties to the Somozas. One was a politician in the Christian Democratic Party who went on to become a member of the Contra National Directorate. The other was a merchant in the city of Chinandega, one of the northern regions in which the Contras were most active. A third woman was much more like the many rural and young non-Somocistas: though she grew up in Managua, her family made its living raising cattle on a ranch in the country.

30. Eleven of the fourteen Contras without links to the Somozas lived in rural areas before the end of the Contra war in 1990. While the average Contra with ties to the Somozas was born in 1954, the average Contra without ties to the Somozas was born between 1962 and 1963. The non-Somocista and rural Contra women were even younger: the average woman in this category was born in 1965, making her only fourteen years old when the Sandinistas came to power in 1979.

31. A 1986 survey of the Contras found that 10 of the 17 top military leaders were former members of Somoza's National Guard, while 200 to 250 of the 17,500 combatants had belonged to the Guard. Put another way, former Guardsmen comprised 58.8 percent of the top commanders but only 1.14 to 1.43 percent of the combatants. See Morales Carazo, *La contra*, 126, 130. Also see Chamorro, *Packaging the Contras*; Dickey, *With the Contras*; and Núñez et al., *La guerra y el campesinado*.

32. Only one woman in this category had a job that was linked to the Somoza regime, and she was not in the kind of prominent military position that was held by many urban Somocistas: she worked as a secretary in the mayor's office in her small town in the north.

tence), rural proletarians (those with no land), and the urban poor tended to support the Sandinistas.[33]

The rural Contra women had largely been left alone by the Somoza regime and often told me that things were better during that time because "you could buy things." In other words, their memory of the Somozas is that they did not intervene in the economy. In fact, the Somozas were highly interventionist on a macroeconomic level in their promotion of agro-exports and the concomitant land concentration,[34] but from the perspective of the middle peasant, economic life was largely untouched. Middle peasants were people who either were not pushed off their land or who managed to acquire new land on the agricultural frontier.[35] They continued to eat at least as well as ever, since they had enough land to grow their own food, and if they had a surplus to sell, they benefited from the high food prices that were devastating to their neighbors.

The Somocista policies and market logic that drove those neighbors into the arms of the Sandinista guerrillas were, for members of the middle peasantry, fairly benign. So when, upon taking power in 1979, the Sandinistas sought to rectify the structural inequalities that had built up over the course of four decades of Somoza family rule, some rural dwellers saw them as undermining a formerly stable order. Just as the Somozas had inadvertently created the conditions that gave rise to a guerrilla movement that would overthrow them, so too the Sandinistas inadvertently helped create a guerrilla movement that did not win militarily but arguably *did* win politically.[36]

Channeling the Crisis

Structural or socioeconomic changes were important in creating the conditions that allowed many women to organize—but by themselves, socioeco-

33. Morales Carazo, *La contra*, 290; Núñez et al., *La guerra y el campesinado*.

34. Booth, *The End and the Beginning*, 63–69.

35. Those who acquired land on the agricultural frontier might have been the beneficiaries of the third Somoza's limited land reform that was carried out by the Instituto Agrario de Nicaragua, known as the IAN. Areas with high concentrations of IAN beneficiaries tended to be strongholds of support for the Somoza regime, and they logically might have been strongholds of later support for the Contras (Anne Larson, personal communication to author, September 1998; on Somoza's agrarian reform, see Enríquez, *Harvesting Change*, 50–52).

36. The fourteen-party coalition that defeated the Sandinistas in the 1990 election included significant numbers of people with ties to the Contras; "around 100 of the top and intermediate leaders of the counterrevolution" came to hold positions in the government headed by Violeta Chamorro (Núñez et al., *La guerra y el campesinado*, 491). The government of Arnoldo Alemán, elected in 1996, is at least as directly tied to the Contras if the employment patterns that I observed while I did research in 1998 are any indication.

nomic changes do not create a revolution or a counterrevolution. Discontent needs to be channeled, and there is nothing preordained about the shape that channel will take. A number of ideological and organizational shifts, beginning in the 1960s, channeled the discontent generated by the structural crisis of the 1950s. The single most important of these changes, for the purpose of explaining female participation in the Sandinista guerrilla movement, was the transformation of the Catholic Church.[37]

Beginning in the mid-1960s, liberation theology, a school of Catholic thought that examined social inequality in the light of the Bible, was to have an explosive impact in Nicaragua.[38] One of the many women who became politicized through religion was Diana. While Diana was unusual in that she would rise far in the guerrilla ranks (in the late 1990s, she was one of only three women on the FSLN's National Directorate), her revolutionary origins in the liberation theology movement were fairly common. Growing up in a mining town on Nicaragua's Atlantic Coast, she attended a series of Catholic schools and later chose to become a missionary. But her religious training was also a form of political training. This is how she answered me when I asked what her first political experience had been.

> Contact with the progressive clergy helped me a lot in reflecting on poverty in Nicaragua. And also the experience of living in the mining sector. . . . I joined the Front while I was a missionary. Four of the eleven of us left to join the guerrillas. Although the others knew about it, they supported us morally and with their silence. And they also served in the rear guard. In 1975 or '76 I joined the Front, we had contact with the base communities. In '76 or '77 we began to create cells, on the coast and in Managua.[39]

Diana was only one of many Sandinistas who pointed to their religious education as being critical in initiating them into political life. Silvia, a student

---

37. While I think the transformation of the Church was the single most important organizational change that set the stage for the Sandinista Revolution, the Church was not the only space in which women who would become Sandinistas were first mobilized. Family networks, student groups, and (to a lesser extent) labor unions all provided opportunities for women to learn how to organize. The role of these preexisting networks in revolutionary politics is considered in much greater detail in Kampwirth, *Revolution in the Real World*.

38. Tommie Sue Montgomery, "Liberation and Revolution: Christianity as a Subversive Activity in Central America," in *Trouble in Our Backyard: Central America and the United States in the Eighties*, ed. Martin Diskin (New York: Pantheon Books, 1983); Philip Williams, *The Catholic Church and Politics in Nicaragua and Costa Rica* (Pittsburgh: University of Pittsburgh Press, 1989).

39. Diana [pseud.], interview by author, Managua, 5 February 1997.

activist who did semi-clandestine work with the FSLN in the 1970s, explained that in her school, "the sisters taught us another way to live out one's religion, it was a very practical way. . . . That left a big impression on me."[40]

Perhaps more surprising was the story of Cristiana. The daughter of a senator from Somoza's party, she would go on to become a student activist against Somoza before 1979 and a leader in Contra support work after 1979. She traced her early activism to the liberal ideology of her father (who tolerated her activities even when he disagreed with her positions), to her mother's spirit of service, and to her religious training.

> I studied in a religious school: the Assumption of León. It was the era of Medellín; there was quite a social focus. From a very young age I participated in community organizations. In high school I participated in fundraising projects, in lay missionary programs. I went for a year to Guatemala, to an indigenous town. That was very important."[41]

Upon returning from Guatemala in the early 1970s, she entered the University of León, joined a student group, and participated in demonstrations against the Somoza regime. But her days as an activist in the radical Church and the student movement came to an end when, in 1973, she married and followed her student husband to France. In 1978, while they were still in France, her father, the senator from Somoza's Liberal party, was assassinated by Sandinista guerrillas. She returned home to Nicaragua and, with her family, went into exile in Guatemala the month before the Sandinistas took power.

> I had to go. I had so much hope for that revolution. And I continue to think that one has to do things for the poor but I felt that I never could work for the government that had assassinated my father. . . . In the first moments of the revolution, despite the pain, I always hoped that things would go well. I had a sort of internal conflict.[42]

Cristiana would live in Guatemala and Honduras until the Sandinistas were voted out of power in 1990. While living abroad, she was active in the Nicaraguan Ladies Association (Asociación de Damas Nicaragüenses), an organization that supported other Nicaraguan exiles. Over time, that support work

40. Silvia [pseud.], interview by author, Managua, 15 January 1997.
41. Cristiana [pseud.], interview by author, Managua, 30 January 1997.
42. Ibid.

would evolve into indirect Contra support and, eventually, direct work with the Contras during the demobilization process.

For Cristiana, as for the majority of the women I interviewed, family was destiny. Of course, there were women who had close family ties to the Somoza regime, and even to the National Guard, who nonetheless were unwavering in their support for the revolutionary project. Yet they were a minority within the Sandinista coalition—perhaps a tiny minority if my relatively small sample is any indication.[43] To say that family was destiny does not mean that these women accepted their families' political views without question. But family ties did shape their opportunities—among them, the likelihood of making contact with a representative of either the Sandinista or Contra guerrillas.

Motivations for Right-Wing Action

While the organizational opportunities that channeled the anti-Somoza movement—such as the rise of liberation theology and the student movement—were discussed explicitly by most of the women who supported the Sandinista guerrillas, the motivations for participation in the Contra movement (except for those women who were Somocistas) were often less clear to me. In response to my questions about their first political experiences, Contra women most frequently pointed to the moment that they joined the Contras. (Sandinista women, in contrast, all told stories of political experiences—often dating to their childhoods—that eventually led them to become Sandinistas.) Jumping right to their experiences as Contras was so surprising to me that I rephrased the question, asking them if they had belonged to any other group prior to joining the Contras, and was consistently told *no*.

While Sandinistas looked back fondly at their participation in various collective actions, Contras were often motivated by the desire to avoid collective actions. In resisting Sandinista efforts to control the market and to mobilize people into popular organizations, Contras defended the value of individualism, one of the dearest values of the middle peasant.[44]

43. Only one of the twenty-four activists who was a Sandinista both before and after 1979 told me that she had close family ties to the Somoza regime. But based on her research on the Somoza period, Victoria González estimated that a much greater portion (perhaps 10 percent) of mid- and high-level Sandinista activists came from middle- and upper-class families that supported Somoza (personal conversation with author, September 1998).

44. Bendaña, *Una tragedia campesina*; Núñez et al., *La guerra y el campesinado*.

Rationing was one of the Sandinista actions that particularly angered the women who became Contras. I suspect that Contra men would have also been angered by rationing, though it probably was a particularly sore point among women, who tended to be responsible for buying the family's food. Several mentioned resentment at the periodic shortages of white sugar that forced them to buy "black sugar," something that had never happened before: "General Somoza gave that sugar to animals."[45]

Sandinista rationing and rules against hoarding created particular hardships for small merchants. Andrea, who was born in 1945 in the provincial city of Chinandega, was a merchant who supported the Sandinista struggle against Somoza: "I was part of the insurrection, I carried arms, I even made Molotov cocktails." But after the Sandinistas took power, she was unhappy with some of their policies. "I didn't like the way Sandinismo worked . . . the rationing of food, the abuse against teenagers [who] had to carry out military service. MICOIN[46] did not allow one to work, it took everything away and my poverty was what made me join. . . . Because of that I decided to go with the Resistance. When I looked at the rationing of food, no, that was not for me." To continue working as a merchant, she had to violate the rule that "nobody could buy more than 3 pounds [of meat] at a time, that nobody could buy things wholesale."[47]

The purpose of the Sandinista rules was to ensure that meat was available at affordable prices for all. But the same rule that made life easier for some who had not been able to afford meat under Somoza made life harder for women like Andrea. Moreover, by forcing them to make illegal purchases, it turned these women into enemies of the state. Once she had become a Sandinista enemy through an action that she felt she had to take to preserve her livelihood, it was not such a great leap to join the Contras.

Other rural Contra women were motivated by a different sort of individualism—a resistance to joining social groups and attending meetings. One of those women was Gladys, who grew up in Managua but maintained strong ties to the countryside through her father's ranch. While she was uninterested in politics as a child, she became concerned "upon seeing the big change. It was communism, there was no freedom of any sort." For young Gladys, an example of the lack of liberty was the pressure she felt to join a student coffee-picking brigade. "I don't think anybody likes that." So in 1983

---

45. Doris [pseud.], interview by author, Managua, 22 July 1998.
46. MICOIN stood for Ministerio de Comercio Interior.
47. Andrea [pseud.], interview by author, Managua, 21 July 1998.

she decided to join her uncle in a Contra training camp. "I found it necessary to resist. I was about to turn 15."[48]

Even the 1980 literacy campaign[49]—consistently mentioned by Sandinistas as the most beautiful moment of the revolution—came under criticism by some Contras. While urban Sandinista supporters saw the campaign as an example of revolutionary sharing, some of their mostly rural students experienced it as revolutionary imposition.

By the age of seven, Tina had never attended school. So when literacy campaign volunteers arrived in her community, she and her siblings decided to attend: "We only went for one day, I think that was because of our misgivings." She didn't like the fact that her teacher wanted to be addressed as "compañero" ("companion" or "comrade") rather than "teacher." But the worst part was the content of the class. That day she learned words like "bomb, rifle, ambush, machine gun, only military things. We said to my Dad, only military things and we're not soldiers."[50] Had she returned another day, Tina would have been exposed to a series of other lessons without military themes. But she never went back, since for her family, the campaign (and perhaps the revolution as a whole) was about the city imposing its concerns on country people who wanted to be left alone.[51]

Similarly, Reina Isabel also objected to pressures to participate in Sandinista-affiliated popular organizations, though unlike Gladys and Tina, she was fairly extensively involved in revolutionary activities: she participated in a labor union and in three coffee-picking brigades. Still, even while she engaged in these activities, she resented "the pressure that was placed on us

48. Gladys [pseud.], interview by author, Managua, 13 July 1998.

49. Only a few months after Somoza's fall, tens of thousands of volunteers, mostly young people from the cities, spent the first five months of 1980 teaching their fellow Nicaraguans to read, the sort of collective action that is only possible at the height of revolutionary commitment. During the crusade, 406,056 people would learn to read and write—reducing Nicaragua's illiteracy rate from over 50 percent to under 13 percent. Deborah Barndt, "Popular Education," in *Nicaragua: The First Five Years*, ed. Thomas W. Walker (New York: Praeger, 1985), 328; Ministerio de Educación, *Cinco años de educación en la revolución: 1979–1984* (Managua: MED, 1984), xvii.

50. Tina [pseud.], interview by author, Managua, 20 July 1998.

51. In her excellent study of the roots of the counterrevolution in the north of Nicaragua, Lynn Horton observes that representatives of the Sandinista government were often seen by locals as urban outsiders, even "foreigners," who had come to meddle in their daily lives. While that view is very consistent with Tina's view, she may have been extreme in her rejection of the literacy campaign. "[M]any Quilalí peasants, including some who later supported the Contras, have positive memories of the literacy campaign in particular and comment that 'it was beautiful' " (Horton, *Peasants in Arms: War and Peace in the Mountains of Nicaragua, 1979–1994* [Athens: Ohio University Press, 1998]).

to participate, to receive one's grades . . . it was a requisite that they asked for in the schools." While Reina Isabel was still in high school, her whole family decided to leave their small town in war-torn Chinandega for exile in Honduras. Living in a refugee camp, she and others in her family came into contact with the Contras and, along with some of her relatives, decided to join them. "Of my family, the only others were some cousins and a brother-in-law. I was the only woman in this group. . . . I already had a son by that point; I was 17 years old. My mother stayed with my son."[52]

Reina Isabel's mention of her son brings me to a third possible reason for participating in both guerrilla movements. Many believe that the defense of motherhood and children is a major motivation for women's participation in radical politics in Latin America and elsewhere.[53] In the case of Nicaragua, many have argued that significant numbers of women entered the Sandinista struggle in defense of their children.[54] Maternalism also played an important role in right-wing politics when presidential candidate Violeta Chamorro successfully used maternalistic rhetoric, especially opposition to the draft, to win the election of 1990.[55] Thinking through the framework of motherhood and politics, I assumed that when significant numbers of women mentioned their opposition to the draft as a major motivation for entering the Contra struggle, it was a further example of maternalism.

But then I thought about the ages of the women who used that explanation. Of all the women who seemed likely to be concerned about Sandinista military service—those old enough to have draft-age children[56]—only one even mentioned the draft. The other five women who were motivated to

52. Reina Isabel [pseud.], interview by author, Managua, 14 July 1998.

53. Jo Fisher, *Out of the Shadows: Women, Resistance, and Politics in South America* (London: Latin American Bureau, 1993) and *Mothers of the Disappeared* (Boston: South End Press, 1989); Marguerite Guzmán Bouvard, *Revolutionizing Motherhood: The Mothers of the Plaza de Mayo* (Wilmington, Del.: Scholarly Resources, 1994); Alexis Jetter, Annelise Orleck, and Diana Taylor, eds., *The Politics of Motherhood: Activist Voices from Left to Right* (Hanover: University Press of New England, 1997); Kristin Luker, *Abortion and the Politics of Motherhood* (Berkeley and Los Angeles: University of California Press, 1984); and Lynn Stephen, *Women and Social Movements in Latin America: Power from Below* (Austin: University of Texas Press, 1997).

54. Collinson, ed., *Women and Revolution*; Murguialday, *Nicaragua, revolución y feminismo*; Margaret Randall, *Sandino's Daughters: Testimonies of Nicaraguan Women in Struggle* (Vancouver and Toronto: New Star Books, 1981).

55. Karen Kampwirth, "The Mother of the Nicaraguans: Doña Violeta and the UNO's Gender Agenda," *Latin American Perspectives* 23, no. 1 (1996): 67–86.

56. Six of the twenty-one were born before 1952, which would have made them at least thirty-two years old in 1984, old enough to have sixteen-year-old sons if they had given birth to them at age sixteen, an age by which many Nicaraguan women have children.

join the Contras by their opposition to the Sandinista draft were born between 1964 and 1968, and so they were far too young during the 1980s to
have had any directly maternal concerns about military service. If their concerns were personal, they worried about a brother or, more likely, a boyfriend. For instance, Irene told me that, in 1986, she left her two children in
her mother's care and joined the Contras, hoping that "maybe I was going
to catch up with the father of my children" who had left her for the Contras
two years earlier. She felt "deceived to realize that the father of my children
had been killed; with more bravery I picked up my rifle and continued
fighting."[57]

While the numbers in this study are too small to support definitive conclusions, they do suggest the need for us to use caution when we hear left-
and right-wing women use maternal rhetoric to justify their public actions.
Is it possible that the language of maternalism is a way to make public participation acceptable more than a political motivation of its own? Certainly,
many women feel the need to justify their actions. A woman who engages in
public participation risks being called a "public woman" *(mujer pública),*
the equivalent of a prostitute.

The language of maternalism is useful even when women's motivations
are not strictly maternal, since it is the language of everyday experience, and
since it is so malleable. For example, Andrea, the merchant who supported
the anti-Somoza insurrection and later supported the Contras, told me about
life under Somoza.

> In Somoza's time never, we never lived [like under the Sandinistas],
> I earned my money for food, I bought whatever I wanted. The only
> thing about Somoza is that he never concerned himself with the
> [National] Guard's great abuse of the people, but that he was a bad
> president, no. The same thing happened to him that happens to
> mothers when we are the last ones to know what our children are
> doing. That was what happened to him. He was not a bad president.
> The only thing is that there were never free elections because he
> wanted to be president forever, but we lived quietly, there was no
> war, there was nothing like that.[58]

Andrea supported the Contras so that she could be left alone, free to be a
merchant. She valued individual freedom so highly that even though she

57. Irene [pseud.], interview by author, Managua, 21 July 1998.
58. Andrea, interview.

opposed Somoza near the end of the dynasty, she had come to reevaluate his actions, forgiving even the violence of the Guard, because at least Somoza allowed her to live quietly.

Ironically, many of the Contra women joined a national and international political effort so as to avoid pressures to become political. Unlike the Sandinista women who joined the guerrillas as a way of coping with the terrible changes in their lives, the Contra women joined the guerrillas as a way of preserving a way of life that was threatened by the revolutionaries. And even if they saw undesirable elements in that old rural way of life, these women might turn those individualistic middle-peasant values to their own advantage by independently going off with the Contras.

Personal Roots of Rebellion

Millions of women experienced the structural crisis and organizational opportunities that transformed Nicaragua in the second half of the twentieth century. But most of those women did not join revolutionary or counterrevolutionary organizations. Instead, most women—and most men, for that matter—did their best to find personal rather than public solutions to the crisis. In short, most people fled from risk. And logically enough: the chance of successfully overthrowing either government was very low, and the cost of defeat was very high. Why did some women seek out public, or collective, solutions to their problems?

I have already made reference to some of the personal factors that informed their political decisions. Family ties were critical for both Sandinistas and Contras. Contact with preexisting networks, including church groups, labor unions, student groups, and other popular organizations, was also key in leading both sets of women into radical actions; the difference was that Sandinista women tended to remember those prior experiences as positive, and Contra women often remembered them as negative. Probably the most important factor, and the one that I think is worth considering in a bit more detail here, is age.[59]

In my study, the women who had been involved in the anti-Somoza movement were born between the years 1935 and 1961. Twenty-four of them were born between the years 1948 and 1961, while only three were born

59. Others have consistently found that guerrillas across the world have tended to be quite young (see, for example, Wickham-Crowley, *Guerrillas and Revolution*, 19–21, 42–43).

before 1948. Very few of them had reached the age of thirty when Somoza's flight ended the Sandinista guerrilla struggle in 1979; a number of them were still teenagers. (This was typical: one study showed that 71 percent of those who died in the guerrilla struggle were between fifteen and twenty-four years old.[60])

Most of the women who became guerrillas chose to cast their lot with the Sandinistas when they were old enough to decide for themselves but young enough not to be burdened with the responsibility of children, or at least not many children. They had usually become guerrillas at an age when they, like other adolescents, tended toward recklessness: they either underestimated the risks involved in supporting the guerrillas or did not care about those risks.

In their youth, the Contra women had a lot in common with their Sandinista predecessors. The twenty-one former Contra women I interviewed were born between 1936 and 1971; fourteen of them were born in the 1960s and 1970s. These findings are consistent with data from the demobilization in 1990. At that point, the majority of former Contras were between the ages of 16 and 25: 27.8 percent were 16–20 years old, and 22.9 percent were 21–25 years old.[61]

For many of the women who threw in their lot with the radical left or the radical right while they were still very young, politics seemed like a genuine opportunity in a country in which there were very few opportunities for poor young people, especially poor young women. Sonia, who was a student activist in her high school, went off with the Sandinistas at the age of seventeen:

> I did not go off with the FSLN because of any great consciousness. No, I think I went off with the FSLN because of rebelliousness. . . . I always criticized the fact that [in my Catholic high school] people were treated differently depending on their social standing. . . . The FSLN was like the possibility of changing my life. And yes, I changed it definitively.[62]

Angry at the multiple inequalities that they had to confront on a daily basis, girls like Sonia tended to see participation in the guerrilla forces as a way to escape the constraints of their daily lives.

Furthermore, joining a guerrilla group (as opposed to participating in a less radical political group) allowed them to leave the tedium of their homes

60. Vilas, *The Sandinista Revolution*, 108.
61. CIAV/OEA, "Cuadros estadísticos."
62. Sonia [pseud.], interview by author, Managua, 19 January 1997.

and to see the world, or at least to see Honduras. Entering radical politics even meant getting a new identity: both the Sandinistas and the Contras gave all new members pseudonyms, which many of them would continue to use long after the wars were over. Explaining the factors that led them to become Contras, many women told me stories that were remarkably similar to the stories told by young women who had become Sandinista guerrillas a decade earlier.

María Elizabeth was only thirteen when she joined the Contras for reasons that were completely personal. When she was six years old, her mother died, and the place where María Elizabeth lived had not been much of a home afterward. In her aunt and uncle's house, she felt unwanted and used: "I never studied, they never gave me that opportunity. [They] never gave me the love of a family, they only tormented me, they treated me like a slave by the end." So she left to join the Contras, "because I no longer found anything to do; it was my only way out."[63]

For María Elizabeth and many teenagers, radical politics became a way to leave home, to get away from difficult relations with parents or other relatives, or to continue their studies. Manuela, for instance, explained that she was attracted by an ad inviting boys and girls to sign up for Somoza's military academy: "upon joining the army we were given the option of continuing our studies."[64] At the age of fifteen, Manuela found a career in the National Guard far more appealing than her other options—continuing to work in the store where she had already been working for a year, or, like her mother, washing and ironing for members of the Guard.

So in their individual motivations, many women of the Contra movement and women of the Sandinista Front faced similar situations and made similar choices. They used different political rhetoric (solidarity, class struggle, and social justice in the case of the Sandinistas; anticommunism, individualism, and economic freedom in the case of the Contras). But when it came down to personal motivations, they were not so different. This suggests that the contrast between the social commitment of the Sandinistas and the rugged individualism of the Contras may be too stark. After all, the women who became Contras chose to submit themselves to a group—quite a hierarchical group. But the key word here is *chose.*

For the women who joined the Sandinista coalition in the 1960s and 1970s, joining felt voluntary, like a true choice. In contrast, by the 1980s,

63. María Elizabeth [pseud.], interview by author, Managua, 25 July 1998.
64. Manuela [pseud.], interview by author, Managua, 16 July 1998.

joining a Sandinista organization did not feel like a choice to some women. In deciding to rebel, the women who came of age in the 1980s had certain things in common with the Sandinistas of the 1960s and 1970s. Both groups of women chose guerrilla groups; both resisted the legitimate authority of their day. Yet despite these similarities, the choices that they made had significantly different implications for their views of themselves as women and for their relationships with men.

Gender Relations and Guerrilla Struggle

Not surprisingly, gender relations under the conditions of guerrilla warfare differed from the gender relations of everyday life. It would have been impossible to perfectly replicate the traditionally gendered division of labor under the nontraditional conditions of guerrilla life; moreover, limiting the duties of female guerrillas would have been a poor choice, given that these organizations desperately needed all willing volunteers. So both Sandinistas and Contras told me stories of significant gender equality during their respective guerrilla struggles. For instance, Diana, the missionary from the Atlantic Coast who became a Sandinista guerrilla, compared relations between men and women during the guerrilla struggle with those of the later revolutionary period.

> There was more equality in the mountains than after the triumph. We shared what we had. We shared the cooking duties, the gun cleaning, the leadership responsibilities. . . . There wasn't gender consciousness in the guerrilla forces, what there was was an incredible solidarity. At any time men as much as women could be killed. Later a *machista* life began, which is Nicaraguan culture. They returned to what they considered a normal life.[65]

Diana's description—of the egalitarianism of the guerrilla struggle, followed by a return to "normal" inequality once the dictatorship had been overthrown—was quite common. Contra women, too, typically described relations with male guerrillas as being characterized by a lot of respect, claiming that they were treated like other soldiers, that these relations were like those between brothers and sisters.

But not everyone remembered such nearly perfect egalitarianism during

65. Diana, interview.

the guerrilla struggle, as illustrated by María's answer to my question about relations between Sandinista men and women:

> Look, I spent a lot of time being annoyed. . . . There was one *compañero* in particular that always wanted the *compañeras* to fuck with him. I myself, for example, had relations with him and I didn't want to. Later it didn't seem right to me. I do think that in many things . . . there wasn't the same level of responsibility.[66]

Some Contra women also told stories of less than perfect gender relations during the guerrilla struggle. Tina, for example, felt that women were frequently treated as less competent, and less valuable, than men. "Women were not seen as capable people, they just made tortillas. Well, they verbally abused them." This deprecation of female Contras could be extreme: women would be traded as though they were commodities, something that never happened to men. "He said, 'we will trade all our women for [Tina].' 'We will exchange a woman for a pair of boots,' it reached that extreme. [One woman commander], she exchanged a woman for a poncho liner . . . she was one of the people who most promoted that. If she did it, why wouldn't the men?" Such views of women, not surprisingly, lent themselves to a casual attitude regarding men's sexual behavior. "There was always the question of abuse of women, and on top of that I worked in the clinic, so I would see such things."[67] But Tina herself was not touched by these mental and physical abuses since, as she made clear to me, she was a valuable Contra, volunteering for dangerous assignments that other women avoided. And—just in case—she always made a point of sleeping with her gun.

María Elizabeth had a story of a very different sort of gender-related abuse. For some reason that she could not explain, one of the Contra commanders, a Cuban-American, "decided he hated me and he made me lose my daughter."[68] Threatening her right to live and work in the Contra camp, the commander convinced María Elizabeth to sign a paper to avoid going to jail. To her horrified surprise, she was then told that she had signed away her legal rights to the baby. Since, in his estimation, she was too young to care for the child, he was going to give the baby to his wife in the United States. After taking a series of photos of María Elizabeth in her uniform so that he would be able to show the baby her birth mother some day, the Contra commander sent the baby to the United States.

66. María [pseud.], interview by author, Managua, 23 January 1997.
67. Tina, interview.
68. María Elizabeth, interview.

Benigna was the only woman I interviewed who said that she did not volunteer for Contra service: "They kidnapped me, I did not want to go with them. At that time I was a girl, I lived with my parents. They raped me. We women suffered a lot."[69] The Contras had not originally intended to kidnap her. They had intended to kill her father, who had been identified to the Contras as a Sandinista by neighbors. (Benigna said that he was not a Sandinista, but merely caught in the middle: "at that time you had to collaborate with both bands.") Since he was not in the house when they arrived, the Contras got their revenge by beating up his pregnant wife and stealing his fifteen-year-old daughter.

Benigna was taken off to Honduras, where she apparently changed her thinking. "Later on I became more conscious. . . . Later I went to fight in the mountains and I saw that it was a just cause, that it was for our own country." I asked her what that cause was and she explained: "to win the war, the situation that we were living with the Sandinistas, there was a war, there wasn't food." Although the men who raped her were never tried for their crimes, she also assured me that the human rights situation improved with time. "Later on they treated me very well, they respected me a lot."

That better treatment could have resulted from the fact that she quickly found a boyfriend among the Contras, a man who probably helped protect her. It might have come from pressure by what Benigna called "the human rights," or external human rights groups. But the main reason that she stayed was neither the better treatment nor her desire to see the Contras win the war. Rather, she stayed because she lacked other options. "I asked God to help me return to my family. But since I was there I had to accept that I'd have to stay. I suffered very much."[70]

Were gender relations within the Contra movement really more violent and less egalitarian than those within the Sandinista movement? It is possible that the Sandinista women had less vivid memories of gender relations in the guerrilla movement because more time had passed than in the case of Contra women. It is also possible that I asked Sandinista women fewer questions about the guerrilla period because I was interviewing them on the events of several decades, while my Contra interviews typically focused on the events of a decade or two.

A third possibility is that the former Sandinista guerrillas might have downplayed gender inequality during the guerrilla days out of loyalty to the

69. Benigna [pseud.], interview by author, Managua, 29 July 1998.
70. Ibid.

Sandinista party. Had I conducted these interviews during the Contra war of the 1980s, these women would have had obvious reasons to refrain from criticizing the Sandinistas to me (a citizen of the country that funded the Contras). Moreover, as many of them told me, in the 1970s and 1980s they had not thought much about gender inequality within the guerrilla army. It was only in the 1990s, when all the left-wing women I interviewed participated in some sort of women's rights work (and many of them repudiated the Sandinista party), that they started to evaluate their guerrilla days through a new framework. That this group of women, all identified in one way or another with feminism, could not come up with many stories of gender inequality in the 1970s makes me think that in fact there was a high degree of gender equality among the left-wing guerrillas in Nicaragua.[71]

It is not surprising that gender inequality and violence against women seems to have been far more prevalent within the Contra forces than within the Sandinista forces. After all, Sandinista guerrillas fought to transform Nicaragua into a more egalitarian place; Contra guerrillas fought to defeat that project. Logically, then, Sandinista life would be expected to be characterized by less violence and inequality than Contra life. Human rights reports seem to indicate that this was the case.[72] Even the human rights group that most sympathized with the Contras, the Asociación Nicaragüense Pro-Derechos Humanos (which was founded and funded by the U.S. Congress), reported more than fourteen cases of women being kidnapped, sexually abused, or raped by the Contras.[73]

The fact that the Contras were largely headed by former members of the National Guard, which was infamous for its use of indiscriminate violence against civilians,[74] may help to explain why violence within the Contra forces was often tolerated. Moreover, as several Contras mentioned to me, the Contra army was a military organization, not a political-military organization like the Sandinista Front. The existence of political study sessions amongst the Sandinistas, in which they read and discussed political essays and novels,

---

71. On the social construction of memory, see Daniel James, " 'Tales Told Out on the Borderlands': Doña María's Story, Memory, and Issues of Gender," in *The Gendered Worlds of Latin American Women Workers,* ed. John French and Daniel James (Durham: Duke University Press, 1997).

72. Stephen M. Gorman and Thomas W. Walker, "The Armed Forces," in *Nicaragua: The First Five Years,* ed. Thomas W. Walker (New York: Praeger, 1985), 109–10.

73. ANPDH, *Segundo informe de seis meses sobre derechos humanos en la resistencia nicaragüense* (San José, Costa Rica: n.p., 1988), 14, 17, 19, 21, 25, 26, 31; also see Morales Carazo, *La contra,* 292–95.

74. Booth, *The End and the Beginning,* 60–61, 72–73, 94–95.

meant that levels of political consciousness (and perhaps unwillingness to accept abuse) were much higher among the Sandinista women even if they, like many Contra women, had originally joined the guerrillas for largely personal reasons.

Greater egalitarianism within the guerrilla forces, and higher levels of political consciousness, help to explain a finding that I mentioned earlier: while most of the leaders of the women's rights movement in the 1990s traced their political roots to the Sandinista struggle, very few had been associated with the Contra struggle. And few of the Contras I interviewed had even heard the word "feminist"; they certainly did not identify as such. Despite many similarities in their initial motivations, and despite the fact that many women on both sides were personally empowered through their participation in guerrilla movements, a comparison of Sandinista and Contra women suggests that women's politicization through radical left-wing politics is far more likely to nurture later struggles for gender equality than politicization through right-wing politics, no matter how radical.

Epilogue: Coalition Building Across Political Lines

In 1990, several decades of guerrilla warfare came to a formal end when the Contras were demobilized. In the years that followed the Contras' demobilization, a number of efforts were made to reconcile those who had been mobilized on opposite sides during the Contra war. Some of those reconciliation efforts involved men and women from both sides of the political divide; a few were coalitions that united women in defense of their gender interests, defined in various ways. In concluding, I will identify four of these coalitions, three of which involved some of the women I interviewed for this chapter.[75]

As Zoilamérica Ortega observed in her excellent account of a series of reconciliation workshops that were given by the Center for International Studies (Centro de Estudios Internacionales) starting in 1991, women were sometimes more likely than men to make coalitions across political lines. For example, in the city of Matagalpa, demobilized women found themselves drawn to the mothers' groups and other women's organizations that were founded during the war, for "at times they were better received by other

75. Those three coalitions all worked at least partially out of Managua, which is where the women I interviewed lived; the final coalition was based in the small town of Waslala.

women than by members of their own organizations whose male leaders did not allow basic issues to be raised."[76]

Another organization that sought to reconcile Sandinistas and Contras, beginning in 1990, was the National Union of Agricultural Producers and Cattle Ranchers (Unión Nacional de Agricultores y Ganaderos, or UNAG). The leaders of the pro-Sandinista UNAG hoped that the fact that many of the union's members were middle peasants would make it possible to reach out to the many middle peasants who had been on the Contra side during the civil war. By 1997, that reconciliation had progressed to the point that a Contra support group, the Association of the Nicaraguan Resistance (Asociación Resistencia Nicaragüense Israel Galeano "Comandante Franklin," or ARNIG), had a tiny office in the national headquarters of the UNAG and received a stipend from the Sandinista labor union.

Like the UNAG, the ARNIG was a predominantly masculine organization; unlike the UNAG, the ARNIG did not have a women's section. But despite the historical tensions between feminist activists and the right, the considerable female presence in the leadership of the ARNIG[77] allowed for some tentative outreach between the two sectors: at the time of my interview, the president of the ARNIG spoke enthusiastically about the possibility of a feminist workshop for the women of her organization.[78]

A third alliance between Contra and Sandinista women involved more than eight hundred mothers and widows of combatants on both sides from the northern town of Waslala, who came together to demand pensions from the state social security agency more effectively. In 1995, they took advantage of the power of maternalism by founding the Association of Mothers and War Victims of Waslala (Asociación de Madres y Víctimas de Guerra de Waslala), which the co-founders described as "an organization without political or religious distinctions."[79] Through that organization, they received their pensions, materials to help them build the "Widows Neighborhood" (comprised of the families of twenty-six women from each side), a revolving loan program, and a small sewing collective, along with promises for a fish-raising farm, a basic grains project, and a construction materials factory.[80]

76. Ortega, *Desmovilizados de guerra,* 61–62.
77. Of the sixty-eight hundred affiliates of the ARNIG at the time of my interview, four hundred were women, including the president and three of the seven members of the board (Galeano, interview).
78. Ibid.
79. "No es lo mismo estar juntas, que ser 'revueltas,' " *La Boletina,* no. 25 (March 1996), 8.
80. Ibid., 6–11.

Working in concert, the Sandinista and Contra mothers of Waslala made considerable material gains. But the same claim to be nonpolitical that made the coalition possible also limited their ability to take public stands on issues. Of course, that apolitical discourse did not mean that they were truly free of opinions: looking forward to a local election, they hinted at their plans to participate quietly as an unified association. "And it will not be a case of 'the Sandinistas are over here, those of the Resistance over there.' Although we are thinking of a woman mayor, who would understand women's interests, so that she would defend them."[81]

Members of a final coalition, analyzed by María Teresa Blandón in the third chapter of this volume, were far less coy about the political nature of their work. Unlike the mothers of Waslala who maintained unity through an apolitical maternal discourse, the members of the National Women's Coalition (Coalición Nacional de Mujeres), founded in 1995, were fiercely partisan and made no claims to unity. Without papering over their political differences, they mobilized around those interests that they thought they held in common as women. Through this coalition, women from nearly the entire range of the Nicaraguan political spectrum were able to defend their interests in gender equality at the same time that they insisted that they—no less than men—had every right to be political actors.

BIBLIOGRAPHY

INTERVIEWS

Andrea [pseud.]. Interview by author. Managua, 21 July 1998.
Benigna [pseud.]. Interview by author. Managua, 29 July 1998.
Cristiana [pseud.]. Interview by author. Managua, 30 January 1997.
Diana [pseud.]. Interview by author. Managua, 5 February 1997.
Doris [pseud.]. Interview by author. Managua, 22 July 1998.
Emilia [pseud.]. Interview by author. Managua, 27 January 1997.
Galeano, Elida María ("Comandante Chaparra"). Interview by author. Managua, 9 July 1998.
Gladys [pseud.]. Interview by author. Managua, 13 July 1998.
Irene [pseud.]. Interview by author. Managua, 21 July 1998.
Manuela [pseud.]. Interview by author. Managua, 16 July 1998.
María [pseud.]. Interview by author. Managua, 23 January 1997.
María Elizabeth [pseud.]. Interview by author. Managua, 25 July 1998.
Palacios, Justo Pastor ("Comandante Indio"). Interview by author. Managua, 30 July 1998.
Reina Isabel [pseud.]. Interview by author. Managua, 14 July 1998.
Silvia [pseud.]. Interview by author. Managua, 15 January 1997.

81. Ibid., 12.

Sonia [pseud.]. Interview by author. Managua, 19 January 1997.
Tina [pseud.] Interview by author. Managua, 20 July 1998.

OTHER SOURCES

Alvarez, Sonia E. *Engendering Democracy in Brazil.* Princeton: Princeton University Press, 1990.
ANPDH (Asociación Nicaragüense Pro-Derechos Humanos). *Segundo informe de seis meses sobre derechos humanos en la resistencia nicaragüense.* San José, Costa Rica: n.p., 1988.
Barndt, Deborah. "Popular Education." In *Nicaragua: The First Five Years,* edited by Thomas W. Walker. New York: Praeger, 1985.
Bendaña, Alejandro. *Una tragedia campesina: Testimonios de la resistencia.* Managua: COMPANIC, 1991.
Booth, John. *The End and the Beginning: The Nicaraguan Revolution.* 2d ed. Boulder, Colo.: Westview Press, 1985.
Brenes, Ada Julia, Ivania Lovo, Olga Luz Restrepo, Sylvia Saakes, and Flor de María Zúniga. *La mujer nicaragüense en los años 80.* Managua: Ediciones Nicarao, 1991.
Brown, Timothy. "Women Unfit for Combat? Au Contraire!" *Wall Street Journal,* 30 September 1997, A22.
Chamorro, Edgar. *Packaging the Contras: A Case of CIA Disinformation.* Monograph Series no. 2. New York: Institute for Media Analysis, 1987.
Christian, Shirley. *Nicaragua: Revolution in the Family.* New York: Vintage Books, 1986.
CIAV/OEA (Comisión Internacional de Apoyo y Verificación de la Organización de Estados Americanos). "Cuadros estadísticos del proceso de desmovilización y repatriación en Nicaragua." Managua, July 1991. Unpublished document.
Collinson, Helen, ed. *Women and Revolution in Nicaragua.* London: Zed Books, 1990.
Diebold de Cruz, Paula, and Mayra Pasos de Rappacioli. *Report on the Role of Women in the Economic Development of Nicaragua.* Managua: USAID, 1975.
Dickey, Christopher. *With the Contras: A Reporter in the Wilds of Nicaragua.* New York: Simon and Schuster, 1987.
Enríquez, Laura J. *Harvesting Change: Labor and Agrarian Reform in Nicaragua, 1979–1990.* Chapel Hill: The University of North Carolina Press, 1991.
———. *Agrarian Reform and Class Consciousness in Nicaragua.* Gainesville: University of Florida Press, 1997.
Fauné, María Angélica. *Mujeres y familias centroamericanas: Principales problemas y tendencias.* Vol. 3. San José, Costa Rica: Litografía e Imprenta LIL S.A., 1995.
Fisher, Jo. *Mothers of the Disappeared.* Boston: South End Press, 1989.
———. *Out of the Shadows: Women, Resistance, and Politics in South America.* London: Latin American Bureau, 1993.
Flynn, Patricia. "Women Challenge the Myth." In *Revolution in Central America,* edited by Stanford Central America Action Network. Boulder, Colo.: Westview Press, 1983.
García, Ana Isabel and Enrique Gomáriz. *Mujeres centroamericanas.* San José, Costa Rica: FLACSO, 1989.
Gorman, Stephen M., and Thomas W. Walker. "The Armed Forces." In *Nicaragua: The First Five Years,* edited by Thomas W. Walker. New York: Praeger, 1985.

Guzmán Bouvard, Marguerite. *Revolutionizing Motherhood: The Mothers of the Plaza de Mayo.* Wilmington, Del.: Scholarly Resources, 1994.

Horton, Lynn. *Peasants in Arms: War and Peace in the Mountains of Nicaragua, 1979–1994.* Athens: Ohio University Press, 1998.

James, Daniel. " 'Tales Told Out on the Borderlands': Doña María's Story, Memory, and Issues of Gender." In *The Gendered Worlds of Latin American Women Workers,* edited by John French and Daniel James. Durham: Duke University Press, 1997, 31–52.

Jaquette, Jane S., ed. *The Women's Movement in Latin America: Participation and Democracy.* Boulder, Colo.: Westview Press, 1994.

Jetter, Alexis, Annelise Orleck, and Diana Taylor, eds. *The Politics of Motherhood: Activist Voices from Left to Right.* Hanover: University Press of New England, 1997.

Kampwirth, Karen. "The Mother of the Nicaraguans: Doña Violeta and the UNO's Gender Agenda." *Latin American Perspectives* 23, no. 1 (1996): 67–86.

———. *Revolution in the Real World: Women and Guerrilla Movements in Latin America.* University Park: The Pennsylvania State University Press, forthcoming.

Long, Kristi. *We All Fought for Freedom: Women in Poland's Solidarity Movement.* Boulder, Colo.: Westview Press, 1996.

Luker, Kristin. *Abortion and the Politics of Motherhood.* Berkeley and Los Angeles: University of California Press, 1984.

Mason, T. David. "Women's Participation in Central American Revolutions." *Comparative Political Studies* 25, no. 1 (1992): 63–89.

Ministerio de Educación (MED). *Cinco años de educación en la revolución: 1979–1984.* Managua: MED, 1984.

Montgomery, Tommie Sue. "Liberation and Revolution: Christianity as a Subversive Activity in Central America." In *Trouble in Our Backyard: Central America and the United States in the Eighties,* edited by Martin Diskin. New York: Pantheon Books, 1983.

Morales Carazo, Jaime. *La contra.* Mexico City: Editorial Planeta, 1989.

Murguialday, Clara. *Nicaragua, revolución y feminismo.* Madrid: Editorial Revolución, 1990.

"No es lo mismo estar juntas, que ser 'revueltas.' " *La Boletina,* no. 25 (March 1996): 4–12.

Núñez, Orlando, Gloria Cardenal, Amanda Lorío, Sonia Agurto, Juan Morales, Javier Pasquier, Javier Matus, and Rubén Pasos. *La guerra y el campesinado en Nicaragua.* Managua: Editorial Ciencias Sociales, 1998.

Ortega, Zoilamérica. *Desmovilizados de la guerra en la construcción de la paz en Nicaragua.* Managua: Imprimatur Artes Gráficas, 1996.

Pardo-Maurer, R. *The Contras, 1980–1989: A Special Kind of Politics.* New York: Praeger, 1990.

Randall, Margaret. *Sandino's Daughters: Testimonies of Nicaraguan Women in Struggle.* Vancouver and Toronto: New Star Books, 1981.

———. *Gathering Rage: The Failure of Twentieth-Century Revolutions to Develop a Feminist Agenda.* New York: Monthly Review Press, 1992.

———. *Sandino's Daughters Revisited: Feminism in Nicaragua.* New Brunswick: Rutgers University Press, 1994.

Reif, Linda L. "Women in Latin American Guerrilla Movements: A Comparative Perspective." *Comparative Politics* 18, no. 2 (1986): 147–69.

Smith, Christian. *Resisting Reagan: The U.S. Central America Peace Movement.* Chicago: University of Chicago Press, 1996.

Stephen, Lynn. *Women and Social Movements in Latin America: Power from Below.* Austin: University of Texas Press, 1997.

Stephens, Beth. "Changes in the Laws Governing the Parent-Child Relationship in Post-Revolutionary Nicaragua." *Hastings International and Comparative Law Review* 12, no. 1 (1988): 137–71.

Vilas, Carlos. *The Sandinista Revolution: National Liberation and Social Transformation in Central America.* New York: Monthly Review Press, 1986.

———. *Between Earthquakes and Volcanoes: Market, State, and the Revolutions in Central America.* New York: Monthly Review Press, 1995.

Walker, Thomas W., ed. *Reagan Versus the Sandinistas: The Undeclared War on Nicaragua.* Boulder, Colo.: Westview Press, 1987.

Waylen, Georgina. "Women and Democratization: Conceptualizing Gender Relations in Transition Politics." *World Politics* (March 1994): 327–54.

Wickham-Crowley, Timothy. *Guerrillas and Revolution in Latin America.* Princeton: Princeton University Press, 1992.

Williams, Philip. *The Catholic Church and Politics in Nicaragua and Costa Rica.* Pittsburgh: University of Pittsburgh Press, 1989.

3 | The Coalición Nacional de Mujeres

An Alliance of Left-Wing Women, Right-Wing Women, and Radical Feminists in Nicaragua

María Teresa Blandón

EDITORS' INTRODUCTION

The following chapter breaks with the pattern of the other chapters in this volume, for it was written by an activist intellectual who was a central participant in the events she discusses; the other chapters, by comparison, were written by academic observers. Given the vantage point of the author, María Teresa Blandón, it is not surprising that this chapter is notably different from the others in its tone, its use of evidence, and its overt sympathies.

Blandón, who is a member of the Malinche Feminist Collective (Colectivo Feminista La Malinche) and director of the Central American Current (La Corriente Centroamericana),[1] is one of the women she describes as "the feminists."[2] As such, she is obviously more sympathetic to the position of the feminists within the National Women's Coalition (Coalición Nacional de

Translated from the Spanish by Karen Kampwirth.

1. The Malinche is a feminist collective that was founded in 1992 with the goal of influencing debate around gender issues in Nicaragua. The Central American Current was founded in 1995 by members of feminist groups in the five Central American countries, with its office and staff in Managua. By 2000, both groups continued to be active, though the Salvadoran group that had helped found the Central American Current, the Dignas, had chosen to withdraw from that regional collective so as to focus its work on feminist organizing within El Salvador.

2. In the chapter that follows, Blandón divides the Coalition's members into four categories: right-wing women, left-wing women, women's movement activists, and feminists. The reader should note that some of these terms overlap. For instance, while many women's movement activists do not identify as feminists, all feminists are part of the women's movement. The women's movement, in its broadest sense, includes all groups that are mainly composed of women and that somehow concern themselves with women's issues (on these categories, see the introduction to this volume). Also, since the vast majority of women's groups in Nicaragua can trace their roots to the Sandinista revolution of the 1970s and 1980s, they could also be categorized within the left, as Blandón sometimes does. The other women in the Coalition were from the left- and right-wing parties. Right-wing women included women from the right-wing parties who would run for office in 1996, women who held political positions in the then-

Mujeres)—the topic of her chapter—than to the positions of the other members of the coalition. This is not to say that she is unfair in her assessment of the coalition, but merely to say that she writes from a particular perspective.

While coalitions of women from widely differing political perspectives were a new phenomenon in late-twentieth-century Nicaragua, women's political activism was not. Campaigns to extend voting rights and educational opportunities to women can be traced back at least to the 1880s. By the 1920s, the first wave of feminist organizations had emerged in Nicaragua; first wave activists fought for the right to vote, along with other goals. These organizations continued to be active through the 1950s, at which point they were largely co-opted by women who sympathized with the Somoza regime.[3]

The roots of the second wave of feminism in Nicaragua are often traced to 1961, the year in which the Sandinista Front for National Liberation (Frente Sandinista de Liberación Nacional, or FSLN) was founded. This is the period with which María Teresa Blandón begins her overview of the women's movement. In part, this choice may reflect the fact that her own personal history closely parallels this national history.[4] But perhaps more significant, late-twentieth-century Nicaraguan feminists consistently date the beginning of the women's movement to the 1960s, not to the 1880s or 1920s.

Through the FSLN, thousands of women were mobilized as guerrilla combatants and as members of the broader revolutionary coalition (including student groups, unions, and women's groups, often called "popular organizations" by Nicaraguans) that provided critical support for the guerrillas. After the 1979 fall of the Somoza dictatorship, women (and men) in the popular organizations took on the task of reconstructing the country, building the revolution, defending the country from the Contras, and—all too often, in the view of many women—promoting the interests of the FSLN

---

outgoing government of Violeta Barrios de Chamorro, and women from the few nongovernmental women's organizations that identified with the right.

3. For more on this history, see González, this volume.

4. María Teresa Blandón was born in 1961 in the small town of Matiguas in the province of Matagalpa; her father worked as a farmer, and her mother was a teacher. Her early experiences were unusual in that her mother valued education—for girls as well as boys—very highly, and strongly encouraged all her children to prepare themselves for professions. But her earliest experiences were shared by many in other ways. She first was introduced to politics as an activist in Christian youth groups and then, at the age of sixteen, she became involved with the FSLN, working with student groups in various forms of protest. After the overthrow of the dictator, she held a number of positions within the revolutionary coalition, in the FSLN, in the Ministry of the Interior, and in the rural workers' labor union (Asociación de Trabajadores del Campo, or ATC). Like many others, over the course of the 1980s she became increasingly disillusioned with the verticalism of the FSLN, and was one of the people who founded the autonomous feminist movement.

over their own interests in challenging gender inequality. In response, some women began to seek autonomy from the FSLN over the course of the 1980s, first within the women's secretariats of the labor unions and then, by the end of the decade, in a few independent women's organizations.

The FSLN lost the 1990 election, and the Contra war ended shortly thereafter; many of the women who had first been mobilized through the revolutionary coalition at last felt free to demand autonomy from the FSLN. The early 1990s were marked by a series of new autonomous women's organizations, women's issues networks, feminist study groups, and well-attended feminist conferences. By the mid-1990s, the autonomous feminist movement in Nicaragua was the most prominent one in Central America—and one of the most significant in Latin America as a whole.[5] It was at that point that many of the newly independent feminists began to seek alliances with women who did not share their leftist roots. This search for allies led to the formation of the National Women's Coalition, a group created for the 1996 electoral campaign that presented what it called a "Minimum Agenda," or series of women's demands, to all the political parties. María Teresa Blandón's chapter analyzes the challenges inherent in such coalition building.

■ ■ ■

One notable aspect of recent Nicaraguan history was the role of women in the struggles against the Somoza dictatorship and in support of the student movements of the 1960s and 1970s. Those political groups were led by young students who were inspired by the ideals of the Sandinista movement and linked to the clandestine structures that were organized by the Sandinista Front for National Liberation (Frente Sandinista de Liberación Nacional, or FSLN). The Sandinista women's movement was first born in the political battles of the 1960s and 1970s.

5. On second wave feminism in Nicaragua, see Florence Babb, *After the Revolution: Mapping Gender and Cultural Politics in Neoliberal Nicaragua* (Austin: University of Texas Press, forthcoming); Norma Stoltz Chinchilla, "Feminism, Revolution, and Democratic Transitions in Nicaragua," in *The Women's Movement in Latin America,* ed. Jane S. Jaquette (Boulder, Colo.: Westview Press, 1994); Ana Criquillón, "The Nicaraguan Women's Movement: Feminist Reflections from Within," in *The New Politics of Survival: Grassroots Movements in Central America,* ed. Minor Sinclair (New York: Monthly Review Press, 1995); Karen Kampwirth, "Confronting Adversity with Experience: The Emergence of Feminism in Nicaragua," *Social Politics* 3, no. 2/3 (1996); Sofía Montenegro, ed., *Movimiento de mujeres en Centroamérica* (Managua: Programa Regional La Corriente, 1997); Clara Murguialday, *Nicaragua, revolución y feminismo (1977–1989)* (Madrid: Editorial Revolución, 1990); Margaret Randall, *Sandino's Daughters Revisited: Feminism in Nicaragua* (New Brunswick: Rutgers University Press, 1994) and *Gathering Rage: The Failure of Twentieth-Century Revolutions to Develop a Feminist Agenda* (New York: Monthly Review Press, 1992).

With the triumph of the Sandinista revolution on 19 July 1979, the first organization within the Sandinista women's movement—the Association of Women for National Concerns (Asociación de Mujeres Ante la Problematica Nacional, or AMPRONAC)—changed its name. The new organization, the Luisa Amanda Espinoza Association of Nicaraguan Women (Asociación de Mujeres Nicaragüenses Luisa Amanda Espinoza, or AMNLAE), was a mass organization of women with a formal membership, a leadership structure, and goals that tried to combine demands for women's rights and dignity with demands that were given to the organization by its vanguard, the FSLN. Ironically, AMNLAE ended up as the main organization through which women could fight for some of their specific rights as women and, at the same time, as a roadblock that forced women to put the brakes on some of their demands as a way of showing their loyalty to the revolution, which they understood as synonymous with loyalty to the FSLN.

The broad-based women's movement that we now know emerged from the very heart of AMNLAE and from the demands of women who were affiliated with the farm workers' unions and the professional associations, all with significant support from leftist intellectual women who represented the more critical currents within leftist thought. This process of consciousness raising and radicalizing of various female Sandinista leaders inevitably led to ideological, political, and grassroots divisions within the Sandinista party as well as within AMNLAE. Those divisions would, in turn, eventually allow women activists to regroup.

At the end of the 1980s and beginning of the 1990s, there was an intense process of critical debate among feminists, leaders of labor unions, women in professional organizations, and the formal leaders of AMNLAE. As a result of those debates—which were often heated—a new alliance emerged among the women's movement leaders who rejected the tutelage of AMNLAE. As a result of this new alliance, specific women's demands reemerged.

The leaders who represented the unions organized a long period of consultation among Sandinista women, including women who were formally affiliated with AMNLAE, with the goal of reaching agreements about the sort of women's movement we needed. Through this process of consultation, a new movement was born—a movement that would be built on the basis of autonomy.

The first half of the 1990s, which coincided with the government of President Violeta Barrios de Chamorro (1990–97), was a period of consolidation of the broad-based women's movement. During those years, the emerging autonomous women's movement openly broke with AMNLAE, and as a result, it rejected the notion of the FSLN as a vanguard organization. Women's initiatives flourished around a wide variety of themes. The discourse within the movement opened up, very slowly giving way to the recognition that women have varied interests. The new leadership made significant advances in its consideration of new schools of thought. New women's organizations and feminist institutions were created that had greater political and financial capacities, and coordinating bodies were created for the women's movement that considered women's own interests and that took on the goal of influencing national politics in a clear way. The autonomous women's movement began to have an influence at an international level.

One measure of the success of the efforts to consolidate the autonomous women's movement was the formation of the first pluralistic alliance of women in the context of the 1996 election campaign. That grouping, which was known as the National Women's Coalition (Coalición Nacional de Mujeres), united women from extremely wide-ranging ideological, political, and social backgrounds.

What Made the National Women's Coalition Possible?

A number of political factors allowed for the formation of the National Women's Coalition, which made its first public appearance in March 1996. Foremost among these factors was the construction of the autonomous women's movement, which resulted from the autonomy struggle of the late 1980s and early 1990s in which activists were highly conscious of the diversity within the movement itself. That movement, with its renewed leadership, was to have a significant presence in society, especially with respect to the state.

The Coalition was born in a context in which the autonomous women's movement could count on coordinating bodies that were more or less stable. Those bodies helped movement leaders act on the goal of intervening in national politics so as to improve women's conditions in all aspects of life. One way that we in the autonomous women's movement sought to meet that goal was by opening up a dialogue with other social movements and with state agencies.

These efforts to reach out politically could be seen in a variety of ways in the years leading up to the formation of the National Women's Coalition. For instance, the National Feminist Committee (Comité Nacional Feminista), along with other groups within the women's movement, formulated various political proposals. Another coordinating body, the Women's Health Network (Red de Mujeres por la Salud), participated in a number of meetings with state officials. In 1995, members of the women's movement were active participants in the national consultation leading to the reform of the Constitution. Finally, members of the women's movement participated in the international conferences organized by the United Nations to improve women's conditions, including the Conference on Population and Development in 1994 and the Fourth World Conference on Women in 1995.

All those changes created the political preconditions that the women's movement needed if it was going to have an influence beyond the grassroots base of the Sandinista party. Once those conditions existed, some of us suggested the idea of forming a National Coalition of Women with the goal of having an influence on the electoral process in 1996.

The women who originally proposed this project were all affiliated with nongovernmental organizations that, in one way or another, had established ties with the recently created Nicaraguan Women's Institute (Instituto Nicaragüense de la Mujer, or INIM).[6] The fact that the women in charge of INIM did not have experience working for women's rights was actually an advantage, from the perspective of many in the women's movement. A number of women's movement activists, from their positions within the existing coordinating spaces, sought to reach out to these government officials, offering them information with the hope of increasing their sensitivity to gender issues.

Certainly, the women who held leadership positions in the government or in right-wing parties needed to connect to the women's movement in order to participate in the election campaign from a position of greater strength, not just for themselves personally, but also for their respective political parties. Similarly, we feminists needed this broad coalition so that we could extend our alliances and make sure that our demands were included in public debates and party platforms.

At the same time that we in the autonomous feminist movement were interested in building alliances in preparation for the 1996 election, some women on the right were also interested in alliance building. So women in

6. INIM traced its roots to the Institute for Research on Women (Instituto de Investigaciones de la Mujer, also known as INIM), which had been founded by the Sandinista administration in the 1980s. After the Sandinistas lost the 1990 election, INIM ceased to have a clear identity for about two years: the library of the institute passed on to the women's movement, while the government agency opened and closed in a series of locations. By 1992, INIM (which changed its name but kept the acronym) once again had strong government funding and a stable location until it was absorbed, in 1997, by the Ministry of the Family (Ministerio de la Familia), newly created by the Alemán administration.—Eds.

the government (and in the nongovernmental organizations that were closest to the government) contacted one of the feminist collectives that best represented the movement. They did so for two reasons: first, the feminist collective could provide philosophical and ideological input for the formation of the Coalition, and second, it could serve as a bridge between their groups and the women's movement. The women who worked for the government, including those of the Women's Institute, were in charge of "convincing" the right-wing women that they should participate in the first event—one of a series of debates. During that event, a very thorough analysis of the situation of women in Nicaragua was presented.

More than seventy women participated in the first debates. They included radical feminists, women's movement activists who did not necessarily identify as feminists, women who held high-level positions within the state, Congresswomen, Sandinistas, anti-Sandinista activists, former Sandinistas, Conservatives, Social-Christians, and representatives of the governing party. In short, women from quite divergent ideological positions and political experiences came together for the debates.

The feminists made a number of philosophical, ideological, and political observations to start the debates. The document that served as a stepping stone for those debates had been written by Sofía Montenegro, a well-known feminist journalist. In that document, Montenegro synthesized a series of previous documents that she and other feminists had written that had already played important roles in building the autonomous women's movement. The following section is a summary of Montenegro's document.

On the Concept of Feminism

Synthesis on previous feminist documents

We feminists would like to establish a women's pact around a feminist proposal. We understand feminism as a project of questioning and challenging the political-social system. It is a project that would transform gender relations as well as a political doctrine that creates the basis for the construction of a movement of empowered women. Feminism as a proposal would require new ethics. It would mean a moral proposal with unprecedented emancipatory dimensions, since it would require the democratization of public and private spaces.

Power feminism is based on the assumption that we women are capable of exercising power in a way that is autonomous, responsible, and inclusive. Feminism would reject sexism without rejecting men, since the emancipation of human beings does not mean eliminating men or disempowering them; rather, it means that we women should also be empowered. Power feminism insists that every person has a right to autonomy, and that includes people's right to live out their sexual orientations.

Feminism demands that women be full participants in the social contract, that they be candidates to elected office, that they aspire to occupy public space as full citizens, equal to men. It recognizes that sexual equality will not guarantee that politics be carried out in a different way, though that would be desirable, and we should support those changes through our movement.

Feminism recognizes that women cannot fully participate in politics without autonomy. We women need power to be able to fully exercise our citizenship rights and believe that a collective of empowered women would allow women to get that power. The women's movement needs leaders who are reliable and committed to these goals. As part of the strategy toward autonomy, we need to elaborate our own agenda and put the demands of women out for public debate. That is the way toward the construction of a new culture, a new set of ethics, a new utopia.

Building consensus does not mean imposing ideas. Rather, it means being tolerant and respectful of differences. It means building bridges between women in the women's movement and women in the political parties, elaborating a common agenda without disqualifying any independent women, regardless of whether they identify themselves as feminists.

Those proposals were part of the general agreement that the participants reached, and for many, the agreement guaranteed that there would be a healthy, respectful, and constructive debate. Comments made during the debate expressed some of the concerns of women on the right and on the left, as well as the concerns of women from the movement. Those comments are summarized here.

- Up until now, political parties have not had the opportunity or the conditions to develop themselves fully. But so far, they have been the only means to power. Through parties, we can make women's struggle for their rights more visible. So there is no contradiction between women participating in a political party and maintaining their own identities.
- This gathering should help women untangle themselves from patriarchal captivity. That is, it will help us search for common ground from which to construct our own platform, using a different voice, allowing us to negotiate our proposal with the political parties.

comments from
during debate

- We really should think more deeply about the demand for quotas for women in political offices. Power should not be exercised just for its own sake. We still need to do more thinking about our attitudes toward, and conceptions of, power itself.
- One major question that we need to address is which women should be promoted as candidates for the political parties and which should run as independents, both for mayoral positions and for Congressional offices.
- One of the problems with female leadership is that women are only recognized as leaders when they hold formal offices. To address this, we need to work on constructing a new political culture, a new set of ethics that recognizes our differences and still looks for the issues that unite us. That way we can create a new politics, leaving behind our old prejudices. This politics would require intuitive, thoughtful, respectful, and nonaggressive leaders.
- We feminists do not seek to get rid of representation itself; we seek to promote solidarity among women around their common interests. Feminism is a radical proposal and the feminist movement cannot speak for the whole women's movement. It is important that feminists are not the only ones who elaborate our proposals, since the social movement activists also have some of their own ideas.

The first step was reaching an agreement about how we understood the national context and what philosophical and ideological goals we would promote through the initiative. Next, the participants were asked to commit to carrying out a participatory process that would involve consulting women both within the women's movement and within the parties as a way of increasing women's participation in public politics. The results of that agreement are summarized in the following section.

Strategies for Political Participation

- To create a contingent of women in positions of power who share an agenda developed though a diverse and consensual process by women of the political parties and the autonomous feminist groups. The basis of that agenda would be the construction of a new set of ethics, recognizing our gender subordination and the need for us to join together to fight for our demands.
- To admit that we women need to participate in political parties, as well as run as independents, in order to get access to public office.
- To broaden the debate around women's issues to include public policy.

Without a clear debate about politics itself, we will never be able to promote our candidates or our agenda.

- To construct alliances between women of the parties and women of the movement, recognizing that the party women need the women's movement, which fights for the citizenship rights of all women, and that they also need the feminists, who provide intellectual support for those struggles.
- To make sure that the new thought, which considers interests of gender, class, and ethnicity, does not get lost at the elite level. Instead, this new thought should be used to help make compromises and build alliances with other sectors.
- To propose concrete goals that candidates can take with them to the mayors' offices and city councils. Furthermore, we should negotiate with the leaders of the parties to make sure that more women become mayors and Congresswomen.
- To support leaders who recognize female subordination and who are committed to try to change the existing relations between women and men.

During our debates, the overarching problem was always that the leaders of the movement and the women of the political parties did not trust each other, a problem that was rooted in their past histories. In response to this lack of trust, an ethical framework was devised that clearly established the moral obligations to which we would all commit. Once the framework in which we would work had been secured, the design of the Minimum Agenda was fairly simple.

The Minimum Agenda

The Minimum Agenda was divided into five sections: Ethical Framework, Politics and the State, Sociocultural Issues, Economics, and Labor Legislation. In general terms, those categories reflected the women's issues about which we could all agree. Within those categories, the whole debate over women's problems and demands could be fit—from domestic and sexual violence to sexual inequality and subordination in all aspects of life. Through the Minimum Agenda, we showed that we needed to construct better means of communication between civil society and the state, to ensure that public policies responded to women's concerns.

The National Women's Coalition presented the Minimum Agenda on 8 March 1996. That was the first time that 8 March, International Women's Day, was celebrated by women from such a wide variety of political schools of thought. The slogan "Diverse, Different, and United" linked a wide array of people: two thousand women, the diplomatic corps, presidents of a number of political parties, members of President Barrios de Chamorro's cabinet, Congressional representatives (both men and women), and representatives of the social movements. Together, they participated in a landmark in the political history of our country.

Overview of the Results, Accomplishments, Limitations, and Impact of the Coalition

It may be that the Women's Coalition was the most heterogeneous political experiment carried out by any social movement in Nicaragua in the twentieth century. It certainly was the first time that leftist women, radical feminists, and women from the traditional political class (otherwise known as the right) all came together. The formation of the Coalition was a turning point, since it was at that moment that women, who up until then had always been the victims of patriarchal pacts, decided to make a pact of their own around their common interests. Through the pact, they were able to negotiate with those who held political power, establishing a precedent in the ongoing efforts to depolarize and democratize society and its structures.

The feminists were to play a key role in the setting of this precedent by defining the conceptual framework, contributing philosophically and ideologically, strategizing, proposing issues, and—finally—developing the ethical framework that allowed us to work together. But even though significant efforts were made to guarantee that the basic terms of the agreement were clear to all participants, there were a few unresolved problems that had a negative impact on relations within the Coalition and between the Coalition and the women's movement. Those unresolved issues included:

- Whether quotas for women's participation in politics were a good idea.
- The relationship between women in the women's movement and female candidates from the different parties.
- Whether the Coalition was capable of defining concrete goals in the case of local as well as national elected officials.

- The future relationship between the women's movement and the Coalition.
- Women's reproductive rights, and especially abortion, to which brief references were made over the course of the debates.

Despite the fact that we were not able to address every problem, the general feeling was that we had succeeded in leading an event of great importance for Nicaraguan women. That euphoric feeling often promoted great human warmth between right-wing women and feminists with roots in the Sandinista movement, women who had been deeply divided for most of the twentieth century (see Chaps. 1 and 2 of this volume).

It was in the Coalition that many of us first talked about our personal histories, about our experiences during the 1980s, the decade of the revolution. Through those conversations, we often discovered that we had experiences that were quite similar to those of women in the mixed-gender organizations. Those gatherings had the effect of reducing the distance between women; furthermore, the old feelings of political or ideological antagonism were replaced by mutual respect.

The seven months that followed the official public presentation of the Coalition, from March to October 1996 (when the election was held), were very intense. From the perspective of the public's view of the Coalition, the group's most important activities were

- the elaboration and wide distribution of the Minimum Agenda;
- the presentation of the Minimum Agenda to the directors of all the political parties, with the exception of the Constitutionalist Liberal Party (Partido Liberal Constitucionalista, or PLC),[7] which refused to meet with a delegation from the Coalition;
- the press conferences during key moments of the electoral campaign; and
- the public tribute to all the female candidates, held at the close of the electoral campaign.

The National Women's Coalition definitely had an impact in the 1996 election. But what of its role in the medium term? To address that question,

7. The Nationalist Liberal Party (Partido Liberal Nacionalista) was the party of the Somozas, who ruled between 1936 and 1979. In October of 1996, Arnoldo Alemán ran for president on the ticket of a party with a similar name, the PLC; both he and the PLC emerged as the big winners in that election. While all the other major parties supported the Minimum Agenda, the significant successes of the Women's Coalition were tempered by the fact that the single biggest party refused to even meet with Coalition members.—Eds.

one needs to consider the results of the effort, considering each of the groups that participated in the process.

Difficulties Within the Women's Coalition

One source of difficulty was that the founders of the Coalition emphasized two different things. On the one hand, the party women who aspired to public office wanted the Coalition to proselytize in favor of their candidates. On the other hand, we feminists were inclined to prioritize other goals, such as broadening political discourse during the election campaign. Additionally, we sought to influence the political parties, to pressure them to support the Minimum Agenda, and to create lists of candidates that included women in more prominent roles.

In addition, party women wanted to use the Women's Coalition events to strengthen their respective parties and to promote their own candidates. So in the public tribute to the candidates that was sponsored by the Coalition, party women displayed the symbols of their parties, which was in violation of an agreement that they had made previously.

Yet another source of tension was party candidates' fears of being seen publicly in a clear alliance with radical feminists. So the candidates tried to restrict the presence of the feminists at the public events, which only weakened the prior agreement that they would be mutually respectful of one another. As if that were not enough, some government officials attempted to present the Coalition as if it were an accomplishment of the governmental Women's Institute, acting alone. That ended up leaving a bad taste in the mouths of the feminists and the women from the other parties.

One of the most heated debates was over the scope of the Coalition. Did the Coalition represent the whole women's movement, or was it simply one of the coordinating spaces within the movement? For some party women, including the government officials, the Coalition represented the whole movement, and it therefore had the right to speak for all women's movement activists. For others, the Coalition was not part of the movement, and so Coalition members did not have to support all the other initiatives that the movement promoted. From the perspective of the feminists, it was clear that even though the majority of women's movement organizations had signed the Minimum Agenda, many were wary of the role that the Coalition would play.

After the first stages of the Coalition's work, some of the Coalition members tried to ignore the existence of the women's movement and everything it had done in previous years. Some of the right-wing women spoke as if the Coalition had originated in their struggles to gain public power and to play a role in electoral politics. That attitude was probably rooted in their strongly felt anti-Sandinismo. If they acknowledged the fact that the women's movement predated their work in the Coalition, then they would implicitly be giving some credit to the Sandinista movement. Other women were simply unwilling to share any credit; they thought only of the short-term gains to be made as they sought elected office.

For their part, few Sandinista leaders chose to participate in the Coalition. Those who did participate in a consistent way tended to keep a low profile and a flexible attitude. They were accepting and respectful of the ideological leadership of the feminists. At the same time, they managed to use the Coalition to promote their own interests, including their negotiations within the Sandinista party, to get assurances that women would be a significant presence on the slates of candidates for electoral offices.

Difficulties in the Women's Movement

Even after signing the Minimum Agenda, many leaders of the women's movement continued to distrust the party women, especially those on the right, suggesting implicitly (and sometimes explicitly) that the right-wing party women were only involved in order to solicit votes for their candidates. They did not distrust Sandinista leaders in such an open way, which is natural, considering the political roots that were shared by activists from the women's movement and the Sandinista party.

In the day-to-day work of the Coalition during the electoral campaign, there were only a few feminists—almost all from the same collective—who actively participated in developing proposals, doing outreach, clarifying working norms, and fundraising in order to cover operating costs. Other leaders of the women's movement only participated in the Coalition's most important public events. So when it was time to make decisions, the absence of many women's movement activists in the day-to-day activities created a balance of power that did not favor the feminists.

It seems that many women's movement leaders were paralyzed by fear—not just a fear that the right would win the election, but also that those right-wing women would then take the place of the movement itself. A few other women still needed to work out the issue of their continued ties to the

Sandinista party. And yet another factor was that many of these women were not fully convinced that pacts like this one, pacts between women, were really strategically important.

Impact of the Coalition on the Political Parties

In a number of ways, the Coalition had a positive impact. For instance, the vast majority of the parties promised to include the demands made in the Minimum Agenda within their own programs. In addition, all the top leaders of the parties included references to women's rights, in one way or another, in their speeches.

Positive

Those facts make it possible to claim that in some way the Minimum Agenda helped teach the politicians to "read." It also had an impact on members of the most conservative sectors of society, who—for the first time—had to confront an agenda that was put together by women who, due to their autonomy, were able to be active citizens. Another notable aspect of the Minimum Agenda is that despite the fact that it did not directly denounce neoliberalism, it implied (and would require) a complete rethinking of the established socioeconomic model.

The majority of the parties included more women in their national and local slates of candidates than had been the case in the past. Nonetheless, those percentages were still quite low. Only two of the twenty-three parties that participated in the election ran a woman as their candidate for president,[8] while another two of the twenty-three ran women as their candidates for vice president.[9]

More ♀

Twenty-two percent of the candidates for representative to the National Assembly, 95 out of 435, were women. But the effective percentage was much smaller: only 11, or 15 percent of the female candidates, were in the first three positions on each slate—the only ones with the real possibility of being elected.[10] Of the 410 candidates for the Central American Parliament,

8. The parties that chose women as their presidential candidates were the Popular Conservative Alliance (Alianza Popular Conservadora) and the Party for Central American Unity (Partido Unionista Centroamérica).

9. The parties that chose women as their vice-presidential candidates were the National Project (Proyecto Nacional) and the Party for Central American Integration (Partido Integracionista de América Central).

10. Elected offices in Nicaragua are determined using a combination of presidential and parliamentary systems. While individual candidates rather than parties run for president, as in a presidential system, individuals do not run for the National Assembly, Nicaragua's unicameral Congress. Instead, voters choose from slates determined by each party, as in a parliamentary system.—Eds.

102 (about 24 percent) were women, but in the first three positions on the slates, there were only 8 women, not even 10 percent of the pool of female candidates. The Liberal party's slate for the Managua mayoral race included a male and a female candidate.

Some party leaders responded suspiciously to the creation of the Coalition. They responded especially poorly to the new competitive, self-confident attitudes of some of the women in their parties, and in a few cases they "punished" them for those attitudes, taking away their candidacies for office or their formal leadership positions within the party. This happened in the cases of the Party of the Nicaraguan Resistance (Partido de la Resistencia Nicaragüense), the National Conservative Party (Partido Nacional Conservador), and the Social-Christian Party (Partido Social-cristiano).

The Sandinista party leaders responded more positively, but there were limits to their support for our agenda. They had promised that 30 percent of the candidates for offices would be women, but when it came time to put together the slates of candidates for parliament, the party leaders maneuvered to put women in the lower positions on the slate, leaving men in more favorable spots. It was only because of the last-minute intervention of some female Sandinista leaders that the situation was partially reversed.

Results of the Election

Of the 145 mayors who were elected in October 1996, 9 were women; 23 of the 145 vice-mayors were women. The number of women in the National Assembly went down, in comparison with the previous legislature. At that time (between 1990 and 1996), 17 of the 92 representatives (or 20 percent) were women, while only 10 of the 93 who were elected to the National Assembly in 1996, or 10.75 percent, were women. Finally, within the executive branch, headed by President Arnoldo Alemán, only one ministry—that of Health—was headed by a woman.

Comparing the composition of both the National Assembly and the mayors' offices in the 1990s with their composition in the decade of the 1980s shows that there was a loss in women's representation. There are a number of reasons for those changes. In the first place, the two parties that won the most offices, especially the Constitutionalist Liberal Party, had reduced the number of female candidates on their lists. And even though the electoral law in effect since the 1990 election has permitted candidates to run as independents, the polarization during the electoral campaign led the majority of voters to choose between the candidates of the strongest parties, candidates who were mainly men. The women who ran as independents usually did not have enough financing to launch serious campaigns. Additionally, those women who were included on the lists of the small parties had no chance of being elected.

Another issue that might have played a role in shaping the perceptions of voters was the dominating presence in the campaign of the two top candidates (Daniel Ortega and Arnoldo Alemán), both men who never really tried to encourage women to participate in public office. To the contrary: Alemán, in particular, used a discourse that reinforced the idea that the role of women was to maintain stable families. Finally, although their criticisms were veiled, the candidates of both the FSLN and the PLC suggested that the outgoing president, doña Violeta Barrios de Chamorro, had done a poor job in overseeing the economic policies of the country.

Aftermath of the Election

Probably one of the Coalition's greatest successes was that most of the press gave significant coverage to gender issues during the campaign. But the fact that women fell behind as a result of the election was disheartening for some candidates. Others thought that such a response only confirmed that those candidates had had self-serving motivations for participating in the Coalition. Some tried to blame the Coalition for the setback, claiming that it had happened because they had not been able to give sufficient support to their candidates.

In the months following the election, the Coalition was no longer able to attract its former crowds, nor was it able to promote its positions as publicly as before. Deprived of the immediate goal of getting women into elected offices, and riddled with internal tensions, the Coalition focused its energies on momentary activities that did not have much of an impact.

It was not until 1997, when the National Dialogue (Diálogo Nacional) was promoted by President Alemán, that the Coalition again mobilized its forces to participate in this event, one that was crucial for national politics. At that time, some party leaders and prominent feminists were called back to revive the Coalition.

In the process of thinking about what positions the Coalition would take within the Dialogue, we clarified the relationship between the Coalition and the women's movement. Those of the Coalition sought a place at the table of the Dialogue, and the feminists organized their own representation along with the women's movement. Although the women of the Coalition and the women's movement activists tried to come to an agreement about their strategies with respect to the Dialogue, it was clear that—for reasons both political and social—a separation was in the making.

The debate over the Ministry of the Family was another event that confirmed the separation between the Coalition and the women's movement. The women's movement criticized the ideological and moralistic character of the proposed Ministry and demanded, instead of a quasi-religious Ministry, that the Nicaraguan Women's Institute should be made into a Ministry. In contrast, the members of the Coalition defended the Women's Institute while remaining silent on the question of a new Ministry.

Looking Back on the Experience: Common Ground

Feminists, left-wing activists, and right-wing activists share an individual will that led all of us—by different paths—to transgress the traditional roles assigned to women. We share a belief that we have the right to take control of our own lives.

We share the experience of having participated in organizations that involved both men and women—parties, labor unions, associations—and having been placed in the minority, due to our gender. That experience was very useful in allowing us to develop certain skills that the majority of women had not been able to acquire. We all felt the benefits as well as the costs of being seen as particularly strong, capable (and therefore dangerous) women.

We share the feeling of being backed into a corner, stuck between those roles that we are supposed to fulfill as women (especially the roles of wife and mother) and our own internal awareness that we have the right to be fully empowered as citizens and individuals. This contradiction implies that we also share the experience of being socially sanctioned, categorized as "public women."

We share the vices of acting compulsively maternal in the public sphere: always caring for others, prioritizing the interests of others, unconditionally giving others our all, idealizing our causes, and not setting limits between our "selves" and others. One similarity that probably will only become clear to some women after they become conscious of gender discrimination and its causes is that we all had similar experiences in our relations with men in the public sphere. These experiences have included discrimination, sexual harassment, feeling used, being undervalued as women, having our work ignored, and being assigned secondary tasks in support of men's work.

Looking Back on the Experience: Points of Disagreement

With respect to the way in which politics is carried out, women on the right and on the left, in particular, found that their experiences had often coincided. Both groups of women tended to communicate in a veiled way, one that covered up real conflicts. In contrast, the feminists tended to communicate in a way that, though sometimes harsh, was more direct.

The right- and left-wing women favored agreements that were informal and friendly, while the feminists tended to prefer "hard-core politics", with respect to debate style, openness about disagreements, and collective agreements. While the women on the left and the right were willing to compromise when negotiating with other social actors (and especially with the state), the feminists tried to stick to principles.

The feminists and the left-wing women tended to hold similar attitudes toward money: both felt a degree of guilt for being paid for their work, and tended to see volunteer work as proof of one's convictions and one's commitment to a cause. On the other hand, right-wing women were more self-confident in this sense, thinking that their work should earn monetary compensation. Those differences were rooted not only in the differences in class backgrounds but also in different experiences as political activists.

Many of our differences were grounded, to a large extent, in the myths of femininity[11] that are promoted in our patriarchal society. Though they are myths, many of them do have an objective material base with tangible effects.

11. When I speak of myths of femininity, I am talking about those characteristics and behaviors that all women are supposed to adopt, since they are consistent with our womanly natures. Based on these myths, most people assume as a basic truth that we women are more emotional than rational, weak in character, insecure, dependent, unstable, and always willing to sacrifice ourselves for the good of others. Another dimension of the stereotypical view of women is that we are able to satisfy our womanly whims through flirting and seduction. Even in the world of formal politics, many men (and also women) assume that women typically use such means to reach positions of power. In fact, there are women who think and act in that way, but there is no evidence that women usually use such means to attain positions of power.

In the cases in which we are viewed as being more aggressive than stereotypical women, we are portrayed as being extremely aggressive, competitive, and prone to infighting with other women. As a result, the message that hides behind this apparent image of strength is that we women are not capable of keeping ourselves balanced, and as a result we are the sorts of people who cannot be trusted with important public responsibilities.

Class differences played themselves out in various ways within the Coalition, including differences in standard of living, personal attitudes, access to politically powerful people, and degrees of sensitivity to social problems. Despite these conflicts, the radical feminists, left-wing women, and right-wing women all agreed that work for the poorest of the poor should be given priority. But even though we agreed on this issue, we approached the task of privileging the poor differently: the left-wing women approached the issue in a populist and maternalistic way, the right-wing women in a Christian and charitable way, and the feminists in an empowering way.

Class differences also shaped the extent to which participants had developed themselves intellectually. During the decade of the Sandinista revolution (1979–90), the radical feminists and left-wing activists had devoted more time and effort to political and intellectual activities than the majority of the right-wing women had. The right-wing women who spent that decade trapped in exile had tended to spend their time on personal activities that were consistent with traditional feminine roles, such as taking care of their families, working on their personal appearance, promoting social and religious activities, and doing charitable work.

Ideologically, there were great differences within the group with respect to levels of consciousness and sensitivity to the impact of patriarchy. The feminists arrived with significant theoretical baggage, while the left-wing activists maintained a dualistic position that ended up being confusing, and the right-wing activists had only begun to think about gender issues. So it was fortunate that the feminists were willing to work hard to strengthen the women's movement as a space from which to empower women.

Even though the National Women's Coalition represented a significant advance in the development of autonomy and democracy within the Nicaraguan women's movement, it left a number of issues unresolved, issues that women from all political backgrounds need to address. We need to learn how to build political bridges ethically that will help free us of our distrust of others. We need to learn how to facilitate communication. And, ultimately, we must learn how to be more effective in our collective political actions.

BIBLIOGRAPHY

Babb, Florence. *After the Revolution: Mapping Gender and Cultural Politics in Neo-liberal Nicaragua.* Austin: University of Texas Press, forthcoming.

Chinchilla, Norma Stoltz. "Feminism, Revolution, and Democratic Transitions in Nicaragua." In *The Women's Movement in Latin America,* edited by Jane S. Jaquette. Boulder, Colo.: Westview Press, 1994.

Criquillón, Ana. "The Nicaraguan Women's Movement: Feminist Reflections from Within." In *The New Politics of Survival: Grassroots Movements in Central America,* edited by Minor Sinclair. New York: Monthly Review Press, 1995.

Kampwirth, Karen. "Confronting Adversity with Experience: The Emergence of Feminism in Nicaragua." *Social Politics* 3, no. 2/3 (1996): 136–58.

Montenegro, Sofía, ed. *Movimiento de mujeres en Centroamérica.* Managua: Programa Regional La Corriente, 1997.

Murguialday, Clara. *Nicaragua, revolución y feminismo (1977–1989).* Madrid: Editorial Revolución, 1990.

Randall, Margaret. *Gathering Rage: The Failure of Twentieth-Century Revolutions to Develop a Feminist Agenda.* New York: Monthly Review Press, 1992.

———. *Sandino's Daughters Revisited: Feminism in Nicaragua.* New Brunswick: Rutgers University Press, 1994.

4 | Right- and Left-Wing Women in Post-Revolutionary El Salvador

Feminist Autonomy and Cross-Political Alliance
Building for Gender Equality

Patricia Hipsher

El Salvador's feminist movement has become a leading political actor in recent Salvadoran history. Since its emergence in the late 1980s and early 1990s, the movement has advanced an agenda that includes political reforms in the areas of domestic violence, education, labor rights, child support, and women's political participation. It has won many of its political victories partly because of its ability to establish strategic alliances with right-wing women in the Legislative Assembly. That left-wing feminists and right-wing female legislators are able to find common political ground, coordinating their actions to achieve reforms for greater gender equality, is remarkable. During the 1980s, these same women saw each other as political enemies. Most of the women involved in today's feminist movement served as guerrillas and political activists for the revolutionary forces that sought the overthrow of right-wing military rule, a regime supported by women of the political right.

This chapter will examine the complex relationship between feminism and the political left and right in El Salvador during the period 1980–98. To address this subject, I will pose two sets of questions. First, what is the relationship between feminism and the political left? How—and to what extent—has the political left facilitated the emergence of feminist movement organizations, and in what ways has it inhibited the movement's autonomous development? Second, what are the possibilities for (and limits to) alliance formation between left-wing feminists and right-wing women around questions of gender equality?

In this chapter I argue that El Salvador's feminist movement has been shaped by women's historical role in the leftist revolutionary struggle against right-wing dictatorship. Even as women's participation in leftist revolutionary

activities allowed the Salvadoran feminist movement to emerge, this participation also placed constraints on the movement. For one thing, the historically close relationship between the revolutionary left and feminism in El
Salvador has served as a major obstacle to organizations' efforts to win autonomy. In addition, the movement's struggle for autonomy and against internal
sectarianism, a product of revolutionary leftist politics, has inhibited the development of an energetic, unified movement. And the movement's historical ties with the left have placed limits on its capacity to create alliances with
women of the political right.

I also maintain that the possibilities for cross-class, cross-political coalition building between feminists and right-wing women in the struggle for
gender equality largely depend on the issue at hand. Feminists and right-
wing women have been able to form strategic, temporary alliances around
issues that relate to political rights and to women's roles as wives and mothers; however, they have not managed to find common ground on issues
that touch on economic and sexual rights. In this sense, the possibilities for
coalition building exist, but coalitions are more likely to form around issues
that affect *all* women to some extent (regardless of class) and that are not
considered culturally or morally sensitive.

I will develop these arguments in three parts. The first part will present
the historical background of the Salvadoran feminist movement. This section
will discuss the opportunities presented by leftist parties and the revolutionary political context for the emergence of feminist movement organizations
in the 1980s and early 1990s. The second part will discuss the implications
of this historical legacy for the movement's ongoing development. There, I
will examine the efforts by leftist parties to prevent an autonomous movement from developing, the consequences of the movement's leftist origins
for its internal unity, and the debates within the movement over supporting
female political candidates in the 1997 and 1999 elections. In the third part,
I will address the potential for alliances between leftist feminists and right-
wing women. This final section will assess the movement's efforts to build
cross-class, cross-political alliances in the Legislative Assembly on several
feminist policy issues.

The evidence for these arguments comes from personal interviews, secondary sources on Salvadoran politics, and Salvadoran newspapers, both
conservative and progressive. From 1996 to 1998, I conducted thirty-eight
interviews with feminist activists and left-wing and right-wing female legislators in El Salvador. In this chapter, interviews with twelve women on the
left—women involved in the women's movement and/or serving as legisla-

tors for the Farabundo Martí National Liberation Front (Frente Farabundo Martí de Liberación Nacional, or FMLN, also known as "the Frente") in the National Congress—and one interview with a prominent female legislator from the National Republican Alliance (Alianza Republicana Nacional, or ARENA) party are cited. The chapter also draws heavily from articles published in the two leading conservative Salvadoran newspapers (*Diario de Hoy* and *Prensa Gráfica*) and the leftist, feminist-friendly newspaper *Diario Co-Latino*.

The Political Left and Opportunities for Feminist Organizing

Throughout the twentieth century, Salvadoran women have acted as protagonists in the political struggles that have shaped their country's political history. In most instances, women's political organizations have had a decidedly "popular" character—that is, they have been composed of working- and middle-class women and have had a strong "counter-hegemonic" theme.[1] In fact, until the late 1980s and early 1990s, most Salvadoran women's organizations did not conceive of themselves as organizations in pursuit of "strategic gender interests"[2] but as organizations that sought broad, class-based interests. It was not until the end of the revolution and the signing of the peace accords in 1992 that women's movement organizations demanded autonomy from the popular movement and developed a distinctly feminist agenda that emphasized women's political, economic, and sexual rights.

Women's popular organizations in El Salvador can be traced back to the 1920s, when middle-class urban reformers and rural revolutionaries began to encourage women's participation in support of their agendas.[3] In 1921 and 1922, respectively, popular-sector women participated in demonstrations against the Meléndez-Quiñonez dictatorship, supporting democratic presidential candidate Miguel Tomás Molina. Ten years later, they again joined the popular struggle, forming women's committees to support the uprising led by Farabundo Martí against General Maximiliano Hernández Martínez.[4]

1. This term is used in Liza Domínguez Magaña, *De acciones de mujeres y olvidos estatales* (San Salvador: IMU, 1995), 57.
2. The term "strategic gender interests" comes from Maxine Molyneux, "Mobilization Without Emancipation? Women's Interests, the State, and Revolution in Nicaragua," *Feminist Studies* 11, no. 2 (1985): 227–54.
3. Domínguez Magaña, *De acciones de mujeres,* 57.
4. Ibid., 58.

Women's participation in the struggle for suffrage can be traced back to 1930, when the Salvadoran poet Prudencia Ayala formally challenged restrictions on women's right to vote. Ayala demanded the right to vote in the 1930 elections and, when denied, presented herself as a presidential candidate. She argued that the Constitution of 1866 gave her citizenship rights, including the right to vote. The Constitution had given citizenship rights to all "Salvadoreños" over the age of eighteen, as well as to those under eighteen who were married or had earned a literary title. It said nothing about restrictions on the basis of sex. The Council of Ministers, which heard her case, ruled that the term "Salvadoreños" made reference to men born in El Salvador and did not recognize women as citizens or as having citizenship rights. Ayala appealed the decision of the Council to the Supreme Court. However, the Supreme Court refused to rule on the case, arguing that the appeal mechanism used by Ayala only covered individual rights, not political rights.[5]

Ironically, it was under the repressive Martínez regime that women's suffrage became incorporated into the Salvadoran Constitution. In 1939 Martínez called a Constituent Assembly, the purpose of which was to consolidate his power. Martínez believed that one way to shore up support for himself and increase the likelihood of his re-election was granting women the right to vote.[6] Thus, one of the proposals presented at the Assembly was women's suffrage. Among the men present at the Assembly, there was general agreement that women's suffrage should be recognized in the Constitution but that its exercise should be conditioned by law. A law, it was reasoned, could be modified more easily than the Constitution "in case it produced unfavorable results."[7] On 5 December 1938 El Salvador became the first Latin American country to recognize constitutionally women's right to vote. However, the law that was to bring women's suffrage into effect was never produced, leaving women effectively without the right to vote for another twelve years.

As Martínez's power waned in the mid-1940s, civic and political organizations, including women's groups, re-emerged. However, in El Salvador—unlike most countries in the region during this period—these organizations did not constitute a broad-based suffrage movement.[8] The three principal women's organizations that surfaced were the Asociación de Mujeres Demo-

---

5. The events surrounding Ayala's case are related in Jorge Cáceres Prendes, "Ciudadanía y cultura política en El Salvador, 1930–1959," in *Identidades nacionales y estado moderno en Centroamérica*, ed. FLACSO (San José, Costa Rica: FLACSO, EDUCA, 1995), 15.

6. Cáceres, "Ciudadanía"; Domínguez Magaña, *De acciones de mujeres*, 60.

7. *La Prensa*, 6 December 1938, quoted in Elsa Moreno, *Mujeres y política en El Salvador* (San José, Costa Rica: FLACSO, 1997), 15.

8. Moreno, *Mujeres y política*, 17; Marilyn Thomson, *Women of El Salvador: The Price of Freedom* (London: Zed Books, 1986), 83.

cráticas (Association of Democratic Women, or AMD), the Frente Democrático Femenino (Women's Democratic Front, or FDF), and the Liga Femenina Salvadoreña (Salvadoran Women's League). Founded in 1944 and 1945, respectively, the AMD and the FDF were closely aligned with the larger movement for democratic reform and the removal of Martínez from power. Only the Salvadoran Women's League, a civic organization promoted by members of the AMD, displayed feminist leanings. Through its publication, "Heraldo Femenino" ("Women's Herald"), the League defended women's rights and called for women's suffrage.[9] According to social scientist Elsa Moreno, the weakness of the suffrage movement is explained by the social repression and cultural isolation that authoritarian rule had imposed on the country since the beginning of the century.[10]

When Salvadoran women won the legal right to vote in 1950, they owed much to a reformist, modernizing regime, not an organized suffrage movement. In 1948, young, reform-minded military officers overthrew General Martínez and placed in his stead one of the leaders of the coup, Lieutenant Colonel Oscar Osorio. Under the leadership of Osorio, the state implemented social, economic, and political reforms, including social security, a labor code, and women's suffrage.[11]

The 1948 coup and the ensuing political reforms served to re-energize civil society and encouraged the re-emergence of popular women's organizations. Beginning in 1957, women associated with the Communist Party revitalized the tradition of popular female organizing, creating the Fraternity of Salvadoran Women. The Fraternity engaged in "cultural, political and educational" activities, seeking the right to social security and labor protection; equal pay for equal work; child care facilities; housing, educational, and recreation centers; and the protection of female market workers' rights.[12] The Fraternity was also actively involved in the protest movement that, in 1960, deposed the regime of Colonel José María Lemus.[13]

Following the outbreak of revolutionary war in 1979, Salvadoran women became incorporated into public life in greater numbers than ever before. Many women on the political left made the decision to participate in the revolutionary movement via political party activity or guerrilla activism.[14] Ilja

9. Cáceres, "Ciudadanía"; Moreno, *Mujeres y política*, 16.
10. Moreno, *Mujeres y política*, 17.
11. Cáceres, "Ciudadanía."
12. Thomson, *Women of El Salvador*, 94.
13. Ibid.
14. See, for example, Claribel Alegría, *They Won't Take Me Alive*, trans. Amanda Hopkinson (London: The Women's Press Limited, 1983); Norma Guirola de Herrera, *La mujer en la revolución salvadoreña* (Mexico City: COPEC, 1983); Linda Lobao, "Women in Revolutionary

Luciak's work (see Chap. 6) on women's political participation during the war indicates that women made up 29.1 percent of FMLN combatants and 35.52 percent of FMLN political personnel during the war. Women commanded troops, worked as radio operators, became demolition experts, and served as mass organizers and public relations officers.

Women's participation in the revolutionary movement directly and indirectly contributed to the emergence of a feminist movement in the late 1980s and early 1990s. The creation of women's auxiliary organizations to the revolutionary parties during the war directly contributed to the developing feminist movement, providing its organizational foundations. More indirectly, women found that their revolutionary activities helped them develop the organizational resources necessary for the formation of the feminist movement; among left-wing women, especially, revolutionary involvement heightened their gender consciousness.

Shortly after the civil war broke out in the late 1970s, revolutionary political parties began to establish women's organizations. The first major women's organization to be established during this period was the Asociación de Mujeres Progresistas de El Salvador (AMPES, or Association of Progressive Women of El Salvador), which was founded in 1975 by women from the Communist Party. Following the creation of AMPES, over a half-dozen party-linked women's organizations burst onto the political scene—including the Asociación de Mujeres de El Salvador (AMES, or Association of Women of El Salvador) in 1978, Asociación de Mujeres por la Democracia Lil Milagro Ramírez (Lil Milagro Ramírez Association of Women for Democracy) in 1980, Comité Unitario de Mujeres Salvadoreños (CUMS, or Unitary Committee of Salvadoran Women) in 1981, Asociación de Mujeres Salvadoreñas (ASMUSA, or Association of Salvadoran Women) in 1983, and Organización de Mujeres Salvadoreñas por la Paz (ORMUSA, or Organization of Salvadoran Women for Peace) in 1983.[15]

Movements: Changing Patterns of Latin American Guerrilla Struggle," in *Women and Social Protest*, ed. Guida West and Rhoda Lois Blumberg (Oxford: Oxford University Press, 1990), 180–204; T. David Mason, "Women's Participation in Central American Revolutions," *Comparative Political Studies* 25 (1992), 63–89. For the figures on female participation in the FMLN, see Ilja Luciak, "Women in the Transition: The Case of the Female FMLN Combatants in El Salvador" (paper presented at the annual meeting of the Latin American Studies Association, Washington, D.C., 28–30 September 1995), 24.

15. Each of these organizations was founded by a leftist political party or movement. AMES was associated with the Bloque Popular Revolucionario (BPR). The Lil Milagro Ramírez Association of Women for Democracy had connections to the Frente de Acción Unificado (FAPU). ASMUSA was founded by the Central American Workers' Party (PRTC). ORMUSA was created by the Movimiento Popular Social Cristiano (Popular Social Christian Movement, or MPSC). CUMS unified women from five parties: FAPU, BPR, PRTC, Ligas Populares 28 de Febrero (the 28th of February Popular Leagues), and the Union Democrática Nacionalista (Nationalist Democratic

By integrating women into the revolutionary struggle, these organizations served to break down the traditional sexual division of labor. Women engaged in production activities, constructed bomb shelters, and defended their communities by performing sentry duty—work traditionally done by men. However, we should not conclude from this that these were feminist organizations. Much of the work performed by women's organizations during this period merely represented the "collectivization of traditional female work"—health brigades, collective kitchens, and community child care programs.[16] Additionally, Norma Guirola de Herrera points out that the objective of these organizations was not the advancement of gender-specific demands: "Rather, their demands [were] those of all the Salvadoran people involved in the struggle—winning power through the anti-oligarchic, anti-imperialist struggle."[17]

With the exception of ORMUSA, this first generation of women's organizations died out in the mid-1980s due to government repression. This gave way to the establishment of a new set of women's organizations, beginning in 1987. Jeannette Urquilla of ORMUSA explains that the impetus for creating women's groups came from a desire to draw unorganized women into the war effort and to attract international funding. "During the 1980s, the empowerment of women became a greater concern within the international community of multilateral and nongovernmental organizations. The parties recognized that projects related to women's empowerment were a way for them to get financial resources. . . . There were many projects developed in the name of women's organizations, but they were not all developed by women, themselves."[18]

Two of these new organizations, Coordinadora Nacional de Mujeres Salvadoreñas (CONAMUS, or National Coordinator of Salvadoran Women) and the Movimiento Salvadoreño de Mujeres (MSM, or Salvadoran Women's Movement), were founded by independent popular women's organizations.[19] A third, CEMUJER, was autonomous from its inception. However,

---

Union, or UDN). See María Candelaria Navas Turcios, "Las organizaciones de mujeres en El Salvador, 1975–1985" (Mexico City: Universidad Nacional Autónomo de México, Facultad de Ciencias Políticas y Sociales, 1987), 51.

16. Arlene Hailey, "El Salvador: Mujeres y proceso revolucionario," *Revista Fem* 46 (1986): 39.

17. Guirola de Herrera, *La mujer en la revolución*, 8.

18. Jeannette Urquilla, interview by author, San Salvador, 26 May 1998.

19. MSM was created by the Asociación de Promotores de Mujer y Niño (Association of Promoters of Women and Children, or APMN), COFEDYES (an organization of unemployed women), and rural women's organizations from La Libertad, Usulután, and near San Miguel. CONAMUS was founded by the women's committees of several unions and community organizations.

most of the new women's groups were founded by or emerged out of political parties. These party-led women's organizations include the Instituto por la Investigación, Capacitación y Desarrollo de la Mujer (IMU, or Institute for Research, Empowerment, and Development of Women), Asociación Mujer Salvadoreña (AMS, or Salvadoran Women's Association), Asociación de Mujeres Salvadoreñas (ADEMUSA, or Association of Salvadoran Women), Mujeres por la Dignidad y la Vida (Las Dignas, or Women for Dignity and Life), and the Movimiento de Mujeres Mélida Anaya Montes (Mélida Anaya Montes Women's Movement, or MAM).[20] Today, these organizations constitute El Salvador's feminist movement.

Similar to the women's groups created by parties in the early 1980s, this new generation of organizations was designed to support the revolutionary movement, not to pursue the gender-specific needs of women. Feminist researcher and activist Mercedes Cañas describes the subordinate character of women's organizations during the war: "Most of the organizations during the war subordinated their specific interests to broader political interests or class interests, and subordinated their own specific demands because that was the political line of the parties and the popular movement, which said, 'Those are secondary interests. Those problems will be resolved after we take power.'"[21]

Notwithstanding the subordinate character of the women's organizations, these groupings were distinct from their predecessors in the sense that they very quickly developed a stronger gender component than earlier organizations had.[22] Morena Herrera indicates that in the case of Las Dignas, "Even though it was a party initiative that gave birth to the organization, we moved away from that from the very beginning. We wanted to struggle for power for women, not just in the popular movement, but nationally."[23]

Leftist political parties encouraged the emergence of feminism not only by providing the organizational foundations for feminist movement organizations but also by stimulating the development of gender consciousness and

20. IMU and ADEMUSA were founded by the Salvadoran Communist Party; Las Dignas was created by Resistencia Nacional (National Resistance, or RN); AMS was established by the Ejército Revolucionario del Pueblo (People's Revolutionary Army, or ERP); and MAM emerged out of the Fuerzas Populares de la Liberación (Popular Forces of Liberation, or FPL).

21. Mercedes Cañas, "El feminismo: Una propuesta para toda la nación," interview by Stefan Ueltzen, in Como salvadoreña que soy: Entrevistas con mujeres en la lucha, ed. Stefan Ueltzen (San Salvador: Editorial Sombrero Azul, 1993), 155.

22. Clara Murguialday, Las mujeres ante, con, contra, desde, sin, tras . . . el poder político (San Salvador: Las Dignas, 1995), 72.

23. Morena Herrera, "Special Report: Women and the Peace Process: El Salvador," interview by Betsy Morgan and Laura Jackson, Connexions 41 (1993): 29.

strengthening leftist women's organizational skills and resources. Through their political efforts, women on the left became more aware of gender issues in three ways: their participation generated internal contradictions regarding the traditional sexual division of labor, opened up opportunities for travel abroad and contact with feminists outside of El Salvador, and created spaces for discussion among women regarding their experiences during the war.

Involvement in revolutionary activities, particularly at the war front, demanded that women assume nontraditional roles in the sexual division of labor and perform so-called men's work.[24] Vázquez et al. assert that these experiences served to empower women and to increase their sense of self-worth and efficacy: "The women demonstrated to themselves and to the rest of society that they could engage in combat and strategize, that they were capable of carrying out the most unlikely of tasks, and of being efficient in so-called men's areas. . . . As a consequence they became less tolerant of the rigid divisions between the private and the public spheres."[25] Testimonies of former female combatants and political activists confirm this hypothesis. In 1988, a fifteen-year-old peasant girl described her experiences as a *guerrillera:* "I practically had to escape from home to be with the units because in my region people believed that girls would leave home only to marry. Upon arriving here my life has changed because I have assumed 'men's affairs.' "[26]

At the same time that leftist political participation presented women with opportunities to challenge stereotypes and traditional sex roles, it did not liberate women: sexism, patriarchy, and discrimination were rampant within the revolutionary movement. Guadalupe Portillo, former member of the Revolutionary Army of the People (Ejército Revolucionario del Pueblo, or ERP), describes the discrimination against women within the student movement: "Women were looked upon as mere sex objects within the student groups. We tried to work on this and to increase the participation of women within the university student movement. In the end, though, we realized that women were never going to be able to do more than be with the *compañeros,* be their girlfriends, or simply be at meetings to serve coffee. They didn't take us seriously."[27]

24. Julio Soro, "Revolución en la revolución: El movimiento de mujeres y la construcción de la democracia" (1993, unpublished paper), 3.
25. Norma Vázquez, Cristina Ibáñez, and Clara Murguialday, *Mujeres–Montaña: Vivencias de guerrilleras y colaboradoras del FMLN* (Madrid: Horas y horas, 1996), 228, 230.
26. "Salvadoran Women: Reasserting Our Rights with New Responsibilities," *Salvadoran Women's Union for Liberation "Mélida Anaya Montes"* 2 (July/August 1988): 2, 3.
27. Guadalupe Portillo, interview by author, San Salvador, 30 June 1997.

At the end of the war, women hoped that their sacrifices would be recognized and compensated in the peace accords and the government's Program for National Reconstruction. However, they were disappointed once again, as their leftist *compañeros* (and *compañeras*) did not negotiate women's rights or programs into the peace accords or the Program.

Irma Amaya and Isabel Guevara, both revolutionaries in the 1980s, commented on the peace accords.

> I had high hopes for the peace accords, but I quickly saw that they did not benefit women. With *compañeras* who were involved in CONAMUS, some of us women began to talk and reflect on our experiences. We began to see that our lives had not changed significantly. It was at this point that our interests began to change. We started thinking more about our own interests as women.[28]

> As we examined the social struggle we realized that the struggle for women's demands had been excluded. Within the peace accords themselves and the negotiations, the women's organizations were excluded. When you figure what we women did during the war—in combat, in the streets—the social movements primarily were composed of women. . . . Yet none of our sacrifices and contributions was recognized. All of these disappointments have pushed women to struggle for their own rights.[29]

Their participation in revolutionary activities allowed women to extend the boundaries of their traditional positions by taking on masculine roles, but they still did not enjoy the power and rights accorded to men. In this way, their involvement produced internal contradictions within leftist women and stimulated their consciousness of the gendered nature of power within the revolutionary movement and in the society at large.

Exile and international travel to conduct party work encouraged the development of gender consciousness by placing women in contact with feminists and feminist theory abroad. During the early 1990s, many exiled women returned to El Salvador, bringing feminist ideas back with them. Of the twenty-six feminist activists interviewed for this chapter, nearly half of them (twelve) had either lived in exile or as refugees or had traveled abroad during the war. Women who spent time abroad during the war tended to character-

---

28. Irma Amaya, interview by author, San Salvador, 14 July 1997.
29. Isabel Guevara, interview by author, San Salvador, 16 June 1997.

ize the experience as a turning point in their development as feminists. Noemy Anaya, an NGO representative to the Beijing conference, stated, "It was through my involvement in an organization called Women for Dialogue, in Mexico, that I began my formation as a feminist. I was involved with them until I returned to the country in 1993. When I returned to the country, I brought these ideas back and started working in this area."[30] The timing of these travels and contacts was crucial, as feminist organization and mobilization in Latin America was in its ascendance in the 1980s and early 1990s. "At the Fifth Latin American Feminist Encounter in Buenos Aires, we made contacts with women from the region, with whom we agreed to form a Central American feminist network. For us, this Central American process was important, as was the support that we received from a group of Mexican women, because it was in this way that we became acquainted with feminist theory."[31]

Finally, women's participation in the revolutionary process facilitated the emergence of a feminist movement by strengthening women's organizational resources. As activists in leftist parties, women learned a variety of skills, including public relations, propaganda work, political education, and organizing, which could be transferred to other institutional realms. As Morena Herrera put it, "For me, it [participating in the war] was a very enriching experience. It had its costs, and there were difficult situations, but it was an experience that gave me the tools for organizing things, analyzing reality, and supporting the women's movement today."[32]

Participation in the political left also provided women with a source of recruits for the feminist movement. Although Salvadoran feminist organizations welcome women of all political persuasions as well as those without militancy, the vast majority of women involved in feminist organizations are leftist militants or sympathizers who have been recruited to the movement by friends or acquaintances from leftist organizations. Urquilla describes the recruitment tactics of ORMUSA in the early 1990s: "Most of the women we worked with were linked in one way or another to the party. For example, we worked with women in cooperatives in the western part of the country. But they were cooperatives linked to the Frente."[33] Similarly, Amaya explains that "at the beginning, nearly all of us in MAM were from the FPL [Fuerzas Populares de la Liberación, or Popular Forces of Liberation]. We were all ex-combatants. We initially worked to influence women from the parties and

30. Noemy Anaya, interview by author, San Salvador, 24 June 1997.
31. Morena Herrera, interview by author, San Salvador, 7 July 1997.
32. Ibid.
33. Urquilla, interview.

popular organizations—women we already knew. A couple of years later, we started working with women who were not yet organized."[34]

Although the political left played a key role in facilitating the emergence of a feminist movement in the early 1990s, we should not conclude that the political left approved of feminist organizing or supported feminist organizational autonomy. In the next section, we shall see that the feminist movement's development has been constrained, in certain ways, by its historical relationship with the political left.

The Political Left and Constraints on Salvadoran Feminism

Women's participation in leftist political organizations may have spurred the emergence of feminist movement organizations in El Salvador; however, leftist parties actively discouraged the development of autonomous organizations. Additionally, feminist organizations' links to leftist parties have constrained the movement by inhibiting cooperation among organizations and among left- and right-wing women. In these ways, the historical and ongoing relationship between the left and feminism in El Salvador has influenced the development of the feminist movement.

Throughout the revolutionary struggle, leftist political parties and popular organizations conceived of women's organizations as little more than groups to support the cause. Julio Soro writes that "in the rigid context of the war, a women's organization was only valued if it fought for 'universal' class interests, for the objectives defined by the leaders with their masculine ideas."[35] The assumption was that "with the overthrow of the system and the installation of a new one, not only would women be liberated, all people would be liberated."[36] As such, party-led women's organizations were discouraged from pursuing activities or interests that did not directly contribute to the war effort.

Even after the peace accords were signed, leftist parties continued to inhibit the autonomous development of feminist organizations. According to activists Carmen Rodríguez (AMS) and Morena Herrera (Las Dignas), one of the ways in which the left undermined feminist organizational development was refusing to finance gender-specific projects:

34. Amaya, interview, 14 July 1997.
35. Soro, "Revolución en la revolución," 3.
36. Guirola de Herrera, *La mujer en la revolución*, 3

We had a lot of difficulties, at first, because there were so many impediments. One of them was economic. Previously, we had gotten all of our financial support from the party. So, when we started working on issues that the party didn't like, like sex workers, the party took away a lot of our funding. We went through a crisis period in which we had to try to support ourselves with our own resources.[37]

It all began when we [Las Dignas] decided to organize a 'women's encounter' as our first public event, instead of a national assembly or mass event, like the party wanted. The party withdrew its economic support for the event. This was in 1990.[38]

Additionally, the political left criticized feminist organizational efforts as divisive; it portrayed feminists as moral, social, and sexual degenerates.

In 1992, at the Party Congress of the Communist Party, a group of us women suggested that a National Women's Secretariat be created within the Party. . . . We won this, but we suffered a great deal. We suffered the criticisms of old-timers in the party, old men who said that our work within the party was subversive, divisive.[39]

We [in CONAMUS] decided that we needed a space of our own, that we needed to learn more about feminism. At this time being a feminist was equated with being a prostitute or a lesbian. . . . In fact, in the social movement [the revolutionary movement] many spaces became closed to us because people were suspicious of us, didn't trust us. Some groups even tried to block us because some of us had lived abroad.[40]

There were very strong clashes of every imaginable type between us [in Las Dignas] and the party. . . . The party began putting pressure on some of us to withdraw from the women's group and on women in the countryside not to associate with us women in the city. The RN [Resistencia Nacional, or National Resistance Party] made various efforts to divide us and carried out a series of campaigns to discredit

37. Carmen Rodríguez, interview by author, San Salvador, 7 July 1997.
38. Herrera, interview by author, 7 July 1997.
39. Deisi Cheyne, interview by author, San Salvador, 13 March 1998.
40. Isabel Ramírez, interview by author, San Salvador, 24 June 1997.

us. They said that we were corrupting the morals of women and that we were whores and lesbians. They also accused us of being right-wing traitors because we were trying to create alliances with all women, not just those of the left.[41]

Partly because of the left's efforts to discourage the development of an autonomous feminist movement, feminist organizations emerged later in El Salvador than in most other parts of Latin America. While other Latin American feminist organizations had won their autonomy by the late 1980s, it was not until 1992 or 1993 that most Salvadoran feminist organizations had become autonomous.

Even after feminist groups won their organizational autonomy from leftist parties, they continued to be constrained by their revolutionary roots. First, the sectarianism and power struggles that characterized the revolutionary movement crept into the feminist movement, making intra-movement unity and cooperation more difficult. Second, the dominance of the political left in the feminist movement and the high incidence of double militancy in certain feminist organizations hindered coalition building between the movement and right-wing women.

Before the FMLN became a single, unitary political party in 1995, it was composed of five separate parties—the Salvadoran Communist Party, the FPL, the ERP, the RN, and the PRTC (Central American Revolutionary Workers' Party). The consequential ideological and organizational pluralism within the FMLN resulted in sectarianism and competition for hegemony within the left. As each feminist organization tended to emerge out of a distinct party or set of organizations on the left, the movement suffered from internal divisions.

We [in the feminist movement] are always questioning the intentions of others because that is what they [in the political left] taught us. In wartime one must be rather distrusting to survive, so we are not used to being transparent in our relations with one another. Also, we inherited the legacy of sectarianism from our earlier political experiences—always wanting to be the best organization. . . . We have inherited this and, at times, translated it to practices in the women's movement.[42]

These divisions were apparent in the Mujeres 94 initiative as well as in the movement's preparations for the Beijing Conference. Mujeres 94 was a

41. Herrera, interview by author, 7 July 1997.
42. Cañas, "El feminismo," 177.

broad-based coordinating group composed of women's organizations as well as independent feminists. It was defined as a "historic and empowering effort by women to influence the political, economic, and social life of the nation, and to influence the formal political and informal social structures of power."[43] The result was a fourteen-point platform demanding political reforms in the areas of land ownership, employment, health, violence against women, and communication.[44]

Generally, Mujeres 94 is hailed as an example of movement unity. However, the self-evaluation of Mujeres 94 reveals that this initiative suffered from "lack of trust because of revolutionary sectarianism" and "difficulties in respecting diversity within feminism."[45] Additionally, the self-evaluation concluded that the "debate over double militancy consumed a great deal of the group's energy and served to weaken relations among women."[46]

The movement additionally suffered from sectarianism and power struggles in its preparations for the 1995 International Women's Conference in Beijing. Noemy Anaya describes how movement organizations fought to control the agenda of the NGO committee: "When we were working on preparations for the Beijing Conference, it became clear that there were political interests at work. That is, some individuals were interested in dominating the political spaces. There was a struggle for power. I see this as being one of the things that we have inherited from the parties."[47] Whether revolutionary sectarianism is the sole cause for the feminist movement's dilemmas is debatable, as struggles for power frequently afflict social movement organizations, even those that do not have revolutionary roots. However, it is undoubtedly one of the factors that has served to divide women (and organizations) from one another. Fortunately, the movement recently has begun to discuss the problem in open forums and to work to respect differences within Salvadoran feminism.[48]

The continued dominance of the political left in the Salvadoran feminist movement and the high incidence of double militancy within many feminist

43. Mujeres 94, "Documento: Definición política del espacio Mujeres 94" (Las Dignas Centro de Documentación, San Salvador, June 1993, unpublished memo), 3.

44. Michelle Saint Germain, "Mujeres 94: Democratic Transition and the Women's Movement in El Salvador," *Women and Politics* 18 (1997): 75–99.

45. Sonia Cansino and Carmen Medina, "Mujeres 94: Evaluación" (Las Dignas Centro de Documentación, San Salvador, 9 April 1994, unpublished memo), 3.

46. Ibid., 4.

47. Anaya, interview.

48. Patricia Hipsher, "From Revolutionary Activism to Feminist Organizing: The Revolutionary Leftist Roots of the Salvadoran Feminist Movement" (paper presented at the annual meeting of the American Political Science Association, Boston, Mass., 3–6 September 1998).

organizations also has constrained the movement by limiting its electoral coalition-building strategies. In particular, the historical role of the political left in the feminist movement has made it difficult for feminists to create strategic electoral alliances with right-wing female candidates. In the 1997 congressional elections, the issue of cross-political coalition building was raised by some women in the movement, but ultimately the close historical ties between feminists and the left kept this idea from being put into practice.

> The movement as a whole never came to an agreement to support specific women candidates. Some women in the movement expressed their support for certain candidates from the FMLN, meaning that they were going to wear a shirt advertising the candidate, help put up posters, clearly support them. But that is something that we never did for women from the right. There were some suggestions, I recall, that we put aside issues of class and work solely on the basis of gender, that is, support all female candidates regardless of their political colors. But that never became a majority position within the movement. . . . Since the movement is composed of leftist women, it is easier for us to talk with women on the left.[49]

> There are distinct opinions, but perhaps there are two dominant positions on the issue of electoral alliances. One is that the women's movement should support all female candidates, regardless of their party affiliations. The other is that we should support women in whom we have an interest—those who are sensitive to women's issues—because it will be easier to make agreements with them. MAM has identified itself more with the latter position. We prefer women who have made a commitment to the women's movement to press for women's demands.[50]

However, it is arguable that even if right-wing women had shown a commitment to the women's movement, many of the feminist organizations would not have supported them. In the case of the Mélidas (MAM), for example, cross-political coalitions were practically unthinkable in 1997: several active members of MAM were FMLN candidates to Congress.[51]

---

49. Cheyne, interview.

50. Irma Amaya, interview by author, San Salvador, 13 March 1998.

51. Ilja Luciak, "Gender Equality and Electoral Politics on the Left: A Comparison of El Salvador and Nicaragua," *Journal of Interamerican Studies and World Affairs* 40 (1998): 39–66.

In the pre-candidate nomination process for the 1999 presidential elections, the feminist movement found itself in a similar position. In late 1997 the major political parties, ARENA and FMLN, began to consider potential candidates for the March 1999 presidential elections. Among the potential nominees whose names were bandied about in the press and within the political parties were several women. According to public opinion polls, Minister of Education Cecilia Gallardo de Caro and First Lady Elizabeth Calderón Sol, leading right-wing female politicians, received high ratings as potential presidential candidates. On the left, the Attorney for Human Rights, Dr. Victoria Marina de Avilés, received considerable public support.[52]

Despite the seeming public support for women candidates on the left and the right, the feminist movement made no effort to encourage ARENA's nomination of a woman candidate. However, it launched a major campaign to encourage the FMLN to nominate Victoria de Avilés. According to Norma Vázquez of the Asociación de Madres Demandantes (AMD, or Association of Mothers Seeking Child Support), fourteen organizations, most of them women's and human rights organizations, were involved in the public campaign to pressure the FMLN to nominate de Avilés as its presidential candidate.[53] The organizations printed and distributed thousands of flyers to their members, detailing the advances made in human rights and women's rights during de Avilés's tenure as Attorney for Human Rights and encouraging them to send telegrams and letters to FMLN headquarters that read, "We want Dr. de Avilés for President." In 1998, Irma Amaya explained the different efforts of the movement to support women candidates of the left and the right:

> Currently, there is speculation that the Attorney for Human Rights Dr. Victoria de Avilés and Minister of Education Cecilia Gallardo may be among the possible candidates for the next elections. . . . Between those two, I would prefer Dr. de Avilés. . . . With Dr. Victoria de Avilés we believe that the potential and possibility for change is greater, because she is a woman committed to human rights and she is a woman who is close and accessible to the women's movement. On the other hand, the Minister is more distant. If the crite-

---

52. In October 1997, Gallup, UTEC, and UCA conducted a poll to discover the public's favorite public personalities. Cecilia Gallardo de Caro was ranked as the favorite by the largest number of respondents (she rated 6.76 on a scale of 1 through 10), followed by San Salvador Mayor Hector Silva (FMLN) at 6.54, Elizabeth Calderón Sol (ARENA) at 6.54, Alfredo Cristiani (ARENA) at 6.50, and Monseñor Fernando Saenz Lacalle and Dr. Victoria de Avilés (FMLN) at 6.33 each. Ricardo Vaquerano, "Mujeres al poder: Utopia," *Prensa Gráfica*, 5 October 1997, 8–9.

53. Norma Vázquez, interview by author, San Salvador, 1 June 1998.

rion is which woman is closer to the movement, I would have to say Dr. de Avilés.[54]

De Avilés did not succeed at winning the party's nomination to the presidency; however, her defeat had less to do with her status as a woman and more to do with the factionalism that plagued the party at its national convention and de Avilés's alignment with the losing side in the conflict. The contest to establish a presidential and vice-presidential slate was particularly difficult: the slate was decided only after months of debate and three national conventions. De Avilés and Dr. Salvador Arias reflected the orthodox faction of the FMLN, while their competitors, Facundo Guardado and María Marta Valladares (Nidia Díaz), represented the reformist faction. In close voting, Guardado and Valladares defeated de Avilés and Arias by only 33 votes—463 to 430.[55]

Right- and Left-Wing Women: Working Together for Gender Equality, Sometimes

The historical identification of the feminist movement with the political left makes the formation of alliances between feminists and right-wing women unlikely. However, since 1994, feminists have managed to win the support of right-wing women on several important issues. In this section, I will discuss three issues on which feminists and right-wing women have formed common cause: quotas for women's participation in political parties and elected office, responsible paternity, and domestic violence. I will then discuss abortion and economic rights, two areas in which they have found themselves at odds.

Organized feminists describe the movement's relationship with conservative women as being based on strategic and temporary alliances in pursuit of concrete, shared interests.[56] According to Irma Amaya, "We have tried to make alliances on the basis of concurrence of interest on concrete issues, that is, issues on which the feminist movement has clear positions that are shared by right-wing women, leaving aside issues that generate conflict be-

---

54. Amaya, interview, 13 March 1998.
55. Allen Jennings, "FMLN Selects Presidential Candidates," Centro Internacional de Solidaridad El Salvador Update (http://jinx.sistm.unsw.edu.au/~greenlft/1998/339/339p19.htm), 27 January 1999.
56. Cheyne, interview; Morena Herrera, interview by author, San Salvador, 19 March 1998; América Romualdo, interview by author, San Salvador, 10 March 1998.

tween us."[57] The issues on which left- and right-wing women have been able to form alliances are either "practical gender interests"—those that emerge out of women's traditional roles as wives and mothers[58]—or are issues that affect all women equally, regardless of class, race, or other differences.

> We are beginning to see coincidences of interests between right- and left-wing women. . . . I don't feel that the difficulties that used to exist between them are as great now as they used to be. This is because we have begun to realize that there are many problems that traverse different social classes. There are problems that affect women that have nothing to do with which party you belong to, ideology, or class.[59]

> We have to look for the points where our interests coincide. The government has all kinds of programs for women, so we are looking for relationships and ways to coordinate. . . . Of course, there are going to be some issues on which we have differences. For example, abortion is an issue that some groups defend, but others are afraid of defending. But there are many other issues to defend that are immediate, such as water, light, education, and child care.[60]

Recently, the issue of women's political participation has ignited a heated political debate and has mobilized a diverse group of women in El Salvador. As in most countries, women's participation in political parties and elected office in El Salvador is very low. Overall, men hold about 90 percent of the country's public offices. Of the 84 deputies in the national legislature, only 13 (15 percent) are women. Of the 262 mayors, 26 are women.[61] In the Cabinet of President Calderón Sol, only three positions were held by women—Minister of Education, Vice Minister of Health, and the Attorney for Human Rights.[62] The percentage of political party leadership positions held by women is also dismally low. With the exception of the FMLN, where women must be present in 35 percent of all internal leadership positions and

57. Amaya, interview, 13 March 1998.
58. The term "practical gender interests" comes from Molyneux, "Mobilization Without Emancipation," 227–54.
59. Urquilla, interview.
60. Norma Vázquez, "El Salvador: Yet Again, the Personal Proves to Be Political," interview by Kathy Bougher, *Off Our Backs* 23, no. 3 (1993): 25.
61. Luciak, "Gender Equality," 56.
62. A new Attorney for Human Rights, a man, was chosen by the legislature in the summer of 1998.

35 percent of all nominations to elected office, women tend to be underrepresented in Salvadoran political parties. FMLN Deputy Lorena Peña argues that the underrepresentation of women in politics is "not because women are not capable but because their rights and capacities are not recognized by the parties. All of the political parties, from the left to the right, are patriarchal."[63]

To rectify this situation, feminist movement organizations and female legislators on the left and the right have proposed reforms to the Electoral Code that are designed to "guarantee the incorporation of women in the political and public life of the country."[64] The reforms require that women constitute at least one-third of the members of all political parties, the internal leadership positions within all political parties, and the candidates nominated by political parties for elected office.[65] In short, the reforms call for a one-third quota for women's participation in political parties and public office.

Supporters of the Electoral Code reforms include the feminist organizations MSM, AMD, MAM, Las Dignas, and IMU, as well as several congresswomen, with the exception of those from Convergencia Democrática (Democratic Convergence, or CD).[66] FMLN Substitute Congresswoman Irma Amaya and Las Dignas's América Romualdo describe the support for the quota:

Women from both sides of the political spectrum agree on the following: First, we agree that it is not true that only men have the ability and merit to participate in politics. Second, we agree that that part of the Constitution that establishes equality of conditions for men and women is, in practice, being violated, because 90 percent of the public positions are held by men. Third, we agree that for women to achieve equality of condition we must implement affirmative action mechanisms that institutionalize the representation of women within the political parties. We are asking for a minimum

63. Lorena Peña, "Discussion Comments" (presentation made to the United Nations High Commission on Human Rights and Technical Cooperation Project on Human Rights in El Salvador, Forum on the Political Rights of Salvadoran Women, San Salvador, 9 March 1998).

64. Iniciativa de Mujeres por la Igualdad en la Participación Política, "Justificación a las propuestas de reforma al Código Electoral" (Las Dignas Centro de Documentación, San Salvador, 6 November 1997, unpublished correspondence to Salvadoran Legislative Assembly), 4.

65. Ibid.

66. Romualdo, interview.

quota of 33 percent; however, some women on the right think that it should be a 50 percent quota.[67]

We [MSM, AMD, MAM, Las Dignas, and IMU] held a meeting with congresswomen from the USC and ARENA and they told us that they were convinced of the need to establish a participation quota. . . . I believe that the congresswomen now see the necessity of having a quota. They have realized that access to opportunities does not come from one's abilities but from structures and obstacles to those structures. There is a great deal of awareness of this among women who are in public office now.[68]

Although the reform generally has not been received well by right-wing parties, it does enjoy the support of some of the leading conservative female political figures, Gloria Salguero Gross (ARENA) and First Lady Elizabeth Calderón Sol. Deisi Cheyne notes, "On issues related to political discrimination, Doña Gloria gets very excited. In her public statements, she has said that she feels that the quota is necessary. Also, Doña Elisa made sure that the demand for a political quota was placed in the National Women's Policy. She always has said that she favors this. In fact, she prefers that there be a quota of 50 percent or more."[69] Conservative women's analysis of the political participation issue reflects a feminist—or, at least, a gendered—understanding of political power. In a 1997 interview with *Prensa Gráfica,* Salguero Gross explained women's underrepresentation in ARENA in terms of sexism: "On a scale from 0 to 10 [with 0 being the least sexist and 10 being the most sexist] ARENA scores between 8 and 9 points. This is a cultural model that has existed for hundreds of years. Let's also keep in mind that the sexism that exists in our country is strong and has deep historical roots, and has not allowed improvements in the status of women. In ARENA, right now, we do not have a single departmental director who is a woman."[70] And the following year, Salguero Gross described the discussions between right- and left-wing women and the commitment of right-wing female legislators to the fight for equality in political participation: "We currently are embarking on a rather difficult struggle for a representation quota for women, which we

67. Amaya, interview, 13 March 1998.
68. Romualdo, interview.
69. Cheyne, interview.
70. Vaquerano, "Mujeres al poder," 9.

would like to see put in place by the next elections. We women legislators from the right and the left have had a series of discussions—fruitful and powerful discussions—about the issue, and we are working very hard on this, knowing that it will be a tough battle."[71]

The main obstacle that the quota faces is resistance from conservative male legislators and attorneys, who argue that the reform violates the Salvadoran Constitution. They argue that by institutionalizing a quota for women, but not for men, the reform discriminates against men. This discrimination, they argue, violates the Constitution's prohibition on sex discrimination.[72] Another obstacle to the reform's approval, says Romualdo, is the public's unwillingness to pass laws that increase the relative power of women vis-à-vis men: "When we talk to the press or the public about the 'poor women' who are discriminated against and who are mistreated, the public pays attention and understands. But when it comes to giving women power, or women becoming protagonists, instead of victims, it becomes more complicated. Issues that involve the protection of women, who are treated like victims, are easier to sell to the public than those that treat women as protagonists and active players."[73]

A second issue on which feminists and right-wing women have joined forces (one that Kelley Ready discusses in Chap. 5 of this volume) is responsible paternity and a woman's right to the *cuota alimenticia*. (The *cuota alimenticia* is similar to child support, in that it requires non-custodial parents to make financial contributions to cover the basic needs of their children.) The issue of responsible paternity, like that of domestic violence, has brought together women of all political stripes because of its universal nature. Amaya says, "In this country the theme of responsible paternity, like domestic violence, is an issue that concerns us women greatly and affects us greatly. . . . What is more, both of these issues affect women of the left and women of the right in the same way. A very rich man, just as easily as a very poor man, can be an irresponsible father."[74]

A third issue on which left- and right-wing women have coordinated their efforts is that of domestic violence. Since 1994, the Salvadoran Legislative Assembly has taken several measures to recognize and combat domestic violence. It has ratified international instruments related to violence against women and approved legislation to prevent domestic violence and punish

71. Gloria Salguero Gross, interview by author, San Salvador, 27 May 1998.
72. Romualdo, interview.
73. Ibid.
74. Amaya, interview, 13 March 1998.

offenders. On 24 November 1994, the Legislative Assembly declared a National Day of No Violence Against Women for 25 November. The following year, on 23 August 1995, the Assembly ratified the OAS Interamerican Convention to Prevent, Punish, and Eradicate Violence Against Women—the Belem do Pará Convention. Then in 1996, the legislature approved the Law Against Domestic Violence. The Law Against Domestic Violence allows members of the community to inform police of suspected cases of domestic violence and permits police to enter homes and make arrests based on the testimony of the plaintiff or neighbors. In addition, the law allows domestic violence victims to file restraining orders against aggressors, establishes special units within the National Civilian Police that are staffed with personnel trained in domestic violence issues, and encourages the establishment of temporary shelters for victims of domestic violence.[75]

Feminists received strong support from right-wing congresswomen for the Law Against Domestic Violence and the Belem do Pará Convention. Gloria Salguero Gross spoke in favor of the Law Against Domestic Violence, and upon its passage, she declared it "a historic act."[76] Rosa Mélida Villatoro, a Christian Democratic congresswoman and President of the National Commission on the Family, Women, and Children, also spoke publicly in favor of the Law Against Domestic Violence.[77] The quick passage of the Belem do Pará Convention was facilitated by the advocacy of right-wing congresswomen. Isabel Guevara, Executive Director of MSM, indicates that Salguero Gross led the fight for the approval of Belem do Pará: "She had committed herself to this as president of some Central American entity, so she had a responsibility to get it passed. Another thing that helped was that this was just a month before the Beijing Conference, and anything related to women was very fashionable."[78]

While women of the left and right have managed to form alliances on certain issues, they have found it difficult to collaborate with one another on others. Lorena Peña observes, "The problem is that we have these party boundaries, and each party—and the men and women in the party—has to defend certain principles. So on issues that touch on these basic principles it is difficult for us to unite."[79] Issues surrounding sexual rights and economic

75. Cecilia Cabrera, "Está por aprobarse ley de la violencia intrafamiliar," *Diario Co-Latino,* 24 April 1996, 17.

76. Luis Lainez, "Aprueban ley contra violencia doméstica," *Diario de Hoy,* 24 April 1996.

77. Jaime García, "PNC allanará casas por maltratos," *Diario de Hoy,* 14 December 1996, 3.

78. Isabel Guevara, interview.

79. Peña, "Discussion Comments."

rights have seemed the most intractable, according to FMLN Congress-woman Peña and ARENA Congresswoman Salguero Gross:

> Really it is not easy to incorporate the women's agenda, much less issues having to do with strategic gender and class demands, into the national political agenda: sexual orientation, motherhood by choice, women's labor rights, and credit policies. These themes are taboo because they affect the neoliberal political economy and the existing patriarchal structure.[80]

> On issues related to the family, the well-being of the family, intra-family violence, and child support, we [congresswomen] have been in agreement and we have supported the legislation. . . . But when there have been established party positions, we women have re-mained separated from one another. This has been true on eco-nomic issues. We [ARENA] want a free-market economy. They [FMLN] believe more in a mixed or socialist economy. Agreement also has been difficult on controversial issues, like abortion, where we are on completely different sides.[81]

Feminist activist Morena Herrera concurs with the legislators' analyses.

> One very difficult issue that we had to deal with last year was the elimination of the exceptions in Article 137, having to do with abor-tion. On this issue it was clear that we [leftist and rightist women] were divided. . . . Another difficult issue for us, although we have not had much experience with it yet but which I suppose will be difficult, is things that have to do with economic policy. Obviously, there are distinct economic interests among Salvadoran women. I imagine that for reasons of class, it will not be easy to construct alliances with right-wing women.[82]

Deisi Cheyne adds, "Our ability to form alliances with women on the right depends on the issue. When it comes to issues that deal with class or moral-ity, gender is going to fall by the wayside. Experience has taught us that."[83]

---

80. Lorena Peña, "Comments," quoted in "Memoria de Encuentro: Relaciones entre el movimiento de mujeres y el estado," by Red de Mujeres por la Unidad y el Desarrollo (San Salvador: Red de Mujeres por la Unidad y el Desarrollo, 20 March 1997), 14.

81. Salguero Gross, interview.

82. Herrera, interview by author, 10 March 1998.

83. Cheyne, interview.

While the feminist movement has received support from right-wing women on practical gender interests and political rights, it has come into conflict with them over the question of abortion. The 1997 abortion battle was over the rewriting of Article 169 of the Penal Code. Article 169 of the old Penal Code defined three conditions under which abortion was not punishable: (1) when it was necessary to save the life of the mother; (2) when the pregnancy was the consequence of rape or incest; and (3) when it was presumed that the fetus would be born with grave deformity. Initially, Article 137 of the new Penal Code bill included almost identical provisions to those found in Article 169 of the old Code. Article 137 allowed abortion when it was necessary to avoid grave danger to the life and physical or mental health of the pregnant woman, when the pregnancy was the consequence of a crime against the woman's sexual will, and when there was presumption that the fetus would be born with grave physical or mental deficiency.

Opposition to Article 137 was led by the Catholic Church and conservative political parties, including right-wing female politicians. Male and female members of the Christian Democratic Party and ARENA solidly opposed Article 137, as did male and female members of the President's Cabinet. First Lady Elizabeth Calderón Sol led the right-wing charge against Article 137, arguing for the sanctity of all life: "Promoting and preserving life have been the principal objectives of the Salvadoran government, and under no circumstances will we allow abortion to be legalized."[84] The Attorney for Human Rights, Dr. Victoria Marina de Avilés, was generally liberal on political issues, but she also opposed the exceptions. She based her position on the premise that life begins at conception and that all humans, even the unborn, enjoy rights.[85] ARENA legislators denounced the bill in press conferences and on the floor of the Legislative Assembly chamber. In a press conference, ARENA Congresswoman Milena Calderón de Escalón expressed unconditional opposition to abortion: "We cannot permit the killing of an innocent life and, for this reason, we are opposed to the three conditions found in Article 137. And ARENA will never approve the legalization of a fourth exception— 'abortion for psychological motives.' If the woman is affected psychologically by remaining pregnant, why did she sleep with the man in the first place?"[86] Christian Democratic congresswomen took similar positions. Congresswoman Rosa Mélida Villatoro argued that it was necessary to eliminate the three exceptions because "medical advances have allowed physicians to

84. "Defendamos la vida," *Diario de Hoy*, 26 February 1997, 9.
85. "Inconstitucional legalizar aborto," *Diario de Hoy*, 6 January 1997, 11.
86. "Jamás ampliaremos el aborto," *Diario de Hoy*, 2 March 1997, 4.

overcome almost all problems that could endanger the life of the mother."[87] She simultaneously promoted adoption of unwanted babies instead of abortion, and encouraged the enactment of more stringent laws to prevent and punish rape and incest, which could result in unwanted pregnancies.[88]

Feminists and left-wing women, on the other hand, supported Article 137. The principal supporters of the Article were FMLN legislators and the feminist organizations Las Dignas, MAM, CEMUJER, and the Coordinator for Women's Organizations (COM). FMLN Congresswoman Marta Valladares suggested that one of the reasons for abortion was the lack of sex education, and she held that it was a mistake to address the issue simply with punitive measures: "The question of abortion must be addressed with preventative strategies . . . and sex education campaigns that begin in fifth grade."[89] Valladares concluded that as long as the economic conditions that encouraged abortions continued to exist, she would support legal abortion.[90]

Ultimately, the forces supporting Article 137 were fewer in number and more poorly organized than their opponents, and they lost the battle. On 26 April 1997, the Legislative Assembly voted 58 to 26 to eliminate Article 137 from the Penal Code and to impose stiff penalties on physicians and others who performed abortions. Under the new law, the maximum penalty for performing abortions is six to twelve years in prison and, in the case of physicians, the loss of one's medical license for up to twelve years.[91]

A second area in which feminists and right-wing women have found it difficult to form alliances is the problem of economic rights, particularly the rights of female workers in free trade zones. In 1995, the Legislative Assembly began to debate reforms to the laws governing *zonas francas* and *recintos fiscales*. *Zonas francas,* or free trade zones, are geographically delimited areas in which industries enjoy freedom from duties and customs; their products must be destined for export. *Recintos fiscales* are industrial areas that are physically outside the designated free trade zones but that enjoy the same privileges as those located within free trade zones.[92] One aspect of the reform was the establishment of a fund into which industries located in free trade zones and *recintos fiscales* would have to make contributions. The

---

87. "La Constitución debe prohibir el aborto," *Diario de Hoy,* 2 March 1997, 5.
88. Ibid.
89. "Hay que prevenir el aborto, no prohibirlo," *Diario de Hoy,* 2 March 1997, 5.
90. Ibid.
91. Ricardo Vaquerano, "Aprueban Código Penal," *Prensa Gráfica,* 27 April 1997, 3A.
92. Victor Pino, "Informe especial: Maquilas," *Prensa Gráfica,* 7 March 1995, 5A.

contributions were designed to guarantee the payment of back wages to employees in the event that the industry closed shop.[93]

Male and female FMLN legislators, feminist organizations (MAM, in particular), and women *maquila* workers saw these reforms as a way of protecting employees from fly-by-night entrepreneurs who, when they shut down their Salvadoran operations, might leave workers uncompensated for work already performed or vacation pay already earned. By the mid-1990s, this kind of irresponsible business activity had become common in El Salvador. In 1995, a Cuban-American-owned textile factory, Confecciones y Ensambles, S.A., closed its doors; its managers fled the country without paying the salaries, vacations, and overtime pay of 1200 employees.[94] The same year, MAQUISALTEX (another U.S.-owned factory) fired 120 workers and refused to pay their back wages.[95] In 1996, in an incident similar to that of Confecciones, the South Korean textile factory GABO closed its doors without paying its 400 employees.[96] What makes this a feminist issue is the fact that women make up the vast majority—79 percent—of workers in the factories in the free trade zones and tax-exempt areas.[97]

The passage of reforms to the Free Trade Zone Law was very difficult, in part because feminists and left-wing legislators did not have the support of right-wing congresswomen. Speaking to a group of feminists, Congresswoman Peña described the intense opposition that she and other FMLN legislators faced on this issue: "I don't know if you are aware of what it meant to fight for the reform of the Free Trade Zone Law. They wanted to sanction and throw out Nidia [Díaz], two male FMLN representatives, and me from the Assembly."[98] According to Deisi Cheyne, the resistance of right-wing congresswomen to the free trade zone reforms was due to class differences: "When we have had to deal with issues like the free trade zones and the *maquilas,* we have not been able to make alliances, because of class differences. The right-wing women think that the *maquila* workers are the best-

93. Mayra García and Hugo Ceceña, "FMLN presentará propuesta sobre fianza en instalación de maquilas," *Diario Co-Latino,* 23 September 1996, 3.

94. Gerardo Lopez, "Inicia embargo contra maquiladora," *Prensa Gráfica,* 28 June 1995, 6A.

95. Ibid.

96. José Mauricio Segura, "Relaciones con Corea podrían deteriorarse," *Diario de Hoy,* 17 September 1996, 14.

97. Isabel Villalta, "Crecimiento económico vs. bienestar laboral," *Diario Co-Latino,* 11 February 1995, 32.

98. Peña, "Comments," quoted in Red de Mujeres, "Memoria," 14.

treated queens of all female workers. They don't understand what it means to be a worker in one of these factories."[99]

This is not to say that cross-class, cross-political coalition building is impossible on economic issues. FMLN Congresswomen Irma Amaya and Norma Guevara are optimistic that left- and right-wing congresswomen may be able to form alliances on some economic questions.

> Right now we are in the midst of a debate on poverty, and we have achieved consensus that poverty principally affects women. And on the basis of this consensus, we realize that women do not have the same rights as men—access to credit, access to work. But we do not have consensus yet on how to resolve the problem. . . . One of the proposals, by MAM, has been the establishment of a women's credit institution. . . . There is a lot of interest in this on the part of female legislators, so we may be able to work on this together.[100]

> One initiative that has been put forward by the Frente has been the creation of a credit institution for women. We have met with women from ARENA to exchange ideas and give them information on this project. They are excited about this measure.[101]

Conclusions

The development of the feminist movement in El Salvador has been conditioned by the movement's relationship with the political left. During the war in the 1980s, women's organizations were closely tied to leftist political parties and tended to perceive of those on the political right, including conservative women, as their foes. However, since the emergence of an autonomous feminist movement, the relationship between feminism and political parties of the left and the right has become more complex.

Women's participation in revolutionary activities facilitated the emergence of feminist organizations by providing women with an organizational foundation and creating opportunities for the development of a feminist consciousness. Despite this positive contribution on the part of the left to the emergence of feminism in El Salvador, one can also point to ways in which

99. Cheyne, interview.
100. Amaya, interview, 13 March 1998.
101. Norma Guevara, interview by author, San Salvador, 26 May 1998.

the movement's relationship with the left has been a political liability. The revolutionary foundation of the feminist movement has spawned internal sectarianism and has created obstacles to potential alliances between feminists and right-wing women.

The feminist movement has managed to transcend—but not abandon—its leftist history, developing a working relationship with right-wing women on a number of political issues. Feminists and conservative female political figures in El Salvador have constructed alliances around the issues of domestic violence, responsible paternity, and women's political participation, issues that can be considered liberal political issues (in the case of participation) and practical gender issues (in the cases of domestic violence and responsible paternity). However, issues that touch on questions of class and sexuality or morality—such as abortion and the free trade zone reforms—tend to divide feminists and right-wing women.

There is good reason to believe that cross-political, cross-class cooperation and coalition building between women on the left and the right will continue. In 1996, women in the Legislative Assembly formed the Women's Political Party Forum of El Salvador, a political space that is similar to the Women's Caucus in the U.S. Congress. By creating a space in which female legislators may discuss issues, find overlapping interests, and develop legislative initiatives to improve the status of women,[102] the Forum "seeks to unify women of all political parties, regardless of ideology."[103]

As the Forum is a newly established entity, predicting the extent to which it will contribute to political coalition building among leftist and rightist women is quite difficult. Members of the Women's Forum tend to concentrate their efforts on issues that will unite women, emphasizing the positive aspects of the Forum and demonstrating its potential to their male counterparts.[104] Thus far, the Forum has been used to discuss issues related to women's political participation and women's access to credit, to develop mechanisms to publicize the political achievements of female legislators, and to establish agreements to defend other female legislators, regardless of party, if they are subject to gender-based attacks.[105] While the Forum serves a civilizing purpose and facilitates coordination among female legislators on the "easy" issues, it is unlikely to contribute to progress on the more difficult, controversial questions. But ultimately, the Forum represents an ef-

102. "Mujeres tras mayor participación política," *Diario de Hoy,* 6 June 1996, 45.
103. Amaya, interview, 13 March 1998.
104. Norma Guevara, interview.
105. Ibid.

fort—albeit one with limitations—to establish cross-political, cross-class alliances on issues that benefit women and advance gender equality.

BIBLIOGRAPHY

INTERVIEWS

Amaya, Irma. Interviews by author. San Salvador, 14 July 1997 and 13 March 1998.
Anaya, Noemy. Interview by author. San Salvador, 24 June 1997.
Cheyne, Deisi. Interview by author. San Salvador, 13 March 1998.
Guevara, Isabel. Interview by author. San Salvador, 16 June 1997.
Guevara, Norma. Interviews by author. San Salvador, 16 June 1997 and 26 May 1998.
Herrera, Morena. Interviews by author. San Salvador, 7 July 1997, 10 March 1998, and 19 March 1998.
Portillo, Guadalupe. Interview by author. San Salvador, 30 June 1997.
Ramírez, Isabel. Interview by author. San Salvador, 24 June 1997.
Rodríguez, Carmen. Interview by author. San Salvador, 7 July 1997.
Romualdo, América. Interview by author. San Salvador, 10 March 1998.
Salguero Gross, Gloria. Interview by author. San Salvador, 27 May 1998.
Urquilla, Jeannette. Interview by author. San Salvador, 26 May 1998.
Vázquez, Norma. Interview by author. San Salvador, 1 June 1998.

OTHER SOURCES

Alegría, Claribel. *They Won't Take Me Alive.* Translated by Amanda Hopkinson. London: The Women's Press Limited, 1983.
Cabrera, Cecilia. "Está por aprobarse ley de la violencia intrafamiliar." *Diario Co-Latino,* 24 April 1996, 17.
Cáceres Prendes, Jorge. "Ciudadanía y cultura política en El Salvador, 1930–1959." In *Identidades nacionales y estado moderno en Centroamérica,* edited by FLACSO (Facultad Latinoaméricano de Ciencias Sociales). San José, Costa Rica: FLACSO, EDUCA, 1995.
Cansino, Sonia, and Carmen Medina. "Mujeres 94: Evaluación." Las Dignas Centro de Documentación, San Salvador, 9 April 1994. Unpublished memo.
Cañas, Mercedes. "El feminismo: Una propuesta para toda la nación." Interview by Stefan Ueltzen. In *Como salvadoreña que soy: Entrevistas con mujeres en la lucha,* edited by Stefan Ueltzen, 153–83. San Salvador: Editorial Sombrero Azul, 1993.
"La Constitución debe prohibir el aborto." *Diario de Hoy,* 2 March 1997, 5.
"Defendamos la vida." *Diario de Hoy,* 26 February 1997, 9.
Domínguez Magaña, Liza. *De acciones de mujeres y olvidos estatales.* San Salvador: IMU, 1995.
García, Jaime. "PNC allanará casas por maltratos." *Diario de Hoy,* 14 December 1996, 3.
García, Mayra, and Hugo Ceceña. "FMLN presentará propuesta sobre fianza en instalación de maquilas." *Diario Co-Latino,* 23 September 1996, 3.
Guirola de Herrera, Norma. *La mujer en la revolución salvadoreña.* Mexico City: COPEC, 1983.

Hailey, Arlene. "El Salvador: Mujeres y proceso revolucionario." *Revista Fem* 46 (1986): 34–39.

"Hay que prevenir el aborto, no prohibirlo." *Diario de Hoy,* 2 March 1997, 5.

Herrera, Morena. "Special Report: Women and the Peace Process: El Salvador." Interview by Betsy Morgan and Laura Jackson. *Connexions* 41 (1993): 29.

Hipsher, Patricia. "From Revolutionary Activism to Feminist Organizing: The Revolutionary Leftist Roots of the Salvadoran Feminist Movement." Paper presented at the annual meeting of the American Political Science Association, Boston, Mass., 3–6 September 1998.

"Inconstitucional legalizar aborto." *Diario de Hoy,* 6 January 1997, 11.

Iniciativa de Mujeres por la Igualdad en la Participación Política. "Justificación a las propuestas de reforma al Código Electoral." Las Dignas Centro de Documentación, San Salvador, 6 November 1997. Unpublished correspondence to Salvadoran Legislative Assembly.

"Jamás ampliaremos el aborto." *Diario de Hoy,* 2 March 1997, 4.

Jennings, Allen. "FMLN Selects Presidential Candidates." Centro Internacional de Solidaridad El Salvador Update (http://jinx.sistm.unsw.edu.au/~greenlft/1998/339/339p19.htm). 27 January 1999.

Lainez, Luis. "Aprueban ley contra violencia doméstica." *Diario de Hoy,* 24 April 1996.

Lobao, Linda. "Women in Revolutionary Movements: Changing Patterns of Latin American Guerrilla Struggle." In *Women and Social Protest,* edited by Guida West and Rhoda Lois Blumberg. Oxford: Oxford University Press, 1990.

Lopez, Gerardo. "Inicia embargo contra maquiladora." *Prensa Gráfica,* 28 June 1995, 6A.

Luciak, Ilja. "Women in the Transition: The Case of the Female FMLN Combatants in El Salvador." Paper presented at the annual meeting of the Latin American Studies Association, Washington, D.C., 28–30 September 1995.

———. "Gender Equality and Electoral Politics on the Left: A Comparison of El Salvador and Nicaragua." *Journal of Interamerican Studies and World Affairs* 40 (1998): 39–66.

Mason, T. David. "Women's Participation in Central American Revolutions." *Comparative Political Studies* 25 (1992): 63–89.

Molyneux, Maxine. "Mobilization Without Emancipation? Women's Interests, the State, and Revolution in Nicaragua." *Feminist Studies* 11, no. 2 (1985): 227–54.

Moreno, Elsa. *Mujeres y política en El Salvador.* San José, Costa Rica: FLACSO, 1997.

Mujeres 94. "Documento: Definición política del espacio Mujeres 94." Las Dignas Centro de Documentación, San Salvador, June 1993. Unpublished memo.

"Mujeres tras mayor participación política." *Diario de Hoy,* 6 June 1996, 45.

Murguialday, Clara. *Las mujeres ante, con, contra, desde, sin, tras . . . el poder político.* San Salvador: Las Dignas, 1995.

Navas Turcios, María Candelaria. "Las organizaciones de mujeres en El Salvador, 1975–1985." Mexico City: Universidad Nacional Autónomo de México, Facultad de Ciencias Políticas y Sociales, 1987.

Peña, Lorena. "Discussion Comments." Presentation made to the United Nations High Commission on Human Rights and Technical Cooperation Project on Human Rights in El Salvador, Forum on the Political Rights of Salvadoran Women, San Salvador, 9 March 1998.

Pino, Victor. "Informe especial: Maquilas." *Prensa Gráfica,* 7 March 1995, 5A.

Red de Mujeres por la Unidad y el Desarrollo. "Memoria de Encuentro: Relaciones entre el movimiento de mujeres y el estado." San Salvador: Red de Mujeres por la Unidad y el Desarrollo, 20 March 1997.

Saint Germain, Michelle. "Mujeres 94: Democratic Transition and the Women's Movement in El Salvador." *Women and Politics* 18 (1997): 75–99.

"Salvadoran Women: Reasserting Our Rights with New Responsibilities." *Salvadoran Women's Union for Liberation "Mélida Anaya Montes"* 2 (July/August 1988): 2, 3.

Segura, José Mauricio. "Relaciones con Corea podrían deteriorarse." *Diario de Hoy,* 17 September 1996, 14.

Soro, Julio. "Revolución en la revolución: El movimiento de mujeres y la construcción de la democracia." 1993. Unpublished paper.

Thomson, Marilyn. *Women of El Salvador: The Price of Freedom.* London: Zed Books, 1986.

Vaquerano, Ricardo. "Aprueban Código Penal." *Prensa Gráfica,* 27 April 1997, 3A.

———. "Mujeres al poder: Utopia." *Prensa Gráfica,* 5 October 1997, 8–9.

Vázquez, Norma. "El Salvador: Yet Again, the Personal Proves to Be Political." Interview by Kathy Bougher. *Off Our Backs* 23, no. 3 (1993): 25.

Vázquez, Norma, Cristina Ibáñez, and Clara Murguialday. *Mujeres–Montaña: Vivencias de guerrilleras y colaboradoras del FMLN.* Madrid: Horas y horas, 1996.

Villalta, Isabel. "Crecimiento económico vs. bienestar laboral." *Diario Co-Latino,* 11 February 1995, 32.

5 | A Feminist Reconstruction of Parenthood Within Neoliberal Constraints

La Asociación de Madres Demandantes in El Salvador

Kelley Ready

In January 1997, Gloria Salguero Gross—the president of the Salvadoran Legislative Assembly, one of the country's largest landowners, and a prominent leader of the right-wing ARENA party—was surrounded by a group of women in the hallway outside the chambers of the Assembly. Several of these women were former militants of the Farabundo Martí National Liberation Front (FMLN), the guerrilla army that had fought against the government in the twelve-year civil war that ended in 1992. However, this was not a hostile confrontation. On the contrary, the former enemies were patting each other on the back for the successful passage of the "Non-Arrears Bill." This piece of legislation required that all candidates for elected office get a legal clearance certifying that they were not in arrears for child support payments.

First developed by the "Legislative Initiative" project of the Mélida Anaya Montes Women's Movement (MAM), the bill was then publicly lobbied for by women from the Association of Mothers Seeking Child Support (Asociación de Madres Demandantes, or AMD). The bill was introduced into the Assembly by leftist legislators from the FMLN—now legally recognized as a political party—and shepherded through the Assembly by the conservative legislative president, Salguero Gross, with the collaboration of the centrist Christian Democratic Party (PDC).

Even in postwar El Salvador, this coalition between women on the left and women on the right was unusual. By 1996, almost five years had passed since the war had ended. Most of the terms of the 1992 peace agreement had been implemented by both the political parties that had previously con-

Research for this chapter was funded by a Fulbright grant and a grant from the Institute for the Study of World Politics. All translations by the author.

trolled the state and by the opposition forces that had become part of the state as a result of the peace accords. As a result, neither reconstruction nor reconciliation remained a primary focus of either sector. Rather, after the peace accords, the modernization of the state and the economy had become a central theme in the discourse of both the left and the right in El Salvador.[1]

The peace accords created a situation in which political actors who had been traditionally excluded from the administration of the state gained increased access to state power. While the legalization of the FMLN and its offshoots had been an important aspect of that process, the ability of formerly excluded groups to participate in elections was only one avenue through which they received increased access to state power. The creation of new state agencies such as the Ombudsman of Human Rights also opened doors through which previously excluded actors could participate in the administration of the state. Organizations that were traditionally aligned with the left, or that, like the women's movement, had emerged from the left, began to organize openly, mobilizing civil society to take advantage of the opportunities and contradictions created by the modernization of the Salvadoran state.

Many of these actors adopted a new view of modernization, rejecting previously held beliefs that reduced the state to an apparatus of bourgeois control, according to Morena Herrera,[2] a former guerrilla and one of the founders of the Mujeres por la Dignidad y la Vida (Women for Dignity and Life, or the Dignas), the Salvadoran feminist organization that started the AMD. During the war, Herrera had seen the state as an institution that had to be destroyed. But in the postwar period, that attitude changed, and the Dignas worked to construct a state that responded to women's needs. The new state would be unlike the one that existed before the war, she contended. Dating back to 1932, the goals of that state had been, first, to protect the landed classes, and then later, the interests of the agro-industrial oligarchy. In the postwar period, she and many others on the left saw the state as an arena—or its institutions as separate arenas—in which "the relation of power between different political forces is materialized."[3] It is with this perspective, combined with a feminist analysis of the condition of women, that the AMD emerged as a force to organize women who were seeking child support.

1. See, for example, Carlos Umaña, *Un nuevo mapa para El Salvador* (San Salvador: Ediciones Tendencias, 1996), 71.
2. Morena Soledad Herrera, interview by author, San Salvador, 13 November 1996.
3. Umaña, *Un nuevo mapa*, 74.

Is there a relationship between the characteristics of the child support system in El Salvador, and its relation to the state in particular, that has brought together women and men from the right and the left to challenge irresponsible fatherhood? What are the specific philosophies and conditions that have motivated Salvadoran feminists to focus on this issue as a key element in their efforts to reconstruct gender relations within the country? This chapter examines why the problems of women seeking child support emerged as a national political issue in the aftermath of the civil war. By describing the institutional response of the state to the issue of "irresponsible fatherhood," I will attempt to explain why this was one of the arenas through which a Salvadoran feminist group, the Dignas, chose to organize women to challenge inequality. I will describe how, in the process, they created a new political identity—mothers seeking child support—and brought these women together to form the AMD, which eventually became an autonomous organization. Finally, the Salvadoran feminist analysis of motherhood that motivated this campaign will be examined, along with the successes they have had in challenging the contradictory ideology and institution of motherhood in El Salvador.

Child Support and the Salvadoran State

The faint outline of the words Procuraduría de los Pobres (Attorney General of the Poor) can still be made out on the facade of the tall concrete building that housed this institution prior to the 1986 earthquake. The structure has been left standing, unusable, spilled files still visible from the doorways that one passes to get to the current offices, a series of crudely constructed wooden buildings erected as temporary replacements after the earthquake. The office was established in the 1950s during the modernization of the state apparatus that accompanied the policy of import substitution;[4] its name was updated in the 1970s to Attorney General of the Republic, or AGR. Its original purpose was to provide some relief to the misery of the old, the infirm, and abandoned children. The AGR's mandate expanded in the 1980s when many trade unions became targets of government repression. As the unions could no longer represent workers' interests, workers turned to the AGR for help

---

4. Norma Vázquez and Clara Murguialday, *Unas + otras × todas = Asociación de Madres Demandantes: Una lucha colectiva por la cuota justa y paternidad responsable* (San Salvador: Las Dignas, 1996).

in addressing their complaints about their unpaid salaries, denied benefits, and inadequate working conditions. In the phase of modernization that was made possible by the signing of the 1992 peace accords, attending to child support became the major function of the AGR, according to its chief executive, Miguel Angel Cardoza Ayala.[5]

El Salvador has a high percentage of female-headed households.[6] The war intensified the conditions that made this situation problematic (poverty, deteriorating social services, unemployment). Additionally, during the war, many women felt constrained from demanding child support. For women on the left, initiating a suit was politically risky, for it meant possible involvement with the police. A suit might also have put a woman's former partner in political jeopardy by giving the police an excuse to detain him. On the other hand, women who had been involved with political figures or men in the army or national police feared that they themselves would become victims of violence, since their former companions often enjoyed immunity from prosecution for far worse crimes.[7]

With the signing of the peace accords in 1992 and the emergence of an autonomous women's movement,[8] it became more possible for women to sue for child support. The cessation of hostilities lessened the threat of political violence. Women could initiate claims for child support without worrying that they would result in the disappearance of the ex-partners. The demobilization of the armies on both sides and of the national police began a process of dismantling a military apparatus, making previously untouchable members of military groups more vulnerable.

Simultaneously, as part of a process that had begun in the late 1980s, women in the different sectors of the FMLN began to reflect upon "the situation and condition" of women in El Salvador and on their experience in the war. This focus eventually included issues of child support. With funding from abroad, these organizations (and the women in them) became increasingly independent from the FMLN. They also became increasingly critical of

5. Miguel Angel Cardoza Ayala, interview by author, San Salvador, 7 January 1997.
6. Ana Isabel García and Enrique Gomáriz, *Mujeres centroamericanas: Ante la crisis, la guerra y el proceso de paz* (San José: FLACSO, 1989), 105; Victor Lagos Pizatti and María Teresa de Mejía, "La situación de la familia y del menor en El Salvador," in *La situación de la familia y el menor en Centro América y Panama* (San Salvador: Secretaría Nacional de la Familia, 1994), 21; Francisco Lazo, *El Salvador en cifras y trazos* (San Salvador: Equipo Maíz, 1996), 76.
7. These observations come from informal conversations with members of the Dignas, the AMD, and other women in the popular movement.
8. See Hipsher, this volume.

male domination in their society, in the institutions of the left, and in their personal relationships.

The peace accords established the conditions under which the modernization of the Salvadoran state could move forward. Douglas Carranza Aguirre, the director of the Office of Information and Reception of the AGR, pointed out that part of this modernization included the first enactment, in 1994, of a separate legislative code that regulated family life.[9] Until then, laws regulating the family had been subsumed in a Civil Code dating from 1960. The new laws reconceptualized "the family" and afforded rights to women in common-law marriages and their children, according to Ana Mercedes Jovel, a lawyer and member of the Legislative Initiative of the MAM.[10] Whereas under the earlier law, illegitimate children did not have inheritance rights, the new law recognized all children equally. In addition to revising the laws governing divorce, the new legislation redefined the points at which women could file child support claims and expanded the criteria that would be used to determine the size of the payments. Previously, women could not have received support until a child was born; under the new law, the men who were sued could be made to contribute to expenses incurred during pregnancy and childbirth. In addition, rather than just contributing to the basic costs of feeding and clothing a child, the cost of the child's education and health care would be considered in calculating the amount of the payment. According to the director of the Department of Family Relations, Hilda Edith Herrera Reyes,[11] the revision not only gave women more rights, but the passage of the code also led to more publicity of those rights.

These changes had a great impact on the work of the AGR and led increasing numbers of women to go to that office as they sought child support. According to the records of the AGR,[12] the number of women coming to initiate claims increased dramatically. In the five years preceding the signing of the peace accords (1988–92), the average number of claims per year was 2,145. Over the four years that followed (1993–96), the number of women per year making claims was 3,751, an increase of 75 percent.

9. Douglas Carranza Aguirre, interview by author, San Salvador, 10 February 1997.
10. Ana Mercedes Jovel, interview by author, San Salvador, 9 June 1997.
11. Hilda Edith Herrera Reyes, interview by author, San Salvador, 10 February 1997.
12. One indicator of the need to modernize the AGR is that there are discrepancies between different sources of data. I arrived at these figures by averaging the figures from the years 1986–90 and the years 1991–95 in the *Libros de Actas.* Those figures are extremely erratic, which is probably more reflective of differences in the way in which data were recorded than of actual annual changes.

Setting the Stage to Reconstruct Gender Relations

According to Miguel Angel Cardoza Ayala, the Attorney General of the Republic, the AGR's current constitutional mandate calls for it "to watch over the
defense of the family and of persons, and the interests of minors and others
incapable of taking care of themselves."[13] This mandate is fulfilled by giving
legal assistance to people who have few resources and by representing them
in court "in defense of their individual liberty and labor rights."[14] The role of
the AGR is very different from those played by similar institutions in other
countries, according to Cardoza. In other places, the Attorney General's office usually represents the state; in El Salvador, the institution was established to provide legal and social services to marginalized sectors of the
population.[15]

But to the women of the organization Mujeres por la Dignidad y la Vida,
the Dignas, the AGR is something very different. They see the institution as
"the largest stage in the country where men and women each day face off
over the fulfillment of their respective roles in caring for children."[16] Poor
women, primarily those who have had common-law marriages, come to the
AGR when they want the fathers of their children to contribute to their daily
maintenance. Eventually, if they are at all successful, these women must meet
face-to-face with the fathers of their children to negotiate the amount that
will be contributed to the children's maintenance. To extend the Dignas'
metaphor, if the AGR has created the stage for these negotiations to take
place, the AMD has become an unexpected actor, sometimes welcomed,
sometimes not, whose improvisations are rapidly changing the scenery on
the stage itself.

In soliciting child support, women cope directly with what is regarded
by many Salvadorans as a cultural trait of Salvadoran men: irresponsible fatherhood. Increasingly recognized as a problem, it is generally seen as an
innate component of traditional Salvadoran masculinity, or *machismo*. But
the Dignas, as well as other Salvadoran women's groups, have rejected the
belief that gender roles are natural and inherent. They have promoted a
feminist perspective that reframes *machismo* as sexism and argues that traditional gender roles were socially constructed to ensure female subordination. The issue of irresponsible fatherhood provides an arena in which to

13. Cardoza Ayala, interview.
14. Ibid.
15. Ibid.
16. Vázquez and Murguialday, *Unas + otras,* 13.

challenge sexist roles directly. Their first study on the topic identified the demand for child support as an ideal vehicle through which the Dignas could link the "practical needs" of thousands of women to a "strategic" critique of motherhood, fatherhood, and the family.[17] Through the AMD, the Dignas built a new organization that sought to organize women seeking child support around those practical necessities, raise consciousness, and challenge the cultural patterns and state institutions that encourage irresponsible fatherhood.

The Dignas combined their analysis of the ideological underpinnings of *machismo* with a political plan of action that called for the women seeking child support to "organize themselves not just to resolve their particular problems but to confront the structural, political, and ideological obstacles [they faced]."[18] The Dignas recognized the growing importance of the state in shaping gender and family relations during the postwar democratization and modernization period in El Salvador. From their perspective, the state's response to irresponsible fatherhood was insufficient: it simply "translate[d] the interests of women (that the fathers contribute to the sustenance of the children) into a legal issue (the right to receive child support) and into an administrative issue (the collection of the payment)."[19] The Dignas believed that the state could use institutions like the AGR to move from merely treating the consequences of irresponsible fatherhood to restructuring Salvadoran gender relations. The Dignas' tactic of organizing women was meant to reshape women's conception of gender roles, specifically the rights and obligations of motherhood and fatherhood. Significantly, it also sought to exert pressure on the state in order to bring about institutional changes that would actively combat irresponsible fatherhood.

Motherhood After the War

In order to understand the Dignas' focus on organizing women around the issue of child support, we must take two facts into account. The first is that the institution and ideology of motherhood is profoundly contradictory (I

17. Sonia Baires, Dilcia Marroquín, Clara Murguialday, Ruth Polanco, and Norma Vázquez, *Mami, Mami, demanda la cuota alimenticia . . . la necesitamos: Un analisis feminista sobre la demanda de cuota alimenticia a la procuraduría* (San Salvador: Mujeres por la Dignidad y la Vida, 1996), 8.

18. Vázquez and Murguialday, *Unas + otras,* 111.

19. Ibid., 16.

will return to this point below). The second is that Salvadoran feminists were organizing during a transitional period. During the 1990s, the state was shifting from an authoritarian regime to one in which new democratic institutions were being developed with the supposed goal of articulating the will of civil society.

The 1992 peace accords created an unprecedented opportunity for this incipient civil society. The organizations that had developed and survived under the extremely adverse conditions of guerrilla warfare were finally able to work in the open. Supported by United Nations Human Rights monitoring and increased access to funding, previously clandestine structures of the FMLN—like the Dignas—were transformed into legitimate entities. Many of the activists in these groups were experienced organizers who had developed their skills by mobilizing urban networks and rural communities that had been under assault during the war. These same activists found a renewed sense of purpose in the postwar period. They built organizations that sought to develop a functioning civil society and created mechanisms through which they could implement their goals.

The second factor that shaped child support activism was the contradictory way in which motherhood and the position of women in the family defined women's gender roles. The Dignas describe motherhood as the center of Salvadoran women's identity.[20] Echoing the title of an oft-quoted article by the late Ignacio Martín-Baró, they point to the conflict and ambiguity that surround women's experience in the family. Martín-Baró noted that while the family incarcerates women in many ways, it also provides them with a safe harbor. But it is a harbor that is partly built, he acknowledged, on "the mythical image of the mother, object of song and poetry."[21]

I will draw upon two very disparate phenomena to illustrate the depth and power of the institution of motherhood in El Salvador. The first is a character from Salvadoran legend: *la Siguanaba*.[22] It is a myth known to all Salvadorans, and the story is even distributed in popular comic book form by vendors who sell the comics in buses and on the streets. *La Siguanaba* was a very beautiful Indian princess who, after she was married, was more concerned with looking at her own image in the river, or going out to

20. Baires et al., *Mami, Mami*, 22.
21. Ignacio Martín-Baró, "La familia, puerto y carcel para la mujer salvadoreña," *Revista de Psicología* 9, no. 37 (1990), 272–73.
22. There are numerous spellings of her name. Another common spelling is *Ciguanaba*. According to Pedro Geoffry Rivas, it comes from the Náhuatl words for women *(sihuat)* and witch *(nahauli)*. See Rivas, *Lengua salvadoreña* (San Salvador: Dirección de Publicaciones e Impresos del Ministerio de Cultura y Comunicaciones, 1987), 52.

dances—depending on the version—than with taking care of her son, *el Cipitío*. As a result, a god (the god of the waters, *Tlaloc*, in the popular version) ordered that she be changed into a horrible ugly woman who would live in the riverbed, forever washing clothes, looking at this ugly reflection of herself.

La Siguanaba is still sighted today. Usually she appears late at night to drunk men who are returning home after romancing a lover. *La Siguanaba* inspires such fear that during the war, a military operation was supposedly canceled by an FMLN unit after one of the soldiers reported having encountered this woman. In the countryside, especially, stories about *la Siguanaba* are common. As in similar legends in other countries, *la Siguanaba* symbolizes the consequences that women risk in failing to meet their maternal obligations. She also embodies the guilt men face when, as expected, they cheat on their wives.

Another manifestation of motherhood's power in society can be seen in the practice of maternal politics by the organization Las CoMadres, the Oscar Arnulfo Romero Committee of Mothers of Political Prisoners, the Disappeared, and the Assassinated of El Salvador. Insisting that their actions were motivated by maternal instincts rather than political ones, the CoMadres organized women who had lost children and spouses in order to publicly challenge the military and paramilitary forces during the civil war. Incorporating key elements from the ideology of motherhood, combined with liberation theology and the discourse of the international human rights movement, the CoMadres carved out a space for resistance by creating a new set of social relations. Like the Argentine Mothers of the Plaza de Mayo, they took their demands to the streets, denouncing the disappearances, captures, and assassinations of their children and other family members.[23]

The status of the CoMadres as self-identified mothers initially provided them with a measure of safety; the government did not take the actions of such women too seriously. But as their tactics became more daring—including their occupation of the Salvadoran Red Cross in 1978—the repression against them became more murderous: their offices were bombed and their members were captured, tortured, and disappeared. Despite the danger, they continued to work publicly. They demonstrated in the streets; they occupied foreign embassies, cathedrals, and government buildings; they sought political and material support from international sources.

The existence of the CoMadres can be understood as part of the broad

23. Jo Fisher, *Mothers of the Disappeared* (Boston: South End Press, 1989).

cultural manifestations that Evelyn Stevens identified as *"marianismo,"* the Latin American exaltation of the Virgin Mary. Claiming that *marianismo* is the female counterpart to *machismo,* Stevens described it as "the cult of female superiority which teaches that women are semi-divine, morally superior, and spiritually stronger than men."[24] These qualities allegedly engender "abnegation, that is, an infinite capacity for humility and sacrifice. No denial is too great for the Latin American woman. No limit can be divined to her vast store of patience with the cruel men of her world."[25] Stevens pointed out that the representation of this image is ubiquitous: "The image of the black-clad, mantilla-draped figure, kneeling before the altar, rosary in hand, praying for the soul of sinful menfolk, dominated the television and cinema screens as well as the oral tradition of the whole cultural area."[26]

While such sweeping generalizations ignore the vast diversity in race, class, ethnicity, experience, and history among "Latin American women,"[27] the Dignas identify abnegation and self-sacrifice as part of the ideology that influences Salvadoran women's sense of motherhood. But they do not see it as an inevitable part of that experience, and their work with mothers who seek child support is meant to challenge that ideology both as it manifests itself within women's consciousness and behavior and in how it is institutionalized in the apparatus of the state.

The Dignas' analysis of motherhood shows how gender roles within the Salvadoran family are naturalized. Motherhood plays a central role in women's identity, they argue. "To be a wife and, above all, a mother—that is, to form a family—is a dream that is nurtured from when we are little; to fail to achieve it is the source of pain, anguish, self-reproach, and social condemnation. While a small group of Salvadoran women has questioned this prototype of femininity that limited a good part of women's capabilities, for the majority of the female population, it continues to be the ideal that they strive to attain."[28]

But fatherhood has no corresponding importance in the Salvadoran male identity. For men, fatherhood is a choice; for women, motherhood is seen as an inevitable and inescapable part of their destiny. According to the

---

24. Evelyn P. Stevens, "Marianismo: The Other Face of Machismo in Latin America," in *Male and Female in Latin America,* ed. Ann Pescatello (Pittsburgh: University of Pittsburgh Press, 1973), 91.
25. Ibid., 94–95.
26. Ibid., 96.
27. Tracy Bachrach Ehlers, "Debunking *Marianismo:* Economic Vulnerability and Survival Strategies Among Guatemalan Wives," *Ethnology* 30, no. 1 (1991).
28. Vázquez and Murguialday, *Unas + otras,* 37.

Dignas, fatherhood is a reality that exists only as long as a father's relationship with his child's mother continues. Once that relationship deteriorates, so does his commitment, both financial and emotional, to his offspring. Socially, there are few sanctions against men who fail to fulfill their obligations to their children. Men often deny that they are the fathers of their children and there are few legal mechanisms to require them to do so. On the other hand, the Dignas acknowledge, women tend to accept this state of affairs and rarely do more than try to exert moral pressure on the men to assume responsibility for their children.

The Dignas use the insights from their analysis to encourage women to both question gender roles and develop political actions based on their roles as mothers. If motherhood is socially constructed, then it can be reconstructed through a feminist praxis of analysis, consciousness-raising, and political action. Their political program targeted those women whose experience best exemplified the contradictions of the institution and the experience of motherhood—mothers who sought child support.

Reconstructing Motherhood

The most effective mechanism the AMD established for providing women with emotional support was a Thursday morning drop-in group. Not coincidentally, it was also the AMD's primary vehicle for raising women's consciousness about their role as women and challenging their attitudes toward motherhood. Excerpts from my edited fieldnotes provide a sense of these meetings.

Thursday [17 October 1996] I went back to the AMD as I was hoping to accompany the promoters as they made their rounds of the waiting rooms at the AGR, but neither Anabel, Reina, nor Vilma was there. But at least one woman was waiting for the "Consciousness Raising Meeting" when I came in. . . . Fifteen women have gathered in the chairs set up in the open space of the second floor office around the corner from the AGR. Montse, one of the psychologists from the Dignas, has spread out colored pieces of paper on the floor. Each one has a feeling written on it: capable, content, cheerful, self-sacrificing, overburdened, guilty. I have asked Montse to introduce me and ask the women if it is okay if I observe their meeting. They respond with applause.

"How does it feel to be a mother?" Montse asks, and she instructs them to select the words that describe how they are feeling today. The women get up from their chairs and pick words. Montse asks, "Who would like to explain why they chose the words they picked up?" The first woman to speak is Angela,[29] who explains that she is angry because her case is not going as fast as she had hoped. She is happy to be with these other women and to see her case is being processed. She feels lucky *(dichosa)* to be responsible for her son, and feels alive because of her work. Montse responds by asking her, "Haven't you made a lot of sacrifices?" "Yes," she responds. Montse seems to be trying to point to the underside of motherhood. As women continue to filter in, she talks about how women have been trained since childhood to be mothers and that it's not all that it is supposed to be. "It's difficult!" she says, characterizing her remarks as "a little reflection." Montse asks for another volunteer. . . . Sara jumps in and tearfully describes her situation. Her oldest daughter is with Sara's mother, who has been deathly opposed to giving her up. Her husband has custody of her son, whom she is trying to get back. But because the father is more lenient and has more money, the son does not want to come back to her. She's terrified that her youngest daughter will decide that she too wants to leave. Montse provides her with toilet paper to wipe away the tears.

Montse's response is that we think our children are "ours, our property, and these are valid feelings." "But," she added, it's necessary "to learn to take time for ourselves." [Later, when I asked Montse about the meeting, she remarked that she was very dissatisfied with it because there was too much idealizing of motherhood for her to deal with it effectively.]

Sofía, one of the women I had chatted with before the meeting, described her situation next. She was left by the father of her three children for another woman. So she took half the furniture in the house and left with it. He has brought charges of robbery against her and there is an order for her arrest. She is terrified that she will be arrested, leaving her children on their own. Many of the women in the room respond. One encourages her to "trust in God," but in recounting her own struggle, she notes that she has also made use of earthly institutions such as Tutela Legal [a Catholic legal rights service], the Institute for the Protection of Children, and the AMD.

Montse also affirms Sofía's right to the things that she took. . . . These last two women have taken up about a half an hour each. Montse gives instructions for the others to keep it short so that more women can speak. Irma has chosen the words responsible, animated, and content. She says that

29. The names of the women in the groups are pseudonyms.

she is proud to have put her daughter through school, and happy that she ranks first in her class. Marina, one of the more middle-class-looking women in the group, is celebrating her one-year separation. She tells the group that she did not leave her house so that she would not lose it. She has grabbed the word *realizada* (self-actualized) because she has been awarded fifteen hundred colones a month (U.S. $173) for six kids. [This is not bad, considering that the AGR reported that 65 percent of all the women who receive support receive less than one hundred colones per month, or about U.S. $11.50.[30]]

Debora speaks next. She cannot pay her daughter's school fees and unless she comes up with some of the money the school is threatening to fail her daughter. Her ex-husband says that he will pay the fees if Debora withdraws her suit against him. Again this generates many responses and support. One young woman explains that she is a teacher and advises Debora to go to higher authorities in the school system to explain the problem, assuring Debora that she can get some more time. Debora also selected cards with the words happy and calm. She says that is how being with these women makes her feel.

One of the participants comments that women can work but no matter how much they work, they are going to need "his help." Montse is quick to correct her: "It's not help. It's their responsibility." With that she calls the meeting to an end.

Most of the women hang around chatting. I turn to the woman who has been sitting beside me. She had continuously tried to talk to me during the second half of the meeting and as politely as possible I tried to discourage her from talking to me, encouraging her instead to talk to the group. She had selected a card that indicated that she was afraid. "I don't have the courage," she told me, so after the meeting I encouraged her to tell me her story. About twelve years earlier, she had been raped by her boss and ended up with twins as a result. She has decided to sue for child support, for as the boys get older, the cost of raising them increases. The father has a good job at *Pollo Campero* [the Salvadoran equivalent of Kentucky Fried Chicken] not far from the office of the Association. . . . When she informed him of this, he threatened her with arrest.

I told her that I didn't think he could have her arrested, and called over to Lorena, the other woman I had chatted with before the meeting. Lorena seems like a real fireball. "I'm not proud to be a single mother," she had

30. Baires et al., *Mami, Mami,* 136.

interjected in the meeting. "I'm tired, mistreated, and sick of it!" Another woman, María, also came over to encourage her. María offered to accompany her to her appointment the next day; Lorena shared the fear that she had felt before going to her appointment earlier that morning. Both talked about the support they had found at the Asociación. I left them talking, noting how the woman, who had struck me as possibly being developmentally disabled, was becoming much more coherent and articulate as she moved beyond the terror that had gripped her throughout the meeting.

The next week I went back again.

Thursday [24 October] I headed over to the AMD for a second "Conscious-ness Raising Workshop." . . . Montse and Larissa [another of the Dignas' psychologists] . . . ask those who are coming for the first time to identify themselves and tell us why they are here.

A woman whose face and arms are covered with burns tells us that she has left her children with someone who is now trying to get permanent custody of them. She has come with Debora, who wants to tell us something else about the woman, but Larissa stops her, saying that she can speak for herself. The woman sitting beside me appears to be very sad and suffocated from her fear. She tells us that her three children are living with their father and she wants to get custody. She was sent by CEMUJER [another women's organization]. Another woman says that she has heard the talks in the wait-ing room [of the AGR] and wants to see what the AMD could offer her. There is a woman who did not discover that her husband had a lover until after he died, a woman with an eight-year-old who has never gotten any support, and a woman sent by Lorena for help with a problem with her husband.

Larissa asks for someone to explain what goes on in the meeting. Irma explains: courage, resolve, peacefulness, counsel, and support. Sara adds that it's emotional support. Larissa emphasizes that "we talk about feelings, we support each other [Larissa stresses mutuality throughout the meeting]. The meeting is to talk about us because we never think about ourselves. It's a network to mutually support each other, to bring us together so that we don't feel alone. It's a space just for us. It's good for us." Debora confirms that "I have changed." Pati says that a friend brought her to see a lawyer who listened to her like she had never been listened to before. She says that she has been helped by the psychologist so that she's no longer afraid.

We engage in an exercise to draw the persons and things that comprise our world. Montse did not give me paper at first, but several of the women point it out to her, and she gives me one on which to draw. Many of the women draw their children at the center of the picture and leave out themselves, something that Montse and Larissa point out and comment upon.

At the end of the meeting, Aracely announces a press conference they are having Tuesday. They have been pressuring the AGR to claim a part of the Christmas bonus for women who are receiving child support and have written a decree that they are going to submit to the Legislative Assembly. Aracely recruits women to attend the press conference.

My notes from the following week included this description:

Larissa built on the exercise by asking the group to draw pictures of our mothers and to put on one side what it is that we don't like about them and on the other side to put what we would change. . . . "What does this have to do with us?" Larissa asks and then explains, "We are a reflection of our mother. What we don't like and don't want to do as mothers, is what we didn't get as children." Several women draw pictures and say there is nothing that they would change about their mothers, that they were wonderful, perfect, and sacrificed everything for them. When one of the women says she wouldn't change anything, Larissa tells her that she doesn't believe her. "Are you the same as your mother?" she asks them. Some say yes, others respond negatively. Unloved, indifferent, ignored are some of the other words that come up. "What do you want to change and what does it have to do with you?" She is not easy with them.

These meetings are designed to provide mothers with a positive image of themselves, an image that counters the prevailing concept of child support as a handout. The discourse of the AMD asserts that child support is a paternal obligation of men to their children. The organization promotes a new ideology of motherhood that demands "the payment of an adequate level of child support, insists that men recognize their children as their own and assume responsibility for them, calls on men to share in meeting the emotional needs of their children, and requires that men assume all the duties and rights that have been traditionally assigned exclusively to women."[31]

31. Vázquez and Murguialday, *Unas + otras,* 75.

From Practical Interests to Rights

The Dignas took up the issue of child support after becoming dissatisfied with their previous emphasis on productive projects such as bakeries, raising livestock, and opening local stores. The strategy behind productive projects was based on theories that divided the motives behind women's organizing into practical and strategic interests.[32] By providing women a means to an income and a legitimate excuse to get out of the house and meet with other women (their practical interests), the Dignas hoped that women would become involved with the feminist ideas the organization was promoting (their strategic interests). Once project participants had had the opportunity to reflect upon their own experiences with the help of the Dignas, it was assumed that they would be motivated to organize as mothers and join the group.

But the strategy did not work as the Dignas had anticipated. The challenges of making the productive projects work overwhelmed the challenges of changing women's consciousness. Despite the fact that the Dignas were successful in channeling some funds into women's hands, few of the projects became economically feasible. After weighing the extensive time spent on these projects against the small number of women they were reaching, some of the Dignas began to question whether the efforts these types of projects required were justified.[33]

The Dignas could have continued to raise money to keep the projects going. However, several other issues made the organization (amidst much contention) decide to shift its orientation, according to Vilma Vásquez, one of the founders of both the Dignas and the AMD.[34] The relationships between the poorer rural participants in the productive projects and the more educated urban women who formed the core of the Dignas had taken on patron-client dynamics that many of these women had experienced during the war while participating in the National Resistance, one of the five political

32. See the introduction to this volume. Also see Maxine Molyneux, "Mobilization Without Emancipation? Women's Interests, the State, and Revolution in Nicaragua," *Feminist Studies* 11, no. 2 (1985), and Caroline O. Moser, "Gender Planning in the Third World: Meeting Practical and Strategic Gender Needs," *World Development* 17, no. 11 (1989).

33. See Mujeres por la Dignidad y la Vida, *Los proyectos productivos y la autonomía económica de las mujeres: La experiencia de Mujeres por la Dignidad y la Vida en el desarrollo de proyectos con y para las mujeres* (San Salvador: Las Dignas, 1993). See also Lynn Stephen, *Women and Social Movements in Latin America: Power from Below* (Austin: University of Texas Press, 1997).

34. Vilma Gladis Vásquez Melgar, interview by author, San Salvador, 20 February 1997.

parties of the FMLN. Dignas members, Vásquez told me, increasingly felt that the participants in the projects saw the Dignas primarily as a source of funds. The Dignas were falling into the practice of giving people things and maintaining their dependency rather than enabling them to help themselves.

In 1992, when the Dignas asserted their autonomy from the party, they did so in part because they rejected clientelistic relationships. What they wanted was to find better ways in which to empower women, and that did not seem to be happening through the productive projects. Consequently, at the annual Dignas assembly at Coatepeque in 1993, a proposal was approved to stop developing productive projects and to focus on organizing women around feminist issues.

At the same time, several of the key activists in the organization, including Vásquez, sued the fathers of their children for child support. In the process, they became aware of the considerable number of women who had had similar experiences at the Attorney General's office. When Vásquez applied for child support, she gained firsthand knowledge of the humiliating and unwieldy process that women were forced to go through in order to get the fathers of their children to contribute to their care. Vásquez's ability to transform that experience into feminist political action came from her personal history.[35] Because she had worked with the state prior to the war, Vásquez knew how to negotiate within that arena. Her history in the FMLN provided her with experience organizing civil society in order to pressure the state. Through her feminist involvement with the Dignas, she became convinced that women could only become protagonists by disentangling "sexuality" and "motherhood." In her view, these were not separate options for women; men, unlike most women, could have sexual relations and leave the resulting offspring behind. Vásquez insisted that changing this dynamic was a major goal of the feminist movement. Because of its interrelationship with the state, she saw the issue of child support as key to enacting feminist changes. All the laws used the nuclear family as a model, Vásquez explained, when the reality is that the prevalent family unit in El Salvador is made up of a woman and her child or children. In the face of this situation, the Dignas would attempt to reshape the ideal to take reality into account.

With funding from Spain, the Dignas began to research the issue of child support. They also started meeting with women in order to advise them of their rights and to treat the emotional distress which, Vásquez asserts, centered on a variety of problems: incest, powerlessness, motherhood, child

35. Ibid.

abuse, and battering. Soon even the Attorney General's office began sending difficult cases to the Dignas for attention. By 1994, the Dignas were providing legal services. Through pressure and negotiation, they succeeded in resolving many difficult cases that had been stalled in the Attorney General's office.

But the work soon went beyond dealing with individual cases. As part of the peace accords, the National Police and several branches of the armed forces had been dissolved. In November of 1994, those who were laid off were given severance pay. Only a few months after they had begun to organize the AMD, the Dignas and the women they had mobilized succeeded in pressuring the Attorney General into announcing that he would deduct the equivalent of twelve months of child support payments from the severance pay of those who were being sued for child support. Unfortunately, despite this change in policy, the mechanisms to implement it were not established in time; many women discovered that the severance pay had already been disbursed by the time they arrived to claim their portion. Other women failed to put in claims because of threats from former partners who had been in the police or the military. But despite its limited success, the campaign mounted by the Association attracted more women to the Dignas and raised awareness of the problem of irresponsible fatherhood. The efficacy of their work was recognized by UNICEF, which in 1994 awarded its first annual Communication Award (in the category of Alternative Media Campaigns) to the Dignas for their work in generating publicity for the issue of child support.

After an initial unsuccessful attempt in 1995 to form a domestic violence support group, the Dignas continued to offer free legal and psychological services for women who were seeking child support. But providing these services was only a means to achieve the ultimate goal of organizing women for political action. Once women came to the Dignas for services, they would be organized, have their consciousness raised about the political implications of their situation, and would be compelled to act.[36] In August of 1995, with funds from the European Union and Canada, the AMD opened an office that was separate from the Dignas—around the corner from the Attorney General's office.

The following month, an opportunity arose for the AMD to exert its political force. President Cristiani offered voluntary retirement to employees in the public sector as part of the process of privatizing the state. The AMD held a news conference and criticized the plan, noting that it did not include

36. Vázquez and Murguialday, *Unas + otras,* 79.

deductions for child support. Two days later, the Attorney General sent a proposal to the Legislative Assembly, one that was rewritten as Decree 568. That decree required that 30 percent of the severance pay be deducted and handed over to the mothers seeking child support. The AMD worked actively to lobby for the passage of the bill. According to Vásquez, they also fought to include a provision that would have required the Ombudsman of Human Rights, an institution set up by the peace accords, to verify timely notification. A woman whose former companion was going to retire would be notified in time to guarantee that she and her children could access the funds. While this amendment was not included, Decree 568 was passed quickly enough to allow women to claim their child support.[37]

The following year, the AMD convinced the Attorney General to propose a decree that would allow the AGR to take child support deductions from workers' yearly bonuses. Each year, workers with a formal salary are awarded an extra month's pay in December, ostensibly to cover the additional expenses of Christmas and New Year's celebrations. But these funds had never been considered part of the total income in determining child support payments—until the passage of this legislation. The bill vividly illustrates how the AMD's efforts at reshaping gender relations intersected with global policies and state formation in postwar El Salvador.

The structural adjustment policies of the World Bank have made it impossible for the Salvadoran government to increase its budget for social services. While the Legislature would not have approved an across-the-board increase in the payments women receive, legislators did accept the Attorney General's proposal for a portion of the bonus to be deducted for child support. Miguel Angel Cardoza Ayala, the Attorney General, pointed to this legislation as one of the principal achievements of the AGR in 1996, and he acknowledged that the initiative came from the AMD.

The AMD's momentum came to bear on the passage of the "Non-Arrears Bill," the requirement that political candidates prove that they were up to date on their child support payments before they would be permitted to assume elected office. The nature of the campaign to get this legislation passed illustrates the contradictory context in which the AMD operates. To pass the "Non-Arrears Bill," the Dignas formed a coalition that included members from the entire political spectrum. Their allies in this process held extremely diverse views, even on issues pertaining to women's rights. For example, during the very session in which the "Non-Arrears Bill" was to be

37. Vásquez Melgar, interview.

considered, a letter was read from the Christian Democratic representative, Rosa Mélida Villatoro, the head of the Assembly's Commission on the Family. While Villatoro's maternalist concerns about poor women and their children made her one of the AMD's primary allies in the Legislature, she took a virulent stance against abortion. That very day she had submitted a statement to the Assembly that called on legislators to eliminate the exceptions under which abortion was permitted.[38]

Lorena Peña, a FMLN representative and the president of MAM, introduced the "Non-Arrears" proposal with the argument that supporting one's children was "a moral value that every legislator, male and female, should have." Representatives of party after party stood up to support the proposal, rising to the cheers of an AMD contingent that sat in the gallery. Even the right-wing ARENA party—which had at least two candidates in default, the AMD suspected—supported the proposal. Yet despite this outpouring of support, the legislators began a debate over whether to vote for the proposal as it stood or to send it to committee for review. One of the representatives on the stage, Gustavo Salinas of the Christian Democratic Party, called for a direct vote; Lorena Peña, however, argued that it should be revised in committee.

During the debate, I was sitting with the women from the AMD behind Villatoro. She turned to consult Vásquez and Nelly Rivera, another AMD staff member. Peña came up to the gallery where we were seated to explain that she worried that if the bill did not go to committee, it might include loopholes or be written in an unconstitutional way. Salguero Gross suggested that Peña call a recess, allowing the legislative committee to meet for twenty minutes in order to decide whether they could come up with a proposal or whether there was a need for more consideration. The committee returned, stating that they needed more time but agreeing that the legislation could be approved without additional amendments. The law's unanimous passage was front-page news the next day.

While the AMD knew that there were candidates from both the FMLN and ARENA who were in default, they did not anticipate that the head of the ARENA youth group, Walter Araujo, owed thirty thousand colones (approximately thirty-five hundred U.S. dollars) to his ex-wife. Araujo was the poster

---

38. While Villatoro's gesture seemed purely polemical at the time, a few months later the Assembly passed a new penal code that eliminated the cases in which abortion had been permitted: rape, incest, malformation of the fetus, and risk to the life of the mother. It was a move that took the Salvadoran women's movement by surprise, one that they were totally unprepared to challenge. (On the abortion issue, see Hipsher, this volume.)

boy of the right-wing party. Young, handsome, and extremely articulate, he was featured prominently in television ads as part of the election campaign claiming that the FMLN was a "terrorist" organization. News of his default generated enormous publicity along with calls for his resignation from the party. While he denied that he had failed to support his son, claimed that the accusations against him were a misrepresentation of the situation, and criticized his detractors for saying things that hurt his child, Araujo paid the debt before receiving his clearance.

The passage of these initiatives was the realization of a political strategy initiated by the Dignas and carried out by the AMD. In those women who gathered outside the AGR to seek child support, the Dignas recognized a potential constituency whose unmet needs embodied the contradiction between the ideology of motherhood and the treatment of mothers by the state. The Dignas organized women into the AMD to confront that contradiction. But the AMD was part of the Dignas' larger agenda—to challenge the construction of gender roles in El Salvador, in which men are inherently irresponsible toward their children and women are naturally self-sacrificing mothers.

The AMD's strategy intersected with the AGR's project of modernization within the limited constraints imposed by the neoliberal policies of the ARENA government. The AMD developed a working relationship with the Attorney General and elaborated proposals that enabled him to expand his budget without violating the neoliberal policies of the state. This collaboration in developing, promoting, and passing legislation—such as the severance pay packages and the Christmas bonuses—enabled the AGR to increase the amount of funds transferred from men to the mothers of their children without leveling new taxes. Thus, the AGR's budget was increased without any new expenditures by the state. The AMD enabled the AGR to improve its services to the children of irresponsible fathers without expanding the welfare state; the AMD worked with the AGR to improve the situation of the women seeking child support by challenging fathers' irresponsibility. Recognizing the limits of the neoliberal policies of the Salvadoran state, the Dignas did not demand that the state provide for the basic needs of women, children, or men.

The critique of irresponsible fatherhood was not invented by the Dignas. It was part of a broader discourse on the state's modernization, a discourse the Dignas and the AMD were able to use to forge the coalitions they needed. Obligating men to contribute part of their severance pay and Christmas bonus to their children required little of the state. And since the Dignas used a moral language that echoed the language of the Salvadoran right, they encountered little opposition to their proposal that children get a portion of their fathers' Christmas bonus. It was equally hard for the representatives to argue that someone who was behind on child support payments should be allowed to take office. The notoriety of Araujo's case generated significant additional publicity for the issue.

The role of the Salvadoran state as the arbitrator between men, women, and children makes it possible for conservative women like Salguero Gross and Villatoro to jump on the bandwagon, condemning irresponsible father-hood. Rather than providing the funds for child support, the state simply collects them from fathers or their employers and redistributes the funds to mothers.[39] While the state must support the AGR, it has not assumed any financial responsibility for the maintenance of children (except those placed in orphanages). The AMD has not challenged this situation; it sees such an effort as futile. As a result, Salvadoran feminists with a radical critique of neoliberalism find themselves on the same side as right-wing women who support the neoliberal agenda.

BIBLIOGRAPHY

INTERVIEWS

Cardoza Ayala, Miguel Angel. Interview by author. San Salvador, 7 January 1997.
Carranza Aguirre, Douglas Francisco. Interview by author. San Salvador, 10 February 1997.
Herrera, Morena Soledad. Interview by author. San Salvador, 13 November 1996.
Herrera Reyes, Hilda Edith. Interview by author. San Salvador, 10 February 1997.
Jovel, Ana Mercedes. Interview by author. San Salvador, 9 June 1997.
Vásquez Melgar, Vilma Gladis. Interview by author. San Salvador, 20 February 1997.

OTHER SOURCES

Baires, Sonia, Dilcia Marroquín, Clara Murguialday, Ruth Polanco, and Norma Váz-quez. *Mami, Mami, demanda la cuota alimenticia . . . la necesitamos: Un analisis feminista sobre la demanda de cuota alimenticia a la procuraduría.* San Salvador: Mujeres por la Dignidad y la Vida, 1996.
Ehlers, Tracy Bachrach. "Debunking *Marianismo:* Economic Vulnerability and Sur-vival Strategies Among Guatemalan Wives." *Ethnology* 30, no. 1 (1991): 1–16.
Fisher, Jo. *Mothers of the Disappeared.* Boston: South End Press, 1989.
García, Ana Isabel, and Enrique Gomáriz. *Mujeres centroamericanas: Ante la crisis, la guerra y el proceso de paz.* San José, Costa Rica: FLACSO, 1989.

39. Though there were rumored cases of women who had been sued for child support, no one in the AGR was aware of any actual cases.

Lagos Pizatti, Victor, and María Teresa de Mejía. "La situación de la familia y del menor en El Salvador." In *La situación de la familia y el menor en Centro América y Panama.* San Salvador: Secretaría Nacional de la Familia, 1994.

Lazo, Francisco. *El Salvador en cifras y trazos.* San Salvador: Equipo Maíz, 1996.

Martín-Baró, Ignacio. "La familia, puerto y carcel para la mujer salvadoreña." *Revista de Psicología* 9, no. 37 (1990): 265–77.

Molyneux, Maxine. "Mobilization Without Emancipation? Women's Interests, the State, and Revolution in Nicaragua." *Feminist Studies* 11, no. 2 (1985): 227–54.

Moser, Caroline O. "Gender Planning in the Third World: Meeting Practical and Strategic Gender Needs." *World Development* 17, no. 11 (1989): 1799–825.

Mujeres por la Dignidad y la Vida. *Los proyectos productivos y la autonomía economica de las mujeres: La experiencia de Mujeres por la Dignidad y la Vida en el desarrollo de proyectos con y para las mujeres.* San Salvador: Las Dignas, 1993.

Rivas, Pedro Geoffry. *Lengua salvadoreña.* San Salvador: Dirección de Publicaciones e Impresos del Ministerio de Cultura y Comunicaciones, 1987.

Stephen, Lynn. *Women and Social Movements in Latin America: Power from Below.* Austin: University of Texas Press, 1997.

Stevens, Evelyn P. "Marianismo: The Other Face of Machismo in Latin America." In *Male and Female in Latin America,* edited by Ann Pescatello. Pittsburgh: University of Pittsburgh Press, 1973.

Umaña, Carlos. *Un nuevo mapa para El Salvador.* San Salvador: Ediciones Tendencias, 1996.

Vázquez, Norma, and Clara Murguialday. *Unas + otras × todas = Asociación de Madres Demandantes: Una lucha colectiva por la cuota justa y paternidad responsable.* San Salvador: Las Dignas, 1996.

6 | Gender Equality, Democratization, and the Revolutionary Left in Central America
Guatemala in Comparative Context

Ilja A. Luciak

To the Guatemalan woman has to be guaranteed, under conditions of equality, her full participation in political, civil, economic, social, and cultural life, and the eradication of every form of gender and sex discrimination that constitutes an obstacle for the full display of her talents and potential in support of the development and progress of the country.

—URNG, *POSICIÓN DE URNG SOBRE LA MUJER GUATEMALTECA,* 1995

On 29 December 1996, the guerrilla forces integrated into the Unidad Revolucionaria Nacional Guatemalteca (Guatemalan National Revolutionary Unity, or URNG) and the Guatemalan government, headed by president Alvaro Arzú, signed historic peace accords that ended a conflict that had traumatized Guatemala for thirty-six years. The human suffering during this period defies the imagination. According to a report by the Historical Clarification Commission, which was charged under the peace accords with establishing the truth about Guatemala's violent past, more than two hundred thousand Guatemalans were killed or disappeared over the course of the conflict.[1] In addition, hundreds of villages were destroyed, and one and a half million people were internally displaced or sought refuge in Mexico.[2]

This chapter is based on a book-length manuscript that analyzes the situation of women in postwar Central America. The author would like to express his gratitude to DIAKONIA-Sweden and Lutherhjälpen-Sweden, which provided financial support for this research project.
1. Historical Clarification Commission, *Guatemala: Memory of Silence* (Guatemala City: Historical Clarification Commission, 1999).
2. Ibid. See also Jack Spence et al., "Promise and Reality: Implementation of the Guatemalan Peace Accords" (Cambridge, Mass.: Hemisphere Initiatives, August 1998), 4.

In the wake of the peace accords, the URNG started the process of becoming a legal political party, seeking to provide political representation for its supporters. It has been argued that the democratization of Guatemala requires a broadening of political participation.[3] Political parties play a key role in facilitating that political participation and thus are important actors in the Central American transition toward more democratic forms of government. In order to consolidate national and even regional democracy, the parties have to democratize themselves and effectively "articulate the demands and perspectives emerging from the newly-mobilized sectors."[4] Women are at the core of these newly mobilized sectors, as the proliferation of a strong women's movement throughout the region will attest. The recent mobilization of women has to be considered in historical context, however: women's demands have traditionally been neglected by a male-dominated party system.

This chapter examines the efforts of the URNG to provide a voice for its female constituents. Gender equality is a central indicator in assessing whether the revolutionary left in Guatemala is fulfilling its promises to its female constituents. I understand gender as a socially produced category, defined in Terrell Carver's terms as "the ways that sex and sexuality become power relations in society."[5] Equality is used as a twofold concept that includes "formal equality, which can be achieved by means of legislation" and "substantial equality, which aspires to being able to deal with relations between individuals in different original positions."[6]

The significant female participation in the Salvadoran and Nicaraguan guerrilla armies during the 1970s and 1980s raises the question of the role of women in the URNG during the war. Even more important, we need to establish the extent of female participation during the URNG's conversion from an armed movement to a political party. Female militants in Central America frequently express the fear that the transition from the popular revolutionary struggle (characterized by mass participation) to the electoral politics of the 1990s has demobilized women. What are the consequences of this transition? Have women obtained significant representation in the emerging

3. Rachel M. McCleary, "Guatemala's Postwar Prospects," *Journal of Democracy* 8, no. 2 (1997), 129.
4. Carlos Vilas, *Between Earthquakes and Volcanoes* (New York: Monthly Review Press, 1995), 185.
5. Terrell Carver, *Gender Is Not a Synonym for Women* (Boulder, Colo.: Lynne Rienner, 1996), 120.
6. Tuija Parvikko, "Conceptions of Gender Equality: Similarity and Difference," in *Equality Politics and Gender,* ed. Elizabeth Meehan and Selma Sevenhuijsen (London: Sage, 1991), 48.

political structures? In the case of Guatemala, what is the impact of the female militants on the formulation of the URNG's political project?

I begin my analysis by examining the extent of female participation in the URNG during the war. I then discuss the peace accords, seeking to determine the extent to which women's needs and rights were recognized. Next, I analyze gender equality in the URNG and examine the initial steps of the URNG's conversion from an armed movement to a democratic political party. I conclude with reflections on the challenges facing the URNG in the near future. The discussion of the URNG tends to emphasize quantitative indicators—and thus formal equality—in the recognition that the struggle to achieve substantial equality is still in its infancy.

Women's Participation in the Revolution

When the URNG signed the 1996 peace accords, the Guatemalan guerrilla movement was composed of four different groups: the Ejército Guerrillero de los Pobres (Guerrilla Army of the Poor, or EGP), the Organización Revolucionaria del Pueblo en Armas (Revolutionary Organization of People in Arms, or ORPA), the Fuerzas Armadas Revolucionarias (Revolutionary Armed Forces, or FAR), and the Partido Guatemalteco del Trabajo (Guatemalan Workers' Party, or PGT). Throughout the struggle there was much speculation as to the strength of the respective groups, with the Guatemalan army claiming several times to have eliminated the guerrillas. Most observers agree that the URNG was considerably weakened by the end of the 1980s. According to Jack Spence et al., "In the last years of the war the URNG was estimated to field no more than 1,000–1,500 guerrillas and militarily became only a nuisance to the Guatemalan army."[7] While speculation will continue regarding the URNG's strength during the war, we have detailed records of URNG personnel at the time of demobilization.

As part of the peace negotiations, the URNG agreed to a definitive cease-fire in an accord signed in Oslo on 4 December 1996.[8] Whereas the implementation of the peace accords was supervised and facilitated by the United Nations Mission for Human Rights Verification in Guatemala (MINUGUA), the demobilization and disarmament of URNG personnel was monitored by

7. Spence et al., "Promise and Reality," 11.
8. MINUGUA, *Acuerdo sobre el definitivo cese al fuego* (Guatemala City: MINUGUA, 1996).

a United Nations peacekeeping mission. A group of 155 military observers, authorized by the United Nations Security Council, was in charge of security for the eight camps (located on six sites) where URNG combatants were concentrated and processed. The URNG agreed to demobilize its forces in three phases over a period of two months following D day, 3 March 1997.[9]

By the end of March, all URNG forces had been concentrated in the established camps. According to Lieutenant Colonel Araujo Lima, the Brazilian who was in charge of the demobilization camp located at Finca Claudia, Esquintla, the URNG presented an initial list of a total of 3,614 combatants. This list was eventually revised down to 3,250. The actual number of demobilized combatants was somewhat lower still and reflected the fact that some URNG members had no desire to go through the demobilization process. Some were already integrated into civilian life, while others did not want to appear in the official demobilization list.[10] As had been the case in El Salvador, some guerrilla fighters had little faith in the viability of the peace agreement.[11] In light of the extreme political violence of the past, they were not prepared to endanger their lives by officially registering as members of the URNG.

At the same time that a part of the URNG membership chose not to demobilize, the URNG members who congregated in the camps were not always actual combatants. In addition to those URNG fighters who went to the camps from their areas of operation inside Guatemala, a considerable number of URNG supporters were brought back from refugee camps in Mexico. Not all in the latter group were URNG combatants, a fact manifested by the considerable number of children in the camps. Based on United Nations records, 125 children below fourteen years of age were demobilized, several of them infants.[12] Some observers maintained that only about half of the URNG personnel in the camps were "actual former combatants."[13] In light of these observations, one needs to take the membership statistics with a grain of salt.

9. Due to the close relations between the Guatemalan government and Taiwan, China opposed the deployment of a United Nations peacekeeping mission in the U.N. Security Council. China withdrew its veto first on 20 January 1998. Thus, China's position delayed the starting day of the demobilization.

10. Araujo Lima, interview by author, Esquintla, 23 April 1997.

11. For an elaboration of the Salvadoran case, see Ilja A. Luciak, "Gender Equality in the Salvadoran Transition," *Latin American Perspectives* 26, no. 2 (1999).

12. These data are based on information provided by Lieutenant Colonel Carlos Tanco in an interview by the author, Guatemala City, 21 November 1997.

13. McCleary, "Guatemala's Postwar Prospects," 138.

Table 6.1

Composition of URNG Combatants by Group, 1997

Group	URNG Combatants (N)	(%)
EGP	1,479	50.3
FAR	1,211	41.2
ORPA	250	8.5
Total	2,940	100.0

Source: **MINUGUA.**

According to data from the United Nations, 2,940 URNG combatants officially demobilized. The EGP and FAR constituted the great majority of the fighters, with 50 and 41 percent, respectively. The ORPA forces constituted less than 10 percent of the total, while the PGT (according to the official record) had no military forces at all. "Carlos Gonzáles" (Ricardo Rosales), the head of the PGT since 1974, explained that although the number of PGT combatants was indeed small, the Communist party did have a military force. The combatants, however, were integrated into the military forces of the other URNG groups. For example, the Frente Unitario (Unified Front), which was established in 1993 and originally consisted only of ORPA fighters, later included 16 PGT combatants.[14]

In addition to the combatants concentrated in the various camps, the URNG demobilized an additional 2,813 members. This latter group consisted of 493 people who belonged to URNG international cadres; the rest were URNG leaders and other personnel who had served the guerrilla movement as political cadres inside the country. Thus, according to United Nations records, the total URNG membership at the time of demobilization was 5,753.[15]

It is interesting to compare these figures to the data from the Salvadoran demobilization process. There, the guerrilla forces integrated into the Frente Farabundo Martí para la Liberación Nacional (Farabundo Martí National Liberation Front, or FMLN) demobilized in 1992. A total of 15,009 FMLN members were registered, including 8,552 combatants, 2,474 wounded non-combatants, and 3,983 political cadres. The number of women in the FMLN

14. "Carlos Gonzáles," interview by author, Guatemala City, 4 March 1999.
15. Data are based on information provided by Lieutenant Colonel Carlos Tanco.

was 4,492, or 29.9 percent.[16] Unfortunately, the Guatemalan data—particularly in regard to gender composition—are not as complete as in the case of El Salvador.[17] This situation reflected the continued climate of fear and the extremely secretive nature of the URNG.[18]

Nevertheless, a European Union-sponsored study of the socioeconomic background of the URNG membership gives a reasonably accurate picture of the URNG's gender composition. URNG members carried out this study during the demobilization phase. The study is based on a survey of 2,778 URNG combatants (of the 2,940 concentrated in the camps) and 1,410 political cadres (of 2,813). Although only half of the political cadres were surveyed, we have an almost complete picture of the URNG combatants.

According to Table 2, women represented 410 (15 percent) of the 2,778 interviewed combatants and 356 (about 25 percent) of the 1,410 political cadres. These data demonstrate that female participation in Guatemala's revolutionary struggle was rather limited, compared to female participation in the Salvadoran and Nicaraguan conflicts.[19] In the case of the Sandinista move-

Table 6.2

Gender Composition of URNG by Demobilization Category, 1997

	Women		Men		Total	
Category	(N)	(%)	(N)	(%)	(N)	(%)
Combatants	410	14.8	2,368	85.2	2,778	100.0
Political cadres	356	25.2	1,054	74.8	1,410	100.0
Total	766	18.3	3,422	81.7	4,188	100.0

SOURCE: URNG, "Personal incorporado: Diagnostíco socio-economico" (Guatemala City: UNRG, May 1997), 2–4.

16. Ilja A. Luciak, "La igualdad de género y la izquierda revolucionaria: El caso de El Salvador," in *Género y cultura en América Latina*, ed. María Luisa Tarres Barraza (Mexico City: El Colegio de México, 1998), 142.

17. United Nations and URNG officials were generally reluctant to discuss membership statistics. Unlike the situation in El Salvador, there are no official data indicating the gender composition of the three groups making up the URNG combatants.

18. An anecdote will illustrate this point: in April 1997, I went out with three women active in the Guatemalan women's movement. During the course of the evening they "confessed" to each other (and to the author) for the first time that all three of them had been active in the URNG for several years. Although they had been close friends for years, they did not consider it prudent to reveal their political work. The three friends also maintained that no one in their families knew about their URNG membership.

19. In light of the fact that many URNG combatants were brought back from refugee camps in Mexico, it is reasonable to assume that some of the demobilized women were not actual combatants. This is probably also the case for a number of the male URNG members.

ment in Nicaragua, the most widely reported estimates state that women constituted between 25–30 percent of the combatants.[20] Patricia Chuchryk, for example, maintained that in Nicaragua the "rate of women's participation in armed combat during the insurrection was the highest of any Latin American revolutionary movement."[21] Unfortunately, there are no hard data to support these estimates. While it is clear that women participated in great numbers in the revolutionary struggle, the FSLN never released official figures on the composition of its guerrilla force at the time of demobilization. For this reason we are left with considerable variation in the reported estimates.

Carlos Vilas, who based his estimates on a review of Sandinista combatants' death certificates, found that women constituted only 6.6 percent of Sandinista forces.[22] His findings differ considerably from the predominant image of a force that was one-third female. However, two observations may help resolve this conflict. One has to do with the concept of "combatant." Vilas's data obviously emphasize arms-bearing combatants, while the definition of "combatant" employed by most other studies tends to be much broader and includes support personnel. Second, it is important to distinguish between women's participation during the final phase of the insurrection and the revolutionary struggle in general. Almost all studies reporting a 30 percent participation rate refer to the final stage of the struggle.[23]

Women did participate in significant numbers and came to occupy important leadership positions; in the early years of Nicaragua's revolutionary struggle, however, female participation was restrained. According to Leticia Herrera, one of the few female commanders, male FSLN militants had a very traditional view of women, and female combatants were only accepted in greater numbers after 1973–74.[24]

While some controversy persists regarding the number of women in the FSLN, reliable figures document the scope of female participation in El Salvador's FMLN. Women represented 29.1 percent of the FMLN combatants at the time of demobilization. They were most strongly represented among

20. Susan E. Ramírez-Horton, "The Role of Women in the Nicaraguan Revolution," in *Nicaragua in Revolution*, ed. Thomas W. Walker (New York: Praeger, 1982), 152.

21. Patricia M. Chuchryk, "Women in the Revolution," in *Revolution and Counterrevolution in Nicaragua*, ed. Thomas W. Walker (Boulder, Colo.: Westview Press, 1991), 143.

22. Carlos Vilas, *The Sandinista Revolution: National Liberation and Social Transformation in Central America* (New York: Monthly Review Press, 1986), 108–9.

23. See Linda L. Reif, "Women in Latin American Guerrilla Movements: A Comparative Perspective," *Comparative Politics* 18, no. 2 (1986), 158; Ramírez-Horton, "The Role of Women in the Nicaraguan Revolution," 152; Helen Collinson, ed., *Women and Revolution in Nicaragua* (London: Zed Books, 1990), 154.

24. Leticia Herrera, interview by author, Managua, 12 November 1997.

the *políticos* (political cadres), constituting 36.6 percent of those engaged in political work. In terms of the overall membership, comprised of combatants, *políticos*, and wounded noncombatants, the 1994 ONUSAL data show 4,492 women, or 29.9 percent.[25] Thus, female participation in the Guatemalan guerrilla movement was significantly less than it had been in El Salvador. Among combatants (where we have the most complete data), URNG women had only 50 percent of the strength of their Salvadoran counterparts. Overall, female participation in the Guatemalan conflict was about half of what it had been in other Central American revolutionary movements.

Whereas lower levels of female participation distinguished the Guatemalan guerrilla movement from its Central American counterparts, similarities were evident in other areas. For example, Nicaraguan, Salvadoran, and Guatemalan women all gave similar reasons for joining the guerrillas and offered comparable descriptions of the nature of gender relations during the war. When asked why they had joined the URNG, female combatants most frequently gave reasons that had little to do with their gender interests. Like their male counterparts, most women joined out of a conviction that conditions in Guatemala had to be changed or because family members had been killed or had joined the guerrillas. Representative statements included "the necessity to move the country forward"; "the knowledge that Guatemala suffered severe repression"; "the death of my mother in combat in 1981"; "ethnic discrimination and the economic situation at the time, and the advice of my father who was a member of the revolutionary party." One combatant said, "my parents were organized before I was born. I joined conscientiously at the age of thirteen."[26]

Despite the sentiments they shared with other Central American revolutionaries, Guatemalan women tended not to participate in the guerrilla movement during its early years. Alba Estela Maldonado ("Comandante Lola"), the most senior female commander, recounted that when she joined the EGP in 1974 she found only two women in her group. It was only in the 1978–80 period that women started to join the movement in greater numbers, but at no time did women's participation surpass 25 percent.[27] Sexual relations were initially strictly regulated by the leadership. Couples had to go through a trial period and had to prove themselves before they could seek permission to form a family. These stringent norms broke down as the guerrilla forces grew in numbers. Many of the new recruits lacked the political

25. Luciak, "Gender Equality in the Salvadoran Transition."
26. These statements are from interviews conducted in 1997 and 1998.
27. Alba Estela Maldonado, interview by author, Guatemala City, 20 November 1997.

education and awareness of the old cadres. In the opinion of the old guard, they exhibited a different level of commitment. Whereas the original cadres held the view that "if we join, it is for life," the new recruits viewed their experience differently, announcing, "I'll join the guerrilla movement for one year."[28] As the movement grew, the strict discipline enforced during the early years started to break down. Interestingly, the experience in the guerrilla movement affected more than gender relations: it reportedly played a key role in breaking down ethnic barriers. According to Maldonado, members of different indigenous groups got to know each other for the first time in a context where "ethnic differences did not play a role in amorous relations."[29]

Traditional gender relations were reinforced and challenged at the same time. In the military command structure, women were the exception. Most female combatants were active in communications, logistics, and rearguard activities. Traditional domestic activities, however, such as preparing meals, washing clothes, cutting firewood, and cleaning, were more equally shared between the sexes. These experiences established important precedents for the postwar period.

Between 15 April and 3 May 1997, the former combatants left the camps to reintegrate themselves into civilian life. The process of reintegration promised to be complex and challenging. For example, six hundred URNG members had to be put into temporary housing upon leaving the camps, since they had no place to go. Many had lost their entire families in the war, while others were afraid to return to their villages of origin, since they would be stigmatized as official URNG combatants.[30] The Ixcán incident of May 1998 was ample proof that their fears were justified. The incident occurred when a group of demobilized ex-combatants sought to return to their communities and some villagers used violent means to prevent them from doing so. What made this a high-profile case was the fact that these communities were considered sympathetic to the URNG.[31]

Of particular concern were the poverty and the ethnic background of the former combatants. The majority of URNG personnel came from Guatemala's twenty-one indigenous peoples and belonged to the most marginalized sectors of society. Among URNG combatants, indigenous people represented 80 percent of the total, while they made up about 50 percent

28. Ibid.
29. Ibid.
30. Captain Hernán, interview by author, Finca Claudia, Esquintla, 23 April 1997. See also McCleary, "Guatemala's Postwar Prospects," 139.
31. For background to this incident, see Spence et al., "Promise and Reality," 19.

of the political cadres.[32] According to Rachel McCleary, "the rank-and-file supporters of the URNG [speak] 16 indigenous languages."[33] The living conditions of Guatemala's indigenous community were—and are—appalling, characterized by great deficiencies in their access to the most basic human needs, including health care, housing, and education. World Bank data revealed that in the countryside, where the overwhelming majority of the indigenous population is located, 90 percent live in conditions of abject poverty.[34] In the case of URNG personnel, government statistics indicated that URNG members tended to come from areas in which 82 percent of the population lived in poverty or absolute poverty.[35]

In a few areas, the socioeconomic profile of URNG members was remarkably different from that of the population in general. For example, only 16 percent of the former combatants and political cadres were illiterate, and an equally large group had some form of technical or university education.[36] In the general population, however, the illiteracy rate was 44 percent.[37] In most regards, however, the URNG members shared the characteristics of the general population. For example, most were of peasant background, and only 16 percent indicated that they had any land. Most were seasonal agricultural workers without access to land or stable employment.[38] Their predicament reflected the conditions prevailing in Guatemala's rural sector, which was characterized by extreme inequality in land tenure and extensive insecurity about property rights. Not surprisingly, the situation was particularly precarious for URNG women. Only 25 had any land, while 635 (out of the 766 interviewed) had responsibility for the support and survival of their families. The burden of responsibility was particularly heavy in the case of the 141 single mothers.[39] Thus, the URNG leadership confronted an enormous challenge when it sought to provide for the needs of its supporters in the wake of the peace accords.

32. URNG, "Personal incorporado: Diagnóstico socio-economico" (Guatemala City: URNG, May 1997), 2–3.
33. McCleary, "Guatemala's Postwar Prospects," 138.
34. World Bank, *Guatemala: An Assessment of Poverty* (Washington, D.C.: World Bank, 17 April 1995), 1–4, cited in Spence et al., "Promise and Reality," 47.
35. URNG, "Personal incorporado," 8. Those who live below a dollar a day live in "absolute poverty." People living in "poverty" cannot meet their basic needs.
36. Ibid., 5.
37. World Bank, *Development 1997* (Washington, D.C.: World Bank, 1997), Table 5, cited in Spence et al., "Promise and Reality," 47.
38. URNG, "Personal incorporado," 9.
39. Ibid., 11.

Gender Equality and the Peace Accords

Luz Méndez, a member of the URNG's commission negotiating the peace accords, was conscious of the importance of incorporating women's rights into the agreements. She had learned from the Salvadoran experience that women's issues received scant (or no) attention in peace negotiations.[40] This was the case in El Salvador, even though "Nidia Díaz" (María Marta Valladares),[41] Lorena Peña ("Rebeca Palacios"), and Ana Guadalupe Martínez, all high-ranking FMLN commanders, participated in the process. Peña, re-elected to the Salvadoran parliament in 1997, affirmed that the special problematic of women was simply not discussed during the negotiations.[42] Now a committed feminist, she recognized that women's emancipation was not an issue during the war and that she had had no idea of gender consciousness at the time of the demobilization.[43]

Awareness of gender issues was also limited in the ranks of the URNG. Within civil society, however, the reality was different. An increasingly vocal women's movement supported the efforts of a few high-ranking female URNG officials to put gender equality on the agenda of the peace negotiations.[44] The Asamblea de la Sociedad Civil (Assembly of Civil Society, or ASC) played a particularly important role. It consisted of ten diverse organizations representing the main sectors of Guatemalan society. The ASC derived its legitimacy from the January 1994 framework agreement, giving it "official recognition as an interlocutor by the parties to the peace talks."[45] A highly visible group within the ASC was the Women's Sector: "Practically the only one with a permanent presence, the Women's Sector in the Assembly of Civil Society influenced . . . the coordination and the content of some of the accords."[46] As a result, women's rights were specifically addressed in four of the seven substantive agreements reached between July 1991 and September 1996. This fact was publicized only days after the signing of the accords; a

---

40. Luz Méndez, interview by author, Guatemala City, 4 April 1997.

41. Several guerrilla leaders have continued to use their *noms de guerre*, since their legal names are often not widely known. I refer to the name most commonly used, and provide the pseudonym in parenthesis, with the *nom de guerre* in quotation marks.

42. See Luciak, "Gender Equality in the Salvadoran Transition," for an analysis of the Salvadoran peace accords.

43. Lorena Peña, interviews by author, San Salvador, 29 July 1993 and 4 May 1995.

44. Ana Leticia Aguilar, "Un movimiento de mujeres embrionario," in *El movimiento de mujeres en Centroamérica*, ed. María Teresa Blandón and Sofía Montenegro (Managua: La Corriente, 1997).

45. Spence et al., "Promise and Reality," 12.

46. Maldonado, interview.

study of the accords, using a gender perspective, was conducted by research-ers from the University of San Carlos and released in January 1997.[47] The emphasis on gender issues in the Guatemalan peace accords indicates that the level of gender awareness in the region had changed since the 1992 Salvadoran agreement.

Indeed, there were a number of important passages on women's rights in the accords. In the accord establishing procedures for the resettlement of populations uprooted during the war, the parties agreed "to emphasize in particular the protection of families headed by women, as well as the widows and orphans who have been most affected."[48] Further, the Guatemalan gov-ernment "committed itself to eliminating all forms of discrimination, factual or legal, against women, and to make it easier [to have] access to land, hous-ing, [and] credit and to participate in development projects. A gender per-spective will be incorporated in the policies, programs and activities of the global development strategy."[49] In the important agreement on the rights of Guatemala's indigenous peoples, considered one of the key achievements of the URNG leadership, indigenous women were given special protection. For example, sexual harassment of an indigenous woman was to be sanctioned particularly severely under Guatemalan law.[50] Women's political rights were also addressed. The accord concerning the strengthening of civil society ad-vocated the introduction of measures of "positive discrimination" to in-crease female participation.[51] The agreement required the signatory parties "to take the corresponding measures in order to ensure that organizations of political and social character adopt specific policies tending to encourage and favor women's participation as part of the process of strengthening civil-ian power."[52]

Luz Méndez affirmed the importance of the international climate during the peace negotiations. For example, discussions on the Socioeconomic and Agrarian accord coincided with the 1995 Fourth World Conference on

47. Universidad de San Carlos de Guatemala, Programa Universitario de Investigación en Estudios de Género, "Proyecto: Mujeres y acuerdos de paz" (Universidad de San Carlos de Guatemala, Guatemala City, mimeograph).

48. United Nations, *Acuerdo para el reasentamiento de las poblaciones desarraigadas por el enfrentamiento armado* (Guatemala City: MINUGUA, 1994), Chapter 2, Article 2.

49. Ibid., Chapter 3, Article 8.

50. United Nations, *Acuerdo sobre identidad y derechos de los pueblos indígenas* (Guate-mala City: MINUGUA, 1995), Chapter 2, Article 1.

51. Measures of "positive discrimination" refer to quotas or other measures intended to benefit women.

52. United Nations, *Acuerdo sobre fortalecimiento del poder civil y función del ejército en una sociedad democrática* (Guatemala City: MINUGUA, 1996), Article 59.

Women in Beijing. The fact that gender issues were on the forefront internationally made it easier to incorporate provisions favoring women's rights into this accord.[53] Finally, there are specific provisions concerning women in the accord on Strengthening Civil Power and the Role of the Military in a Democratic Society. In general, the various accords' provisions concerning women can be seen as part of women's practical gender interests. Nevertheless, it appears that the accords have contributed to a rethinking of women's role in Guatemalan society. At least at a formal level, women are now acknowledged as key protagonists in Guatemala's future development.[54] The challenge remains, however, to implement the provisions in the accords in a way that transforms Guatemalan society.

Spence et al. emphasize that "the Guatemalan agreement contains more wide ranging language on social and economic areas, by far, than the Salvadoran accord, but a great many of the provisions are stated in sufficiently general terms as to make them virtually unenforceable."[55] The authors point to the Achilles' heel of the accords. David Holiday has argued that the guerrillas were considered "relatively weak actors with minority support within society," and therefore "lacked the kind of leverage exerted by revolutionaries in neighboring El Salvador."[56] There is strong consensus that the URNG's weakness at the bargaining table made it impossible for the guerrilla leadership to negotiate more specific, enforceable agreements, a reality that is likely to impede the full realization of the provisions in the accords that concern women's rights.

Thus, the Guatemalan accords, while unique in terms of addressing the role of women in society and advocating change toward greater gender equality, were strong on rhetoric and weak on implementation. The influence that civil society had on the formulation of the accords did not translate into effective pressure during the implementation phase. Not surprisingly, early evaluations of the impact of the peace accords sounded a pessimistic note. Leaders of the women's movement argued "that the demands of women in respect to the implementation of the accords lacked tangible results. Fourteen months after they took effect, it is difficult to perceive how these commitments have been converted into actions; the reality is that six

53. Méndez, interview.
54. Gobierno de Guatemala, *Política nacional de promoción y desarrollo de las mujeres guatemaltecas plan de equidad de oportunidades 1997–2001* (Gobierno de Guatemala, Guatemala City, July 1997, mimeograph).
55. Spence et al., "Promise and Reality," 14.
56. Holiday, "Guatemala's Precarious Peace," *Current History* 99, no. 634 (February 2000).

out of every ten Guatemalan women live in rural areas and the absence of public services is common."[57] The government was criticized for "failing to have an idea of how to attend to women's historic problems" and for lacking a strategy of action designed to ensure that the provisions of the accords would not remain empty words.[58]

Gender Equality and Democracy in the URNG

In 1996, as the end of the peace negotiations came into view, the URNG leadership agreed to unify and dissolve the historic structures of the four constituent groups. This move was an effort to initiate the difficult transition from a secretive, hierarchical, political-military movement to a democratic party. In neighboring El Salvador, following the peace accords, the FMLN had suffered from intense infighting among its five groups, which led to the 1994 exodus of two of its constituent groups. The FMLN finally decided in 1995 to dissolve its five historic organizations. The URNG, having learned from this experience, decided to accelerate the process. In October 1996, the FAR was the first URNG group to dissolve officially. Its example was followed in February 1997 by the EGP and in March 1997 by ORPA and the Communist Party. The dissolution process was difficult for the members, since many shared a strong identification with the political-military project of their respective organizations. In the case of the Communist Party, two high-ranking militants refused to join the URNG and preferred to remain outside the evolving URNG structures.

During the war, the two key URNG structures had been the Comandancia General, consisting of the commanders of the four groups, and a National Directorate made up of seven representatives from each group. Similar to the FMLN, the URNG guaranteed equal representation for each group, regardless of its troop strength. In 1996, this body of twenty-eight was enlarged to forty-four. It was this Directorate that in April 1997 elected the Provisional Executive Committee, the highest decision-making body of the party in formation. Table 3 shows the new URNG structures.

In the elections for the new party authorities, the group quotas were no longer observed. Instead, the composition of the new Executive Committee reflected the relative military strength of the four groups. In addition to the

57. "Demandas de las mujeres y acuerdos de paz," *La Cuerda,* 8 March 1998, 11.
58. Ibid.

Table 6.3
The Party Structure of the URNG, 1997

Level	Party Authorities
National	National Assembly Executive Committee
Department	Department Assembly Department Executive Committee
Local	Municipal Assembly Municipal Executive Committee

SOURCE: URNG.

four seats reserved for the four comandantes, the EGP had five representatives, the FAR three, ORPA two, and the PGT one. This outcome was interesting in light of the fact that the elections were secret. "Rolando Moran," the EGP leader, was elected party president, while "Pablo Monsanto" became vice president.[59] The new party leadership faced the challenging task of building a viable movement. The dissolution of the original structures had left a vacuum and the leadership struggled to reconnect with its historic base while it sought to recruit new members.

During the thirty-six years of conflict, specific statements on women's rights in the manifestos and programs of the four groups integrating the URNG were notably absent. Women's issues were part of URNG platforms only in the most general fashion. Comandante Lola attributed this to different priorities during the conflict. "I believe there were errors, justified in their great majority. It wasn't that we didn't consider it [the consideration of gender issues] important, but that our life was very hard, full of activity directly related to combat, to military activities, to the recruitment for military units. Thus it was not a priority at that moment."[60] It is also important to point out that the Guatemalan guerrilla forces had their origins in the first wave of Latin American guerrilla movements (1956–70). Gender equality was hardly on the agenda then, and few women participated in combat. The traditional views espoused by the URNG leadership during the 1960s and early 1970s were difficult to overcome.

The four URNG groups differed somewhat in the space provided to their

59. Monsanto succeeded Moran following the president's death on 11 September 1998.
60. Maldonado, interview.

female constituents. Comandante Lola affirmed that the EGP was late in taking up gender issues: "I couldn't say it was in the last years, rather in the last
months, that an effort was made to have discussions among ourselves [the
women]. . . . This is one of the lacunae that we have, but I think that all
organizations were in the same situation, because we didn't consider it necessary, it was a lack of vision."[61] In the case of the FAR, however, women
succeeded somewhat earlier in getting their views incorporated into official
documents. In 1991, a FAR meeting ended with the resolution that "In Guatemala, women's liberation is an inseparable part of society's liberation." One
can even find specific references to gender equality: "It is our fundamental
goal to promote the effective and efficient incorporation, participation and
representation of the Guatemalan woman in the political, social, and economic process as part of the integral development of Guatemalan society, in
the context of the search for democracy, peace, and the construction of a
New Guatemala, where gender equality will be one of the elements that define the democratic character of society."[62] The views expressed in the resolution of the 1991 FAR Congress became the basis of a September 1996 FAR
document that elaborated the group's position on the gender dimension in
revolutionary thought. The document uses Maxine Molyneux's concepts of
strategic versus practical gender interests to discuss the challenges confronting women in Guatemala. It emphasizes that only a focus on the realization
of women's rights would lead to a fundamental restructuring of society, one
that would guarantee gender equity.[63] Thus, of the four constituent groups,
the FAR appears to have played the key role in formulating an agenda on
women's rights. The URNG as a whole only recently started to emphasize
women's rights. According to high-ranking leaders, it was only in 1994 that a
section on women's rights was incorporated into an official URNG document.

Within the Central American women's movement there has been heated
discussion over the issue of a women's secretariat within parties on the left.
In the case of the FMLN in El Salvador, such a secretariat was established
following the 1992 peace accords. While it had little autonomy in its first
years, it became an effective advocate for women's rights within the party.
The Sandinistas in Nicaragua established a women's secretariat first during

61. Ibid.
62. FAR, "Documento resoluciones sobre el trabajo de la mujer, Asamblea Nacional de
Cuadros de las FAR" (Guatemala City: FAR, May 1991).
63. FAR, "La dimension de género en nuestra concepción revolucionaria" (Guatemala
City: FAR, September 1996), 14.

the May 1998 party congress. Nicaraguan feminists opposed the creation of a secretariat, fearing a repetition of the events of the 1980s: at that time, the women's movement was subordinated to the party.

Female URNG militants differed in their views on how to advance an agenda of women's rights most effectively within the emerging political party. Following the signing of the peace agreement, women organized the first meeting of female militants in January 1997 and formed the Espacio de Mujeres (Women's Space) in the URNG. Several key protagonists in the struggle for women's rights held the position that one should not advocate the creation of a women's secretariat within the party. Having observed the fight for gender equality within the FMLN and FSLN, they were concerned that such a secretariat would stifle women's autonomy and allow the party to control the agenda. Most women who held this position eventually changed their point of view and agreed to the necessity of creating an institutional space to fight for women's rights.[64] Thus, when the initial structures of the new party were created, a Secretaría de Asuntos Políticos de la Mujer (Secretariat for Women's Political Matters) was set up, one that was headed by Comandante Lola.

A key issue for the newly formed secretariat was the fight to implement measures of positive discrimination that were intended to strengthen female representation in the party structures. Female leaders argued for a 30 percent quota, following the standard employed by the FMLN in El Salvador. After considerable discussion, the URNG leadership made a political commitment, stating that neither gender should have more than 70 or less than 30 percent representation in the new structures. Such a commitment was indeed important, especially in light of the composition of the provisional executive committee of the URNG: Comandante Lola was the only woman among fourteen men (that is, men made up 93.3 percent of the executive committee). This situation was critically characterized by members of the women's movement as *"Lola y los catorce"*—Lola and the fourteen guys.

When asked why only one woman was elected to the executive committee, male leaders argued that women simply did not have sufficient support to get elected and that one had to accept the outcome of a secret, democratic election. Women's participation was barely more significant in the URNG's National Council, which had four women among its forty-four members. Men thus represented 90.9 percent of the council, while women made up only 9.1 percent. Female leaders recognized that much work lay ahead of

64. Méndez, interviews.

them for the new quota to be adhered to in the elections for the permanent party authorities. Comandante Lola affirmed that given the low historic level of female representation, increasing women's representation was a long-term project; one could not expect to reach a 30 percent base immediately.[65]

El Salvador's FMLN represented the Central American vanguard in guaranteeing women's representation within its decision-making structure. In its 1997 party congress, the FMLN used separate ballots to ensure that the agreed-upon quota would be observed. The leadership's commitment to strengthen women's participation translated into female militants holding one third of the seats on the Executive Committee while having 40 percent of the seats on the fifty-two-member Political Council. In addition, Violeta Menjívar, who obtained the most votes, was elected vice president. The Salvadoran experience demonstrated that a commitment to gender equality can indeed be translated into significant improvements for female militants. Nicaragua, on the other hand, could not boast the same success. Historically, women had been excluded from the party leadership. Once a quota was established in 1994, five women were elected to the fifteen-member FSLN Directorate. In the 1998 party congress, the quota was observed, yet gender equality came under attack. What particularly concerned Nicaraguan feminists was the replacement of female leaders who had a strong record in support of gender equality with militants known to toe the (male) party line.

It will be interesting to see whether the URNG will follow the Salvadoran or the Nicaraguan lead. It is important to emphasize that the challenges confronting women in the URNG were even greater than those of the other parties on the revolutionary left. The URNG had a female constituency with a complex ethnic composition (a number of female militants did not speak Spanish) and a high incidence of illiteracy. The agreed-upon strategy was for female militants to assess their current strengths and weaknesses in order to subsequently train and educate women to fill the available positions of leadership. The URNG was still some time away from using mechanisms such as separate ballots to guarantee a female quota.

While the URNG leadership created the secretariat with the intention of giving women greater representation within the party, it also sought to reach out to Guatemalan women in general. This was an important decision, because the URNG had come under increasingly vocal criticism from female leaders who were disenchanted with the URNG's policies following the peace accords. One bridge that connected the URNG to those sectors of

---

65. Maldonado, interview.

Guatemala's social movement that were sympathetic to the URNG's social and political agenda was the Unión Nacional de Mujeres Guatemaltecas (National Union of Guatemalan Women, or UNAMG).[66] UNAMG had originally emerged in 1980 as a result of several years of organizing by women close to the guerrilla movement. The organization suffered greatly from the repression unleashed by the Guatemalan government in the 1980s. For example, in 1985, Silvia Galvez, a cofounder and general secretary of UNAMG, was disappeared. Due to these difficult circumstances, the organization became defunct. It was resurrected in 1997 under the leadership of Luz Méndez. Méndez, a key URNG leader with a recognized record of fighting for women's rights, emphasized that UNAMG was autonomous from the party. Some sectors of the women's movement, however, that rejected the notion of *doble militancia* (active participation in the women's movement *and* in a political party) considered UNAMG to be subordinate to the URNG. Whereas only time could clarify the degree to which UNAMG was independent, it represented an important link between women sympathetic to the political project of the URNG and the women's movement at large.

Conclusion

Any evaluation of gender equality and democratization within the URNG has to emphasize the enormous task facing the URNG leadership and its female militants. The peace process is still in its early stages and the URNG has yet to complete its transition from a political-military organization into a democratic political party. In this context, gender equality is simply not a priority in the minds of many key officials. Female leaders affirm that the URNG—and Guatemalan society at large—lacks gender awareness.

URNG militants debated many of the key issues that their counterparts in Nicaragua and El Salvador encountered, such as *doble militancia* or the autonomy of the women's movement. In addition to these debates, however, URNG women confronted problems specific to Guatemala's reality. Most important, militants of both sexes were overwhelmed by the demands that the demobilization and the creation of a political party placed on them. A central challenge facing the women who sought to advance gender equality within

66. The UNAMG was actually a recreation of a woman's movement that was set up in March 1980 by URNG militants.

the emerging party structures was the fact that they were still in the process of getting to know each other. The problem had two roots: first, the majority of the female URNG members had only recently acknowledged their militancy in a public way; second, despite advances in the unification process and the dissolution of the historic structures of the four constituent groups, many militants were only slowly shedding their identities as members of the subgroups in order to assume a URNG posture. Female militants from these distinct groups had to overcome years of mutual distrust in their efforts to find a common platform for their struggle. It appeared that women were the vanguard in the effort to forge an URNG identity. In the eyes of some leaders, the bonds of solidarity among women from the four groups helped heal the divisions among the organizations.

It is certain that gender equality and democracy can only flourish in the URNG if it successfully completes its transformation into a political party. As the former guerrilla movement proceeds with this transformation, it should learn from the experiences of the revolutionary left in El Salvador and Nicaragua. During the 1980s, the FSLN subordinated the fight for women's rights to the survival of the revolution in Nicaragua. As a result, female militants had only limited success in their struggle to transform gender relations within their party. Following the 1990 electoral defeat of the Sandinistas, an autonomous women's movement emerged and female militants renewed their efforts to achieve gender equality within the FSLN. Although they could point to some positive results, female leaders faced great challenges in extending their organizing efforts from the national level to intermediate party structures. At the same time, the Nicaraguan women's movement was increasingly successful in putting women's rights on the national agenda.

El Salvador presented the opposite picture. There, female FMLN militants demonstrated a remarkable ability to increase their representation in the party's decision-making structures and in the Salvadoran parliament. The women's movement, on the other hand, failed to mount a strong organizational effort in the 1997 elections and suffered from internal divisions. Two key lessons can be derived from these experiences for Guatemala. Efforts by female URNG militants to strengthen gender equality in the party will bear fruit if measures of positive discrimination are strictly enforced during the early stages of the fight for women's rights. For this to happen, alliances with male party leaders must be formed. Simultaneously, these partisan efforts need to be broadened into pluralist coalitions if they are to affect gender relations. Unity and lack of infighting are the preconditions that must be met in order for Guatemalan women to strengthen gender equality within the political parties—and within Guatemalan society.

BIBLIOGRAPHY

INTERVIEWS

Hernán, Captain. Interview by author. Esquintla, 23 April 1997.
Herrera, Leticia. Interview by author. Managua, 12 November 1997.
Lima, Araujo. Interview by author. Esquintla, 23 April 1997.
Maldonado, Alba Estela ("Comandante Lola"). Interview by author. Guatemala City, 20 November 1997.
Méndez, Luz. Interviews by author. Guatemala City, 4 April 1997 and 20 November 1997.
Morales, Ricardo ("Rolando Moran"). Interview by author. Guatemala City, 22 November 1997.
Peña, Lorena. Interviews by author. San Salvador, 29 July 1993 and 4 May 1995.
Rosales, Ricardo ("Carlos Gonzáles"). Interview by author. Guatemala City, 4 March 1999.
Soto, Jorge ("Pablo Monsanto"). Interview by author. Guatemala City, 22 November 1997.
Tanco, Carlos. Interview by author. Guatemala City, 21 November 1997.

OTHER SOURCES

Aguilar, Ana Leticia. "Un movimiento de mujeres embrionario." In *El movimiento de mujeres en Centroamérica,* edited by María Teresa Blandón and Sofía Montenegro. Managua: La Corriente, 1997.
Carver, Terrell. *Gender Is Not a Synonym for Women.* Boulder, Colo.: Lynne Rienner, 1996.
Chuchryk, Patricia M. "Women in the Revolution." In *Revolution and Counterrevolution in Nicaragua,* edited by Thomas W. Walker. Boulder, Colo.: Westview Press, 1991.
Collinson, Helen, ed. *Women and Revolution in Nicaragua.* London: Zed Books, 1990.
"Demandas de las mujeres y acuerdos de paz." *La Cuerda,* 8 March 1998.
FAR (Fuerzas Armadas Revolucionarias). "Documento resoluciones sobre el trabajo de la mujer, Asamblea Nacional de Cuadros de las FAR." Guatemala City: FAR, May 1991.
———. "La dimension de género en nuestra concepción revolucionaria." Guatemala City: FAR, September 1996.
Gobierno de Guatemala. *Política nacional de promoción y desarrollo de las mujeres guatemaltecas plan de equidad de oportunidades 1997–2001.* Gobierno de Guatemala, Guatemala City, July 1997. Mimeograph.
Historical Clarification Commission. *Guatemala: Memory of Silence.* Guatemala City: Historical Clarification Commission, 1999.

Holiday, David. "Guatemala's Precarious Peace." *Current History* 99, no. 634 (February 2000): 78–84.

Landau, Saul. *The Guerrilla Wars of Central America.* New York: St. Martin's Press, 1993.

Luciak, Ilja A. "La igualdad de género y la izquierda revolucionaria: El caso de El Salvador." In *Género y cultura en América Latina,* edited by María Luisa Tarres Barraza. Mexico City: El Colegio de México, 1998.

———. "Gender Equality in the Salvadoran Transition." *Latin American Perspectives* 26, no. 2 (1999): 43–67.

McCleary, Rachel M. "Guatemala's Postwar Prospects." *Journal of Democracy* 8, no. 2 (1997): 129–43.

MINUGUA (Misión de las Naciones Unidas para la Verificación de los Derechos Humanos en Guatemala). *Acuerdo sobre el definitivo cese al fuego.* Guatemala City: MINUGUA, 1996.

Parvikko, Tuija. "Conceptions of Gender Equality: Similarity and Difference." In *Equality Politics and Gender,* edited by Elizabeth Meehan and Selma Sevenhuijsen. London: Sage, 1991.

Ramírez-Horton, Susan E. "The Role of Women in the Nicaraguan Revolution." In *Nicaragua in Revolution,* edited by Thomas W. Walker. New York: Praeger, 1982.

Reif, Linda L. "Women in Latin American Guerrilla Movements: A Comparative Perspective." *Comparative Politics* 18, no. 2 (1986): 147–69.

Spence, Jack, et al. "Promise and Reality: Implementation of the Guatemalan Peace Accords." Cambridge, Mass.: Hemisphere Initiatives, August 1998.

United Nations. *Acuerdo para el reasentamiento de las poblaciones desarraigadas por el enfrentamiento armado.* Guatemala City: MINUGUA, 1994.

———. *Acuerdo sobre identidad y derechos de los pueblos indígenas.* Guatemala City: MINUGUA, 1995.

———. *Acuerdo sobre fortalecimiento del poder civil y función del ejército en una sociedad democrática.* Guatemala City: MINUGUA, 1996.

Universidad de San Carlos de Guatemala, Programa Universitario de Investigación en Estudios de Género. "Proyecto: Mujeres y acuerdos de paz." Universidad de San Carlos de Guatemala, Guatemala City. Mimeograph.

URNG (Unidad Revolucionaria Nacional Guatemalteca). "Propuesta a la sociedad: Cuatro objetivos, nueve cambios, cuatro prioridades." Guatemala City: URNG, April 1995.

———. "Personal incorporado: Diagnóstico socio-economico." Guatemala City: URNG, May 1997.

Vilas, Carlos. *The Sandinista Revolution: National Liberation and Social Transformation in Central America.* New York: Monthly Review Press, 1986.

———. *Between Earthquakes and Volcanoes.* New York: Monthly Review Press, 1995.

PART II

Radical Women in
South America

CHRONOLOGY OF ARGENTINA

1823   The Beneficent Society (Sociedad de Beneficencia) is formed.

1911   The League of Argentine Catholic Ladies is formed.

1919   The right-wing Argentine Patriotic League (LPA) is formed to suppress labor activism and the Left.

1930   President Hipólito Yrigoyen is overthrown by a military coup led by fascist sympathizer José Uriburu.

1931   The rightist Argentine Civic Legion is formed with thirty thousand members. A feminine association within the organization is created, attracting seven hundred members.

1932   The Argentine Association for Women's Suffrage has over eighty thousand members. The "Motherland and Home" Association of Argentine Ladies is formed to fight communism and women's suffrage. The pro-Nazi National Socialist Movement (MNS) is formed, attracting about twenty thousand followers.

1943   A military coup overthrows president Ramón Castillo. Juan Domingo Perón, a participant in the coup, becomes Secretary of Labor.

1944   Perón becomes vice president.

1946   Perón is elected president.

1947   Women win the vote. Evita Duarte, Perón's charismatic wife, establishes the Eva Perón Foundation.

1949   Evita Duarte proposes a Peronist Women's Party.

1952   Evita Duarte dies of cancer. Juan Perón starts second term as president.

1955   A military coup led by Eduardo Lonardi ousts Perón, who goes into exile. Lonardi is then replaced by Pedro Aramburu in another military coup.

1966   Another military coup takes place.

1969   The Montoneros, an urban guerrilla group influenced by Che Guevara and Peronism, is formed.

1970   The Montoneros kidnap and execute former president Aramburu.

1973   Juan Perón returns from exile and is elected president. His third wife, María Estela Martínez, known as Isabel Perón, is elected vice president.

1974   Juan Perón dies. Isabel Perón becomes the first woman president in the Americas.

1974   The Center for the Study of the Argentinean Woman (CESMA) is formed.

1975   Terrorist activity on the left and the right leaves over seven hundred dead.

1976   The military, led by Jorge Rafaél Videla, overthrows Isabel Perón and takes over the government.

1977   The military is formally accused of killing over two thousand people, arresting ten thousand, and disappearing twenty thousand. The Mothers and Grandmothers of the Plaza de Mayo organize the first public protest against the dictatorship and begin searching for their missing relatives.

1978   The Grandmothers of the Plaza de Mayo find missing grandchildren in Chile.[1]

1981   Videla is replaced by Roberto Viola, who is then replaced by Leopoldo Galtieri.

1982   Galtieri leads Argentina into war with Great Britain over the Malvina Islands. Britain wins the war, and as a result, Galtieri is replaced by Reynaldo Bignone. The National Housewives' Movement is formed.

1983   Raúl Alfonsín wins presidential elections, bringing an end to military rule.

1984   The Women's Multisectorial, a multi-class coalition of women, is formed.

1986   A government department for women is created.

1987   Divorce is legalized.

1989   Carlos Menem is elected president.

1990   The fiftieth disappeared grandchild is restored to his family.[2] The Fifth Latin American and Caribbean Feminist Congress meets in Argentina.

1992   Relations with Great Britain are restored.

1995   Menem is re-elected.

2000   Fernando de la Rua becomes president.

   1. Jo Fisher, *Out of the Shadows: Women, Resistance, and Politics in South America* (London: Latin American Bureau, 1993), 102.
   2. Ibid.

CHRONOLOGY OF BRAZIL

1909 The League of Catholic Ladies of Bahia, an antifeminist organization, is formed.

1920 The Nationalist Social Action (ASN), a right-wing federation of 250,000 members, is established in Rio de Janeiro.

1930 Getúlio Vargas comes to power.

1932 Women win the vote, in part due to the efforts of suffragists like Bertha Lutz. The right-wing Brazilian Integralist Action (AIB) is formed. A women's division, called the Green Blouses, is created within the organization. By 1937, the AIB boasts approximately two hundred thousand followers. Twenty percent of these are women. The Green Blouses have their own magazine, *Brasil Feminino*.

1936 The Green Blouses hold a congress in Rio de Janeiro.

1937 Vargas establishes the Estado Novo, eliminating elections and suppressing popular protest. As a result, first wave feminism disappears.

1945 Vargas is ousted by the military.

1949 Vargas is re-elected president.

1954 Vargas commits suicide.

1960 The Women's League of the State of Guanabara is formed.

1964 Through a coup d'état, the military replaces president-elect João Goulart with Humberto Castelo Branco, beginning two decades of military rule. In the aftermath of the coup more than seven thousand people are arrested and nine thousand are removed from office. Among those arrested are members of the Women's League. Right-wing women organized in the Women's Campaign for Democracy (Campanha de Mulher pela Democracia) support the military coup.

1967   General Artur da Costa e Silva becomes president.

1969   General Emílio Garrastazu Médici becomes president.

1972   First National Women's Congress is held in Rio de Janeiro.

1973   General Ernesto Geisel becomes president.

1975   Luís Inácio da Silva, known as Lula, becomes president of the Metalworkers Union of San Bernardo and Diadema.

1975   A Meeting for the Diagnosis of the Situation of Women is held in São Paulo.

1975   *Brasil Mulher,* the first women's newspaper of the contemporary women's movement, is founded in Paraná.

1977   Divorce is legalized.

1978   The First Congress of Women Metalworkers is held in Osasco.

1978   Lula suggests the creation of a Workers' Party. Popular protests against the dictatorship increase.

Late 1970s/early 1980s   Women's groups proliferate.

1979   General João Baptista Figueiredo becomes president.

1980   The Workers' Party (PT) is founded.

1982   All-female police stations are created.

1985   Military rule comes to an end. José Sarney becomes president, establishing a National Council for the Rights of Women.

1985   The Third Latin American and Caribbean Feminist Congress meets in São Paulo, attracting 950 women, including 300 from Brazil.

1988   Chico Mendes, rubber tapper activist, is assassinated.

1989   Presidential election takes place. Fernando Collor de Mello wins against Lula in second round.

1992   Collor de Mello resigns amidst impeachment procedures against him.

1993   Itamar Franco is named interim president.

1994   Fernando Henríque Cardoso wins presidential election with thirty-four million votes against Lula's seventeen million.

1997   Henrique Cardoso is re-elected with 53 percent of the vote. The PT obtains 31 percent of the vote.

CHRONOLOGY OF CHILE

1912 The League of Chilean Ladies is formed.

1932 Arturo Alessandri becomes president. The Nazi National Socialist Movement (NSM) is formed, attracting twenty thousand followers.

1935 The Movement for the Emancipation of the Women of Chile (MEMCH) is formed. It pursues "the integral emancipation of women, especially the economic, juridical, biological and political emancipation."[1]

1938 Popular Front rules the nation.

1942 Juan Antonio Ríos becomes president.

1946 Gabriel González Videla becomes president.

1949 Women win the vote. The final push is made by a coalition of women's organizations, the United Committee pro-Women's Suffrage, which came together in 1947.

1952 Carlos Ibáñez returns to the presidency.

1958 Jorge Alessandri becomes president.

1964 Eduardo Frei, the Christian Democratic candidate, wins presidential election. His administration sponsors a network of Mothers' Centers.

1970 Marxist candidate Salvador Allende wins presidential election with 36 percent of the votes.

1971 A protest of empty pots is held against the Allende administration.

1972 Feminine Power (PF), a coalition of center-right women, mobilizes along with the Housewives' Front (FRENDUC) and Solidarity, Order, and Liberty (SOL) against the Allende government.

1973 Tens of thousands of women march to demand Allende's resignation.

1973 A military coup brings an end to the Allende government. General Augusto Pinochet comes to power. Over two thousand people are

---

1. Asunción Lavrin, *Women, Feminism, and Social Change in Argentina, Chile, and Uruguay, 1890–1940* (Lincoln: University of Nebraska Press, 1995), 311.

murdered by the military in the years following the coup. A military government rules Chile until 1989.

1974   Lucía Hiriart, Pinochet's wife, reorganizes the Mothers' Centers (CEMA) and inaugurates the National Secretariat of Women (SNM), two volunteer organizations.

1974   An Association of Relatives of the Detained and the Disappeared is formed.

1982   A Movement of Shantytown Women (MOMUPO) is formed.

1983   Sebastián Acevedo commits suicide by lighting himself on fire in order to protest the disappearance of his two sons.

1983   Women for Life (MPLV), a coalition of sixteen center-left female leaders, mobilizes against the dictatorship by organizing protests, demonstrations, hunger strikes, discussions, and press conferences.

1983   The Christian Democratic Party creates the Democratic Alliance (AD), a coalition of center-left parties that advocate a peaceful transition to democracy. Another coalition, the Popular Democratic Movement (MDP), forms the same year and advocates armed struggle.

1983   A protest of empty pots is held against the military dictatorship.

1983   The Independent Democratic Union (UDI), a right-wing party, is formed. It opposes divorce, abortion, and feminism.

1983   MEMCH83 is formed.

1986   The rightist party National Renovation (RN) is created.

1988   Lucía Hiriart launches another pro-Pinochet organization, Women for Chile. CEMA already has more than 10,000 centers with a total of 6,000 volunteers and 230,000 members.[2]

1988   A plebiscite takes place to decide whether the military should remain in power. The "No" receives 55 percent of the votes. Women's groups proliferate.

1989   Patricio Aylwin, an anti-Allende Christian Democratic leader, is elected president. Twenty thousand women celebrate International Women's Day.

1991   A National Women's Service (SERNAM) is created by the government.

---

2. Patricia Chuchryk, "Feminist Anti-Authoritarian Politics: The Role of Women's Organizations in the Chilean Transition to Democracy," in *The Women's Movement in Latin America: Feminism and the Transition to Democracy*, ed. Jane S. Jaquette (Boston: Unwin Hyman, 1989), 160.

1993   Eduardo Frei Jr., the Christian Democratic candidate, becomes president.

1998   Pinochet is arrested in London on charges of murder, terrorism, and genocide.

2000   Economist Ricardo Lagos, the candidate of a center-left coalition, wins the presidential election runoff.

7 | Spreading Right-Wing Patriotism, Femininity, and Morality
Women in Argentina, Brazil, and Chile, 1900–1940

Sandra McGee Deutsch

Like other women of Brazilian Integralist Action (Ação Integralista Brasileira, or AIB), the Brazilian fascist party of the 1930s, Dâgmar Cortines wore a green blouse with the Greek letter sigma on her right sleeve and cap. Her movement spied upon Jews and assaulted union members and communists in the streets. Regardless of whether she personally ignored or endorsed such activities, Cortines believed that the AIB defended God, family, and fatherland. Humanity was splitting into Satan's forces on the left and God's on the right, and the Integralists were on God's side. There was no middle, for Jesus had said that those who were not with him were against him. Resembling the devout Spaniards who had rebelled against the atheistic Republic, Integralists were "extremists of the 'right' . . . thank God!" The female Integralist's task was to help form the "new men" who would protect a Christian Brazil from leftist extremism.[1]

Dâgmar Cortines and other women in extreme right-wing groups bely the progressive maternalist images of womanhood that feminist and leftist female scholars have constructed. The latter believe that women's experiences in the home have tended to develop their capacities as nurturing and loving beings. Such attitudes, along with their concern for protecting their families, have predisposed women to empathize with victims of poverty and discrimination and to participate in progressive causes, according to these

The Beveridge Fellowship of the American Historical Association, CIES-Fulbright, and grants from the American Council of Learned Societies, American Philosophical Society, National Endowment for the Humanities, and University Research Institute of the University of Texas, El Paso, funded the research for this chapter. I also thank Margaret Power, Victoria González, and Karen Kampwirth for their comments and Elisa Fernández for inviting me to her campus to present some of these ideas.
1. *A Offensiva*, 18 July 1937, 12.

researchers. Cortines and other radical rightists also have constructed women as caring mothers, but ones who nurture a different agenda. Extreme right-wing movements in Argentina, Brazil, and Chile (ABC) between 1900 and 1940 recruited women for the task of inculcating conservative notions of patriotism and morality in their families. As an extension of these motherly and wifely tasks, women would use their customary educational, philanthropic, and religious labors as vehicles for spreading such views—along with a conservative sense of femininity—within the broader society as well. Upholding the class hierarchy, this type of motherhood was anti-leftist.

Radical right-wing Argentine, Chilean, and especially Brazilian women now and then stepped beyond the prescribed female roles and trespassed into forbidden territory. Some betrayed a desire for autonomy, the expansion of rights, or the use of new rights—a desire that one could see as feminist and that their male comrades tried to curb. Occasionally, right-wing women shared goals with feminists, but they did not seek to ally with them.

These women joined the extreme right, which stridently opposed democracy, leftism, and other factors that seemed to threaten authority, privately owned property, and the particularities of family, locality, and nation. This opposition often took the form of actions outside electoral politics. Such rightist groups arose in the ABC countries from 1900 to 1940, and they reached their height in the 1930s. This was also the time of European fascism, which greatly influenced rightist currents in Latin America. Unlike those in Germany and Italy, however, the movements under study did not achieve lasting control of their governments.

In this chapter, I will discuss female participation in the extreme right during the first four decades of the twentieth century, a time that gave rise to three distinct periods of rightist activity in the ABC countries. In the years before World War I, the extreme right originated in a Catholic-influenced cultural context; during the war (and in the early postwar years), the bourgeois Leagues—with state assistance—battled militant workers; finally, the late 1920s inaugurated an age of fascism. Each period had its own characteristic forms of female involvement. Despite some differences among the women and countries under study, the similarities were paramount. The women's main goal was to safeguard rightist notions of family, country, and religion.

The Origins of the Extreme Right

The years leading up to World War I witnessed the origins of the modern extreme right. The evolution of the ABC countries' export economies promoted the formation of lower and middle classes, which demanded sweeping democratic—and, in the case of many workers, revolutionary—political and economic changes. In response, members of the upper social sectors began to formulate an ideology that rejected these groups' demands for greater autonomy and control but also sought to lure them into the existing system by offering minor reforms. This ideology was heavily influenced by Social Catholicism, a movement that proposed social welfare measures to alleviate poverty and weaken the left's appeal.[2]

Social Catholicism was a worldwide reformist campaign that grew out of the struggle against nineteenth-century attempts by liberal governments to curtail the power of the Church. Catholics' opposition to this anticlericalism led them to question other aspects of liberalism as well, such as free-market economics. Hurt by liberal policies, laborers had caught the attention of the Church in Europe; the fact that many workers had left the flock in favor of "atheistic" leftist movements and unions also influenced its vision. To cut further losses by widening the Church's appeal and forestalling the growth of the left, Pope Leo XIII urged Catholics to work with the poor in *Rerum Novarum* (1891) and other encyclicals. In Argentina and Chile, where the labor movements were relatively strong, Social Catholics founded schools, housing projects, mutual aid societies for laborers, and so-called workers' circles, which were led by priests and upper-class men. The desire to stamp out revolutionary views and worker autonomy set these efforts apart from those of socialists, anarchists, and union members.

Female participation in what would become the extreme right began with Social Catholicism. The Church stressed women's maternal roles within and outside the home: nurturers, educators, and helpmates within the family, women were also philanthropists and guardians of purity in society at large. Daughters of the elite received their education at schools administered by nuns. The religion-laden curriculum and the networks formed among pupils influenced many to work in Social Catholic-sponsored charities and female organizations.

Upper-class women had long been active in charitable endeavors. One important example was the Beneficent Society (Sociedad de Beneficencia) of Argentina, founded in 1823, which utilized government funding to administer orphanages and other social services. By the turn of the century, however, aid to the poor took on new meaning. Women formed a significant portion of the industrial labor force—about 24 percent in Argentina in 1909,

2. For information on the broader context of extreme right-wing activity and Social Catholicism, see Sandra McGee Deutsch, *Las Derechas: The Extreme Right in Argentina, Brazil, and Chile, 1890–1939* (Stanford: Stanford University Press, 1999).

28 percent in Chile in 1907, and 36 percent in Brazil in 1920—and participated in unions and strikes.[3] Some members of the upper classes were dis-
tressed about the conditions in which the poor lived and worked, yet labor
activism alarmed them even more, and some turned to Social Catholicism
for solutions.

As the Chilean Teresa Ossandón Guzmán pointed out, female Catholic
social action was a response to the problems that "tend to create conflicts
between the social classes." Women played only a limited role in the political
and economic arenas, but they could exert substantial influence in the moral
realm. To heal the rift in society, Ossandón advised Catholic women to direct
their efforts toward female laborers and their children.[4] María Rosario Ledesma, an Argentine Catholic activist, echoed her remarks. Bringing the social classes together, she noted, was part of the woman's mission to
strengthen the fatherland and family.[5]

Chile

Several groups in Chile embraced these goals. The Sisters of the Sacred
Heart, who educated girls of upper-class families, encouraged their former
students to join the Daughters of Mary, who were dedicated to uniting the
social classes through charitable works.[6] Another group, the League of Chilean Ladies (Liga de Damas Chilenas), was founded by aristocratic women in
1912 to moralize theatrical productions, fashion, and publishing—but it also
reached out to female workers. It formed the first Catholic women's labor

3. For the statistics, see Asunción Lavrin, *Women, Feminism, and Social Change in Argentina, Chile, and Uruguay, 1890–1940* (Lincoln: University of Nebraska Press, 1995), 58; June E.
Hahner, *Emancipating the Female Sex: The Struggle for Women's Rights in Brazil, 1850–1940*
(Durham: Duke University Press, 1990), 103; Elizabeth Quay Hutchison, "Working Women of
Santiago: Gender and Social Transformation in Urban Chile, 1887–1927" (Ph.D. diss., University
of California, Berkeley, 1995), 45. The figure for Argentina includes women in manual arts,
probably meaning textile workers in cottage industries (Lavrin, *Women*, 57). On women in labor
activities, see these same works, as well as Maria Valéria Junho Pena, *Mulheres e trabalhadoras:
Presença feminina na constituição do sistema fabril* (Rio de Janeiro: Paz e Terra, 1981),
182–89; Maria Valéria Junho Pena and Elça Mendonça Lima, "Lutas ilusórias: A mulher na política operária da primeira república," in *Mulher, mulheres*, comp. Carmen Barroso and Albertina
Oliveira Costa (São Paulo: Cortez Editora, Fundação Carlos Chagas, 1983), 26–27; Marysa Navarro, "Hidden, Silent, and Anonymous: Women Workers in the Argentine Trade Union Movement," in *The World of Women's Trade Unionism: Comparative Historical Essays*, ed. Norbert
C. Soldon (Westport, Conn.: Greenwood, 1985), 167–86.
    4. *Actividades femeninas en Chile* (Santiago: Imprenta La Ilustración, 1928), 571–72.
    5. María Rosario Ledesma de García Fernández, *Una época a través de mis escritos* (1920;
reprint, Buenos Aires: Talleres Gráficos Zaragoza, 1949), 27, 40.
    6. Ibid., 317.

"unions," organizing government and retail employees in 1914 and seam-stresses the following year. By 1922 it had organized 350 seamstresses and, by 1928, 535 employees. The autonomy of the unions grew over time; how-ever, in their early years, the unions were subordinated to the authority of the League and the Church. They enjoyed access to medical and educational services, a library, inexpensive meals, religious retreats, a vacation house, and a cooperative store. Members spoke of but did not act upon their desire for better salaries and working conditions. These "white" (i.e., anti-"red") unions, as the Ladies called them, were the counterparts to militant unions. They were designed to Christianize and tame working women—and thus preserve the Ladies' position at the top of the class hierarchy.[7]

Argentina

The League of Argentine Catholic Ladies (Liga de Damas Católicas Argenti-nas) had similar goals. Established by a Jesuit priest in 1911, this League instituted economical restaurants and a savings bank for female workers as well as a shelter in which recently arrived immigrant or migrant women could live safely.[8] Through such efforts, the Ladies hoped to protect the vir-tue of working-class women and give them a stake in the capitalist system.

In the Blanca de Castilla Studies Center (Centro de Estudios Blanca de Castilla), created in 1916, upper-class girls studied Catholic social doctrine. The center also formed Catholic unions of female laborers, store employees, and seamstresses in 1917 and 1918; by 1919, these unions had 719 members. Like their Chilean counterparts, the Argentine unions provided educational, religious, employment, and other services. President María Rosario Ledesma noted approvingly that the unions controlled by her center peacefully re-sisted both evil employers and the "tyranny of revolutionary societies" that despised Christianity and the social order. She and her collaborators favored some feminist goals, such as the vote and equal pay for equal work. Never-

7. Ericka Kim Verba, "The *Liga de Damas Chilenas* [League of Chilean Ladies]: Angels of Peace and Harmony of the Social Question" (paper presented at the Latin American Studies Association meeting, Guadalajara, Mexico, April 1997), especially 6–8; *Actividades,* 575, 585–90; Liga de Damas Chilenas, *Memoria correspondiente al año 1929* (Santiago: Imprenta Arturo Prat, 1929), 14–15; Blanca Subercaseaux de Valdés (Carmen Valle), *Amalia Errázuriz de Suber-caseaux* (Buenos Aires: Emecé Editores, 1946), 226–28. I thank Carlos Maldonado for the League pamphlet.

8. José Elías Niklison, "Acción social católica obrera," *Boletín del Departamento Nacional del Trabajo,* no. 46 (March 1920), 274–75, 277.

theless, they refused to join forces with what they condemned as "revolutionary feminism" to achieve such measures.[9]

Argentine Catholic women also took to the streets to voice their opposition to labor militancy. Workers' mobilization reached a peak during 1909 and 1910, culminating during the centennial celebrations of Argentine independence in May 1910. Angered by the timing of labor rallies and strikes, upper-class men responded, and their counterdemonstrations often sparked violence against labor. Encouraged by the prominent Social Catholic cleric Miguel de Andrea, the members of the Sisters of Mary, the League, and other upper-class female Catholic organizations held a mass celebrating independence on 21 May 1910. They paraded from the church to the tomb of José de San Martín, the father of Argentine independence, defiantly singing the national anthem.[10] Appealing to Argentine "tradition," they identified their views with the nation, and charged workers (most of whom were immigrants) with foreignism.

Brazil

The Brazilian labor movement was less active than those of the other two countries during these years, so its Social Catholic movement was also weaker. Women joined the Associations of Catholic Ladies (Asociações das Damas Católicas) and the Sisters of Mary, counterparts of the groups in Argentina and Chile. The League of Bahian Catholic Women (Liga das Senhoras Católicas Bahianas), later called the League of Brazilian Catholic Women (Liga das Senhoras Católicas Brasileiras), was founded in 1909. It aimed to clean up carnival celebrations, fashion, and the media, and it opposed feminism, which was beginning to gain recruits among the growing numbers of female professionals.[11]

9. Celina Arenaza de Martínez, interview by author, Buenos Aires, 15 July 1981; Celina de Arenaza, *Sin memoria* (Buenos Aires: Ronaldo J. Pellegrini, 1980), 24–25; Niklison, "Acción," 266–69; Ledesma de García Fernández, *Una época*, 13, 15–16 (quotation on 16), 18, 21–23, 38–39, 44–49.

10. Celia La Palma de Emery, *Discursos y conferencias: Acción pública y privada en favor de la mujer y del niño en la República Argentina* (Buenos Aires: Alfa y Omega, 1910), 247–49; Ambrosio Romero Carranza, *Itinerario de Monseñor de Andrea* (Buenos Aires: Compañía Impresora Argentina, 1957), 69–70; *El Pueblo*, 2 May 1910, 3 May 1910, and 12 May 1910.

11. On these and other female Catholic groups, see John Wirth, *Minas Gerais in the Brazilian Federation, 1889–1937* (Stanford: Stanford University Press, 1977), 199; Riolando Azzi, *Presença da igreja católica na sociedade brasileira*. Cadernos do ISER, no. 13 (Rio de Janeiro: ISER, n.d.), 11; Jeffrey Needell, *A Tropical Belle Epoque: Elite Culture and Society in Turn-of-the-Century Rio de Janeiro* (Cambridge: Cambridge University Press, 1987), 58–60; Dain Borges, *The Family in Bahia, 1870–1945* (Stanford: Stanford University Press, 1992), 175–79; Hahner, *Emancipating*, especially 104–5, 119–20.

Women's earliest experiences on the right, then, were in Social Catholicism. Reflecting the relative strength of local Social Catholic movements—which in turn reflected the strength of the working class—female involvement was greater in Chile and Argentina than in Brazil. The upper-class "ladies" offered models of womanhood for poorer women to follow, ones that differed from those of the anticlerical and combative left. They tried to induce young women into becoming Christian mothers and wives and creating moral, anti-leftist, and "patriotic" families. (In Argentina, there was the added goal of "nationalizing" foreigners, a goal that would become more explicit in the next phase of rightist action.) While the Catholic activists were concerned with some issues that appealed to feminists, such as women's ability to earn a decent living independently, they tended to oppose feminism, which they associated with anti-Catholic and leftist views.

The Age of the Leagues

Near the end of World War I, the battle lines between right and left sharpened. Bourgeois extreme rightist groups such as the Argentine Patriotic League (Liga Patriótica Argentina), Nationalist Social Action (Ação Social Nacionalista) of Brazil, and Patriotic Leagues (Ligas Patrióticas) of Chile asserted their nationalism in the face of several threats: war and revolution abroad; border conflict, in the case of Chile; and, in particular, the mobilization of workers. While rightist women continued to serve in Social Catholic organizations, in this polarized atmosphere they moved toward more visible and militant activities. They entered the first two groups and supported the third, thereby endorsing the Argentine and Chilean Leagues' repression of labor.

Chile

From 1918 to 1920, Chile experienced worker protests and tensions with Peru, which had asserted its claim to areas seized by Chile in the nineteenth century. The Santiago-based Military Patriotic League (Liga Patriótica Militar) and the Patriotic Leagues found in many localities held large rallies supporting the Chilean side of the diplomatic controversy. Some, such as the demonstration in Valparaíso on 21 July 1920, attracted many "ladies, young society women, and women of the people" *("damas, señoritas, y mujeres del pueblo")*, according to a reporter. The Leagues tied the border conflict to the social question, claiming that subversives allied with Peru were responsible for labor agitation. This rhetoric and League activity reached its height with the July 1920 election of Arturo Alessandri, presidential candidate of the mildly progressive Liberal Alliance. Despite his moderate platform, Alessandri's populist campaigning style convinced the elite that he was a dangerous demagogue.[12] In mid-July, the border dispute prompted the outgoing conservative government to send troops to the north. Alessandri's supporters feared that the administration would use the mobilization to remove pro-Alessandri troops from Santiago or otherwise keep the popular favorite from assuming office. Given the mobilization's right-wing tone, the act of accompanying one's menfolk to the train station became a political one for women.[13]

The discord between left and right sparked bloodshed. As an ally of both labor and Alessandri, the Student Federation in Santiago criticized the mobilization. Denouncing student pacifism and worker demands, upper-class youths destroyed an anarchist press on 19 July and the Federation headquarters two days later. In response, most likely, to the attack on the student organization, a group carrying the red flag assaulted some young right-wing demonstrators, shooting and killing Julio Covarrubias, the son of a prestigious Conservative family. This act provoked outrage in rightist circles.[14]

The murder of Covarrubias pushed women into the streets. The lengthy cortege that accompanied Covarrubias's casket to the cemetery included about three thousand women, many of them members of the Red Cross, a largely upper-class association. These mourners claimed the streets to declare their opposition to the left and to Alessandri.[15]

Argentina

More significant was female activism in Argentina, where the Tragic Week, a week of violent conflict between workers and the forces of order, sparked

---

12. After Alessandri assumed office, his repression of labor demonstrated his essential conservatism—as did his later presidency (1932–38).

13. *El Mercurio* followed all these events closely; on women, see 22–23 July 1920. Also see Philip Joseph Houseman, "Chilean Nationalism, 1920–1952" (Ph.D. diss., Stanford University, 1961), 72, 78, 85. On the Patriotic Leagues, see Sergio González Miranda, Carlos Maldonado Prieto, and Sandra McGee Deutsch, "Las Ligas Patrióticas: Un caso de nacionalismo, xenofobia, y lucha social en Chile," *Canadian Review of Studies in Nationalism* 21, no. 1–2 (1994), 57–69.

14. Houseman, "Chilean Nationalism," 80–81; *El Mercurio*, 22–25 July 1920; Guillermo Kaempfer Villagrán, *Así sucedió, 1850–1925: Sangrientos episodios de la lucha obrera en Chile* (Santiago: n.p., 1962), 177–88. The *Boletín de Sesiones Ordinarias* (Santiago, 1920) of the Chilean Senate and Chamber of Deputies also covered these events.

15. *El Mercurio*, 22–25 July 1920; Felicitas Klimpel, *La mujer chilena (el aporte femenino al progreso de Chile), 1920–1960* (Santiago: Andrés Bello, 1962), 236.

the creation of the Argentine Patriotic League (LPA). Dedicated to suppressing labor and the left, the LPA arose on 20 January 1919, a few days after the Tragic Week ended. Its president was Manuel Carlés, a professor and former congressman, who believed that women's philanthropic experience would allow them to instill morality and patriotism among female immigrant workers, who then would spread such notions among their children. Female League members would also teach their charges deportment appropriate to their sex and station. He distinguished these duties from politics, which he declared inappropriate for women, and from feminism, which he claimed inverted the gender order by making women masculine and men feminine. The LPA delegated the tasks of nationalizing households and feminizing female workers to separately organized groups of society matrons (Señoras), young society women (Señoritas), and female teachers. By the 1920s there were approximately 41 Señoras' "brigades" around the country, along with small groups of Señoritas; at the same time, men formed about 550 brigades. Probably about 820 women and 11,000 men made up the militant core of the LPA. The rank and file of the men's and teachers' brigades came primarily from the middle sectors, while most of the national male authorities were upper-class. In contrast, virtually all of the leaders and ordinary members of the Señoras and Señoritas were of the elite. These brigades drew from a narrow group of women united by family ties, attendance at elite Catholic schools, and participation in charity work.[16]

While men busied themselves with repressing strikes, drawing up antirevolutionary doctrine, lobbying, and speechmaking, women designed social welfare projects to help the needy and reduce dissatisfaction with the capitalist system. These projects also served to obscure the violence of the LPA, making it seem peaceful and even beneficent toward workers. The Señoras hosted day care facilities for children of working mothers, free medical services, neighborhood schools, maternity clinics, distributions of cradles and clothing, and patriotic celebrations for the poor. Many of these programs disseminated anti-leftist and religious messages intended to "Argentinize" immigrant mothers and their children. Such messages also infused the curriculum of the Señoritas' free schools for female laborers in factories and workplaces. By 1927, at least nineteen of these schools existed, and as late as 1950 the LPA claimed that over fifty were still operating. The schools imparted basic skills, domestic arts, lessons in civics and the catechism, and

16. Unless otherwise stated, information on female LPA members comes from Sandra McGee Deutsch, *Counterrevolution in Argentina, 1900–1932: The Argentine Patriotic League* (Lincoln: University of Nebraska Press, 1986), 87–94, 107–11, 155–63.

traits valued by employers. Their aim was to convert working-class women into obedient laborers and patriotic Christian mothers.

The Señoras saw it as part of their task to honor native-born women who performed traditional crafts in the home. One of their main projects was the annual textile fair, featuring cloth produced by indigenous and mestizo women of the interior. Sales of their woven and embroidered goods helped women who labored in their abodes, thus promoting the LPA's ideal of keeping them within the family unit. In addition, as Hortensia Berdier, president of the Señoras, put it, these fairs highlighted the talents of creole women who had inherited their techniques from previous generations and who lived in regions that were poor yet imbued with nationalist sentiments. We must help not only female factory workers but local industries as well, she told other League members.[17] Promoting a model of Argentine-born womanhood, nationalism, and tradition in this manner, then, was another part of the Señoras' mission.

The textile fairs and other projects sponsored by the Señoras and Señoritas were designed to raise female income levels, enhance women's skills, and provide services to needy families. In part, they represented concrete efforts to improve conditions for women. Nevertheless, they did so in ways that were designed to spread right-wing values and constrain workers' freedom of action.

Although the LPA opposed feminists, there was some overlap between the two groups. LPA women administered funds and large projects, conducted parliamentary-style meetings in which they chose their own leaders, and gave speeches in public. The skills they acquired within the LPA were precisely those that feminists sought for women in the wider society. Yet female League members never commented on the feminist goal of women's suffrage, which Argentines were debating in the 1920s, or on the feminist-backed revision of the Civil Code in 1926, which increased the rights of married women. Perhaps they followed the lead of Carlés, who proclaimed that women were not interested in rights they did not need. It is also likely that they disapproved of the feminists' secular, middle-class, and leftist or democratic ties.[18]

17. Liga Patriótica Argentina, *Discursos pronunciados en el acto inaugural y veredicto del jurado de la Tercera Exposición Nacional de Tejidos y Bordados* (Buenos Aires: n.p., 1922), 1, and *Discursos pronunciados en el acto inaugural y veredicto del jurado de la Cuarta Exposición Nacional de Tejidos y Bordados* (Buenos Aires: n.p., 1923), 2.

18. On Argentine feminism, see Lavrin, *Women;* Marifran Carlson, *Feminismo! The Woman's Movement in Argentina from Its Beginnings to Eva Perón* (Chicago: Academy Chicago, 1988). For views on feminism, including Carlés's (163), see Miguel J. Font, *La mujer: Encuesta*

At any rate, women's autonomy within the LPA was limited. They could not cast ballots for the movement's presiding officers, even though they were subordinate to them. The fact that Carlés headed the female as well as the male branches reflected the LPA's belief in male rule inside and outside the home.

Brazil

Brazil's entry into World War I—and labor mobilization in the years 1917–20—sparked the creation of groups similar to the LPA. The largest of these was Nationalist Social Action (ASN), which was established in February 1920 and centered in Rio de Janeiro. Catholic, anti-leftist, and anti-Portuguese, the ASN was a federation of nationalist and civic groups with a combined membership of perhaps 250,000. The rank and file came from the middle sectors, who resented the economic prowess of Portuguese immigrants, but members of the elite joined its leadership, and President Epitácio Pessoa (1919–22) served as honorary president. Ties to the ruling class facilitated the passage into law of several measures favored by the ASN, including price controls on primary foodstuffs and restrictions on the hiring of foreigners. The ASN approved of government crackdowns on leftism, which it identified with foreigners.[19]

The ASN aimed to "emancipate" women and incorporate them into its struggle. Catholic activists, the wives and relatives of members, adherents of a few female groups, and other middle-class women responded to its call. Writer Anna César, the president of one of these female groups—the Legion of the Brazilian Woman (Legião da Mulher Brasileira)—observed that ASN women would guide and inspire their menfolk: "Patriotic love, invigorated by the love of the mother, wife, sister and daughter, accomplishes miracles, [and] transforms small numbers of men into legions of valiants." Further underlining their customary roles, she added that women would cultivate patriotism with the same care they used in cultivating their gardens and ap-

---

feminista argentina: Hacia la formación de una Liga Feminista Sudamericana (Buenos Aires: Imprenta Costa Hermanos, 1921).

19. Steven Topik, "Middle-Class Brazilian Nationalism, 1889–1930: From Radicalism to Reaction," *Social Science Quarterly* 59, no. 1 (1978), 97–101, and "Economic Nationalism and the State in an Underdeveloped Country: Brazil, 1889–1930" (Ph.D. diss., University of Texas, Austin, 1978), 277–79; Alvaro Bomilcar, *A política no Brazil ou o nacionalismo radical* (Rio de Janeiro: Editores Leite Ribeiro & Maurillo, 1920), 143–45, 183–84; Alcibiades Delamare Nogueira de Gama, *Linguas de fogo: Discursos e conferencias* (Rio de Janeiro: Typographia do Annuario do Brasil, 1926), 189–96; *Gil Blas,* 13 February 1920.

pearance. (This image of femininity contradicted one offered by a male ASN leader. He cast Joan of Arc, with her nationalism, Christian faith, bravery, and self-sacrifice, as a fitting model for ASN women, yet her image was scarcely a maternal one.[20])

Another ASN member, however, appealed to motherhood. Writing in *Gil Blas* (the organ of the ASN), Rachel Prado urged Brazilian daughters, sisters, wives, and especially mothers of all colors, religions, and classes to love Brazil and pass on this love to their children. True Brazilians, she said, must oppose leftists and Portuguese merchants, foreigners who had abused Brazilian hospitality. But she widened the female nationalist space by asking women to be active patriots in their workplaces and schools as well as their homes.[21]

It is difficult to form a picture of women's activities, since the nationalist press mentioned them infrequently. Women raised funds for ASN affiliates and for the project to construct the statue of Christ the Redeemer, which was completed in 1931. They also attended ASN demonstrations and other functions and provided entertainment for them. A few exceptional women wrote in the press and gave speeches for the nationalist cause.[22]

It was unusual for women to serve as publicists; the right-wing Brazilian women who did so were more conspicuous than their Argentine or Chilean counterparts. One such figure was the poet and teacher Maria Rosa Moreira Ribeiro, who belonged to the ASN affiliates Legion of the Brazilian Woman and Nationalist Pedagogical Center (Centro Pedagógico Nacionalista) as well as the Red Cross. The government of São Paulo had delegated her to work with the ASN. Ribeiro directed the performances of a nationalist drama group (another ASN affiliate), wrote for *Gil Blas,* and addressed audiences. Her drama group, she pointed out, demonstrated how the educated Brazilian woman could contribute to the "sacrosanct battle to aggrandize the loved Fatherland," once she was freed from "antiquated ideas that . . . [she] should not separate herself from the home, where the man created for her a chimerical throne." Though she did not necessarily agree with female emancipation from the home in general, Ribeiro justified such emancipation if it allowed women to engage in nationalist activities.[23]

Like Ribeiro and several men in the organization, the ASN orator Maria

20. *Gil Blas,* 13 February, 23 September, and 30 September 1920; 5 May, 13 May, and 4 August 1921. On the Legion of the Brazilian Woman, see Hahner, *Emancipating,* 136.

21. *Gil Blas,* 5 May 1921.

22. For examples of such activities, see *Gil Blas,* 31 March, 5 May, 19 May, and 26 May 1921.

23. Ibid., 31 March, 13 May, and 7 July 1921.

Junqueira Schmidt praised the Brazilian Federation for Feminine Progress (Federação Brasileira pelo Progresso Feminino, or FBPF), the main suffragist organization, and endorsed female suffrage and access to higher education, the professions, and public administration. While admitting that women were capable of ruling society, this young professor and Catholic activist nevertheless concluded that their main task was to rule the home. Although her views seemed more conservative than Ribeiro's, both women tied the women's cause to nationalism. Schmidt defined feminism merely as raising children with patriotic values.[24]

By situating women in the household, Schmidt did not differ greatly from the moderate FBPF. Moreover, both ASN spokespersons and FBPF feminists tended to vindicate women's liberation in terms of broader causes: nationalism and social reform, respectively. Yet the strong Catholic character of the ASN separated it from the suffragist organization. The FBPF did not antagonize the Church, and many of its members were observant, but it was still secular in orientation. Nationalists did not criticize the FBPF specifically; however, they found fault with other women's groups that were not tied to the Church. The ASN's views more closely approximated those of the popular *Revista Feminina*, which spread its conservative "Catholic feminism"— including support for the vote—among numerous readers. They had little, if anything, in common with anarchist and communist feminists who urged sexual liberation and social revolution.[25]

Rightist women in this period enlarged their sphere of activity. They moved outside the Church, although the lingering Catholic ties of the rightist groups smoothed female entry by providing a sense of continuity and making the women seem nonpolitical. Women took part in new ventures, such as demonstrations, public speaking, and writing.

Whether they moved in the direction of autonomy or feminism is another matter. Maternalist justifications for women's political activity tended to pervade the right in the three countries (although there were some exceptions), and the goal of creating model patriotic mothers was evident in Brazil and Argentina. It was equally clear that the extreme right's notion of motherhood reinforced the existing class hierarchy. Women may have carved out more independence for themselves in the ASN, but the LPA limited their

---

24. Schmidt in *Gil Blas*, 29 December 1921 and 6 January 1922. For other ASN statements approving of feminism, see *Gil Blas*, 29 July 1920, 7 July 1921, and 22 September 1921.

25. *Gil Blas*, 18 March 1920; Susan K. Besse, *Restructuring Patriarchy: The Modernization of Gender Inequality in Brazil, 1914–1940* (Chapel Hill: The University of North Carolina Press, 1996), 166–92; Hahner, *Emancipating*, 127–38, 148–55.

ability to do so. Although the ASN supported moderate feminist positions and the LPA fostered the development of skills among its female members within the organization, not even the ASN would work with feminists to achieve any concrete goal. The religious nature of right-wing nationalism precluded such alliances, as did the leftist and democratic affiliations of the Argentine women's movement.

The Age of Fascism

From the late 1920s through 1940, the ABC countries witnessed the rise of fascist-influenced groups, usually paramilitary in nature, that opposed liberalism, democracy, leftism, and Jews. Such organizations as the Argentine Civic Legion (Legión Cívica Argentina), Brazilian Integralist Action (Ação Integralista Brasileira), and the National Socialist Movement (Movimiento Nacional Socialista) of Chile fought socialists, workers, and even moderate democrats in the streets. At the same time, expanding on ideas developed earlier by Social Catholics, they emphasized the need for drastic (albeit non-Marxist) change along nationalistic lines. Their martial orientation and support for male dominance seemed to preclude female participation. Nevertheless, despite some male opposition, women joined these radical rightist movements.

Argentina

In Argentina, a coup led by General José F. Uriburu toppled a democratic government and installed a fascist-leaning one in 1930. Supported by the Nationalists, as the radical rightists called themselves, the administration recognized the largest Nationalist group—the Argentine Civic Legion, formed in February 1931—as its partner in maintaining order and promoting nationalism. Trained by military officers, uniformed Legionnaires repressed workers and other opponents of the regime.

Legionnaires and other Nationalists opposed women's activity outside the home, strongly objecting to female suffrage. They also found fault with male voting, partly for ideological reasons and partly because they saw no possibility of winning elections, given widespread fraud.[26] Despite the Na-

26. I explore the ABC extreme right's views on voting in "What Difference Does Gender Make? The Extreme Right in the ABC Countries in the Era of Fascism," *Estudios interdisciplinarios de América Latina y el Caribe* 8, no. 2 (1997), 5–21.

tionalist hostility toward them, however, some women who wanted to fight subversive ideas and protect the family saw the Legion as a vehicle for such activity. In June 1931, the Feminine Group of the Legion was formed; fearing that the depression would foment instability, the Group set up free housing for the jobless and directed soup kitchens. Its vocational schools helped housewives of modest means acquire skills that would enable them to earn some money while remaining at home. Later in the decade, it also hosted tearful vigils at the grave of General Uriburu, who died shortly after leaving office in 1932 and became a Nationalist martyr. The Group characterized these efforts as neither political nor military, thus attempting to make them acceptable to Legionnaires and to the larger society. Lest even these limited duties foster a sense of autonomy, the Legion appointed a male "technical advisor" to oversee the Group.[27]

By mid-1931 there were an estimated thirty thousand Legionnaires and seven hundred members of the Feminine Group, all organized in brigades around the country. The Legion's male leaders and female members were largely upper-class, but somewhat less so than was the case in the LPA. The disillusionment with liberal democracy that was fostered by the depression, the conviction that fascism was the wave of the future, and the spread of Catholic militancy into the middle class had helped broaden the extreme right's appeal.[28]

Despite the fact that their male "comrades" did not particularly welcome them, some women continued to join such groups as the Alliance of Nationalist Youth (Alianza de la Juventud Nacionalista) and the National Association of High School Students (Asociación Nacional de Estudiantes Secundarios, or ANDES). Perhaps because they wanted to assume responsibility for their own affairs, other female Nationalists created their own organizations. In June 1932, for example, they formed the "Fatherland and Home" Association of Argentine Ladies (Asociación de Damas Argentinas "Patria y Hogar") to fight communism and factious ideas such as female suffrage. The Ladies sponsored radical rightist speeches on the radio and a school offering free courses on home economics, vocational skills, and patriotism for working-

27. Unless otherwise stated, the material on the Legion and women's activity in other Nationalist groups comes from my *Las Derechas,* 236–38.

28. On Catholic mobilization, see Austen Ivereigh, *Catholicism and Politics in Argentina, 1810–1960* (New York: St. Martin's Press, 1995), 76–84; Lila Caimari, *Perón y la iglesia católica: Religión, estado y sociedad en la Argentina (1943–1955)* (Buenos Aires: Ariel Historia, 1994). On Catholicism and Nationalism, see Loris Zanatta, *Del estado liberal a la nación católica: Iglesia y ejército en los orígenes del peronismo: 1930–1943* (Quilmes: Universidad Nacional de Quilmes, 1996).

class women, courses which resembled those of the Feminine Group and the LPA. In addition, they commemorated Uriburu's death and attended Nationalist parades and ceremonies. Occasionally the aristocratic Ladies, including wives and relatives of male Nationalists, gave speeches at such gatherings. Not all female Nationalists opposed votes for women. A member of ANDES and of the elite, Isabel Giménez Bustamante, publicly endorsed suffrage. Regarding women as mothers above all else, Giménez praised them for maintaining stability through their roles in the home. Voting by literate native-born women, she claimed, would reinforce social cohesion and counter the destructive tendencies of foreign-born electors, who were included in the ranks of the leftists.[29]

Giménez's position overlapped that of one of the main feminist organizations, the Argentine Association of Feminine Suffrage (Asociación Argentina del Sufragio Femenino), which favored the vote for literate Argentine-born women and for naturalized women who had long resided in the country.[30] Perhaps these moderate feminists thought that only a limited voting proposal could win congressional approval in a rightist-dominated political context. There is no sign, however, that feminists and Nationalists worked together to promote this bill (which did not become law) or to achieve any other goal.

Giménez's views and the courses for women offered by the Legion and Ladies were examples of female Nationalist maternalism. So, too, was a speech given by Miss María Esther Méndez of the feminine section of the Santa Fe Nationalist Union (Unión Nacionalista Santafesina). The "Argentine and Nationalist woman," she claimed, knew how "to be the light of a home, to coo to a child, . . . to love with the saintly love of a mother, a wife, a sister, a fiancée." She and her collaborators believed that Soviet communism was destroying women by pushing them from home and family into men's work.[31] Female Nationalists hoped to prevent a similar catastrophe in Argentina.

Chile

Like their peers in Argentina, radical rightist men in Chile in the 1930s were reluctant to welcome women into their associations. The radical right's main group was the National Socialist Movement (MNS, or Nacis), which attracted

29. *La Fronda*, 5 August 1932, 6.
30. Lavrin, *Women*, 277–79.
31. *Crisol*, 16 December 1941 (Méndez), 3; also see 8 May 1942, 2.

about twenty thousand followers, largely Chileans of German descent and members of the middle and working classes. When it originated in 1932, it parroted the beliefs of German National Socialism, but to counter the local leftist surge, it became a particularly combative and populist variant of fascism. Nacis defined their movement and mission as "virile and manly," apparently excluding women, whom they viewed exclusively as mothers. Unlike their Argentine counterparts, however, the Nacis saw possibilities for advancement through electoral politics. Thus, when women won the right to vote in municipal elections in 1934, they became eligible for membership in the MNS. Several hundred women affiliated with feminine brigades in Santiago and other major cities. Perhaps of Social Catholic backgrounds, these women seem to have been of higher social rank than most male Nacis.[32]

However much it shifted in other respects, Naci ideology about women's place was consistently maternalist. When the MNS decided to admit women, spokesmen claimed that their duties would not be political in nature. Women would work "as women" in Nacism, attending to the sick and to needy mothers and children. Then they wrote that it was women's duty to enter Naci politics, focused as it was on the common welfare, and to uphold the Naci version of "feminism," which emphasized familial roles. Female "soldiers" would form "phalanxes of the future mothers of the Naci State."[33]

Female Nacis dedicated themselves to charity and other activities in which they illustrated "proper" female deportment. Their efforts were supposed to forestall communism, which the MNS blamed on government neglect of the impoverished. Naci women distributed goods to hospital patients, children, and the poor; visited poverty-stricken homes; ran health clinics and an employment agency for Naci clients; hosted parties for children; and raised money to finance these projects. An important duty was to inspire their menfolk in the cause. As one female Naci sympathizer noted, they gave "spiritual help to those who fight for the liberty of a people enchained to misery." According to the MNS newspaper *Trabajo*, women could engage in these chores without compromising "in any respect their femininity." Indeed, within Nacism, they groomed themselves as models of purity, modesty, and domesticity, thus "feminizing themselves" and inspir-

32. Michael Potashnik, "Nacismo: National Socialism in Chile, 1932–1938" (Ph.D. diss., University of California, Los Angeles, 1974), especially 235–37, 242–48; *El movimiento nacional-socialista (MNS)* (Santiago: Editorial del Pacífico, 1933), 22; *Trabajo*, 16 November 1935, 2; 11 December 1935, 3; 21 March 1936, 2; 28 March 1936, 2; 6 August 1936, 7; 12 August 1937, 6; 21 December 1938, 2; 25 March 1939, 2; 26 March 1939, 4.

33. *Acción Chilena* 5, no. 1 (1936), 51–55; *Trabajo*, 11 December 1935, 3; 14 December 1935, 3; 17 April 1936, 6.

ing other women to do the same. Instead of playing bridge, indulging in luxury, walking shamelessly in the streets, and sitting in bars with their legs crossed—unlike other well-off women, according to the MNS—they were training themselves for motherhood.[34]

Like Naci social action, the feminization of the MNS was largely a response to the Marxist threat. The leftist Pro-Emancipation of Women of Chile Movement (Movimiento Pro-Emancipación de las Mujeres de Chile, or MEMCH) led feminist forces who advocated contraception, divorce, equal rights and equal salaries for men and women, and, in general, a socialist program. By claiming that women were in an inferior position to men and advising them to demand entry into the male arena, these socialist feminists, according to the MNS, hoped to destroy the home. It warned that women who followed their admonitions were obeying the "serpent." In contrast, the feminization of women returned them to the home and to maternal tasks, thus ensuring order, hierarchy, and peace within the household and society at large. MEMCH spokeswomen retorted that returning home would mean degradation and poverty for women and their families. While both MEMCH and female Nacis claimed maternalist goals and opposed liberal neglect of the poor, the ideological gulf between them precluded joint action.[35]

Nacis even justified women's public appearances in terms of femininity. In November 1936, Naci women joined the funeral procession of a young Naci killed by leftists, Raúl Lefevre Molina. Staving off possible criticism of women in military formation, a writer in *Trabajo* ascribed their participation to their desire to maintain the home and social structure. She praised the elegance and "natural feminine coquetry" of their uniforms and their wish to share the grief of Lefevre's parents. She also, however, lauded the untutored arrogance of their stride—not a particularly feminine quality.[36]

The fact that this and other presumably female contributors to the Naci newspaper wrote under pseudonyms—even when their articles appeared on its women's page—suggests their lack of voice and agency. So, too, does the fact that *Trabajo* rarely mentioned the names of female Nacis. Nor did women fill all the leadership posts in their chapters; a man served as the director of the feminine brigade of Santiago province. Yet some women left

34. For notices of female activities and for gendered rhetoric, see *Trabajo* between 1936 and 1939, especially 11 January 1934, 3; 22 April 1936, 2; 25 April 1936, 2; and 13 August 1937, 3. The words of the Naci sympathizer come from *Trabajo*, 4 March 1938, 3.

35. *Trabajo*, 8 February 1934, 3 and 16 July 1936, 10; *Acción Chilena* 4, no. 2 (1935), 105. On MEMCH, see its periodical, *La Mujer Nueva*, especially 8 November 1935, 1, 3; see also Lavrin, *Women*, 310–12 and passim.

36. *Trabajo*, 6 November 1936, 6.

their homes to participate in marches and meetings in other cities, indicating at least some sense of autonomy in relation to their family tasks.[37]

Brazil

Although women were active in the MNS and in Nationalism, their role in Brazilian Integralist Action (AIB) was far more significant. The AIB, formed in 1932, was the largest single group in the three countries; moreover, the Integralists were also the first nationally organized legal mass party in Brazil.[38] Since it was seeking to fill an electoral vacuum in a context where feminists had won the vote for literate women, the AIB, unlike Nacis and Nationalists, sought female followers from the start. AIB leaders also understood that if they recruited the entire family, they could strengthen the movement and more thoroughly infiltrate society. By 1937 there were perhaps two hundred thousand Integralists, 20 percent of whom were women, or Green Blouses, as distinguished from the male Green Shirts. Boys and girls, or Plinians (named after the movement's leader, Plínio Salgado), formed another 10 to 20 percent. While women occasionally belonged to and even officiated over male nuclei, most joined the separate feminine sections or departments. By 1936 the AIB grouped these and the children's units together, significantly, under a single secretariat. The male rank and file came from the lower middle and lower classes, and the leaders emerged from the upper middle class and the liberal professions. Unlike their Argentine and Chilean counterparts, Integralist women, many of whom were related to male Integralists, seem to have come from social backgrounds similar to those of the men.[39]

Like women in the other movements—and similarly inspired by antileftist motives—AIB women construed their function partly as one of helping the poor. They founded inexpensive working-class restaurants, milk dispensaries for needy expectant mothers and children, free medical clinics, and literacy schools for children. They offered women training in domestic arts

37. *Trabajo*, 6 August 1936, 7 December 1936, and 9 December 1936, 1.
38. In terms of percentage of the population, Nationalism was larger than Integralism. Nationalism, however, comprised various constituent groups. The Communist Party arose in Brazil in 1922, but the government banned it from time to time.
39. On the general characteristics of the AIB, see Hélgio Trindade, *Integralismo (o fascismo brasileiro na década de 30)* (São Paulo: Difusão Européia do Libro, 1974). Also see Elmer R. Broxson, "Plínio Salgado and Brazilian Integralism, 1932–1938" (Ph.D. diss., Catholic University, 1972), 197; Hélgio Trindade, interview with Margarida Corbisier, São Paulo, n.d. I thank Trindade for sharing the interview with me. *A Offensiva* contained much information on the Green Blouses between 1934 and 1937.

and vocational skills, and a group of AIB women visited the sick. Often they gave toys to children at Christmas. By 1937, Green Blouses claimed to have distributed aid—much of it in motherly fashion—to five million people.[40]

Class conciliation involved more than addressing the needs of the poor: one had to moralize society and rid it of bourgeois egoism. Like their counterparts in Argentina and Chile, Green Blouses partly defined their role as one of influencing other women by offering themselves as models of womanhood, demonstrating piety, self-sacrifice, patriotism, obedience, decorum, and domesticity. Rather than fight to end differences in wealth, they spurned ostentatious displays of wealth and emphasized charity. Female leaders entreated their followers to avoid sexually explicit movies, dances, novels, and fashions, recommending chaste sports, spiritually uplifting books, and modest dress as substitutes. Unlike their predecessors in the Brazilian Catholic groups and the ASN, they attributed immorality to subversive Jewish influences in the media.[41]

Green Blouses were not always limited to politicized versions of maternal or "feminine" roles. Female Integralists listened to lectures on Brazilian finances and other topics not related to the domestic sphere. They took part in demonstrations and congresses with men and spoke at the meetings of male nuclei. Six women were in the movement's governing bodies by 1937; vastly outnumbered by the male leaders, they still helped rule over men. Women voted in the plebiscite that chose Salgado as the AIB standard-bearer for president, bestowing a sense of order and respect on the proceedings, according to Iveta Ribeiro, editor of the Integralist women's magazine. They also campaigned for Salgado and other Integralist candidates for the election scheduled for 1938, which President Getúlio Vargas eventually cancelled. As only the literate could cast ballots, Green Blouses taught potential voters to read and helped them register. A few female Integralists ran for office, one of them winning a city council seat in the state of São Paulo. While they did not fight leftists in the way the Green Shirts did, women engaged in passive resistance in at least one bloody encounter at an Integralist rally in São Paulo in October 1934. Many expected this event to spark violence between left and right; thus, female attendance was an act of courage. Despite intermittent shooting, the members of a female honor guard lifted their arms in the Integralist salute, sang the national anthem, and stood their ground as the

40. *Brasil Feminino*, no. 38 (November 1937), 24; *A Offensiva*, 3 January 1935, 1, 8; 3 January 1937, 15; 18 July 1937, 12, 14.

41. *Brasil Feminino*, no. 38 (November 1937), 15, 33; *A Offensiva*, 13 September 1936, 16 and 17 January 1937, 13.

men streamed in. The male leaders took their places in front of the women, who in effect served as a shield for them. Even as they sneered at the men's cowardice, bystanders applauded the women's bravery.[42]

AIB speakers, both male and female, echoed Naci views: women's proper place was in the home; their main task was to educate future leaders. Women should abstain from lowly partisan politics, but instead join a force dedicated to renovating society. Socialist feminism destroyed women and the family, but a mild, Christian, and national feminism would strengthen them. One Green Blouse, Maria Ribeiro dos Santos Fe'res, compared the female role in the movement to "obscure roots that, unseen, penetrate the profundity of the soil to give life to a magnificent tree." Similarly, as mothers, wives, sisters, and educators, women would nurture, encourage, and inspire present and future Integralists. The domestic and moderate character of such statements did not differ markedly from the statements of mainstream feminists, although the Catholic tone and disapproval of liberal democracy did.

Clearly, the AIB women's duties were broader and more varied than those of women in the other groups studied; in addition, the AIB's views on women were more complex. Rosa Malta Lins Albuquerque, an officer of the women's secretariat, advised women to end their submissive, timid ways and acquire a sense of their "autonomy" and worth. The chief of the secretariat, Dr. Irene Freitas Henriques, told women to force their husbands to comply with Integralist duties, if necessary. (Apparently the strength of the AIB assumed priority over male rule within the household.) Another Integralist leader, Dr. Dario Bittencourt, justified Brazilian women's political activity inside and outside the AIB by placing it in an international context: women everywhere were entering the public arena.[43]

There were other signs of female autonomy—and of the male apprehension it stirred. Unlike Nacis, Green Blouses wrote under their own names in the weekly women's page in the Integralist newspaper of Rio de Janeiro, *A Offensiva*, and in their own magazine, *Brasil Feminino*.[44] They also held

---

42. *A Offensiva*, 28 June 1934, 1; 11 October 1934, 1, 7; 24 January 1936, 4; 23 March 1936, 5; 17 October 1936, 3–5; 8 December 1936, 1; 1 May 1937, 1–2; 10 June 1937, 3; 2 November 1937, 2. Also see *Brasil Feminino*, no. 36 (June 1937), 25. On the AIB rally in São Paulo, see Eduardo Maffei, *A batalha da Praça da Sé* (Rio de Janeiro: Philobiblion, 1984). For details on the AIB's changing organizational and governance structures, see Trindade, *Integralismo*.

43. *Anauê*, no. 15 (May 1937), 59; *Brasil Feminino*, no. 38 (November 1937), 22–23; *A Offensiva*, 13 September 1936, 16; 11 October 1936, 15; and 17 January 1937, 13.

44. The page began on 13 September 1936, 16, and *Brasil Feminino* officially became an Integralist publication in June 1937.

their own congresses, including one in Rio de Janeiro in October 1936 that attracted delegates from various states. Salgado opened and closed the proceedings, thus asserting his control over them. Hinting that women should not make too much of their new roles, he reminded his listeners that the practice of voting was outmoded. Two male meetings overlapped the female one, and the AIB press covered the men in much greater detail than the women, concealing the latter from public view.[45] These are indications that the male authorities tried to keep women from asserting too much independence. An alliance with moderate feminists might have shored up their position, but the Green Blouses never sought one.

During the era of fascism, women entered large, paramilitary organizations of the right. They continued to dedicate themselves to dispensing alms, diffusing a bourgeois and maternal model of femininity, and bestowing upon otherwise violent groups a benign face, yet they departed from the past by appearing publicly in uniform in Brazil and Chile and moving into leadership positions in Brazil. Men allotted women some space in movements they generally defined as male, and women tried to acquire even more. Their desire to improve the economic standing of the poor (enabling female wage earners to return home) was shared by many feminists in these years, but their Catholicism and hostility to democracy and leftism separated radical right-wing women from those in the other camp.

Conclusion

In this analysis, some differences emerge among the ABC countries. The most striking one is that initially there was less extreme rightist female activity in Brazil than in Argentina and Chile, but by the 1930s the former boasted the largest mobilization of women. Furthermore, starting in the 1920s, Brazilian women seemed more vocal, assertive, and likely to be of middle-class origin than their counterparts. The stature and gains of middle-class feminism in Brazil, along with the brief democratic opening that the country experienced in the 1930s, helps account for these distinctions.

The similarities among the three nations, however, outweigh the differences. In each country, upper- and middle-class women joined the extreme right as an extension of their activities in the Catholic Church. They envisioned their role as one of spreading patriotism, morality, and bourgeois

45. *A Offensiva*, 16–18 October 1936.

notions of femininity (particularly among the poorer and immigrant social sectors deemed prey to leftist subversion). Establishing social welfare and worker education projects, serving as helpmates to their male comrades, and offering themselves as models of womanhood were their primary means of achieving these goals. Such functions persisted over time, as they moved from Catholic organizations to Leagues to fascist-influenced movements. Through their activism, they honed their skills as organizers, speech-givers, voters, and administrators—skills that their male counterparts were not necessarily eager for women to exercise in the broader society. Participation in the radical right may have given women a sense of greater autonomy, another consequence that most men in the movements had not intended. In fact, some extreme rightist women moved in the direction of moderate feminism as a response to their sense of independence, the abilities they had refined, their concern for impoverished families, and their interest in suffrage. The ideological differences between the radical right and feminism, however, were too sizable to bridge.

Men and women of the far right tended to visualize women as mothers and helpmates, justify their activities in these terms, and utilize these roles for political purposes. This rightist maternalism, however, differed markedly from typical scholarly depictions of progressive maternalism (the notion that women's nurturing qualities have nudged them toward the left). For the extreme right, familial notions usually reinforced hierarchy within the home, which symbolized the desired hierarchical order in society. Harnessing bourgeois women through their customary duties also served practical ends. Mothers spread their radical rightist political ideas to their children, and sisters and wives supported their menfolk in the cause. As mothers in a broader social sense, women disseminated their anti-leftist views through charitable works and moralization campaigns. When radical right-wing youths died in combat with their ideological foes, women marched in sympathy as mothers and sisters. By the 1930s, some radical rightists thought that the votes of Christian patriotic mothers could offset those of immoral leftist women. By influencing women, the far right could gain access to families, neighborhoods, and institutions throughout society.[46] Dâgmar Cortines and her female comrades in Argentina, Brazil, and Chile were not only extremists of the right but also, for the most part, mothers, sisters, and wives, and their presence as such strengthened the movements to which they belonged.

46. Kathleen Blee, "Mothers in Race-Hate Movements," in *The Politics of Motherhood: Activist Voices from Left to Right,* ed. Alexis Jetter, Annelise Orleck, and Diana Taylor (Hanover: University Press of New England, 1997), 252–55.

BIBLIOGRAPHY

PRIMARY SOURCES

Newspapers

Acción Chilena (Santiago)
Anauê (Rio de Janeiro)
Brasil Feminino (Rio de Janeiro)
Crisol (Buenos Aires)
La Fronda (Buenos Aires)
Gil Blas (Rio de Janeiro)
El Mercurio (Santiago)
La Mujer Nueva (Santiago)
A Offensiva (Rio de Janeiro)
El Pueblo (Buenos Aires)
Trabajo (Santiago)

Interviews

Arenaza de Martínez, Celina. Interview by author. Buenos Aires, 15 July 1981.
Corbisier, Margarida. Interview by Hélgio Trindade. São Paulo, n.d.

Other Primary Sources

Actividades femeninas en Chile. Santiago: Imprenta La Ilustracion, 1928.
Bomilcar, Alvaro. *A política no Brazil ou o nacionalismo radical.* Rio de Janeiro: Editores Leite Ribeiro & Maurillo, 1920.
Chile. Congreso. Cámara de Diputados e Senado. *Boletín de Sesiones Ordinarias.* Santiago, 1920.
De Arenaza, Celina. *Sin memoria.* Buenos Aires: Ronaldo J. Pellegrini, 1980.
Delamare Nogueira de Gama, Alcibiades. *Linguas de fogo: Discursos e conferencias.* Rio de Janeiro: Typographia do Annuario do Brasil, 1926.
Font, Miguel J. *La mujer: Encuesta feminista argentina: Hacia la formación de una Liga Feminista Sudamericana.* Buenos Aires: Imprenta Costa Hermanos, 1921.
La Palma de Emery, Celia. *Discursos y conferencias: Acción pública y privada en favor de la mujer y del niño en la República Argentina.* Buenos Aires: Alfa y Omega, 1910.
Ledesma de García Fernández, María Rosario. *Una época a través de mis escritos.* 1920. Reprint, Buenos Aires: Talleres Gráficos Zaragoza, 1949.
Liga de Damas Chilenas. *Memoria correspondiente al año 1929.* Santiago: Imprenta Arturo Prat, 1929.
Liga Patriótica Argentina. *Discursos pronunciados en el acto inaugural y veredicto del jurado de la Tercera Exposición Nacional de Tejidos y Bordados.* Buenos Aires: n.p., 1922.
————. *Discursos pronunciados en el acto inaugural y veredicto del jurado de la Cuarta Exposición Nacional de Tejidos y Bordados.* Buenos Aires: n.p., 1923.
El movimiento nacional-socialista (MNS). Santiago: Editorial del Pacífico, 1933.
Niklison, José Elías. "Acción social católica obrera." *Boletín del Departamento Nacional del Trabajo,* no. 46 (March 1920).

Romero Carranza, Ambrosio. *Itinerario de Monseñor de Andrea*. Buenos Aires: Compañía Impresora Argentina, 1957.
Subercaseaux de Valdés, Blanca (Carmen Valle). *Amalia Errázuriz de Subercaseaux*. Buenos Aires: Emecé Editores, 1946.

SECONDARY SOURCES

Azzi, Riolando. *Presença da igreja católica na sociedade brasileira*. Cadernos do ISER, no. 13. Rio de Janeiro: ISER, n.d.
Besse, Susan K. *Restructuring Patriarchy: The Modernization of Gender Inequality in Brazil, 1914–1940*. Chapel Hill: The University of North Carolina Press, 1996.
Blee, Kathleen. "Mothers in Race-Hate Movements." In *The Politics of Motherhood: Activist Voices from Left to Right*, edited by Alexis Jetter, Annelise Orleck, and Diana Taylor. Hanover: University Press of New England, 1997.
Borges, Dain. *The Family in Bahia, 1870–1945*. Stanford: Stanford University Press, 1992.
Broxson, Elmer R. "Plínio Salgado and Brazilian Integralism, 1932–1938." Ph.D. diss., Catholic University, 1972.
Caimari, Lila. *Perón y la iglesia católica: Religión, estado y sociedad en la Argentina (1943–1955)*. Buenos Aires: Ariel Historia, 1994.
Carlson, Marifran. *Feminismo! The Woman's Movement in Argentina from Its Beginnings to Eva Perón*. Chicago: Academy Chicago, 1988.
González Miranda, Sergio, Carlos Maldonado Prieto, and Sandra McGee Deutsch. "Las Ligas Patrióticas: Un caso de nacionalismo, xenofobia, y lucha social en Chile." *Canadian Review of Studies in Nationalism* 21, no. 1–2 (1994): 57–69.
Hahner, June E. *Emancipating the Female Sex: The Struggle for Women's Rights in Brazil, 1850–1940*. Durham: Duke University Press, 1990.
Houseman, Philip Joseph. "Chilean Nationalism, 1920–1952." Ph.D. diss., Stanford University, 1961.
Ivereigh, Austen. *Catholicism and Politics in Argentina, 1810–1960*. New York: St. Martin's Press, 1995.
Kaempfer Villagrán, Guillermo. *Así sucedió, 1850–1925: Sangrientos episodios de la lucha obrera en Chile*. Santiago: n.p., 1962.
Klimpel, Felicitas. *La mujer chilena (el aporte femenino al progreso de Chile), 1920–1960*. Santiago: Andrés Bello, 1962.
Lavrin, Asunción. *Women, Feminism, and Social Change in Argentina, Chile, and Uruguay, 1890–1940*. Lincoln: University of Nebraska Press, 1995.
Maffei, Eduardo. *A batalha da Praça da Sé*. Rio de Janeiro: Philobiblion, 1984.
McGee Deutsch, Sandra. *Counterrevolution in Argentina, 1900–1932: The Argentine Patriotic League*. Lincoln: University of Nebraska Press, 1986.
———. "What Difference Does Gender Make? The Extreme Right in the ABC Countries in the Era of Fascism." *Estudios interdisciplinarios de América Latina y el Caribe* 8, no. 2 (1997): 5–21.
———. *Las Derechas: The Extreme Right in Argentina, Brazil, and Chile, 1890–1939*. Stanford: Stanford University Press, 1999.
Navarro, Marysa. "Hidden, Silent, and Anonymous: Women Workers in the Argentine Trade Union Movement." In *The World of Women's Trade Unionism: Comparative Historical Essays*, edited by Norbert C. Soldon. Westport, Conn.: Greenwood, 1985.

Needell, Jeffrey. *A Tropical Belle Epoque: Elite Culture and Society in Turn-of-the-Century Rio de Janeiro.* Cambridge: Cambridge University Press, 1987.

Pena, Maria Valéria Junho. *Mulheres e trabalhadoras: Presença feminina na constituição do sistema fabril.* Rio de Janeiro: Paz e Terra, 1981.

Pena, Maria Valéria Junho, and Elça Mendonça Lima. "Lutas ilusórias: A mulher na política operária da primeira república." In *Mulher, mulheres,* compiled by Carmen Barroso and Albertina Oliveira Costa. São Paulo: Cortez Editora, Fundação Carlos Chagas, 1983.

Potashnik, Michael. "Nacismo: National Socialism in Chile, 1932–1938." Ph.D. diss., University of California, Los Angeles, 1974.

Quay Hutchison, Elizabeth. "Working Women of Santiago: Gender and Social Transformation in Urban Chile, 1887–1927." Ph.D. diss., University of California, Berkeley, 1995.

Topik, Steven. "Economic Nationalism and the State in an Underdeveloped Country: Brazil, 1889–1930." Ph.D. diss., University of Texas, Austin, 1978.

———. "Middle-Class Brazilian Nationalism, 1889–1930: From Radicalism to Reaction." *Social Science Quarterly* 59, no. 1 (1978): 93–104.

Trindade, Hélgio. *Integralismo (o fascismo brasileiro na década de 30).* São Paulo: Difusão Européia do Libro, 1974.

Verba, Ericka Kim. "The *Liga de Damas Chilenas* [League of Chilean Ladies]: Angels of Peace and Harmony of the Social Question." Paper presented at the Latin American Studies Association meeting, Guadalajara, Mexico, April 1997.

Wirth, John. *Minas Gerais in the Brazilian Federation, 1889–1937.* Stanford: Stanford University Press, 1977.

Zanatta, Loris. *Del estado liberal a la nación católica: Iglesia y ejército en los orígenes del peronismo: 1930–1943.* Quilmes: Universidad Nacional de Quilmes, 1996.

8 | Changing the System from Within?
Feminist Participation in the Brazilian Workers' Party

Liesl Haas

The PT intends to be the expression of the popular movements, pure and simple.

—LULA, FIRST PRESIDENT OF THE PT

We want the right to decide about the society in which we live. For us women, this is new. Because often we let others speak for us while we remain quiet. Many times we struggle but we let others decide. Now we will talk, decide, and participate in politics.

—CLARA CHARF, PT CANDIDATE

Two of the most significant political developments to occur in Brazil since the imposition of authoritarian rule in 1964 were the creation of the Workers' Party (Partido dos Trabalhadores, or PT) and the emergence of the Brazilian women's movement.[1] The Workers' Party was created to represent those

An earlier version of this chapter was presented as a conference paper at the Nineteenth International Conference of the Latin American Studies Association, Washington, D.C., September 1995.

1. Some caveats are in order regarding my use of the term "women's movement." As many analysts have rightly argued, there is no one movement that represents women in Brazil. Rather, there is a multitude of movements, some overtly feminist (seeking to challenge existing gender roles), some explicitly nonfeminist (accepting traditional gender roles). There are also differences among movements regarding the degree to which they consider themselves political or seek to change state or party policy. While my focus is on the feminist movement, it is impossible to discuss the emergence and development of the feminist movement in Brazil without taking note of the wider women's movement of which it is a part. However, when

social elements—namely, the new labor movement, new social movements, and elements of the left—that were unrepresented by traditional Brazilian parties. The Brazilian women's movement stands out among the women's movements that arose throughout Latin America due to its size, diversity, and strength, which are evidenced by the significant social and political gains that it made for Brazilian women in the 1985 transition to democracy and in the first democratic administration (1985–89). While scholars have studied the political development of the Workers' Party and the evolution of the women's movement, little attention has been focused on the historical and ideological similarities between the two.

The feminist discourse of the women's movement shares with the PT a vision of social transformation that goes beyond piecemeal legislative change or the demand for more opportunity in the existing social and political system. In theory, the ideal society envisioned by feminists is not much different from that proposed by the PT: the PT calls for "radical democracy" and for popular participation in politics; the feminist movement calls for "the democratization of daily life." Both also emphasize internal democracy, collective decision making, and accountability of the leaders to the organization's members. Both are suspicious of the political process and strive to maintain their links to the popular base even as they work with elites in the existing political system.[2] And both have taken their most fundamental goals to be the mobilization and political representation of underrepresented sectors of the Brazilian population. A closer look at the relationship between the Brazilian feminist movement and the PT reveals much about the PT's claim to speak for the politically marginalized and to signal a fundamental change

---

discussing the participation of women within the PT and the adoption by the party of a progressive gender agenda, I concentrate on the feminist wing of the women's movement in order to distinguish these women from the nonfeminist women who participate in the parties (mostly on the right). Likewise, policies are evaluated from a feminist perspective to distinguish among those policies that address women in their traditional roles as mothers (for example, in calls for better schools) and those policies that seek to alter those roles and focus on women as individuals (such as the decriminalization of abortion or the promotion of policies to end employment discrimination). (See Maxine Molyneux [1985] for further elaboration of this point.) In sum, I use the term "women's movement" to refer to the collectivity of women's groups that emerged in Brazil under authoritarian rule. I use the term "feminist movement" to refer to those groups espousing a feminist ideology.

2. Emir Sader and Ken Silverstein explain that a significant level of general distrust exists between the traditional Brazilian left and the PT. The PT's ideology and practice are quite distinct from those of the Communist Party (the PT has avoided a rigid definition of socialist ideology), and Sader and Silverstein go so far as to describe the PT as in some respects closer to a popular movement than a political party. See Sader and Silverstein, *Without Fear of Being Happy: Lula, the Workers' Party, and Brazil* (New York: Verso, 1991).

from Brazilian politics as usual. In addition, the relationship has important implications for the ability of the feminist movement to translate effective opposition tactics into long-term, institutionalized political change.

Throughout Latin America, the transitions to democracy and the return of party politics presented the social movements which had arisen under the dictatorships with a difficult choice. During the dictatorships, when political parties were illegal, social movements played a critical role in opening spaces in civil society for political discussion and resistance. As part of a diverse political opposition, social movements were crucial in weakening the hold of the authoritarian regime.[3] However, with the return of democracy, political parties reclaimed their position as the interlocutors of public demands to the state. Social movements that opted for autonomy vis-à-vis established political parties found themselves excluded from political debates and their demands ignored. At the same time, those movements that sought to institutionalize their demands by becoming incorporated into the parties found that the return to democracy was in many ways a return to politics as usual, as social movement demands were placed low on the parties' lists of priorities.[4]

The Workers' Party, however, was both a new party and a different one from other parties in Brazil. Emir Sader and Ken Silverstein explain that the PT is not only the largest explicitly socialist political party in South America but also the most diverse, uniting "radical unionists, landless peasants, shantytown activists and the progressive wing of the country's powerful Roman Catholic Church."[5] The PT also signified a departure from the norm of Brazil-

---

3. See, for example, Jane S. Jaquette, ed., *The Women's Movement in Latin America: Participation and Democracy* (Boulder, Colo.: Westview Press, 1994); Arturo Escobar and Sonia E. Alvarez, eds., *The Making of Social Movements in Latin America* (Boulder, Colo.: Westview Press, 1992); John Burdick, *Looking for God in Brazil: The Progressive Catholic Church in Urban Brazil's Religious Arena* (Berkeley and Los Angeles: University of California Press, 1993); and Scott Mainwaring and Eduardo Viola, *New Social Movements, Political Culture, and Democracy: Brazil and Argentina* (Notre Dame, Ind.: Helen Kellogg Institute for International Studies, 1984).

4. See Jane S. Jaquette and Sharon L. Wolchik, eds., *Women and Democracy: Latin America and Central and Eastern Europe* (Baltimore: The Johns Hopkins University Press, 1998); Angela Borba, Hildete Pereira, Jacqueline Pitanguy, and Wania Sant'anna, "O feminismo no Brasil de hoje," *Estudos feministas* 2 (Fall/Winter 1994); Jacqueline Pitanguy and Eli Diniz, "Leila Dinz e a antecipação de temas feministas," *Estudos feministas* 2 (Fall/Winter 1994); Francis Hagopian, "After Regime Change: Authoritarian Legacies, Political Representation, and the Democratic Future of South America," *World Politics* 45 (April 1993): 464–500; and Daniel H. Levine, ed., *Constructing Culture and Power in Latin America* (Ann Arbor: University of Michigan Press, 1993).

5. Sader and Silverstein, *Without Fear of Being Happy*, 3.

ian politics, in that it sought to be the authentic political voice of the workers and the poor, internally democratic, and accountable to its members. Margaret Keck notes:

The singularity of the Workers' Party derives in part from its attempt, within the transition process, to create a political identity that broke both with the pattern of relations characterizing the authoritarian period and with historical traditions. In the other Southern Cone countries, this organizational space was historically occupied by parties that predated the military regime and retained a substantial legitimacy among their constituencies. In Brazil, the problem was not only to occupy that space but also to create it.[6]

The PT rose from obscurity in the late 1970s to prominence in Brazilian politics, forcing a second-round vote for president in the 1989 elections. In light of this strong performance, Sader and Silverstein[7] concluded that the PT had established itself as one of Brazil's major political forces. Although the victory of Fernando Cardoso's PSDB (Brazilian Social Democratic Party)—in coalition with the conservative PFL (Party of the Liberal Front)—in the 1994 presidential elections was a disappointment for the PT, the fact that the PSDB and the PT were the only major contenders for the presidency is evidence that the PT continues to be a powerful force in Brazilian politics.

Like the Workers' Party, the Brazilian women's movement also traces its origins to the late 1970s. Moreover, many of the same political and economic factors that spurred the development of the PT gave rise to the women's movement. Throughout Latin America, women organized in opposition to authoritarian rule. They protested the effects of neoliberal economic policies, human rights abuses, and lack of government services in working-class communities. Middle-class feminist women organized on a mass scale to protest gender discrimination in the home and workplace.[8] Throughout Latin America, women formed an important part of the political opposition, yet

6. Margaret E. Keck, *The Workers' Party and Democratization in Brazil* (New Haven: Yale University Press, 1992), 39.

7. Sader and Silverstein, *Without Fear of Being Happy*, 6.

8. Discussed in Norma Stoltz Chinchilla, "Women's Movements in the Americas: Feminism's Second Wave," *NACLA Report on the Americas* 27, no. 1 (1993); Jo Fisher, *Out of the Shadows: Women, Resistance, and Politics in South America* (London: Latin American Bureau, 1993); Cornelia Butler Flora and Helen I. Safa, "Production, Reproduction, and the Polity: Women's Strategic and Practical Gender Issues," in *Americas: New Interpretive Essays*, ed. Alfred Stepan (New York: Oxford University Press, 1992); Sonia E. Alvarez, *Engendering Democracy in Brazil* (Princeton: Princeton University Press, 1990); and Kathleen Staudt, ed., *Women, International Development, and Politics* (Philadelphia: Temple University Press, 1990).

the women's movement that emerged in Brazil was "arguably the largest, most diverse, most radical, and most successful women's movement in contemporary Latin America."[9] With the return to democracy, women's organizations faced the same participation-versus-autonomy dilemma that other social movements confronted. And many of these women (like the founders of the Workers' Party) harbored deep suspicions about the political system, which they viewed as inherently *machista* and opposed to the social and political advancement of women. Many feminists feared that the internal democracy they had tried to foster in the women's groups would be eroded within the hierarchical structure of the parties.[10]

During the transition period, many feminists active in the women's movement did join political parties, predominantly the PMDB (Party of the Brazilian Democratic Movement),[11] the PSDB, and the PT. Other groups chose to remain autonomous, planning to pressure the parties and state to address feminist demands from a position of independence.[12] The creation in the early 1980s of State Councils on Women's Rights (first in São Paulo, and then in several other states), followed by the creation of the National Council on Women's Rights (CNDM) in 1985, testified to the political power that women had gained in Brazil. With broad advisory powers, a feminist majority, and ministerial rank, the National Council let its presence be felt in policy making; it played a critical role, for example, in the drafting of progressive family planning legislation.[13]

After the creation of the National Council in 1985, women in Brazil lost political ground. The gradual turn to the right of the Sarney administration, succeeded by the election of the conservative Collor government, under-

9. Alvarez, *Engendering Democracy*, 3. Alvarez explains: "By the mid-1980s, tens of thousands of women had been politicized by the women's movement and core items of the feminist agenda had made their way into the platforms and programs of all major political parties and into the public policies of the New Brazilian Republic."

10. Borba et al., "O feminismo no Brasil de hoje"; Céli Regina Jardim Pinto, "Donas-de-casa, mães, feministas, batalhadoras: Mulheres nas eleições de 1994 no Brasil," *Estudos feministas* 2 (Fall/Winter 1994): 297–313. Borba et al. describe the two major dilemmas within Brazilian feminism as (1) the struggle to maintain a high level of representation and internal democracy within the movement itself, and (2) the difficulty of maintaining links to the autonomous movement while simultaneously participating in the parties and government.

11. The MDB (Brazilian Democratic Movement) was the official opposition party created by the government following the coup in 1964. When parties were relegalized in 1979, the MDB changed its name to PMDB (Party of the Brazilian Democratic Movement).

12. Borba et al. explain that "the feminist movement in Brazil has always considered the state its interlocutor" ("O feminismo no Brasil de hoje," 523).

13. See Alvarez, *Engendering Democracy*, for an extended description of the development of the state and federal family planning programs.

mined the gains women had made at the state level. The National Council itself was disbanded as part of Collor's commitment to trim down the federal bureaucracy, and many other organizations created during the transition period and the first democratic administrations also dissolved as their funding disappeared. In the face of these setbacks, many feminists in Brazil expressed frustration with the state of the movement and spoke of a "return to the base," working on the grassroots level to mobilize women.[14]

Both the PT and the feminist movement challenged the fundamentally elitist nature of Brazilian politics. Yet their shared hope—to see Brazil become a more participatory democracy—was frustrated in the years after the transition: the Brazilian system retained its historically exclusive character. As a relatively new party, however, the PT was in a unique position to democratize the existing system by giving voice to those elements that remained unrepresented. To what extent did the PT give voice to the demands of Brazilian women? I draw two conclusions from an examination of the relationship between the PT and the Brazilian feminist movement: on the one hand, the PT adopted a more progressive gender agenda and promoted more feminist candidates than any other party, but on the other hand, significant obstacles to cooperation between the party and the feminist movement remained.

A look at the evolution of the PT's position on several critical gender issues, dating from the party's founding to the 1994 electoral campaign, provides evidence that progress was made in incorporating women into the party and in promoting women as candidates. In addition, the party's position on issues such as abortion reflects a feminist influence. At the same time, I would argue that the fundamental barrier to greater feminist participation within the PT and to the PT's adoption of progressive positions on gender issues was that the most powerful factions in the party—namely, labor, the left, and the Catholic Church—were conservative in regard to the role of women in society. Though these factions were progressive on many other social questions, their influence within the PT kept gender issues (and women themselves) from gaining ground within the party. Labor, the left, and the Church were the most powerful players in the party's formation, and their early participation served in large degree to cement their power within

14. Frustration with the present state of the women's movement was expressed by many of the feminists interviewed by the author in São Paulo, Belo Horizonte, and Rio de Janeiro between June and August 1994. It was also a major theme of the conference "Formação, Pesquisa e Edição Feministas na Universidade: Brasil, França e Quebec," held in Rio de Janeiro, 6–10 June 1994.

the party. Angelo Panebianco emphasizes the importance of an institution's founding moment:

> The way in which the cards are dealt out and the outcomes of the different rounds played out in the formative phase of an organization, continue in many ways to condition the life of the organization even decades afterwards. The organization will certainly undergo modifications and even profound changes in interacting throughout its entire life cycle with the continually changing environment. However, the crucial political choices made by its founding fathers [sic], the first struggles for organizational control, and the way in which the organization was formed, will leave an indelible mark.[15]

When the PT was in its formative period, the women's movement was also growing—but was emphasizing its autonomy. Many of the active feminists were former members of leftist parties who had become disillusioned with the parties. A number of feminists saw in the PT a new way of doing politics, but others had left political parties expressly to develop autonomous organizations. While women were present at the PT's founding, many feminists did not participate, and as a result, women's voices were not heard as clearly as they could have been. Although the PT evolved over time to become more broad-based and more appealing to the middle class, the early power players continued to influence the party's position on women and to form a significant obstacle to closer links between the PT and the feminist movement.

The PT's Official Position on Women

The interests of the PT and of the women's movement overlap at several points, and the ideologies of the two are in many ways clearly compatible. What was the official party line on gender issues?

With the re-legalization of multiparty opposition in 1979, the PT, like all the major parties, actively courted the female vote. While many professional and academic feminists supported the PMDB (and later the PSDB), other feminists, especially those who had been active in the left, saw the PT as the potential voice of the popular movements within the political system. Because of the visible presence of PT militants in social movements in many

15. Angelo Panebianco, *Political Parties: Organization and Power* (Cambridge: Cambridge University Press, 1988), xiii.

marginal neighborhoods, especially in São Paulo, neighborhood activists felt a natural affinity toward the PT. In addition, women frequently played a prominent role in these urban organizations, and for those women without previous political experience, the PT was the party with which they were most familiar.

By the 1982 election campaign, the PT boasted a higher proportion of female members than any other party, surpassing 40 percent in São Paulo County. The number of female candidates promoted by the party (twenty-three) was surpassed only by the twenty-four launched by the PDS (Social Democratic Party), the reconstituted government party, whose female candidates had no links to the women's movement. Although not the most successful party electorally, the PT adopted the most progressive platform on gender issues. The party advocated the creation of government-funded public *creches* (day care centers), a proposal long supported by the woman's movement;[16] it also defined motherhood as a social rather than a natural condition, calling for the increased availability of contraceptives and the improvement of women's medical care in general. In the PT's national platform, the problem of discrimination against women was linked to the general struggle of workers:

> Woman is treated like a second class being. The worst jobs and lowest salaries are reserved for her, besides being submitted to a double workday, since she is responsible for all household chores as well. She is constantly subjugated and humiliated, oppressed not only as a worker, but also as a woman. . . . We demand equality in the laws that rule the family, labor, and society. [We demand the] right to employment, to professionalization and the extension of workers' rights to all women workers, such as domestic workers, and respect for equal pay for equal work.[17]

Most important, the PT declared in an addendum to the party program that "discriminations are not secondary questions, as the problems of female workers, segregated in the factories, in the fields, and also in the home, are not secondary."

Another way in which the PT distinguished itself from other Brazilian parties was in its decision not to form a women's department within the party. The debate over the creation of such an organization had been the

16. Borba et al., "O feminismo no Brasil de hoje," 518.
17. Partido dos Trabalhadores, "Plataforma Nacional," 1982 (quoted in Alvarez, *Engendering Democracy,* 172).

cause of much contention among female party members. Some feared that a women's department would marginalize women from party debates and would relegate such "women's issues" as contraception, day care, etc., to consideration solely by women instead of by all party members. Others, however, considered the negative past experience of women in the left, and they argued that it was unrealistic to expect the majority male party to address women's concerns seriously. Such concerns would most likely be given low priority within the party, and without a women's department, these issues would never be discussed at all. In the end, a compromise between the two groups led to the creation of a "women's division" that was linked to the Party Secretariat for Popular Movements. The purpose of the women's division was not to be the focal point for discussion about women's rights. Rather, the PT women's division was conceived—and feminists hoped that this would distinguish it from traditional party "women's departments"—as an oversight mechanism within the Workers' Party that could agitate more effectively for the inclusion of feminist concerns within broader party programs. The women's division would advise and educate party leaders and militants on women's issues and promote PT participation in women's movement activities, while respecting the autonomy and self-determination of existing women's organizations.[18] The document that explained this decision stated:

> [W]e are perhaps the only party which did not constitute a feminine department. . . . It is because we conceive of women's participation in the party differently. In the first place, we understand that women should be shoulder to shoulder with the men in our party, and not separate from them. . . . In the second place . . . there is a [women's] movement which is growing, assuming its own forms of organization. . . . We are a Party that is born with the registered mark of respect for the entities, the forms of organization of the working people. It would be absurd if we had a feminine department or any other institution that would swallow the movement, instead of strengthening it.[19]

On paper, the PT's position regarding women and gender issues appears significantly more progressive than that of the other parties. In 1993, after

18. Alvarez, *Engendering Democracy,* 173.
19. Partido dos Trabalhadores, Comissão da Mulheres, "A Participação do PT no III Congresso da Mulher Paulista," 1981, issued by the Women's Commission for the International Women's Day celebrations that year (quoted in Alvarez, *Engendering Democracy,* 174).

several years of debate, the PT adopted a quota rule stipulating that at least 30 percent of leadership posts in the party must go to women.[20] PT discourse does not marginalize women and gender issues, forcing them to occupy a separate sphere of party activity, but integrates considerations of women into its analysis of class relations and other pertinent party debates. How does this progressive discourse play itself out in actual party practices?

Theory and Reality: Obstacles in the Relationship Between Women and the PT

An analysis of the PT's progressive policies on gender issues reveals that party leaders addressed women's demands and incorporated them into party programs only in response to sustained, organized pressure by party feminists. For example, none of the speakers at the party's founding convention addressed "the specificity of women's oppression within class relations," and PT feminists responded by developing a "women's platform," presenting it to the National Executive, and pressuring the party to fund a national PT women's convention before the elections.[21] It was during this second convention that women drafted a document regarding the creation of a women's division. The organized presence of women at the 1982 nominating convention led to the incorporation of many of their concerns into the party's electoral program. However, while the party did address the need for contraception, pressure from the Church prevented it from responding to female members' demands that it endorse the decriminalization of abortion.

The situation improved only marginally after 1982. For example, the adoption of the quota law came about only after fierce debate—and in fact, the law was passed against the wishes of most of the party's feminists. The law had originally been proposed as a result of the failure of the party to elect significant numbers of women to leadership positions in the party or to promote them as candidates. However, many feminists feared that the quota law would freeze women's membership in leadership posts at 30 percent, and interestingly, the most sexist members of the party voted for the law, while most feminists voted against it.[22] Feminist party members asserted that a tremendous gap between the PT's discourse on women and the reali-

20. Jardim Pinto, "Donas-de-casa, mães, feministas, batalhadoras."

21. Alvarez, *Engendering Democracy,* 172.

22. Federal congresswoman Sandra Starling, interview by author, Belo Horizonte, Brazil, 6 July 1994.

ties of the PT's practices was still in place, almost two decades after the party's founding. A closer look at the relationship between women and the PT's founding organizations—labor, progressive sectors of the Catholic Church, and the political left—will elucidate the specific barriers to women's equal participation in the PT.

Labor and Women

From the beginning, the PT has consisted of various social movements and leftist groups as well as labor activists, but the party has its roots and its most important base of support in the new labor movement, which arose in the late 1960s as a result of state-led industrialization. Margaret Keck differentiates the PT from other workers' parties, such as the Labour Party in Britain, because the PT was not created by unions *qua* unions. However, the PT was legitimated by its close relationship with the unions, which played a key role in the building of a dominant coalition within the party. In order to consider the relationship between women and organized labor, one must therefore examine both the Workers' Party itself as well as the central union organization, the CUT (Central Unica dos Trabalhadores) with which it is organically (though not institutionally or juridically) linked.

Sandra Starling, a PT federal deputy from Belo Horizonte, finds it not at all surprising that such a strong sexist element exists in the party. She traces the PT's sexist character to the power of the founding *operarias* and claims that the labor leadership is even more traditional in its views on women than the labor rank and file.[23] Starling asserts that Lula (Luís Inácio da Silva, the first president of the PT) typifies the attitude of labor leaders: in his dealings with women in the party, he adopts a manner that is alternately contemptuous or seductive. Feminists in the PT, who believe the party to be the best (if far from ideal) vehicle for change, have worked hard to prep Lula for public appearances and speeches to prevent him from saying inappropriate things about gender issues, things that would hurt the party's popularity. Starling explains that many men in the party feel threatened by the increasing presence of women in the PT. They see women party militants not as partners in the party's social project but as a challenge to their authority.

Discrimination in the party is seen not so much in official documents as in the daily workings of the party, the atmosphere in meetings, and in the

23. Ibid.

low number of women in leadership positions. Women who are subject to sexual harassment by male party members are made to feel disloyal if they seek legal action against their *"companheiros."*[24] In addition, despite the hopes of the founders of the party's women's division, it has functioned in practice in essentially the same way as typical women's departments. "Women's issues" are kept separate from general party concerns and are discussed primarily by women.[25] This is in direct contradiction to the aim of the CUT, as defined in its documents: to treat women's discrimination as a problem for everyone, especially the working class, and not a problem solely for women to discuss.[26] The fight for day care *creches,* for example, which was a notable part of the party's program before the 1982 elections, is now an issue primarily discussed among female party members. Ironically, the issue of day care has been a problem within the party itself. Party meetings are timed for men's convenience, often at times when women cannot attend due to household and child care responsibilities, and most party meeting places do not provide child care services.[27] For this reason, the women who have achieved leadership positions within the party are those like Luiza Erundina de Souza (former mayor of São Paulo) and Bernadette da Silva (senator from Rio de Janeiro), who are older and no longer have child care responsibilities. In fact, since the CUT's founding in 1983, there have been almost no changes to the condition of women in the CUT unions.

The Resolutions from the Fifth National Plenary of the CUT state that "the feminine work force is utilized by capitalism to increase the level of exploitation of the [working] class as a whole."[28] Yet women's participation in the PT and the CUT has so far failed to convince either group to address the horrendous conditions of many female workers adequately. Researchers and feminist activists are focusing their attention on the abuse of female factory workers. Maria Cecilia Camargo has researched the conditions of women in Brazilian factories, for example, and describes the conditions at the de Millus lingerie factory as typical. In addition to the common company practices of hiring minors, paying less than minimum wage, demanding con-

24. Ibid.
25. See Pitanguy and Diniz, "Leila Dinz," for a discussion of the "ghettoization" of gender issues in the parties: they note that only women discuss issues like day care, contraception, and the like because these are deemed to be "women's issues."
26. Resoluções do V Plenario da CUT (internal document), São Paulo, July 1992, 27.
27. Ibid. See Borba et al., "O feminismo no Brasil de hoje," for a more detailed discussion on the lack of government action on this issue.
28. Resoluções do V Plenario da CUT, 27.

stant overtime work, and providing minimal break time,[29] women in the de Millus factory were required to undergo pregnancy tests before they were hired (this was repeated annually for underage female workers), and were forced to comply with daily strip searches to make sure they were not stealing from the factory. Sexual harassment of female workers by male owners and managers is a common occurrence in factory life.[30]

As a result of demands from the women's movement, maternity leave legislation was included in the new Brazilian constitution.[31] However, the notorious lack of oversight in Brazil has allowed employers to respond to the legislation by increasing their vigilance about female employees' fertility; often, employers insist on sterilization certificates before women can be hired. Sterilization was legalized in June 1994 as a result of legislation authored by PT congressman Eduardo Jorge. On the positive side, this legalization means that the procedure will be a safer option for women who choose it. However, if the causes of Brazil's exceptionally high sterilization rate are not addressed,[32] many women will continue to be forced to undergo sterilization, either because safe contraceptive alternatives are unavailable or because lack of oversight of factory conditions continues to allow employers to monitor the fertility of employees.

The document from the Fifth National Plenary of the CUT devotes several pages to illustrating the gap between theory and practice in the CUT's stance on women. For example, the demands of female workers are rarely incorporated into CUT collective negotiations, and there is little research undertaken by the unions on the actual number of female workers or on the conditions under which they labor. Efforts to analyze the impact of gender on the relationship between the worker and capital are rarely made. And there is no attempt to educate and sensitize the majority male membership to gender issues outside of the efforts of the women themselves.[33]

29. Women workers were allowed to use the bathroom once a day and were given one twenty-minute break for lunch. See Maria Cecilia Camargo, "Constitution and Reality: Women and Labour Law," in *Women in Brazil*, ed. Caipora Women's Group (London: Latin American Bureau, 1993), 37.

30. Ibid., 37–38. See bibliography for more citations on this topic.

31. Section 2 of the 1988 Constitution stipulates the right to 120 days of paid maternity leave without loss of job or pay. For a discussion of the lack of enforcement of these constitutional rights, see Céli Regina Jardim Pinto, "Mulher e política no Brasil: Os impasses do feminismo, enquanto movimento social, face às regras do jogo da democracia representativa," *Estudos feministas* 2 (Fall/Winter 1994): 256–70.

32. For a recent analysis of reproductive rights and sterilization in Brazil, see Shyamala Nataraj, *Private Decisions, Public Debate: Women, Reproduction, and Population* (London: Panos, 1994).

33. Document from V Plenario da CUT, 28–30.

The Catholic Church and Women

Much has been written about the crucial role played by the Brazilian Catholic Church under authoritarian rule.[34] The Church protested the abuses of the military regime, participated in grassroots efforts to improve the lives of those most marginalized by the regime, and provided needed support and legitimation for the political opposition. Not only was the institution of the Church a powerful influence on its own, but Church activists also constituted a substantial percentage of the membership of many social movements, influencing the stand that the movements took on gender issues. With regard to Church influence on PT policy, therefore, one must consider both the influence of the institution of the Catholic Church within Brazilian society as a whole and the more specific role of Catholic activists within many of the sectors that composed the PT.

The progressive wing of the Catholic Church was extremely active during the dictatorship. Ecclesiastical Base Communities (CEBs) were an important means of mobilizing the popular sectors, and membership in CEBs often led to participation in other social movements, such as movements for housing, health care, basic services in poor areas, land rights, and human rights. So important was Church support for the formation and survival of many social movements that, according to Herminia Maricato, "without [the Church], 90 percent of the urban social movement organizations in São Paulo would not exist."[35] Catholic activists were also engaged in the labor movement, and their presence helped forge links between labor and other social movements, thus broadening the base of support for the creation of the PT beyond the unions.[36]

However, the Church's relationship to women is more complicated. While the Church encouraged the mobilization of women around economic or human rights issues and supported female workers as part of its general support for labor, the Church has not been sympathetic to most feminist demands, especially those dealing with reproductive issues.[37] In general, the

34. See Carol Ann Drogus, *Women, Religion, and Social Change in Brazil's Popular Church* (Notre Dame: University of Notre Dame Press, 1997); Burdick, *Looking for God in Brazil;* Rowan Ireland, *Kingdoms Come* (Pittsburgh: University of Pittsburgh Press, 1991); Scott Mainwaring, *The Catholic Church and Politics in Brazil, 1916–1985* (Stanford: Stanford University Press, 1986).

35. Herminia Maricato, *Em Tempo* 42 (18 December 1978), 4, cited in Alvarez, *Engendering Democracy*, 131.

36. Sader and Silverstein, *Without Fear of Being Happy*, 35–37.

37. See, for example, Borba et al., "O feminismo no Brasil de hoje."

Church's discourse on women supports their traditional roles or their mobilization as workers, but the Church is critical of feminist attempts to redefine established gender roles, including the unequal burden shouldered by women in the gendered division of labor. Jane Jaquette concludes, "Although the Church cooperated with women's groups in the democratic opposition, the Church—even its progressive wing—tends to be critical of the feminists' strategic agenda. The Church organizes women in competition with the feminist movements, building mass support by meeting women's 'practical' gender interests."[38] The Church takes a conservative stand on many issues of concern to the feminist movement, particularly issues related to sexuality. For instance, the Church continues to oppose feminists' calls for increased availability of contraception, and it opposes abortion for any reason.

The Church's support of the democratic opposition under the dictatorship has bolstered its political profile since the transition.[39] When Church positions conflict with feminist demands, the PT has shown itself to be more concerned with losing the support of the Church than that of women. For example, in the 1994 elections, the PT was the only party to advocate the decriminalization of abortion, and the party's original program outlined its position on this issue. Under pressure from the Church, both within and outside the party, the PT recanted and removed the mention of abortion from the party program. This was a major setback for party feminists, who had felt that they were making progress after years of not being able to broach the issue of abortion as a subject for party debate.[40] Paola Cappellin shares the belief of many Brazilian feminists: in post-transition politics, she says, the Church is one of the leading obstacles to the advancement of feminist claims.[41] Given the slow pace of change within the Church, its conflict with feminists is unlikely to be resolved in the near future.

38. Jane S. Jaquette, "Conclusion: Women and the New Democratic Politics," in *The Women's Movement in Latin America: Feminism and the Transition to Democracy* (Boulder, Colo.: Westview Press, 1991), 195. "Practical" versus "strategic" gender demands is a distinction originally formulated by Maxine Molyneux (1985). Practical gender demands (such as improvements in community services) are those rights or resources that allow women to fulfill their traditional roles. Strategic demands (such as for the legalization of abortion) challenge the very legitimacy of those roles.

39. For a discussion of this phenomenon in the Chilean context, see Liesl Haas, "The Catholic Church in Chile: New Political Alliances," in *Latin American Religion in Motion,* ed. Christian Smith and Joshua Prokopy (New York: Routledge, 1999).

40. Paola Cappellin, interview by author, Rio de Janeiro, 19 June 1994.

41. Ibid.

The Left and Women

The history of women's participation in parties and movements on the left has been one of extremes: women have contributed immensely to causes on the left, but they have also been frustrated by the left's deferred attention to women's rights. Although the political left has focused much more sharply on women's equality than other political groups have, specific actions taken by leftist parties and movements still fall short of their promises. From the Nicaraguan Sandinistas to the Cuban Revolution to El Salvador's FMLN guerrillas-turned-political-party, numerous accounts have detailed the difficulties women have faced in their attempts to participate as equals in the organized left.[42] Brazilian women are no exception to this frustrating experience. Research has illustrated that female guerrillas in the militant left participated in the same military actions as the men, but in the hierarchical structure of the leftist organizations, few women achieved leadership positions. In addition, women militants found the men unsympathetic to their particular challenges as women. Women in the underground movements who struggled to raise children, for instance, complained that they received little help or support from the men. Caring for the children born to group members was considered solely the responsibility of women.

A continuing source of tension between female militants and the male leadership within the left has concerned the proper prioritization of the women's movement within the larger struggle for political change. The majority of male leaders believed that concerns specific to the struggle for women's emancipation could only be addressed after the "larger" battle for socialism had been won. Feminists, however, felt that the struggle for women's rights should be fought simultaneously with the broader struggle of the opposition. Many female leftist feminists developed their own theories of gender oppression that were based on the writings of Marx and on their own experiences. Norma Stoltz Chinchilla explains that in the past two decades, progress has been made in bridging this rift between traditional and feminist Marxists.

> Feminism is seen by a growing number of Latin American Marxists as not only compatible with [traditional Marxism] but essential to it. The very existence of new social movements in Latin American soci-

42. Chinchilla, "Women's Movements in the Americas"; Margaret Randall, *Gathering Rage: The Failure of Twentieth-Century Revoluions to Develop a Feminist Agenda* (New York: Monthly Review Foundation, 1992); Alvarez, *Engendering Democracy*.

eties (i.e., the multiplicity of class, sectorial, and other opposition groups that challenge some aspect of authoritarian relationships, exploitation, or alienation) challenges left political parties to develop more tolerant, democratic, and pluralistic political practices in spite of a weak democratic tradition.[43]

Some of these women abandoned leftist organizations altogether to start autonomous movements in which questions of gender and of women's equality would not be secondary ones.

Women's experiences of sexism in leftist organizations have made many feminists disillusioned with party politics and cynical about the PT's claim to be different from other parties, especially given the prominent position of leftist organizations within the party. Nevertheless, many feminists have found the PT to be a more hospitable place than traditional parties of the left. For example, Lurdinha Rodrigues, the current president of the União de Mulheres, a São Paulo-based feminist organization, is one of several União members who were expelled from the Communist Party for their feminist views and who are now members of the PT.[44] She explains that female PT militants must still confront sexism within the party, but the eclectic nature of the party makes it more open to different points of view, including feminist perspectives. In contrast, the Brazilian Communist Party has a more difficult time moving beyond a traditional class analysis that is incapable of incorporating feminist arguments into the ideology of class struggle.[45] The difference in character between the PT and the Brazilian Communist Party stems from the fact that, as home to an eclectic group of movements, the PT is less dogmatic than the Communist Party. Although it is formally a socialist party, the official goal of the PT is, in fact, not to promote a socialist form of government but to make the Brazilian system more democratic.[46]

Feminist PT Candidates in the 1994 Elections

Several telling points regarding the relationship between women and the political parties can be made from an analysis of female candidates in the

43. Chinchilla, "Women's Movements in the Americas," 49–50.
44. From interviews with União members, São Paulo, July 1994.
45. For leftist feminists, class and gender exploitation are related phenomena; see, for example, Chinchilla, "Women's Movements in the Americas."
46. Starling, interview.

1994 elections. First, the overall number of female candidates—from the left and the right—increased,[47] demonstrating the expanded space available to women in general in Brazilian politics. However, the majority of these women, predominantly those from the right and the center-right, were not feminists and had no ties to the organized women's movement. Most of the conservative women were relatives of politically powerful men, such as Roseana Sarney of Maranhão state, the first female governor in Brazil's history and daughter of the former president. Feminist candidates came from the left, predominantly the PT (and, to a lesser extent, the PSDB). Despite the larger political space for women, space for feminists is apparently found only in a few parties of the left, and especially in the PT.[48] Reflecting on the relatively high number of feminist candidates from the PT, Céli Regina Jardim Pinto concludes that this is not due solely to the progressive position of the party on gender issues but also to the internal democratic organization of the party, which makes it easier for women to participate. She states that in less stratified parties like the PT, the leadership is less consolidated, and women therefore have an easier time filling available candidate spaces.[49]

A closer look at the PT female candidates reveals that all of them were feminists and had participated in the unions and social movements. However, almost none of them explicitly promoted a feminist agenda in their campaigns. For example, Esther Grossi and Maria Luiza Jaeger, former municipal Secretaries of Education and Health, respectively (from Rio Grande do Sul), went to great lengths to justify their candidacies by emphasizing their educational backgrounds and their past work for the party. Jardim Pinto

47. Jardim Pinto, "Mulher e política no Brasil," 507–9. Jardim notes that twelve women ran for the National Senate, twelve for State Governor, twelve for Assistant Governor, and two for Vice President (these last two were Iris Rezende and Gardênia Gonçalves, who ran on the tickets of Amin and Quércia, respectively). Jardim Pinto explains that neither of these tickets had any chance of winning, and so the presence of female vice-presidential candidates signals not the progressive nature of their parties as much as the fact that the two campaigns were lost causes. Elections in the state of Rio Grande do Sul are indicative. Thirteen women ran for the National House of Representatives and twenty-two for the State House of Representatives, corresponding to less than 6 percent of the candidates from all the parties (ibid.).

48. Jardim Pinto notes that many nonfeminist candidates incorporated elements of feminist discourse into their campaigns. For example, conservative female candidate Carmen Dreyer of the PPR stated in her television campaign spot, "I come before you today trusting that old prejudices have been destroyed, because women are becoming more active with each passing day, particularly in the major issues facing our society" ("Mulher e política no Brasil," 513). The fact that such candidates use feminist rhetoric without supporting a feminist agenda is evidence that candidates from the right as well as the left recognize the political importance of at least addressing the issue of women's equality. This is significant in that it points to a change in traditional conceptions of women and of the political influence of feminism in Brazil.

49. Ibid., 512.

states that "this exaggerated concern over proving one's professional competence in the campaign leaflets appears to indicate a need to counterbalance one's very condition as a woman (i.e., the traditional wife, mother, and grandmother)."[50] Both women stressed the economy, political corruption, and other general issues in their campaigns, which in and of itself is of course not unusual. However, Jardim Pinto emphasizes that both Grossi and Jaeger focused on general issues to the veritable exclusion of feminist concerns. Although both women were active in the feminist movement, neither used her participation in that movement as an indication of her competence for office, and both conscientiously avoided taking positions on issues clearly identified with the feminist movement. Grossi "never once mentioned women's conditions or the need to defend women's rights in her brief TV appearances or abundant campaign leaflets," and Jaeger, despite having been a municipal Secretary of Health, never "link[ed] her platform in defense of public health to any of the demands from the women's or feminist movements."[51] This latter omission is especially significant, given the priority of women's health issues for both the feminist movement and the women's movement as a whole.

An exception to this pattern was the campaign of Helena Bonumá, who ran for the State House in Rio Grande do Sul. Bonumá explicitly linked the struggle of women against gender oppression to the larger struggle for democracy in Brazil. She specifically addressed the problem of mass sterilization of women and the danger to women's health of illegal abortions, in addition to speaking of more general issues, such as the need for improved working conditions for the entire working class.

An examination of the 1994 elections, then, reveals that on the one hand, the PT was relatively progressive; in comparison to other parties, it nominated feminist candidates and promoted more of the feminist agenda. In addition, the fact that nonfeminist candidates incorporated elements of feminist discourse into their campaigns gave evidence that traditional conceptions of women are changing and that some basic feminist ideas (for example, that women should participate in politics) are becoming more accepted. However, the reluctance of feminist candidates to promote a feminist agenda as part of their campaigns also indicates a continuing social resistance to feminism. Finally, although the overall number of female candidates increased, women still constituted a small percentage of the candidates

50. Ibid., 513.
51. Ibid., 513–17.

for each party, including the PT. Women occupied a position within the PT that was still far from equal to the position of men.

Conclusions

The social and political power of women should be a central concern for the left and consequently for the PT, if for no other reason than the exploitation of women in the market—including substandard wages and mistreatment in the workplace—undermines the strength of the working class as a whole. As long as women can be hired for less than the minimum wage and be forced to work long hours without benefits, the bargaining position of labor in general is weakened. For this reason, even those elements of labor and the left who are not concerned with the advancement of women, or who may even be threatened by it, have a stake in the struggle for women's rights. However, the rhetoric of the PT implies an inclusion of women and of feminist concerns that goes beyond mere instrumentality.

This analysis of the relationship between the feminist movement and the Workers' Party in Brazil has yielded important insights for the study of links between the feminist movement and the political parties. On the one hand, it is obvious that there are significant barriers to women's increased participation in the PT and to the PT's adoption of feminist theory and praxis. These obstacles were greater than might have been expected, given the rhetoric of the PT and the considerable ideological overlap between the PT and the feminist movement. Yet feminists did not abandon the PT, and as a result of their work within the party, the PT nominated more feminist candidates and promoted more of the feminist agenda than any other party in the 1994 elections. Feminist efforts to work within the PT also had a concrete impact on the proposals and practices of the party.

While the difficulties inherent in forging stronger links between the feminist movement and the PT might leave one pessimistic about the chances for similar links between other social movements and more conservative parties, there is reason for optimism. It is true that almost no candidate ran on an openly feminist campaign platform in the 1994 elections. However, the fact that nonfeminist candidates from conservative parties utilized elements of feminist discourse as part of their campaigns is an indication of the influence feminism has gained in society at large and of the gradual change taking place in social attitudes. Even if conservative parties borrow the discourse of women's rights only for short-term electoral gain, the fact that the political right deems it necessary to develop some level of familiarity with these topics is a testament to the influence of the women's movement and of feminism in Brazil.

In many ways, post-transition Brazilian politics has resisted women's participation. Yet it would be inaccurate to conclude that the political landscape in Brazil is not changing and that feminists exert no influence on politics. As the case presented here suggests, the relationship between the women's movement and the Workers' Party illustrates that progress is being made, even if needed changes are occurring more slowly than feminists had originally expected. As the example of the feminist movement and the PT indicates, feminist activism within the PT had an impact on party programs and praxis. There is reason to hope that, with time, links between feminists and political parties may become more numerous and may lead to the consolidation of a more representative democracy in Brazil.

BIBLIOGRAPHY

INTERVIEWS

Cappellin, Paola. Interview by author. Rio de Janeiro, 19 June 1994.
Starling, Sandra. Interview by author. Belo Horizonte, 6 July 1994.

OTHER SOURCES

Alvarez, Sonia E. *Engendering Democracy in Brazil.* Princeton: Princeton University Press, 1990.
———. "The (Trans)formation of Feminism(s) and Gender Politics in Democratizing Brazil." In *The Women's Movement in Latin America: Participation and Democracy,* edited by Jane S. Jaquette. Boulder, Colo.: Westview Press, 1994.
Alvarez, Sonia E., Patricia Chuchryk, Marysa Navarro-Aranguren, and Nancy Saporta Sternbach. "Feminisms in Latin America: From Bogotá to San Bernardo." *Signs,* vol. 17 (Winter 1992): 393–434.
Borba, Angela, Hildete Pereira, Jacqueline Pitanguy, and Wania Sant'anna. "O feminismo no Brasil de hoje." *Estudos feministas* 2 (Fall/Winter 1994): 428–43.
Boschi, Renato Raul. *A arte de associacão: Política de base e democracia no Brasil.* São Paulo: Vertice, 1987.
Bruschini, Cristina. "O trabalho da mulher brasileira nas décadas recentes." *Estudos feministas* 2 (Fall/Winter 1994): 179–202.
Burdick, John. *Looking for God in Brazil: The Progressive Catholic Church in Urban Brazil's Religious Arena.* Berkeley and Los Angeles: University of California Press, 1993.
Camargo, Maria Cecilia. "Constitution and Reality: Women and Labour Law." In *Women in Brazil,* edited by Caipora Women's Group. London: Latin American Bureau, 1993.

Cappellin, Paola. "Viver o sindicalismo no feminino." *Estudos feministas* 2 (Fall/Winter 1994): 271–91.

Chinchilla, Norma Stoltz. "Women's Movements in the Americas: Feminism's Second Wave." *NACLA Report on the Americas* 27, no. 1 (1993): 17–23.

Craske, Nikki. *Women and Politics in Latin America.* New Brunswick: Rutgers University Press, 1999.

Drogus, Carol Ann. *Women, Religion, and Social Change in Brazil's Popular Church.* Notre Dame: University of Notre Dame Press, 1997.

Escobar, Arturo, and Sonia E. Alvarez, eds. *The Making of Social Movements in Latin America.* Boulder, Colo.: Westview Press, 1992.

Fisher, Jo. *Out of the Shadows: Women, Resistance, and Politics in South America.* London: Latin American Bureau, 1993.

Flora, Cornelia Butler, and Helen I. Safa. "Production, Reproduction, and the Polity: Women's Strategic and Practical Gender Issues." In *Americas: New Interpretive Essays,* edited by Alfred Stepan. New York: Oxford University Press, 1992.

Froehlich, Christiane, and Erika Fuechtbauer. "Women in Base Christian Communities." In *Women in Brazil,* edited by Caipora Women's Group. London: Latin American Bureau, 1993.

Haas, Liesl. "The Catholic Church in Chile: New Political Alliances." In *Latin American Religion in Motion,* edited by Christian Smith and Joshua Prokopy. New York: Routledge, 1999.

Hagopian, Francis. "After Regime Change: Authoritarian Legacies, Political Representation, and the Democratic Future of South America." *World Politics* 45 (April 1993): 464–500.

Hewitt, W. E. *Base Christian Communities and Social Change in Brazil.* Lincoln: University of Nebraska Press, 1991.

Ireland, Rowan. *Kingdoms Come.* Pittsburgh: University of Pittsburgh Press, 1991.

Jaquette, Jane S. "Conclusion: Women and the New Democratic Politics." In *The Women's Movement in Latin America: Feminism and the Transition to Democracy.* Boulder, Colo.: Westview Press, 1991.

———, ed. *The Women's Movement in Latin America: Participation and Democracy.* Boulder, Colo.: Westview Press, 1994.

Jaquette, Jane S., and Sharon L. Wolchik, eds. *Women and Democracy: Latin America and Central and Eastern Europe.* Baltimore: The Johns Hopkins University Press, 1998.

Jardim Pinto, Céli Regina. "Donas-de-casa, mães, feministas, batalhadoras: Mulheres nas eleições de 1994 no Brasil." *Estudos feministas* 2 (Fall/Winter 1994): 297–313.

———. "Mulher e política no Brasil: Os impasses do feminismo, enquanto movimento social, face às regras do jogo da democracia representativa." *Estudos feministas* 2 (Fall/Winter 1994): 256–70.

Keck, Margaret E. *The Workers' Party and Democratization in Brazil.* New Haven: Yale University Press, 1992.

Levine, Daniel H., ed. *Constructing Culture and Power in Latin America.* Ann Arbor: University of Michigan Press, 1993.

Mainwaring, Scott. *The Catholic Church and Politics in Brazil, 1916–1985.* Stanford: Stanford University Press, 1986.

Mainwaring, Scott, and Eduardo Viola. *New Social Movements, Political Culture, and Democracy: Brazil and Argentina.* Notre Dame, Ind.: Helen Kellogg Institute for International Studies, 1984.

Miller, Francesca. *Latin American Women and the Search for Social Justice*. Hanover: University Press of New England, 1991.

Molyneux, Maxine. "Mobilization Without Emancipation? Women's Interests, the State, and Revolution in Nicaragua." *Feminist Studies* 11, no. 2 (1985): 227–54.

Nataraj, Shyamala. *Private Decisions, Public Debate: Women, Reproduction, and Population*. London: Panos, 1994.

Panebianco, Angelo. *Political Parties: Organization and Power*. Cambridge: Cambridge University Press, 1988.

Pitanguy, Jacqueline, and Eli Diniz. "Leila Dinz e a antecipação de temas feministas." *Estudos feministas* 2 (Fall/Winter 1994).

Radcliffe, Sarah A., and Sallie Westwood. *Viva: Women and Popular Protest in Latin America*. London: Routledge, 1993.

Randall, Margaret. *Gathering Rage: The Failure of Twentieth-Century Revolutions to Develop a Feminist Agenda*. New York: Monthly Review Foundation, 1992.

Sader, Emir, and Ken Silverstein. *Without Fear of Being Happy: Lula, the Workers' Party, and Brazil*. New York: Verso, 1991.

Safa, Helen I. "Women's Social Movements in Latin America." *Gender and Society* 4, no. 3 (1990): 354–69.

Schultz, Susanne. " 'Having Children? That's Our Decision!' The Women's Health Movement and Population Policy." In *Women in Brazil*, edited by Caipora Women's Group. London: Latin American Bureau, 1993.

Souza-Lobo, Elisabeth. *A classe operária tem dois sexos*. São Paulo: Espolio, 1991.

Staudt, Kathleen. *Policy, Politics, and Gender: Women Gaining Ground*. West Hartford, Conn.: Kumarian Press, 1998.

———, ed. *Women, International Development, and Politics*. Philadelphia: Temple University Press, 1990.

9 | Nonpartisanship as a Political Strategy
Women Left, Right, and Center in Chile

Lisa Baldez

The ideology of "antipolitics" uniformly motivated the actions of military governments throughout Latin America in the 1960s and 1970s. Military rulers seized power from civilian politicians throughout the region on the grounds that " 'politics' was largely responsible for the poverty, instability, and economic backwardness of their nations."[1] According to this view, the demagoguery and factionalism associated with partisan politics—*politiquería*— threatened national unity, impeded national development, and necessitated the intervention of the military as neutral administrators of order and growth.

The military is not the only constituency that has placed the blame for gridlock and underdevelopment at the feet of party leaders. The "politics of antipolitics" in Latin America extends far beyond the domain of the military and does not necessarily entail authoritarian solutions. Women, as an organized political constituency, are foremost among the civilian groups that have framed their mobilization in terms of their opposition to the party system. When women mobilize as political outsiders, declaring their opposition to male party leaders, they forward their own version of antipolitics—and their rationale for doing so has a uniquely gendered slant. This chapter examines both the conditions under which women mobilize on the basis of their

The research for this chapter was conducted in Santiago, Chile, in 1993–94 under the auspices of a dissertation grant from the Fulbright Commission. Earlier versions were presented at annual meetings of the Midwest Political Science Association and Latin American Studies Association. I would like to thank Margaret Power, Victoria González, Karen Kampwirth, Elisabeth Friedman, Elizabeth Hutchison, and Suzanne Marilley for their exceptionally cogent comments and suggestions. Any remaining errors are mine.
    1. Brian Loveman and Thomas M. Davies, Jr., eds., *The Politics of Antipolitics: The Military in Latin America* (Wilmington, Del.: SR Books, 1997), 5.

identity as political outsiders and the political consequences of this strategy for women and for overall policy.

This chapter compares two very different cases in which women mobilized against the regime in power in Chile. The first case concerns Poder Femenino (Feminine Power, or PF), a center-right coalition of women that mobilized to oust the democratically elected government of Salvador Allende in the early 1970s. This group, one of the more prominent organizations in the anti-Allende women's movement, helped consolidate support for the military regime that would rule Chile for sixteen years (1973–89). The second case is Mujeres Por la Vida (Women For Life), a coalition of sixteen female leaders from center-left political parties. This group, which formed in 1983 in the context of Chile's transition to democracy, became a leading force among the women's organizations that mobilized to put an end to the military government and to forward gender-specific concerns in the political arena.

These two cases differ fundamentally. The idea that they are at all comparable will undoubtedly strike many people as unorthodox. They represent diametrically opposed periods in Chile's recent history. Poder Femenino mobilized to bring the military into power, while Mujeres Por la Vida mobilized to get the military out of power. The tensions between supporters and opponents of the military regime have not abated over time; they have only grown more intense since the arrest and detention of General Pinochet in London in October 1998. In interviews, activists insisted that these two groups had nothing in common. Although women on both sides mobilized on the basis of their identity as women, they viewed each other skeptically. Many of the women who *opposed* the military government did not consider Poder Femenino to have been a women's organization at all. Rather, they saw the PF as a conservative upper-class group defending its economic interests. Many of the women who *supported* the dictatorship viewed groups such as Mujeres Por la Vida in similar terms. Pro-military women maintained that the women who mobilized against the dictatorship used their feminine identity to mask support for communism and class-based revolution. These organizations also differed in terms of their view of women's roles. The women of Poder Femenino pointedly eschewed a feminist agenda and did not seek to change the status of women per se. The leaders of Mujeres Por la Vida, on the other hand, explicitly supported the expansion of women's rights and actively pressed for the incorporation of women's demands in the political agenda.

Despite the stark contrasts between them, these two organizations shared important characteristics. First, both groups were constituted primarily by women who served in leadership roles within their respective political parties. Poder Femenino included leaders of the women's divisions of the National Party and the Christian Democratic Party as well as prominent women from independent sociopolitical groups. Mujeres Por la Vida consisted of women from all the main political parties that opposed the military, including the Christian Democrats and the Socialist Party. Despite their partisan affiliations, however, both groups emphasized women's ability to overcome conflict among political parties. These organizations portrayed women as uniquely able to transcend partisan conflict; male politicians, by comparison, were viewed as inevitably mired in factional fights that prevented them from dealing with important, substantive issues. Both Poder Femenino and Mujeres Por la Vida framed their opposition to the existing government in terms of women's ability to stand above the fray of party politics, and both articulated their demands in terms of the need for unity across parties. In both cases, women mobilized as nonpartisans precisely at moments of intense partisan conflict and in the context of intense disagreement about strategy. Well-known female party leaders organized as women—across party lines—in order to reorient the political agenda toward new concerns. Finally, both groups claimed to represent the concerns of women in the context of more general demands for regime change. They maintained that a climate of crisis rendered real unity among political parties a moral imperative. Mobilizing as nonpartisans reflected the women's sincere belief that the political parties had failed to handle a crisis situation and that alternative measures had to be pursued.

Mobilizing across party lines is not unique to women. Nonpartisanship has long been a central part of Chilean political culture. In forming cross-partisan coalitions, women in these organizations pursued a strategy commonly followed by their male counterparts in the parties; indeed, the Chilean electoral system has always required parties to form coalitions in order to win elections and to pass legislation. The need for agreement across ideologically distinct parties is an essential component of political negotiation. The names of the governing coalitions—the Popular Front, the Popular Unity, the Coalition of Parties for Democracy—suggest the importance of appeals to cross-partisan unity.

Nonetheless, political parties are notoriously strong in Chile. Chilean political parties enforced strict discipline on their members (especially prior to

1973), and party influence penetrated deep into political culture.[2] Party affiliation determined not only what people believed politically but also where they went to school, where they worked, and even how they dressed and where they vacationed. Given the profound extent to which the parties controlled Chilean society, the reluctance of female party leaders to side with their parties in moments of crisis is puzzling. Why did these women respond to crisis by mobilizing outside their parties while the men remained loyal to the decisions made by party leadership? In the cases of the PF and the MPLV, women offered a feminine version of nonpartisanship, one that was based on a different rationale and that offered different rewards. Members of these groups attributed political crisis to male party leaders and to the party system overall. Female party activists formed separate coalitions for the express purpose of demonstrating the possibilities for cooperation to their male counterparts.

This strategy had significant consequences for practical politics. A nonpartisan strategy allowed both Poder Femenino and Mujeres Por la Vida to build alliances and mobilize the support of thousands of women precisely at points at which the parties were deadlocked and unable to reach accord. Women mobilized as political outsiders to maximize their leverage over political decisions. Their capacity to mobilize other women sent an important signal to male party leaders, who were eager to predict women's electoral behavior. In addition, women's appeals to nonpartisanship shaped the nature of popular support for regime change, albeit in different ways. Poder Femenino's version of nonpartisanship masked deep divisions between moderates and extremists within the anti-Allende opposition and contributed to the acute polarization that characterized the Popular Unity years. This strategy played easily into the military's "antipolitics" agenda and reaffirmed the belief that women were essentially conservative, the natural allies of the Pinochet regime. Mujeres Por la Vida, on the other hand, used nonpartisan appeals to defuse partisan conflicts and to demonstrate that women could be counted on to support the democratic process—although conflicts between moderates and extremists cut through this organization as well.

Poder Femenino

The phrase "a peaceful road to socialism" encapsulates the central aim of Salvador Allende's Popular Unity government. Allende, a career politician

2. Arturo Valenzuela, "Party Politics and the Crisis of Presidentialism in Chile," in *The Failure of Presidential Democracy: The Case of Latin America*, ed. Juan J. Linz and Arturo Valenzuela, vol. 2 (Baltimore: The Johns Hopkins University Press, 1994).

who had run for president three times prior to his election in 1970, aimed to implement a socialist regime within the confines of Chile's well-established democratic process. To do so, Allende promoted participation on a mass scale, nationalized industries, and accelerated the process of agrarian reform that had begun in the 1960s. He vowed to abide by the Chilean constitution, to hold free elections, and to respect civil liberties—commitments made in 1970 to secure the support of the centrist Christian Democratic Party. Over the course of his tenure in office, however, institutional mechanisms proved increasingly ineffective in resolving the conflicts that emerged within the governing coalition and between the government and the opposition. Myriad factors stymied Allende's efforts to accomplish his goals, including divisions between reformers and radicals within his own governing coalition, covert action by the U.S. government, and intense opposition from conservatives threatened by the prospect of a Marxist-Leninist revolution in democratic disguise.

Women played a prominent role in mobilizing domestic opposition to the Popular Unity government.[3] The anti-Allende women's movement is most famous for the March of the Empty Pots (*Marcha de las Cacerolas Vacías*), in which women marched through the streets of Santiago banging on pots and pans to protest food shortages and a worsening climate of violence. Women's ability to work across party lines in this demonstration indirectly prompted men to do the same, thus helping cement a coalition between the conservative National Party and the more centrist Christian Democrats. Women organized the march for numerous reasons—to express their opposition to Allende, to protest the violence that had broken out weeks earlier in protests at the University of Chile, and to embarrass Allende in front of Cuban president Fidel Castro, who had been in Chile on a widely

3. See María Correa Morande, *La guerra de las mujeres* (Santiago: Editorial Universidad Técnico del Estado, 1974); María de los Angeles Crummett, "*El Poder Femenino:* The Mobilization of Women Against Socialism in Chile," *Latin American Perspectives* 4 (Fall 1977): 103–13; Teresa Donoso Loero, *La epopeya de las ollas vacías* (Santiago: Editorial Nacional Gabriela Mistral, 1974); Michelle Mattelart, *Women, Media, and Crisis: Femininity and Disorder* (London: Comedia Publishing Group, 1986) and "Chile: The Feminine Side of the Coup, or When Bourgeois Women Take to the Streets," *NACLA's Latin America and Empire Report* 9 (September 1975): 14–25; Camilla Townsend, "Refusing to Travel *La Vía Chilena:* Working-Class Women in Allende's Chile," *Journal of Women's History* 4, no. 3 (1993): 43–63; Georgina Waylen, "Rethinking Women's Political Participation and Protest: Chile 1970–1990," *Political Studies* 40, no. 2 (1992): 299–314; Margaret Power, "Right-Wing Women and Chilean Politics: 1964–1973" (Ph.D. diss., University of Illinois, Chicago, 1996); and Lisa Baldez, "In the Name of the Public and the Private: Conservative and Progressive Women's Organizations in Chile, 1970–1996" (Ph.D. diss., University of California, San Diego, 1997).

publicized month-long visit. The publicity that the march attracted demonstrated to male party leaders a high level of domestic opposition to Allende.[4] The march ended in chaos and rioting among the youth factions of the various political parties, and scores of women were injured. This aroused public indignation at the government's mistreatment of women. The violence that erupted lasted several days and prompted Allende to declare a state of siege. In an eerie but certainly unintentional foreshadowing of the future, Allende placed none other than General Augusto Pinochet, then commander of the Santiago army garrison, to oversee the emergency zone.

In response to this crisis situation, the two main opposition parties, the National Party and the Christian Democrats, jointly moved to impeach Allende's Minister of the Interior, Jose Tohá, for his inept handling of the March of the Empty Pots. The National Party had introduced several impeachment measures *(acusaciones constitucionales)* against government officials during the previous year, but this effort marked the first time that the opposition parties had acted in concert. Shortly afterwards, the two parties created a formal coalition, the Confederación Democrática (CODE). Women's nonpartisan efforts thus led indirectly to an alliance among the male party leaders.

Women's groups organized scores of events aimed at defending their families and mobilizing popular opposition to Allende's efforts to build a socialist regime in Chile. They defended grocery stores from being taken over by the government and they commandeered radio stations sympathetic to the Popular Unity. Women organized protests aimed at provoking the military and shaming them into taking power; they taunted the military, throwing chicken feed at soldiers and sending them chicken feathers in the mail.

Poder Femenino served as an umbrella organization for numerous groups of women who opposed the Allende government. It formed in early 1972, a few months after the March of the Empty Pots, when activists from the women's divisions of the opposition political parties joined forces with the independent women who had organized the march. The leadership of this group consisted of a coordinating council of between sixteen and thirty-three women, each of whom represented a particular organization. The Coordinating Council included representatives from the women's departments of the National Party, the Christian Democratic Party, and the Radical Democracy Party; women's professional trade organizations; and civic organizations

4. Newspaper accounts of the march offer a wide range of attendance figures, from ten thousand to one hundred thousand. Given the strong political alliances of all media during this period, it is difficult to establish the validity of these estimates.

such as Solidarity, Order, and Liberty (Solidaridad, Orden y Libertad, or SOL), Fatherland and Liberty (Patria y Libertad), and a group called Javiera Carrera.[5] While the leadership was composed almost exclusively of women from the upper classes, it formed alliances with working-class and poor women, particularly those already organized by the Christian Democratic Party.

Women's groups within the opposition insisted on their nonpartisanship. Poder Femenino repeatedly invoked the spirit of unity among women who represented various parties: the "only salvation of Chile lies in the union of all the democratic sectors. . . . Neither political affiliation nor membership in different parties or movements matters [to us]."[6] A leader of Solidarity, Order, and Liberty stressed that although all the opposition parties were represented within the group, SOL itself "did not pertain to a particular party."[7] Literature disseminated by the Housewives' Front (Frente de Dueñas de Casa, or FRENDUC) stressed nonpartisanship as well. One ad for this group, published in an opposition newspaper, read, "There is not one political party behind our organization, we repeat, not one political party. The housewives who belong to FRENDUC can support whatever party or sympathize with whatever democratic organization they want."[8] Another article on FRENDUC published in *Eva,* an opposition women's magazine, stated: "No one asks what political party the other [members] belong to. In reality, no one is interested in this. But one thing is clear: they aren't Marxists."[9]

Women in Poder Femenino, SOL, and FRENDUC claimed that moral imperatives necessitated unifying along nonpartisan lines. As with other events organized by women in the opposition, the question of whether the March of the Empty Pots was a political act was at the center of public discussion. In an advertisement announcing the march, the organizers underscored its nonpartisan and nonviolent nature:

In this demonstration, although female party militants will participate, political considerations are not fundamental. We women are going to protest because there is no meat to make soup for our babies and as a result, they get sick from diarrhea; we are going to denounce the fact that our husbands are obligated to attend political meetings in order to keep their jobs. . . . We want our children to be educated in liberty and democracy and we protest against the

5. See *Tribuna,* 20 October 1972, 8.
6. *Eva,* 1 September 1972, 41.
7. Interview by author, Santiago, Chile, 1 December 1993.
8. Ad for FRENDUC, *Tribuna,* 10 May 1972, 6.
9. *Eva,* 9 June 1972, 49.

brainwashing that occurs in the schools. We will march to tell the Ramona Parra Brigade[10] that before brandishing chains, acid, and sticks and assaulting the students, let them remember that they are young and have other tasks at hand besides sowing violence and hate. We women are disposed to unite to prevent our society from being formed in hate.[11]

Women insisted that an impending crisis required people to put aside partisan differences and work together to stop Allende's reforms. The nonpartisan nature of the march was reflected in one of the unorthodox ways in which participants were recruited: the organizers posted flyers in beauty salons. "We're not going to go around picking up people or hiring buses to take people to the march like the political movements do," one of the organizers insisted.[12]

Although other groups opposed to Allende portrayed themselves in nonpartisan terms, women's logic for embracing this strategy differed from men's. Women presented themselves as uniquely capable of rising above party conflict. They claimed that men impeded the progress of the opposition as a whole because they could not see beyond party affiliation. Poder Femenino sought to encourage male party leaders to "imitate [women's] example of unity." At one point the group suggested locking up all the male leaders of the various political parties in a single room until they reached an accord.[13] Women perceived their role as being able to cut through the political rhetoric of empty promises and the partisan loyalties that prevented men from accomplishing any concrete goals. The women who participated in the March of the Empty Pots sought in part to send a signal to their own husbands, "who are always wrapped up in the quarrels of *criollo* politics or bound by political loyalties that create real walls between brothers."[14] One sympathetic journalist claimed that as a result of the March of the Empty Pots, "the opposition, at the level of masculine leadership, would have to draw the conclusion that the Chilean woman is not averse to uniting without respect for political differences, when there are more profound interests at stake, affecting the home, her husband, her children and Chile as a whole."[15]

10. The Ramona Parra Brigade was the youth division of the Chilean Communist Party at the time.
11. *La Tercera de la Hora,* 1 December 1971, 5.
12. *El Mercurio,* 30 November 1971, 19.
13. *Eva,* 1 September 1972, 41.
14. *La Tercera de la Hora,* 4 December 1971, 3.
15. Ibid., 5 December 1971, 5.

Poder Femenino portrayed itself as being above the fray of party politics, but most of the group's leaders were themselves prominent in political parties. They claimed a nonpartisan status in order to forge unity among the parties of the opposition; at the same time, they remained deeply involved in conventional partisan activities. Indeed, PF leaders had ample experience as party activists, because they had worked for years in getting-out-the-vote activities and staffing the polls on election day. A number of them came from prominent families and knew many of the opposition political leaders personally. In *La guerra de las mujeres (War of the Women)*, PF leader María Correa's account of the movement, women met frequently with members of Congress and greeted them on a first-name basis.[16]

At election time, women's appeals for unity across party lines conflicted with their need to go "into the trenches" to support their own parties. This proved particularly true during the 1973 congressional elections, which both the government and the opposition viewed as a kind of referendum on the Allende government. Poder Femenino temporarily disbanded prior to the campaign so that its members could work full-time in support of their respective parties: "When the hour arrived for an electoral battle in the recent parliamentary elections, Poder Femenino did not make its voice felt, nor its pots and pans. Months before, its members began to disband, for a completely human and understandable reason: because of their personal preferences for a particular candidate. They didn't go to the [electoral booth] as Poder Femenino, but separately as members of a particular political party or as independents."[17] PF leaders saw no contradiction between their organization's claim to nonpartisanship and the partisan activities of its members; these were simply two different strategies they pursued in their efforts to unseat Allende. The ability of women to cross the boundaries between conventional partisan activity and mobilization on behalf of nonpartisan issues is particularly remarkable, given that party affiliation has always functioned as a powerful source of collective identity in Chile.

Although Poder Femenino was a small organization, with fewer than forty full-time members, it claimed to speak on behalf of all women and was apparently aware of women's electoral clout. María Correa's account of her participation recalls a meeting with leaders from the two main opposition parties: "We women will not permit the party leaders to abandon the country this way. It's also our land and the land of our children, and we women

16. Correa, *La guerra de las mujeres.*
17. *El Rancagüino*, 9 March 1973, 6.

outnumber the men. Either you bring about the unity that can save us from Marxism, or we will never vote for you again."[18] The fact that men and women voted in separate polling places—and still do—meant that politicians tended to be responsive to women's concerns, if only while campaigning.[19]

On the one hand, women's appeal to nonpartisanship tended to reinforce the predominant view (at least among men) that women did not belong in politics. During a congressional hearing on the March of the Empty Pots, a member of the House of Deputies read from a list of the women injured during the march in order to demonstrate the extent of the injuries the women received and to show that not all the women who participated were women from upper-class neighborhoods. As the congressman read the women's names, another deputy interrupted him to ask with which party the women were affiliated. "What does it matter?" the congressman responded. "They are only women!"[20]

On the other hand, some of the leaders of the anti-Allende movement successfully translated their participation in the movement into electoral capital for female candidates. Several activists in the movement ran for congressional seats in the 1973 election and emphasized their relationship to the movement in their campaigns. Silvia Pinto, a well-known journalist who ran for Congress as a National Party candidate, printed campaign literature that featured pictures of empty pots and identified herself as a representative of the heroic Chilean woman (la valienta mujer chilena), a phrase frequently used to refer to the female opposition to Allende. Several female candidates, including Christian Democrats Wilna Saavedra and Carmen Frei, won their elections with the large majorities (primeras mayorías) that indicated a broad popular mandate. Women's representation in Congress reached a historic high in that election, with women holding 14 of 150 seats, or 9.3 percent. Efforts to increase women's representation since the transition to democracy have not been as successful. Women have held an average of 6.5 percent of Chile's congressional seats since 1990.[21]

Despite women's success as candidates for the opposition, the 1973

18. Correa, La guerra de las mujeres, 81.

19. Lisa Baldez, "Democratic Institutions and Feminist Outcomes: Chilean Policy Toward Women in the 1990s." Washington University Department of Political Science Working Papers, no. 340, 1997.

20. Diario de Sesiones, Cámara de Diputados (República de Chile), Legislatura Extraordinaria, sesión 38a, 6 January 1972, 2816.

21. Cited in María Elena Valenzuela, "Women and the Democratization Process in Chile," in Women and Democracy: Latin America and Eastern and Central Europe, ed. Jane S. Jaquette and Sharon L. Wolchik (Baltimore: The Johns Hopkins University Press, 1998), 67.

elections failed to demonstrate a clear popular mandate for either the ruling coalition or the opposition. The Popular Unity candidates won 44 percent of the vote, a greater share than they expected, with important increases among the poor and working class (especially women). The opposition won 55 percent of the vote, a clear majority but well short of the two-thirds needed to impeach Allende. For many in the opposition, these disappointing results meant the exhaustion of the possibilities for ending the crisis within institutional bounds. Tensions between the government and its opponents mounted, and popular support grew for military intervention to end the crisis. Women's activities intensified after the election, culminating in a demonstration of tens of thousands of women in front of La Moneda, the presidential palace, on 5 September 1973. They demanded Allende's resignation on the grounds that he had promised to step down if the people asked him to do so. Six days later, the military seized power, sending a shower of bombs down on La Moneda with Allende and some of his most loyal supporters still inside. In the weeks following the coup, the armed forces credited *la mujer chilena* (the Chilean woman) with having played a central role in liberating Chile from Marxism.

Poder Femenino's reliance on the discourse of nonpartisanship directly affected political outcomes. The rhetoric of female unity disguised deep and bitter partisan divisions and contributed to the climate of polarization. The unity touted by Poder Femenino really entailed conformity with the more conservative, more ardently anti-Allende line espoused by the rightist National Party. The National Party women resented the Christian Democratic Party for continuing to advocate the idea of a compromise with Allende. As María Correa recalled,

> Poder Femenino continued its struggle to obtain total unity within the opposition, but the Christian Democrats insisted in maintaining a "dialogue" with the government, under pressure from Cardinal Silva Henriquez and some of [the PDC's] more leftist leaders. . . . It was inexplicable that [the Christian Democrats] just didn't see. . . . We gave them solid and well-founded arguments, we made them see the responsibility that was before them, we showed them how public indignation was rising against them . . . but it was all useless. After hours of discussion, they remained steadfast in their meek tactics . . . thus permitting the inexorable advance of the Marxist pawns.[22]

22. Correa, *La guerra de las mujeres,* 77–78.

At the same time, the Christian Democrats criticized the Nationals for exacerbating tensions between the government and the opposition. Carmen Frei, a senator from the Christian Democratic Party and a leader in women's activities against Allende, criticized Poder Femenino for polarizing the political situation and eliminating the possibilities for compromise. As she recalled in an interview: "Poder Femenino became fanatical, so that in the end it was a blind fight against communists. Things polarized to such an extent that in the end there were only the communists and the anticommunists. I believe that this was the greatest damage that we all did to democracy in our country. . . . This brutal polarization permitted the military coup to occur."[23] Despite these divisions among women in the anti-Allende opposition, their collective identity as women fostered the widely held perception that women were essentially conservative.

After the coup, the military capitalized on women's mobilization and used it for its own purposes. Poder Femenino's version of nonpartisanship meshed easily with the military's efforts to reconstruct the country and restore order. The military demobilized the movement but recast women's participation to legitimate the military's "antipolitics" solution. Pinochet incorporated women into his regime as the "natural allies" of the military government. He viewed women's participation as complementary to the military's role in extirpating politics and *politiquería* from the Chilean scene. In so doing, however, Pinochet took women's claims to nonpartisanship far more seriously than did most of the women who had framed their actions in those terms. Pinochet and his wife, Lucía Hiriart, created new organizations to carry out the legacy of Poder Femenino.[24]

While Pinochet disbanded Poder Femenino, he appointed several of its leaders to positions of authority in his government. However, he enlisted only those women and women's organizations that had no formal ties to any of the opposition parties. María Eugenia Oyarzún, a prominent journalist and spokeswoman for the female opposition, was named mayor of Santiago; Carmen Grez, a leader of the Las Condes neighborhood council (*junta de vecinos*), served as director of the National Women's Secretariat; Sara Navas, who headed a national parent-teacher organization, served as Chile's representative to the Women's Council of the Organization of American States; and Alicia Romo, a member of Poder Femenino's coordinating council, advised Pinochet on women's issues. None of these women had been a mem-

---

23. Carmen Frei, interview by author, Santiago, 24 May 1994.
24. See María Elena Valenzuela, *La mujer en el Chile militar: Todas íbamos a ser reinas* (Santiago: ACHIP-CESOC, 1987).

ber of a political party. Female leaders within the opposition parties were surprised to find themselves frozen out of the new government on the grounds of their party affiliations, even though many of them supported the military regime and "wanted to help out."

The women who participated in PF—and a majority of Chileans overall—supported the coup and believed that the military's tenure would be brief. They expected that the military would restore order quickly and would act within the bounds of the law before it returned power to civilians. Few anticipated the violence and terror that the military would unleash once in power, and they did not foresee the extent of the military's project to restructure Chilean society. However, many (but not all) activists in Poder Femenino had sought a military solution from the very day that Allende was elected. After the coup, these women actively supported the military's efforts to rid society of subversives and communists, arguing that Chile was in the midst of a civil war that justified extreme measures. These women continued to express support for the Pinochet regime even as information about the extent of human rights abuses became widely known.

Women's mobilization against Allende contributed to the process of democratic breakdown by legitimating the resolution of conflicts outside the arena of conventional democratic political institutions, particularly outside the jurisdiction of political parties. By mobilizing as political outsiders, women helped consolidate public support for an antipolitical solution. The military regime profited from the nonpartisan discourse espoused by the anti-Allende women's movement and reinterpreted that discourse to fit its own purposes. The state incorporated women on the basis of their putatively natural affinity for the military regime; in this context, however, different female constituencies began to mobilize against the regime, challenging the military's violations of human rights and offering yet another reinterpretation of women's proper roles. In the section that follows, I examine Mujeres Por la Vida, one of the leading organizations in the movement of women against Pinochet.

Mujeres Por la Vida

When General Pinochet took power in 1973, his efforts to reconstruct the country extended far beyond temporarily replacing civilian leaders with military officials. Pinochet attributed Chile's problems to democracy itself. He began by physically eliminating politicians, arresting and disappearing thousands of people and committing tens of thousands more to exile. Pinochet sought to demobilize society completely; he banned political parties and restricted civil liberties, shut down Congress and replaced university professors with military personnel. To modernize the economy, the military government privatized hundreds of state-owned enterprises and adopted free-market neoliberal economic reforms. By the time he stepped down in 1990, Pinochet had left a lasting mark on every political institution from electoral laws to the budget process.[25]

A vibrant and diverse women's movement opposed to the dictatorship emerged as an unintended consequence of the regime's policies. Amid a climate of fierce repression, women organized to protest the disappearance of their loved ones, the economic crisis that forced them into poverty, and the climate of fear that made it impossible to conduct the business of everyday life. Women whose relatives disappeared at the hands of military officials organized to demand information on their whereabouts and to denounce human rights violations. Poor and working-class women who were forced into poverty by the regime's economic policies formed soup kitchens, shopping collectives, and craft workshops to help feed their families. Feminists formed organizations to challenge the regime's policies toward women and to forward a concrete agenda of women's rights.[26]

In retrospect, it is easy to identify these diverse groups as belonging to a common groundswell of female opposition to the military regime. Prior to 1983, however, women's efforts to join together were relatively restrained, locally based, and in most cases, isolated from one another. Many women's groups were unaware of the existence of the others. The climate of fear and repression under the military regime required the women who were active in such organizations to remain extremely cautious about acknowledging their participation to any but a few trusted friends; thus, the possibilities for building networks with other groups were quite limited.

This situation changed dramatically in 1983. A devastating economic recession in 1981–82 challenged the regime's legitimacy and prompted some

25. Lisa Baldez and John M. Carey, "Executive Agenda Control: Lessons from General Pinochet's Constitution," *American Journal of Political Science* 43, no. 1 (1999).

26. On the Chilean women's movement, see Patricia Chuchryk, "From Dictatorship to Democracy: The Women's Movement in Chile," in *The Women's Movement in Latin America*, rev. ed., ed. Jane S. Jaquette (Boulder, Colo.: Westview Press, 1994); Waylen, "Rethinking Women's Political Participation"; Alicia Frohmann and Teresa Valdés, "Democracy in the Country and in the Home: The Women's Movement in Chile," in *The Challenge of Local Feminisms: Women's Movements in Global Perspective*, ed. Amrita Basu (Boulder, Colo.: Westview Press, 1995); and Baldez, "In the Name of the Public and the Private."

sectors to criticize the government publicly. On 11 May 1983, the Confederation of Copper Workers, Chile's largest union, called for a national protest against the regime. At 8:00 P.M., thousands of people began banging on pots and pans and honking on horns throughout the city of Santiago. Amazingly, this protest reversed the meaning of the *cacerola,* the empty pot, turning it from a symbol of support for the coup to a symbol of condemnation of the regime's economic failure. The success of this demonstration launched a cycle of monthly protests, known as *las protestas,* that would last for three years.

The political parties, which had been underground for ten years, moved quickly to assume leadership of the protests. Yet despite this display of widespread opposition to the regime, the opposition parties still faced the daunting problem of agreeing upon an alternative political program. Deep and longstanding conflicts on substantive issues and personal grounds divided the parties of the left and center. Activists in the leftist parties distrusted the Christian Democrats for having opposed Allende and having supported the coup in 1973. Within the left itself, relations among the parties were fraught with conflicts over strategy that had originated long before Allende took office but had intensified in the three years of the Popular Unity government. Ultimately, the Christian Democrats agreed to cooperate with the moderate left on two conditions: acceptance of democratic institutions and support for a capitalist economic system. In August 1983, the Christian Democratic Party formed the Democratic Alliance (Alianza Democrática, or AD), a coalition that included moderate factions of the Socialist Party and other leftist parties committed to social democracy. In September of that year, three radical left parties formed the Popular Democratic Movement (Movimiento Democrático Popular, or MDP). These three parties—the Communist Party, a militant wing of the Socialist Party, and the Revolutionary Left Movement (MIR)—favored armed confrontation with the regime rather than a negotiated return to democratic rule.[27] A central point of contention between the two coalitions was whether to participate in the plebiscite scheduled for 1988, which would determine whether an election would be held the following year. Debate centered on whether the regime would permit a fair election and respect the results. The AD insisted that adhering to the regime's schedule for elections was the only chance the opposition had of winning. The MDP maintained that the election would be inevitably fraudulent, and that partici-

27. See Jeffrey M. Puryear, *Thinking Politics: Intellectuals and Democracy in Chile, 1973–1988* (Baltimore: The Johns Hopkins University Press, 1994), and Paul W. Drake and Ivan Jaksic, eds., *The Struggle for Democracy in Chile,* rev. ed. (Lincoln: University of Nebraska Press, 1995).

pating in it would legitimize the regime and eliminate another chance for a peaceful transition until 1997.[28]

The climate of antipolitics under Pinochet served to exacerbate the disagreements within the party coalitions. In the ten years since the coup, Pinochet had continuously harangued *"los señores políticos"* as being responsible for the election of Allende and the chaos that ensued. Censorship and repression of the media prevented the public expression of any competing messages. The extent to which the military government vilified political parties and politicians made it difficult for the parties to reestablish credibility. For many Chileans, the conflicts that emerged between the AD and the MDP in 1983 proved Pinochet's point that political parties inevitably violated the national interest in pursuit of their own partisan goals.

Mujeres Por la Vida (Women for Life) emerged in this context. In part, the organization sought to demonstrate that the opposition parties were not inevitably corrupt but in fact could articulate a leadership role against the wrongdoings of the dictatorship. Like Poder Femenino, the women in MPLV sought to establish unity between the opposition political parties and claimed that women possessed a superior ability to transcend partisan divisions. MPLV sought to provide an example for men to follow; indeed, the group claimed that men *must* follow their example if the opposition was to succeed in ousting the military. To this extent, women opposed to Pinochet relied on some of the same rhetorical strategies as women opposed to Allende. However, while the nonpartisan mobilization of women against Allende led to the breakdown of democratic institutions, groups like Mujeres Por la Vida helped to rebuild democratic institutions.

Mujeres Por la Vida formed in November 1983; its sixteen members represented each of the various parties within the center-left opposition. These women were sufficiently well known within their respective parties to serve as public signifiers of those parties. As María de la Luz Silva, one of the founders of MPLV and a member of a political party known as MAPU (Movimiento de Acción Popular Unitaria, or Movement of Unified Popular Action), recalled, "When I joined MPLV, people from MAPU knew that we approved of this [organization], we were a point of reference for our people. Because we couldn't sign as members of a party, the [founding members of the group] became political referents. . . . So if I was involved with something, MAPU was involved, if Fanny Pollarolo was there, the Communist Party was there, if Graciela Borquez was there, the Christian Democrats were there."[29] How-

---

28. Puryear, *Thinking Politics.*
29. María de la Luz Silva, interview by author, Santiago, 25 May 1994.

ever, while their individual partisan affiliations were clear, these women did not represent their parties in an official capacity. Mujeres Por la Vida organized independently of the parties.

The group's founding members had come to know one other while participating in human rights organizations during the early years of the dictatorship. Their decision to organize was precipitated by an atrocious event: the suicide of Sebastián Acevedo, a fifty-two-year-old man who had lit himself on fire in front of the main cathedral in Santiago to protest the disappearance of his two children. As Silva remembered, "This event struck us all as something extremely painful that could not go on. It was at this point that we women said, 'Women support life against the culture of death that is the dictatorship.' "[30] In response to Acevedo's death, Mujeres Por la Vida sought to promote unity among the center-left parties, maintaining that such accord was a "necessary prerequisite for taking decisive action against the dictatorship." As Silva claimed, MPLV sought "to demonstrate that we, the women, were [in favor of] life, and that life mattered more than the party struggles, the positioning and the strategizing. We were going to demonstrate that when you introduce a higher interest, such as life itself, we can all go forward together."[31] The women in MPLV claimed that they were able to orchestrate a united front by focusing on the issues they all confronted, rather than those specific to their respective parties: "The pain provoked by this system of death and injustice united us, a pain that we transformed into conscience and a fear that we transformed into active solidarity. . . . [W]e had the conviction that either the end of the dictatorship was imperative or we would all be victims of another collective tragedy. What united us was the conviction that we were all indispensable in the reconstruction of democracy."[32]

Mujeres Por la Vida perceived its agenda in gendered terms: its leaders saw the task of inspiring unity within the opposition as one that women were uniquely qualified to carry out. Fanny Pollarolo, one of the group's founding members and a Communist Party leader, claimed that the MPLV's task was "to inspire the spirit necessary to unify the opposition, to overcome the ineffectiveness of the men."[33] The organization drew upon specifically feminine qualities in its efforts to mobilize others. Fabiola Letelier, a well-known human rights lawyer, described the specific contribution that MPLV sought to make to the opposition movement: "The active participation of women is

30. Ibid.
31. Ibid.
32. *Análisis,* January 1984, 18.
33. *La Época,* 4 January 1988, 10.

of paramount importance because women are the ones who are most affected by the horrors of these years and have been in the front lines of battle."[34] MPLV built upon the participation of women in human rights groups and sought to push the opposition further along in the struggle for democracy and change.

On 29 December 1983, Mujeres Por la Vida held a massive rally that brought together women from all the factions within the opposition, the Democratic Alliance as well as the Popular Democratic Movement. The women organized the event in response to widespread and deep frustration over the inability of the opposition parties to reach accord regarding how to bring about the end of the regime. As Patricia Verdugo, a journalist and one of the organizers, remarked at the time: "The recent acts sponsored by the Opposition had been characterized by spending more energy in loudly proclaiming divisions and mutually insulting one another than in charging our batteries to put an end to the [military] regime. The challenge was to construct real unity."[35] MPLV sought to make active opposition to the regime a moral imperative. A pamphlet distributed prior to the event read: "We come together to express the decision to act today and not tomorrow to put an end to the signs of death: torture, hunger and unemployment, *detenidos-desaparecidos,* exile, arbitrary detentions . . . repression and abuses of power."[36]

This gendered appeal struck a nerve; nearly ten thousand women attended the rally, which took place in the Teatro Caupolicán in downtown Santiago and became known as the *caupolicanazo.*[37] It served as the benchmark against which all future events would be measured. Before the *caupolicanazo,* "the Communist Party and the Christian Democrats had never gotten together, and were absolutely incompatible, like water and oil," said María de la Luz Silva.[38] The Caupolicán rally brought leaders from the two parties together: Graciela Borquez, a member of the political commission of the PDC, and Fanny Pollarolo, the Communist Party leader, both appeared. The theme of unity was carried out to the most minute detail. The organizers prohibited participants from carrying party flags or banners. Instead, the co-

---

34. *Análisis,* January 1984, 19.

35. Ibid., 17–21.

36. "Mujeres al Caupolicán" (mimeograph).

37. The *"azo"* suffix indicates a blow or explosion: *puñetazo* is a punch with the fist *(puño),* for example. In this case, the *"azo"* suffix signifies the force and impact of the event.

38. Silva, interview. Christian Democratic Senator Carmen Frei maintained that women from the Christian Democratic Party and the Communist Party had been meeting together since the early years of the dictatorship.

ordinating council of the group designed a banner in which all the flags of the various parties were arranged in a circle around the national symbol, "so that none would be on top of the others. It was like a wheel that spun around."[39] They did not permit men to attend the event, added Silva, because "we were afraid that we would be infiltrated by violent extremists," but also because they wanted to teach the men a lesson.[40]

Between 1983 and 1988, MPLV organized and participated in more than 170 events, including protests, demonstrations, and hunger strikes, as well as roundtable discussions, meetings with officials, and press conferences.[41] MPLV provided a safe forum for women's organizations to join together and articulate a common view of how women could act against the military regime. The participation of notable female party leaders played a key role in this regard; their presence signaled that it was safe for other organization members to attend and that attending might have some impact. In 1986, MPLV sent a representative to the Asamblea de la Civilidad (Civic Assembly), a forum to reconvene the disparate groups within the opposition and articulate a political agenda. The organization established a secure foothold for women's concerns in these early efforts to develop the opposition platform. As María Elena Valenzuela notes, "Women for Life became the reference point for political organizations on women's issues as well as the most important arena for convening and discussing the social mobilization of women."[42]

MPLV was one of several umbrella organizations that formed in late 1983 within the women's movement. Another group, MEMCH83 (Movimiento Por la Emancipación de la Mujer Chilena, or Movement for the Emancipation of the Chilean Woman), focused on changing the status of women and achieving gender equality. In 1984, MEMCH83 developed a feminist policy statement, the Plataforma de la Mujer Chilena (Chilean Women's Platform), that "closely follow[ed] the contents of the United Nations Convention on the Elimination of All Forms of Discrimination Against Women (1979)."[43] The appearance of MPLV on the scene frustrated some feminists, who saw the group as exemplifying a more traditional way of participating in politics.[44]

39. Ibid.
40. Chuchryk, "From Dictatorship to Democracy."
41. Teresa Valdés, one of the founding members of Mujeres Por la Vida, documented these events in "Mujeres Por la Vida: Itinerario de una lucha" (Santiago, 1989, mimeograph).
42. María Elena Valenzuela, "The Evolving Roles of Women Under Military Rule," in *The Struggle for Democracy in Chile,* rev. ed., ed. Drake and Jaksic (Lincoln: University of Nebraska Press, 1995), 172.
43. Valenzuela, "Women and the Democratization Process," 54.
44. Ibid.

The MPLV was criticized as a vehicle of the parties rather than a representative of women's concerns per se.[45] These tensions were fueled by the fact that MPLV emerged precisely at the point at which feminists were beginning to articulate a new way of "doing politics."[46]

What differentiated MPLV from other coalitions among women's organizations was the breadth of its support. No other entity proved as capable of sustaining cooperation among women across the entire spectrum of positions taken by those who opposed the military government. However, even MPLV ultimately succumbed to partisan divisions. The decision to participate in the 1988 plebiscite, and the convening of the Committee for Free Elections, eventually split Mujeres Por la Vida as it had split other organizations. MPLV continued to exist after 1987, but it no longer represented the same constituency. Many of the women who supported the upcoming election joined the Comando por el NO, the coalition of center-left parties convened to oppose the continuation of Pinochet's tenure in power. The Comando would later form the basis for the Coalition of Parties for Democracy (Concertación de Partidos por la Democracia), the coalition that would take power after the return to civilian rule in 1990. MPLV remained in control of a smaller group of women. This new incarnation ultimately supported the election and participated in the plebiscite, but adopted a critical stance toward the upcoming vote. The group organized a campaign that emphasized the regime's responsibility for human rights abuses, countering the more carefree and upbeat tenor of the "No" campaign. As Teresa Valdés describes it:

> In the midst of the debate within the opposition, this campaign seemed to us a great support for the NO, inasmuch as it made present the feelings of many Chileans that they were not represented in the plebiscite strategy. We tried to suffuse the NO with the spirit of those who had suffered so severely during the dictatorship. We took out an ad that had a picture of a fingerprint on it, with the words "Where do they vote: the exiled, the political prisoners, the disappeared, the dead? They cannot vote. Do not forget them when you vote NO."[47]

45. Sandra Lidid and Kira Maldonado, eds., *Movimiento feminista autónoma* (Santiago: Ediciones Número Crítico, 1997).
46. Julieta Kirkwood, *Ser política en Chile* (Santiago: FLACSO, 1986).
47. Valdés, "Mujeres Por la Vida," 29.

Regardless of these tensions within the opposition, the plebiscite proposal was defeated. More important, perhaps, a majority of women voted against the plebiscite (52.5 percent of women voted "No"), signaling that Pinochet could no longer count on women as his primary constituency and that perhaps women were not as inherently conservative as many had thought previously. In the period between the plebiscite and the presidential and congressional elections in December 1989, female party leaders and independent women's organizations took advantage of the gender gap to pressure the opposition parties to incorporate women's demands in the agenda of the incoming government.

It is difficult to discern the precise impact that MPLV had on electoral politics, largely because so many women's organizations were active at the time. Up until the plebiscite, MPLV had successfully maintained a coalition that included women's organizations from all points on the opposition spectrum. Male party leaders, on the other hand, remained divided between the two stances represented by the AD and the MDP. The split between the AD and the MDP resulted not only from strategic differences on how to put an end to the dictatorship but also from the AD's acceptance of the conditions set by the military government, which a majority viewed as a necessary evil. It was clear that the military would not tolerate the participation of the Communist Party in the transition process. The isolation of the Communist Party from the transition, and its subsequent political marginalization following the transition, was one of the great costs that Pinochet imposed on the democratization process.

MPLV's power had derived from its ability to maintain alliances between women from all sectors of the opposition, including AD and MDP adherents as well as other groups that eschewed any party affiliation. MPLV used this "convocational" power to press for the inclusion of women's concerns on the opposition agenda. The split that occurred as the plebiscite neared forced MPLV members to make difficult decisions about where their loyalties lay—and seriously weakened the group's capacity to represent and push for the implementation of women's demands.

Conclusion: Gendered Coalitions

Both Poder Femenino and Mujeres Por la Vida relied on similar discursive strategies to justify their participation in the political arena and to influence political outcomes. Despite their incompatible political agendas, these two organizations framed their activism in terms of women's status outside the conventional political sphere. Both groups maintained that women—even women who were party leaders and who could expect to pursue a career in their parties—could put aside their partisan differences in response to situations characterized by extreme strife. They claimed that women could transcend partisan divisions and provide an example for men to follow. Poder Femenino criticized men in the opposition political parties for continuing to rely on institutional means of protecting the status quo and for failing to cooperate with one another to combat the crisis at hand. The women in Mujeres Por la Vida also viewed the conflicts between the two coalitions within the opposition as men's inability to see the forest for the trees.

My interviews with the women who participated in these organizations suggest that they mobilized in response to a genuinely felt moral imperative. Their decision to act reflected sincere concerns and profound frustration at the inability of political parties to address the crises that were at hand. Women tended to talk about their participation in ways that did not reflect strategic considerations. The women of Poder Femenino viewed the political and economic instability that had emerged under the Allende government as a dire threat to their way of life. For the women of Mujeres Por la Vida, the military's practice of torture and disappearances evoked a visceral response that demanded unified action. The suicide of Sebastián Acevedo highlighted the years of standing by helplessly while the military tortured and disappeared people. The juxtaposition of this event and the return of party infighting enraged women and forced them to take action. In this sense, nonpartisanship was not a strategy at all, but an honest reflection of the deep frustration they felt about the way political events had unfolded.

Considered strategically, however, nonpartisanship afforded female party activists several advantages. Mobilizing as political outsiders allowed women to build broad constituencies that crossed party lines—as evidenced by the thousands of women who participated in both the March of the Empty Pots in 1971 and the *caupolicanazo* in 1983. Poder Femenino demonstrated public support for the ouster of Allende against the wishes of more moderate sectors in the opposition. Mujeres Por la Vida used its ability to mobilize women across party lines to press the opposition to address women's gendered concerns.

Both organizations included women who engaged in double militancy, simultaneously working in political parties and autonomous women's groups. But both organizations also encompassed women who were deeply skeptical about democratic institutions and the politics of compromise, albeit for very different reasons and in very different contexts. Many of the women in Poder Femenino opposed electoral democracy on the grounds that it had enabled a Marxist regime to come to power and thus presented a profound threat to their economic interests. Many of the women in Mujeres Por la Vida opposed electoral democracy on the grounds that it had been negotiated in such a way as to protect the interests of the military regime. However, the broader appeal to women that both of these groups issued masked these conflicts, and facilitated their incorporation into the ensuing regime.

For women in the anti-Allende movement, the antipolitics strategy actually enhanced women's ability to ascend to positions of political power, although not in the way most of them might have anticipated. Pinochet put women's frustration with party politics to use in his efforts to eliminate the parties entirely. He revealed the limits of the women's strategy when he promoted the participation of only those women who really had no involvement in party politics, leaving out those who framed their partisan activities in opposition to male politicians and the party system. A gendered antipolitics strategy did little to strengthen the political clout of the individual leaders of MPLV, on the other hand. Fanny Pollarolo was the only member of this organization who would go on to convert her leadership into political power; she has now served three terms as a member of the House of Deputies.

This unorthodox comparison of Poder Femenino and Mujeres Por la Vida suggests that women's mobilization shares rhetorical and institutional features that transcend ideological differences. The intensity of the political conflicts that surrounded these two groups only makes the similarities between them more intriguing. Juxtaposing these two cases may also force us to examine our own ideological commitments regarding the status of women in the political arena.

BIBLIOGRAPHY

NEWSPAPERS AND MAGAZINES

Análisis (Santiago)
La Época (Santiago)
Eva (Santiago)
El Mercurio (Santiago)
El Rancagüino (Rancagua, Chile)
La Tercera de la Hora (Santiago)
Tribuna (Santiago)

INTERVIEWS

Frei, Carmen. Interview by author. Santiago, 24 May 1994.
Silva, María de la Luz. Interview by author. Santiago, 25 May 1994.

OTHER SOURCES

Baldez, Lisa. "Democratic Institutions and Feminist Outcomes: Chilean Policy Toward
    Women in the 1990s." Washington University Department of Political Science
    Working Papers, no. 340, 1997.
————. "In the Name of the Public and the Private: Conservative and Progressive
    Women's Organizations in Chile, 1970–1996." Ph.D. diss., University of Califor-
    nia, San Diego, 1997.
Baldez, Lisa, and John M. Carey. "Executive Agenda Control: Lessons from General
    Pinochet's Constitution." American Journal of Political Science 43, no. 1
    (1999): 29–55.
Chuchryk, Patricia. "From Dictatorship to Democracy: The Women's Movement in
    Chile." In The Women's Movement in Latin America, rev. ed., edited by Jane S.
    Jaquette. Boulder, Colo.: Westview Press, 1994.
Correa Morande, María. La guerra de las mujeres. Santiago: Editorial Universidad
    Técnico del Estado, 1974.
Crummett, María de los Angeles. "El Poder Femenino: The Mobilization of Women
    Against Socialism in Chile." Latin American Perspectives 4 (Fall 1977): 103–13.
Donoso Loero, Teresa. La epopeya de las ollas vacías. Santiago: Editorial Nacional
    Gabriela Mistral, 1974.
Drake, Paul W. and Ivan Jaksic, eds. The Struggle for Democracy in Chile. Rev. ed.
    Lincoln: University of Nebraska Press, 1995.
Frohmann, Alicia, and Teresa Valdés. "Democracy in the Country and in the Home:
    The Women's Movement in Chile." In The Challenge of Local Feminisms: Wom-
    en's Movements in Global Perspective, edited by Amrita Basu. Boulder, Colo.:
    Westview Press, 1995.
Kirkwood, Julieta. Ser política en Chile. Santiago: FLACSO, 1986.
Lidid, Sandra, and Kira Maldonado, eds. Movimiento feminista autónoma. Santiago:
    Ediciones Número Crítico, 1997.
Loveman, Brian, and Thomas M. Davies, Jr., eds. The Politics of Antipolitics: The
    Military in Latin America. Wilmington, Del.: SR Books, 1997.
Mattelart, Michelle. "Chile: The Feminine Side of the Coup, or When Bourgeois
    Women Take to the Streets." NACLA's Latin America and Empire Report 9 (Sep-
    tember 1975): 14–25.
————. Women, Media, and Crisis: Femininity and Disorder. London: Comedia
    Publishing Group, 1986.
Power, Margaret. "Right-Wing Women and Chilean Politics: 1964–1973." Ph.D. diss.,
    University of Illinois, Chicago, 1996.
Puryear, Jeffrey M. Thinking Politics: Intellectuals and Democracy in Chile, 1973–
    1988. Baltimore: The Johns Hopkins University Press, 1994.
República de Chile. Cámara de Diputados. Legislatura Extraordinaria. Diario de Sesi-
    ones. Sesión 38a, 6 January 1972.
Townsend, Camilla. "Refusing to Travel La Vía Chilena: Working-Class Women in
    Allende's Chile." Journal of Women's History 4, no. 3 (1993): 43–63.

Valdés, Teresa. "Mujeres Por la Vida: Itinerario de una lucha." Santiago, 1989. Mimeograph.

Valenzuela, Arturo. "Party Politics and the Crisis of Presidentialism in Chile." In *The Failure of Presidential Democracy: The Case of Latin America,* edited by Juan J. Linz and Arturo Valenzuela. Vol. 2. Baltimore: The Johns Hopkins University Press, 1994.

Valenzuela, María Elena. *La mujer en el Chile militar: Todas íbamos a ser reinas.* Santiago: ACHIP-CESOC, 1987.

———. "The Evolving Roles of Women Under Military Rule." In *The Struggle for Democracy in Chile,* rev. ed., edited by Paul W. Drake and Ivan Jaksic. Lincoln: University of Nebraska Press, 1995.

———. "Women and the Democratization Process in Chile." In *Women and Democracy: Latin America and Eastern and Central Europe,* edited by Jane S. Jaquette and Sharon L. Wolchik. Baltimore: The Johns Hopkins University Press, 1998.

Waylen, Georgina. "Rethinking Women's Political Participation and Protest: Chile 1970–1990." *Political Studies* 40, no. 2 (1992): 299–314.

while a belief in
the world is that
Latin American & are a-political, the
women in Chile by show their through
were political and social as shown
in their political and social In order to
support or apposition of General
Augusto Pinochet in the 1970s and 1980s

*refute this statement

stereotypes
— Madonna virgin vs Jezabel

whether women saw
Pinochet as their savior
or _____, they became politically
active

10 | Defending Dictatorship
Conservative Women in Pinochet's Chile
and the 1988 Plebiscite

Margaret Power

The October 1998 arrest of General Augusto Pinochet in London, England, and his possible extradition to Spain to stand trial on charges of murder, terrorism, and genocide unleashed a storm of protest among Chileans who supported the former dictator. Conservative women rallied to express both their anger at his arrest and their love and admiration for the man who, they believed, had saved them from communism. In order to mobilize public support for the release of Pinochet, these women led demonstrations against the British and Spanish embassies, organized a campaign in December 1998 to send Christmas cards to Pinochet, wore yellow ribbons to express their belief that the general was "an illegally seized hostage,"[1] and even took over and shut down the Panamericano, the main highway into and out of Santiago.

The fact that Pinochet ruled Chile dictatorially for seventeen years is indisputable.[2] Yet an exclusive focus on the repressive aspects of his regime obscures the fact that a sizable number of Chileans defended his rule. His most passionate and visible supporters were—and still are, as the above examples illustrate—women. Why did these women support Pinochet?

In order to answer this question, the following pages will examine the beliefs and actions of the rightist women who supported the military dictatorship and, in the process, will challenge several ideas that have defined

1. They wore yellow ribbons to draw parallels between the arrest of Pinochet and the seizure of U.S. hostages by Iranians in the early 1980s. In both cases, the yellow ribbons are a reference to the song "Tie a Yellow Ribbon" performed by Tony Orlando and Dawn.

2. After seizing power in the September 1973 military coup that overthrew the democratically elected government of Salvador Allende, General Pinochet proceeded to suspend civil liberties, declare a state of siege, shut down Congress, disband the political parties, and arrest, torture, imprison, exile, or murder thousands of his opponents.

much of the existing scholarship on these women.[3] Contrary to most studies, this chapter argues that conservative women were neither static nor inflexible; they did not hail exclusively from the upper classes. They cannot be described and dismissed summarily as *viejas momias* (old mummies),[4] since right-wing women in Chile are both young and old, rich and poor. It is equally inaccurate to define them merely as women inescapably mired in the past and tradition. As this chapter will demonstrate, when conditions changed in Chile, especially in the period leading up to the 1988 plebiscite, rightist women adapted to the exigencies of the new situation. One clear example of this change is their public transformation from apolitical mothers, which is how both they and the dictatorship had defined the military's female enthusiasts, to political actors who played a central role in the 1988 plebiscite.

Another misconception is that rightist women are a monolithic force. A corollary of this belief is that they share a unified political vision and operate in substantial unison, if not total harmony, with each other. Nothing more clearly shows the error of this assumption than the emergence of the Unión Democrática Independiente (UDI, the Independent Democratic Union) in 1983 and Renovación Nacional (RN, National Renovation) in 1987, two distinct parties on the right, each of which had its own politics and strategy. Although differences in gender politics were not the primary factor that defined and distinguished the parties, they did diverge on issues relating to women (as will be discussed below).

Tens of thousands of women belonged to a third sector of conservative women, the volunteer movement led by First Lady Lucía Hiriart de Pinochet. The volunteer movement both represents an alternative expression of conservative womanhood than the one offered by the parties and illustrates the tensions that arose between women on the right. The volunteer movement certainly reflected the military's program for middle-class and poor women. But to understand it only in this light is to ignore the role Lucía Hiriart played in building and shaping it. Lucía Hiriart may have defined herself as the wife of Augusto Pinochet, but she was much more; she was also the leader of the

<hr />

3. Giselle Munizaga, *El discurso público de Pinochet: Un análisis semiológico* (Santiago: CESOC/CENECA, 1983); Teresa Valdés and Marisa Weinstein, *Mujeres que sueñan: Las organizaciones de pobladoras en Chile, 1973–1989* (Santiago: FLACSO, 1993); and María Elena Valenzuela, *La mujer en el Chile militar: Todas íbamos a ser reinas* (Santiago: Ediciones Chile y América/CESOC, 1987).

4. During the Popular Unity years (1970–73), the leftist government and its supporters routinely referred to those who opposed it as *momias* (mummies) to convey the idea that they were members of the dead bourgeois class.

largest civic movement that existed during the dictatorship. And, as this chapter will show, she was a very ambitious woman. For much of her married life, Hiriart concentrated on her husband's career. As she recently remarked in an interview, she "had found the 'subjection' of her husband within the military hierarchy hard to take, and . . . she urged him to strive for higher office."[5] However, she also took advantage of available opportunities to promote herself. She saw the plebiscite as an opportunity to advance herself politically, both openly (as the loyal defender of General Pinochet) and more subtly (as a political actor in her own right).[6] One factor that prevented her from doing so, I argue, was the emergence of the rightist parties that, although loyal to Pinochet in varying degrees, had their own agendas—which gave high priority to building their own organizations.[7]

The period preceding the 1988 plebiscite offers a window into the thinking and activity of conservative women and illustrates some of the tensions and conflicts between them. Since the outcome of the plebiscite would determine the future of military rule and strongly affect the future of the right, the months leading up to the vote heightened political tensions and struggles. Despite all the limitations and repressive measures the military imposed during this period, it was also the first time since 1973 that Chileans could openly participate in a political campaign, albeit in a limited fashion. The impact this had on the anti-Pinochet forces has been explored elsewhere.[8] This chapter examines what it meant for rightist women. Since this period intensified the politicization of the right, it also allows us to analyze the beliefs and activities of the conservative women who chose to align themselves with a military dictator.

Many of Pinochet's female supporters agreed with him that motherhood is the fundamental expression of womanhood. Disturbed by what they per-

---

5. Jon Lee Anderson, "The Dictator," *The New Yorker*, 19 October 1998, 46.

6. Hiriart comes from a political family. Her father was a Radical Party senator and subsequently an interior minister. In fact, her more prominent family "looked down upon [Augusto Pinochet]" when they first married, since his middle-class family lacked any such distinguished members. Pamela Constable and Arturo Valenzuela, *A Nation of Enemies: Chile Under Pinochet* (New York: W. W. Norton and Company, 1991), 45.

7. Lucía Hiriart experienced the impact of the political parties most directly. In the 1989 senatorial elections, Hiriart indicated that she would be willing to be a candidate for the Fourth Region, the district her father had represented. However, the rightist party Renovación Nacional (National Renovation, or RN) put forward its own candidate and ignored her offer. My thanks to Patricio Navia for this information.

8. Paul W. Drake and Ivan Jaksic, eds., *The Struggle for Democracy in Chile, 1982–1990* (Lincoln: University of Nebraska Press, 1991), and Constable and Valenzuela, *A Nation of Enemies*, 241–46, 260–67, 296–320.

ceived to be the chaos and uncertainty of the Allende years, they looked to the military to restore patriarchal order in society and their families and welcomed the affirmation of traditional gender roles. Haunted by the vision of shortages and lines that defined their memories of the Popular Unity government, they embraced Pinochet's neoliberal economic policies and basked in the reflected glow of what they perceived to be Chile's "economic miracle." Defining themselves as patriots, they cloaked their enthusiasm for the dictatorship in the mantle of nationalism.

One of the most remarkable qualities of right-wing women during this time was the rapidity with which they transformed their public identity. Since 1973, the military and conservative women had defined women as mothers outside the political sphere whose function was to serve their families and the nation. As apolitical mothers, the dictatorship encouraged women to join the volunteer movement, which was tantamount to being unpaid social workers in the service of the dictatorship. The overtly political nature of the plebiscite and the challenge the opposition posed to Pinochet's continued rule forced a change in the definition of conservative Chilean womanhood: instead of being apolitical mothers, women had to become citizens who actively defended the military regime. This chapter examines how that transformation took place.

Background on the Plebiscite

The 5 October 1988 plebiscite on the Pinochet regime was nothing if not direct. In it the Chilean people either voted "Sí" if they were in favor of Pinochet's continued rule or "No" if they opposed it. If the No vote won, then the 1980 constitution mandated that presidential elections be held the following year. If the Sí vote triumphed, then Pinochet would remain as president until 1997. Before entering into a discussion of pro-Pinochet women and the plebiscite, it is first necessary to recount some of the more important developments that took place in Chile during the 1980s, because they influenced the conditions under which the plebiscite took place.

In 1980 the military was at the apogee of its power. Through repression and terror, the regime had weakened the opposition; moreover, the economy was stronger than it had been in the years immediately following the 1973 coup. Given these two factors, the Pinochet dictatorship felt that 1980 was an auspicious moment to institutionalize itself and, hopefully, legitimize itself in the eyes of the international community. It therefore held a referen-

dum on the constitution it had designed and, in an atmosphere that precluded much (if any) dissent from being openly voiced, claimed that 67
percent of the Chilean people had approved it.[9] The intervening years
showed, however, that the dictatorship's confidence was misplaced. In 1982
a severe economic crisis hit Chile, and mass public protests shook Santiago
between 1982 and 1986.

   By 1988 the economy had improved and the opposition appeared
weaker and more divided than it had in the early 1980s, so Pinochet and his
advisers decided to hold the plebiscite. Deceived by his own propaganda,
Pinochet believed that he would win and thought that the vote, and his
victory, would legitimize his rule. Another factor that influenced the armed
forces' decision to hold the plebiscite was that they had publicly committed
themselves to doing so in the 1980 constitution, and to refuse to do so would
entail not only charges of hypocrisy but also a loss of face.[10] Given the military regime's desire to win the plebiscite, it was only natural that the Sí campaign would turn to women and the volunteer movement, its most loyal
supporters, in the hope that they would supply the Pinochet forces with the
numbers and enthusiasm they needed to win.

The Military Regime Thanks Its Female Supporters—
and Relies on Them for Ongoing Support

In his first presidential message following the 1973 coup, General Augusto
Pinochet extolled Chilean women who "exposed their lives and abandoned
the tranquillity of their homes to implore the intervention of the uniformed
institutions."[11] The women who had opposed Allende and called on the military to overthrow his government returned the compliment. On 11 September 1974, members of Feminine Power, the anti-Allende women's
organization that had spearheaded female opposition to Allende (see Chap.
9 of this volume), wrote a public letter stating that

    9. International Commission of the Latin American Studies Association to Observe the
Chilean Plebiscite, "The Chilean Plebiscite: A First Step Toward Redemocratization" (Pittsburgh:
LASA Secretariat, 1989), 1.
    10. For a more detailed discussion of why the armed forces proceeded with the plebiscite,
see International Commission, "The Chilean Plebiscite," 3–4, and Antonio Cavallo, Manuel Salazar, and Oscar Sepúlveda, *La historia oculta del regimen militar: Chile 1973–1988* (Santiago:
Editorial Antártica, 1990), 554–64.
    11. Augusto Pinochet, "Un año de construcción," *Mensaje Presidencial 11 de septiembre
1973–11 de septiembre 1974* (Santiago: n.p., 1974), 2.

the Chilean woman, whose suffering, humiliation and heroism kept
Chile's hope for liberty alive during three years of Marxist government, fervently thanks the Armed Forces who, on the anniversary of
our national independence, returned freedom to the fatherland.

Feminine Power calls on all Chilean women to once again demonstrate their unquenchable spirit of sacrifice and to collaborate
with the Armed Forces.[12]

Such mutually congratulatory statements characterized both conservative women's and the military's public references to each other for the next
sixteen years. However, much more was involved than a verbal love fest.
Contained in these self-serving declarations was a clearly defined sense of
what conservative women and the military thought it meant to be a woman
in Pinochet's Chile.

Above all, they believed that a woman in Chile was a patriot and a mother
whose life centered on her children and her husband. According to this
definition, women stood above politics and rejected the corruption and dirty
dealing that it necessarily entailed. Because a woman essentially lived for
someone and something else—i.e., her family and the nation—she was fundamentally more moral and spiritual than a man. The word used most frequently in interviews with and about these women, and in the publications
of the women's organizations associated with the dictatorship, is *abnegada,*
self-denying.[13] As Giselle Munizaga notes in her analysis of Pinochet's discourse, the military believed that "the Chilean woman should not develop
any activity that she defines for herself or that is based on her own needs or
expectations. Her role is to serve the government, to understand and support it, and to create or, even better, to perpetuate the mechanisms of its
reproduction."[14]

In her study of women during the Pinochet regime, *La mujer en el Chile
militar,* María Elena Valenzuela writes that once the military government
took power, it reified the image of women as mothers "whose contribution
was defined by their qualities of *abnegación* and of postponing their own
needs. [The military government] did not call on women to share power but
to form their own organizations, through which the apolitical image of

12. *El Mercurio,* 14 September 1974, 2.
13. The National Secretariat of Women published a monthly magazine, *Amiga* (Friend),
and CEMA had frequent, if sporadic, publications that expressed its beliefs and activities. I base
this observation on the seventy-five interviews I did with Chilean women in 1993–94 and on an
examination of these publications.
14. Munizaga, *El discurso público de Pinochet,* 44.

women was reinforced."[15] This apolitical image of women dovetailed, to a certain extent, with the military's projection of itself. The armed forces defined themselves by their "spirit of self-sacrifice" and "commitment [to the fatherland] that is silent, total, and [based on] self-denial."[16] The tangible expression of these qualities was the military's unswerving devotion to Pinochet, the commander-in-chief, and its unquestioning acceptance of duty.

One clear indication of the dictatorship's plans for women is that in 1974, shortly after the first anniversary of the coup, the military asked Feminine Power to disband. As one activist acknowledged, while it was true that the overthrow of Allende meant that Feminine Power's goal had been met, she believed that the military did not want an independent women's organization to exist.[17] The dictatorship had other goals for women.

During its first year in power, the military instituted a program of National Reconstruction. The nation, according to the armed forces, needed to recover from "the effects of the tragedy that ravaged the country for three years." This tragedy, claimed the military, resulted from the Popular Unity's "immorality [and] inefficient administration, [which was] compounded by hatred and sectarianism."[18] The program of National Reconstruction had two purposes: first, to collect needed funds to carry out the Junta's policies, and second, to galvanize the civilian population's support for these policies and for military rule. The military looked to women as the main civilian force willing and able to aid the Junta with its plans. The wives of military officials took the lead in demonstrating their support for national reconstruction by donating their jewelry to the cause. In "a simple activity held in the Ministry of Defense" women "gave . . . rings, pearl necklaces, earrings, pins, medals and watches." Some women even contributed their wedding rings, stating that their gift "of such great sentimental value symbolized their profound hopes for the recuperation of the fatherland."[19] Once this project produced enough money and generated a satisfactory display of public enthusiasm for military rule, the military proceeded to implement its larger program for women: the creation of a massive volunteer movement, based on the unpaid labor of women, which would work to build civilian support for military domination and policy.[20]

15. Valenzuela, *La mujer en el Chile militar,* 99.
16. Munizaga, *El discurso público de Pinochet,* 98–99.
17. Elena Larraín, interview by author, Santiago, 30 June 1994.
18. Pinochet, "Un año de construcción," 1.
19. *El Mercurio,* 20 September 1973, 20.
20. See Ximena Bunster, "Watch Out for the Little Nazi Man that All of Us Have Inside: The Mobilization and Demobilization of Women in Militarized Chile," *Women's Studies International Forum* 11, no. 5 (1988), 487.

The two most significant volunteer organizations, both in terms of numbers and impact, were the national Centros de Madres (the Mothers' Centers, or CEMA Chile) and the Secretaría Nacional de la Mujer (the National Secretariat of Women, or SNM). Lucía Hiriart de Pinochet inaugurated CEMA Chile in October 1973 and became its national leader.[21] According to Hiriart, her leadership would ensure that "the members of CEMA would never again be the objects of political maneuvering, as they had been so often in the past."[22] Hiriart also founded the National Secretariat of Women in October 1973. She summarized the goals of this organization as follows: "to disseminate patriotic and family values, to train women on all levels, to maintain a center that investigates the cultural and legal situation of women, and to promote and channel women's support for the government."[23]

The volunteer movement served several purposes for the dictatorship. It organized huge numbers of women to carry out the regime's programs and substituted women's unpaid labor for what had been, under previous governments, a state-subsidized network of social services and social workers. The volunteers worked to maintain what they, and the military, considered proper gender roles based on an authoritarian and patriarchal model. And, by defining their work as apolitical, the volunteers worked to depoliticize Chilean society and, most particularly, Chilean women.

Furthermore, the volunteer movement helped to cushion, however minimally, the impact of the military's economic policies. After it seized power, the Chilean military eliminated most of the welfare policies that the state had practiced. Following the neoliberal precepts of the "Chicago Boys," the dictatorship proceeded to privatize the economy, cut subsidies to local industries, gear production (particularly that of wine and fruit) to export, and open the door to imports. These policies resulted in unemployment and underemployment, lower salaries, and a vastly decreased availability of health

---

21. As part of its program to incorporate the urban and rural poor, the Christian Democratic Party and President Eduardo Frei (1964–70) established mothers' centers throughout Chile. The centers allowed the Christian Democratic Party to establish a base of support for itself among women in the more impoverished neighborhoods of Chile. During the Popular Unity government (1970–73), the centers were sites of intense political struggle as both leftist and Christian Democratic women attempted to win the female members' allegiance. For more on the historical and political significance of CEMA, see Valdés and Weinstein, *Mujeres que sueñan;* and Margaret Power, *Right-Wing Women and Chilean Politics, 1964–1973* (University Park: The Pennsylvania State University Press, forthcoming).

22. Lucía Hiriart, *La mujer chilena y su compromiso político* (Santiago: Editorial Renacimiento, 1984), 21.

23. Ibid., 39.

care, education, and social services for a huge number of Chileans.[24] Instead of attempting to secure employment or provide state-funded social services, the military regime offered volunteers and charity to poor women through the National Secretariat of Women and CEMA.

The organizations operated on two different levels. The National Secretariat worked to "propagate patriotic and family values" by holding seminars for the middle- and upper-class wives of government officials and diplomats and the volunteers from other military-sponsored organizations.[25] The women who staffed CEMA attended these seminars, absorbed the military's message, and transmitted it to the poor and working-class women who attended the mothers' centers. The volunteers taught the poor women basic domestic skills, organized them to attend pro-Pinochet rallies, and made sure that no opposition political activity took place in the centers.[26]

For many poor women, the benefits CEMA offered were not sufficient, but they were better than nothing. As a member of a mothers' center, a woman could possibly obtain medical care, legal assistance, scholarships for her children's education, housing, and food.[27] In addition, the mothers' centers offered women a socially sanctioned reason for getting out of their houses and for meeting with other women.

"Citizens as well as mothers": The Volunteer Movement and the 1988 Plebiscite

After years of decrying the evils of politics, in 1987 Pinochet found himself the principal candidate in the upcoming plebiscite.[28] Given the political na-

24. Phil O'Brien and Jackie Roddick, *Chile: The Pinochet Decade* (London: Latin American Bureau, 1983). The term "Chicago Boys" refers to the group of economists who occupied key government positions during the Pinochet dictatorship. A significant number of them had studied economics at the University of Chicago under the tutelage of free-market theorists Milton Friedman and Arnold Harberger.

25. *La Tercera de la Hora*, 2 December 1986.

26. For a discussion of how the middle-class volunteers used the mothers' centers to build support for the military regime and to prevent any oppositional politics from emerging, see Norbert Lechner and Susana Levy, *Notas sobre la vida cotidiana III: El disciplinamiento de la mujer* (Santiago: FLASCO, 1984).

27. Fundación CEMA Chile, "La artesanía de un país es la más fiel exponente de su cultura" (Santiago: Fundación CEMA Chile, n.d.).

28. The armed forces claimed that political parties in Chile created the economic chaos and the political disorder that compelled the military to step in and overthrow the Allende government. In his crusade against politicians (in whose numbers he did not include himself), Pinochet first abolished the parties that had made up the Popular Unity government and then, in 1977, suspended the rest of them.

ture of this challenge, the military and its female supporters had to adjust their appeal to women, and women had to create and/or project a different identity for themselves than the one they had been using since 1973. For fourteen years, both Pinochet and his female supporters had defined women as apolitical mothers and the volunteer movement as a form of social work, not as an expression of political involvement.

While these attitudes had served Pinochet well during the years that he had ruled Chile with an iron fist, they failed to provide him with the political mobilization he needed to win the plebiscite. Recognizing this, he and his female followers recalibrated their language and their identities to facilitate women's active participation in the upcoming political battles. An editorial in honor of the military-sponsored "Women's Day" in *El Mercurio,* the conservative, pro-Pinochet newspaper, summed up the new approach well. "Women will play the decisive role in projecting the progressive and liberatory work carried out by the government of President Pinochet, not only because they were in the vanguard of the struggle to defend liberty in Chile [their work to oppose Allende], . . . but because during all these years [of Pinochet's rule] they have steadfastly defended peace, tranquillity, order and the family, even as the extremists and their fellow travelers attempt[ed] to destroy them."[29]

As both the head of the volunteer movement and the First Lady, Lucía Hiriart took the lead in projecting a political identity for conservative women. After she assumed leadership of CEMA and the National Secretariat of Women in 1973, Hiriart used her position to extol the virtues of motherhood and women's apolitical nature and to project the significant role she played as head of the volunteer movement.[30] In a 1979 interview, she reflected on her six years as First Lady. "The work of the volunteers has been women's most significant contribution to this government. Through it women have committed themselves totally to the social goals of the government. The self-denial, enthusiasm, and preparation demonstrated by the volunteers have made it possible [for the government] to carry out its good works for the

29. *El Mercurio,* 4 December 1986. In 1976, the military government named 2 December "Women's Day" in honor of the women who had participated in the anti-Allende March of the Empty Pots and Pans. The government hoped to replace the more commonly recognized and celebrated International Women's Day (8 March) with a National Women's Day on 2 December to emphasize the importance of women's activity against Allende and support for the dictatorship.

30. *Amiga* (the monthly magazine of the SNM) and the various publications of CEMA always featured Hiriart's speeches and activities and continually projected her as the formal leader, the most active member, and the key ideologue of these organizations.

general welfare of the population."[31] This self-congratulatory sentiment typifies both Hiriart's and the military's definition of the female volunteers. The work of the volunteers supported the goals designed by the government; indeed, in many cases it made those goals possible. The thousands of hours of unpaid labor that the volunteers donated to the military government facilitated the implementation of its policies. Yet women were not part of the political leadership, nor did they design the regime's policies. The main compensation the middle-class volunteers received for their labor was verbal praise. In 1987, as the Pinochet regime began to prepare its forces for the upcoming referendum, it once again turned to the volunteer labor of its female fans for help. Only now, these women would be members of a political campaign and important political actors, not unpaid social workers.

Lucía Hiriart used the occasion of her public birthday celebration, held in 1987 in Las Condes (one of Santiago's wealthiest neighborhoods), to urge women to be politically active in the campaign for the Sí vote. Before she stepped to the podium, the crowd sang "Happy Birthday" to her. Sara Vivencio, one of four members of the Women's Commission of Las Condes, welcomed her and promised (as a birthday present?) that all the women present would "register to vote before the end of the year." Hiriart then delivered her message to the assembled women. She began by defining herself as "the most apolitical woman in Chile," and then laid out her political program and called on women to participate in the campaign for the Sí vote, since "no woman can stand on the sidelines, watching what happens. In the future, when the country's leaders are elected, we must be present."[32] Hiriart announced the formation of the so-called Women's Independent Movement throughout the country. The role of this movement, she assured the crowd of women, was "to support men's decisions and to slowly integrate women into the political life of the nation."[33] She added that this movement will only take "well-thought-out steps into politics and will not create obstacles for men in our nation."[34] Thus, she simultaneously urged women to get involved in politics, reminded them of their subordinate status in relationship to men, and reassured men that women's involvement would not challenge the former's superior position in politics. In order to allay any fears that she might be suggesting the creation of a feminist movement, she added that "This will not be an extreme women's movement because I just do not agree with

31. *Cosas,* 27 September 1979.
32. *La Época,* 11 December 1987.
33. *El·Mercurio,* 11 December 1987.
34. *Cosas,* 21 December 1987.

that." She rejected that type of women's movement because, as she put it, "I believe that the family, made up of children and a husband, is the pillar of society, and you must maintain good communication and understanding with them."[35] The "birthday party" ended with the "spontaneous" chanting of "Sí."[36]

It appears that her call did not meet with the enthusiasm she initially hoped to generate, since no further mention is made of the "Women's Independent Movement." However, Hiriart persisted in her efforts to establish herself as the leader of a pro-Pinochet women's movement. In June 1988, the so-called Movimiento Independiente Pinochetista de Chile (Independent Pinochet Movement of Chile) announced the formation of the Departamento Femenino Lucía Hiriart de Pinochet (Lucía Hiriart de Pinochet's Women's Department). The department's goal was to "organize women [under the direction of Hiriart] . . . to ensure that the current ruler [Pinochet] is the only candidate in the plebiscite."[37]

Hiriart may not have been successful in creating the women's political organization that she desired, but this was not due to a lack of effort on her part. In July 1988 Hiriart launched yet another pro-Pinochet women's movement, Mujeres por Chile (Women for Chile). The symbol of the new women's group was appropriately feminized: the word "Sí" had a star between each letter and a heart to replace the accent mark. The goal of this organization was to "unite the [female] volunteers and the independent and civic women's groups." It was open to all women "except those who are totalitarians" (which is how the dictatorship and its supporters referred to leftists). Although the organization would not become a party, Hiriart hoped that it would be represented in Congress and, we can only suspect, anticipated that she would be one of its elected representatives.[38]

Even as Hiriart worked to develop the women's political organizations mentioned above, she apparently understood that the volunteer movement she had built over the last fourteen years was her surest base of support. In 1988, according to Hiriart, close to 145,000 women were members of the volunteer movement.[39] Fully aware of the important role these women could play—both in terms of their own votes and in their capacity to mobilize other people to vote for Pinochet in the plebiscite—Hiriart instituted special "civic

35. Ibid.
36. *El Mercurio,* 11 December 1987.
37. *La Época,* 4 June 1988.
38. Ibid., 29 July 1988. (See also footnote 6 to this chapter.)
39. The exact number was 144,948. *El Mercurio,* 21 April 1988.

education" classes for them in April 1988, six months prior to the plebiscite. The goal of the classes was to teach the volunteers "the meaning of each of the options in the upcoming plebiscite."[40] In order to increase the number of votes for her husband and strengthen her own stature as a political leader, Hiriart also announced that CEMA Chile would sponsor classes for the husbands and children of the members.[41]

The National Secretariat of Women (SNM) also strove to educate its seven thousand women volunteers about the plebiscite. The organization planned close to one hundred seminars for 1988, all of which, according to María Isabel Saenz, its secretary, would "emphasize the challenge that is coming up: the next plebiscite." Saenz expected to convert the seven thousand volunteers into enthusiastic campaigners for Pinochet. Realizing that this represented a new role for the volunteers, she pointedly argued that "as women, we need to remember that we are citizens as well as mothers. There is no reason why women should limit themselves to their homes. This is why the SNM has been training women in civics for fourteen years, so we can be qualified to act."[42]

In the months leading up to the October plebiscite, Hiriart used her dual position as head of CEMA Chile and First Lady to wage her political campaign. She combined her ability to distribute resources to a needy population with an overt appeal to poor women to vote Sí in the plebiscite. On 5 July 1988, she opened a Centro Abierto, a childcare center for poor children, with facilities for eighty infants in the impoverished Santiago neighborhood of Renca.[43] Later that same morning she met with three thousand women who were activists in the Sí campaign in Renca. It appears that Hiriart's visit was a success. The women "thanked Señora Lucía Hiriart for her generous support . . . in favor of the most needy sectors." They also declared "their willingness to work unconditionally in favor of the government." Hiriart thanked them and declared that "I have complete faith that your efforts will move mountains and that we will celebrate the triumph of the Sí. This victory will enrich our nation and our children."[44]

The story of Rosa, a woman who lived in Renca and was a longtime

40. Ibid.

41. *El Mercurio,* 13 April 1988. Hiriart always made a distinction between the volunteers, who were mainly middle-class women, many of them married to military officers, and the members, who were poor women whom the volunteers "helped."

42. Ibid., 5 January 1988.

43. According to Hiriart, there were 510 such centers throughout Chile in 1988 and they helped "more than forty-five thousand pre–school age children." *Cosas,* 21 July 1988.

44. Ibid.

member of her local Mothers' Center, offers some insight into how Lucía Hiriart attempted to use CEMA to achieve her political goals. Rosa had initially supported the Allende government in 1971, but by 1972 she grew frustrated with it due to the shortages in essential goods and the hardship that standing in line to get food imposed on her. Although she did not support the military government, she joined the local Mothers' Center because it offered her free classes in crafts, hygiene, and cooking, the ability to socialize with other women, and benefits, such as access to medical care. Prior to the plebiscite, Rosa recalls that the CEMA volunteers went around to the Mothers' Centers in Renca and organized the members to staff the voting booths during the plebiscite. They took Rosa aside and subtly explained that if a woman was unsure about how to fill out the ballot, Rosa should encourage her to either leave the ballot blank or to vote Sí. Since she opposed Pinochet, Rosa did just the opposite on the day of the vote.[45]

Why—despite her fifteen years of work at the head of the volunteer movement—weren't Hiriart's efforts to form and lead a pro-Pinochet women's movement successful? One reason has to do with the reconstitution of the rightist political parties. Although these parties campaigned for the Sí, they also constituted an alternative organizational and political reality that, to some extent, competed with Hiriart for women's allegiance. The emergence of the UDI and RN and the reassertion of the political party system pulled women out of the volunteer movement and into the parties. In addition, since the volunteer movement had portrayed itself as devoid of politics, the dynamics of the campaign for the Sí favored the dominance of the parties—even as the parties relied on the volunteer movement for both resources and campaigners.

A second factor that explains why Hiriart's movement failed to achieve the goals she set for it is that it did not attract the conservative middle-aged women who had belonged to the rightist National Party prior to the overthrow of the Popular Unity government. During the Allende government, these women had relished their prominent position as opposition leaders and activists both in the party and, for some, in Feminine Power. Although they had applauded the coup and generally supported the dictatorship, they welcomed the return to politics and embraced the opportunity to be political actors again. Most of them had not served in the volunteer movement and disagreed with the regime's efforts to limit women's contributions to social services.

45. Rosa, interview by author, 26 November 1993.

For example, two of the principal leaders of Feminine Power, Elena Larraín (an independent) and Victoria Armanet (one of the National Party's representatives to the women's group), were dismayed when the military ordered them to end the group. Instead of joining the volunteer movement, they formed an arts group and traveled.[46] María Correa Morandé, another of the National Party's representatives to Feminine Power and a longtime political activist, disagreed with the military's decision to rely on the wives and friends of military officers to organize women through the volunteer movement. She informed the military that they were "not taking advantage of some very valuable people," but they paid her no attention because, she concluded, "the military is very closed."[47] These women welcomed the return to politics, campaigns, speeches, and elections, and they saw in them the chance to be political activists once again. While they actively campaigned for the Sí, they had no intention of doing so under the leadership of Señora Lucía. They preferred to build their own parties or work with the newly-formed ones to reassert their own independent role in politics. And since many of these women were highly intelligent, well-educated, and wealthy, they could only regard Hiriart, who was middle-class and not as well educated as they were, as their social and intellectual inferior. They were happy that Pinochet got rid of the "communists," but that did not mean that these highly class-conscious women wanted to socialize with his wife or join organizations in which she would be their leader!

The Emergence of Rightist Political Parties and of Conservative Women's Political Identities

The emergence in the early 1980s of a mass militant movement that opposed Pinochet not only illustrated the depth of popular discontent with the dictator; it also had political ramifications within the right. As Edgardo Boeninger, a prominent leader of the centrist Christian Democratic Party, noted, "another important trend in the civilian political arena has been the progressive disillusionment and estrangement from the regime of a substantial part of the Chilean right."[48] The "disillusionment" of these sectors stemmed from

46. Victoria Armanet, interview by author, Santiago, 17 March 1994; Larraín, interview.
47. María Correa Morandé, interview by author, Santiago, 4 January 1994.
48. Edgardo Boeninger, "The Chilean Road to Democracy," *Foreign Affairs* 64, no. 4 (1986), 822. Boeninger attributes the right's loss of confidence in Pinochet to Chile's ongoing international isolation, human rights abuses, and the fear that Pinochet's presence in power

the awareness that the growing strength and radical nature of the left and popular movements threatened not only the dictatorship and its economic project but also the power of the right. These rightist elements, especially the RN (Renovación Nacional, or National Renovation), feared that the growing strength of the left could produce a situation in Chile similar to those in the Philippines and Nicaragua, where popular rebellion, not a transition controlled from above, had ended the Somoza dictatorship in 1979 and threatened to end that of Marcos as well. They understood that the new conditions created by the popular movement demanded that they organize themselves into parties and engage in the upcoming political battles. Otherwise, they could not hope to contest the challenge posed by the opposition.

In response to the increased popular opposition to the dictatorship and the political opening this helped to spark, two rightist political parties emerged in the 1980s. The Unión Democrática Independiente (the Independent Democratic Union, or UDI) began its life as a political movement in 1983, and RN formed in 1987.[49] That same year, the UDI merged with RN; under the RN name, they jointly confronted the challenge of the plebiscite. However, political differences and personal struggles for power within RN led UDI forces to leave the party in April 1988 and to create their own party. The political differences that led to the formation of two distinct parties centered primarily on issues of human rights, democratization, and each party's relationship to the military government.

Quite a few UDI members had served as the principal ideologues to (and held central positions within) the Pinochet regime. Jaime Guzmán, the UDI's principal leader, wrote much of the 1980 constitution. The UDI defined itself as unswervingly pro-Pinochet, fiercely anticommunist, and fervently Christian. It declared that the patriarchal family was central to society, and it defined women's roles within the family as mothers and wives. It opposed divorce, abortion, and feminism.[50] The party styled itself as an organization of technocrats, and many of its members were instrumental in implementing the free-market policies devised by the University of Chicago School of Eco-

---

"offer[ed] permanent war against Marxism instead of development and progress," which could lead to "the danger of an eventual leftist regression" (823). The Christian Democratic Party is a centrist party that initially supported the coup but then moved into the opposition by the late 1970s.

49. For histories of these parties, see Patricia Hipsher, "The New Electoral Right in Chile and the Poor: Strange Bedfellows," *Southeastern Latin Americanist* 39, no. 3/4 (1986): 17–34, and Karina Berrier, *Derecha regimental y coyuntura plebiscitaria: Los casos de Renovación Nacional y la UDI* (Santiago: Servicio Universitario Mundial, 1989), 9.

50. See Berrier, *Derecha regimental,* and Hipsher, "The New Electoral Right in Chile."

nomics. In fact, many of the Chicago Boys—and, to a lesser extent, the Chicago Girls—who introduced the neoliberal economic programs to Chile in the 1970s joined UDI in the 1980s. María Teresa Infante was one of the few Chicago Girls. Although she was not an UDI activist, in many ways she embodied UDI's approach to politics. She studied economics at the University of Chicago and worked in various ministries during the Pinochet regime. She defined herself as a technocrat who was indifferent toward politics. As she remarked, "Politics is a subject that holds no interest for me. What I like is public service. I worked a lot with the Pinochet government." Even though she claimed to be apolitical, she campaigned for Carlos Bombal, the UDI candidate for Senator from Las Condes in the 1993 elections, and her picture appeared in an ad supporting his candidacy.[51]

Unlike the UDI, RN did not offer the Pinochet government unconditional support. While RN supported the regime's economic program, members of the party criticized the military's abuse of human rights and its dictatorial methods.[52] They supported a return to democracy and looked forward to obtaining their share of political power.

Although a conservative party, RN's position on women was somewhat more liberal than that of the UDI. RN's 1987 Declaration of Principles stated that "the family is the basic nucleus of society and it must be respected and strengthened." It also upheld the "market economy based on the private ownership of the means of production, private initiative, and social harmony." Then, in an interesting section entitled "Women and Society," the declaration called for "equal rights for women in all spheres of activity, in work and elsewhere . . . the party will work to achieve greater opportunities for women and opposes all forms of unjust social and economic discrimination against women." In recognition of the fact that a large number of Chilean women worked outside the home, the party promised to "work to make it easier for women to carry out both their social activities and their individual functions [as wife and mother], especially those related to maternity, the raising of children, and the care of the family."[53]

Despite the fact that the parties had different positions on Pinochet and,

51. María Teresa Infante, interview by author, Santiago, 15 December 1993. The UDI took out paid ads in *El Mercurio* and distributed posters with the pictures and titles of prominent Chileans who supported Bombal.

52. See an interview with Ricardo Rivadeneira, the first president of RN. In it he vehemently opposes the military's policy of sending its opponents into exile: "Everyone, everyone must return. Put simply, exile must end. . . . It has been a serious abuse of individual liberty." "Partido Nuevo . . . Cuenta," *El Mercurio,* 15 March 1987, 2.

53. "Declaración de principios de Renovación Nacional," *El Mercurio,* 3 May 1987.

to a lesser extent, on gender issues, they—along with the women of the volunteer movement—supported the dictatorship. Why?

Conservative women agreed that Pinochet's economic program had made Chile the "economic miracle" of South America. The Sí vote represented the continuity of these policies and was one of the primary reasons the right supported Pinochet. As Pinochet stated in one of his first campaign speeches, "Chile lives a moment of major importance. We approach the plebiscite with two roads to choose from: to continue along the path we have chosen or to leap into the void." If the former option is taken, Pinochet continued, then Chile will "obtain its goal of becoming a developed country and a model for the rest of South America in the twenty-first century."[54]

The Sí campaign proclaimed that Pinochet's neoliberal policies were a huge success, and a large number of women from different classes appear to have agreed with this assessment. In order to reinforce the message, the Sí campaign repeatedly reminded Chileans of the economic problems that had besieged them during the Allende government. Women who campaigned for the Sí vote went door to door talking to the housewives they found at home. They said to them, "Señora, remember the lines, the shortages, all that we had to suffer [under Allende]."[55] This theme had a particular impact on women, since they had most directly experienced the privations, high prices, and lines that had plagued Chile from 1972 until September 1973. As mothers, they felt themselves to be responsible for the welfare of their children. When shortages made it difficult to provide for their family's needs or when they had to get up very early in the morning to go stand in lines for food, they felt anguish and anger. The Sí campaign used the threat that Chile would return to a similar situation and emphasized the uncertainty as to what a change in government represented to scare women into voting Sí.

The Sí campaign portrayed the Pinochet regime as the defender of order, tranquillity, and security, and this appealed to many women. As María Elena Valenzuela points out, "the curfew loses its repressive characteristics and becomes an ally for women since it forces men to return to their homes every night at a reasonable hour."[56] In short, for many women, the curfew meant that their husbands had to be in the house instead of outside fooling

---

54. *El Mercurio,* 11 December 1987.
55. Ibid., 17 April 1988.
56. Valenzuela, *La mujer en el Chile militar,* 101. For many people the curfew is a clear sign of authoritarian government. During the early years of its rule, the regime declared that anyone found outside after the curfew could be shot or arrested. In general, it restricted people's movement and social activity and confined them to their homes.

around with other women or spending money. Rightist women often recall the Allende years as a time of unbearable violence, chaos, fighting in the streets, and upheaval. Children who had challenged authority and questioned their parents during the Allende years were brought into line under Pinochet. School regulations were rigidly enforced while young people were taught to respect the military and internalize its rigid and authoritarian approach to life. Patriarchal rule was restored in politics and in the family.

Using the language and identities developed by the women who had opposed Allende, pro-Pinochet women defined themselves as patriots who were fighting for the good of the nation. In the early 1970s the anti-Allende women's movement had defined itself as a nationalistic and patriotic movement, in contradistinction to the leftists who, they claimed, followed the orders of Cuba and the Soviet Union. When the military overthrew Allende, it claimed that it acted, in part, to defend the nation from foreign political forces. The Sí campaign appealed to Chilean nationalist sentiment again in 1988 by criticizing foreign intervention in domestic affairs—only this time the list of foreign enemies included, most prominently, the U.S.[57] Pinochet denounced the U.S. government's funding of the opposition in the plebiscite and repeatedly defined Chile as the victim of unjustified international condemnation, an attitude he attributed to envy of Chile's progress among other nations. This inaccurate portrayal of what was in reality the international community's criticism of the military's abuse of human rights allowed Pinochet to pose as the defender of Chilean nationalism.[58] As Pinochet expressed it, "the plebiscite will be the target of the most brutal campaign that the country has ever experienced, because when they [other nations] see that we are rising up and becoming strong, they attack us."[59]

Right-wing women from both RN and the UDI condemned what they saw as the U.S. government's lack of loyalty to Pinochet. In one conversation, RN supporters indicated that they could not understand why the U.S. had turned against Chile. As one of them declared, "We have never understood this and really, it has been very disillusioning for us."[60] However, instead of undermining their support for Pinochet, the U.S. government's criticisms of him served to reinforce conservative women's sense of patriotism and their belief that Chile, under Pinochet, was defending its national honor against a world gone soft on or dominated by the international forces of communism.

57. *El Mercurio*, 1 December 1987 and 4 December 1987.
58. Following Pinochet's October 1998 arrest in London, his supporters repudiated his detention as an example of "colonialism" and an attack on "national sovereignty."
59. *El Mercurio*, 1 December 1987.
60. Olga Braun, interview by author, Santiago, 11 April 1994.

The U.S. government's "betrayal" of Pinochet served to rally rightist women in his defense. In June 1988, for example, a group of women demonstrated in front of the U.S. embassy in Santiago for the Sí vote and against U.S. support for the opposition. Wearing sunglasses and scarves to cover their faces and hide their identities, the women carried signs in English and Spanish and chanted, "Defend the world instead of fleeing from it," "Intervention is disguised as donations," "The 'No' vote is the U.S.'s Waterloo." The only woman to identify herself publicly was Amalia de Yévenes, whose son Simón Yévenes had been an active member of the UDI before he was murdered in a rather confusing action.[61] Carrying a map that showed the Soviet Union's advances in the world, she announced, "We are here to demonstrate that we are grateful to this president for the freedom he has given us. Everything done against him is the product of envy."[62]

Lucía Maturana had participated in an anti-Allende women's group, SOL (Solidarity, Order, and Liberty). In 1987 she was the only woman on the political commission of RN. She joined RN both because she agreed with its politics and because she saw it as the best way to organize women. Like many in RN, Maturana considered herself an independent who believed that "history will evaluate this government [of Pinochet] as one of the very best governments Chile has had" and, at the same time, declared that we need to "recognize the positive and negative aspects of this government. All governments are susceptible to errors." She planned to organize women to vote Sí in the plebiscite "by educating them about civics since women are fifty percent of the population and we have a lot to say . . . about the future."[63]

Another group of rightist women also emerged during the campaign for the plebiscite. These women, who supported either the UDI or RN, had come of age during the dictatorship. Some of them came from conservative families who had been longtime supporters of the National Party. Few of them had any prior political experience in parties, although many of them had participated in anti-Allende activities. They were educated, middle-class women who had better things to do with their time than get involved in Lucía Hiriart's volunteer movement.

61. According to Juanita Flores, his widow, members of the FPMR (Frente Patriotico Manuel Rodríguez, or the Manuel Rodríguez Patriotic Front, a clandestine organization that fought against Pinochet) killed her husband. However, as she herself points out, after the convicted members of this group were released by President Aylwin in 1993, they recanted the confessions that had been used to convict them and said that the confessions had been extracted under torture. Juanita Flores, interview by author, Santiago, 3 March 1994.

62. *La Época,* 28 June 1988.

63. *El Mercurio,* 12 March 1987.

María Pía Guzmán is one such woman. She studied to be a lawyer in the Catholic University, where she met Andrés Allamand[64] and was greatly influenced by his politics. During the Pinochet years she concentrated on her studies, her career, and her family. When the plebiscite approached, she registered in Maipú, a poor community on the southwestern outskirts of Santiago, rather than in Las Condes, where she lived, because her husband (whose family had a farm in Maipú) told her that her "vote matters more in Maipú than in Las Condes." Like many in RN, her feelings toward the dictatorship betray a certain ambiguity. On the day of the plebiscite, she staffed the booth in support of the Sí vote, although, she said, "I would have voted 'No' except for my position!" Following Pinochet's loss in the plebiscite, she joined RN and educated "RN members and poor people" about politics.[65]

Marta Cousiño is a middle-class woman who "has always worked" outside the home. She participated in the marches against Allende, became politically active again during the plebiscite, and subsequently joined the UDI. She became a member of the UDI because she wholeheartedly supports its "free-market economics." Although she realizes that "many people think UDI is very rigid," she appreciates that the party has "one single line." She "love[s] General Pinochet," and adds, "he was a brilliant man, . . . [but] I do not believe he helped women for one simple reason . . . [during his government] women were always involved in unimportant things like CEMA." Cousiño accepts that CEMA provided resources and training to poor women, but it did not develop them politically. Although she maintains that "*machismo* is everywhere, in politics, at work" and that "women are tenacious and must do twice the work a man does to get ahead" (a sentiment that would bring a smile of agreement from many feminists), she also believes that a woman's primary responsibility is to her family and opposes divorce for Catholics who married in the Church.[66] She upholds the idea that "if you choose to marry in the Church you have the responsibility to know God's commands and the demands of the Church." While she "struggles for women, for reforms for women, I also struggle so that women will never forget why they were put here on earth: to be mothers."[67]

During the campaign for the Sí, Cousiño joined the Mujeres por el Sí,

---

64. During the Popular Unity years, Allamand had led the youth section of the National Party. He was a lawyer and one of the founders of Renovación Nacional.

65. María Pía Guzmán, interview by author, Santiago, 4 November 1993.

66. Divorce is not legal in Chile.

67. Marta Cousiño, interview by author, Santiago, 10 March 1994.

one of the pro-Pinochet women's groups Hiriart started. According to her, the movement included women from both the UDI and RN, as well as CEMA and the National Secretariat of Women. Since Cousiño had worked in a bank, Hiriart put her in charge of the finances for the organization and she traveled throughout the country to mobilize women for Pinochet. She argued that women should support Pinochet "because of the economic growth experienced by the country and the future projects that the country could undertake if it were under the leadership of General Pinochet." Reflecting the refusal of many rightists to acknowledge Chileans' repudiation of the human rights abuses under Pinochet's regime, Cousiño remarked simply that "Pinochet lost because the country needed a change."[68]

The Plebiscite

On 16 October 1988, in an atmosphere of tension and excitement, Chileans lined up to cast their votes. The turnout indicated the significance of this vote: "90 percent of the eligible population turned out to vote, the highest percentage in the nation's history."[69] The No vote won, garnering 54.71 percent of the vote, while the Yes vote received 43.01 percent.[70]

As has been traditionally true in Chilean elections, more women than men voted for the conservative candidate, in this case Pinochet; in fact, more women than men voted.[71] Out of a total of 7,251,943 votes cast, 3,734,496 were from women and 3,517,447 from men. Forty-six percent of women nationally voted for Pinochet, while 39.5 percent of men did. In short, almost half of all women who voted supported Pinochet, while only about two-fifths of the men did.

The No victory shocked and devastated pro-Pinochet women. In response, the CEMA women called an urgent meeting of the Centers. According to Rosa, "they were all crying and hugging each other. It was chaotic. I thought, one of the *viejas* had died, or one of their husbands! I asked them, 'What's the matter? Who died?' They said, 'Rosa, don't you know what hap-

---

68. Ibid.
69. International Commission, "The Chilean Plebiscite," 10.
70. República de Chile, "Resumen votación por regiones de plebiscito 5 octubre 1988" (Santiago: Servicio Electoral, 1988).
71. In Chile, men and women vote separately, so it is possible to determine how each gender votes.

pened? We lost! The No vote won and all this will end.' As if that were the end of the world!"[72]

Nine days later, CEMA celebrated its fifteenth anniversary. Lucía Hiriart addressed the crowd of twenty-five hundred volunteers and members of the Mothers' Centers. Although the No victory had shaken her, she remained a consummate political organizer. She recognized her husband's defeat and reflected on the work of CEMA, commenting that "the training [of the volunteers and members] that has meant so much sacrifice and money did not give us the expected payoff *(los frutos esperados)*. This is a pity, because maybe they did not understand our ideals or maybe they just did not care." She rallied to remind the crowd that "CEMA Chile has always been closely linked to the principles and proposals of the government." As a result, she exhorted the women to remember that "we have to continue defending it. We must continue to be united because the strength of our unity will guarantee our victory."[73]

The defeat of the Sí vote meant that presidential elections would be held on 14 December 1989. They were, and Patricio Aylwin, a leader of the Christian Democratic Party and of the opposition Concertación coalition, handily defeated the two candidates of the right, Hernan Büchi and Francisco Javier Errázuriz. On 11 March 1990, Patricio Aylwin became the first democratically elected president of Chile to hold office since 1973.

Conclusion

Conservative women felt deep respect, gratitude, and support for General Pinochet. In their eyes, he not only made Chile the economic success story of South America but also modernized the Chilean economy. They felt safer in their homes and in the streets with him as their leader. Even though the Catholic Church criticized the military for its abuse of human rights, these women saw Pinochet as a strong defender of Christian morality and traditions. Above all, his continual praise for them and affirmation of their role as mothers confirmed their own sense of self and elevated their role in society to the place they knew it deserved.

When Lucía Hiriart issued her call for the formation of a pro-Pinochet women's movement, she failed to understand that the reappearance of the

72. Rosa, interview by author, 26 November 1993.
73. *El Mercurio,* 26 October 1988.

left, the upsurge in mass protests, and the emergence of RN and the UDI had altered the political landscape. She mistakenly assumed that rightist women would respond unfailingly to her appeal to create a conservative women's movement independent of the parties and under her leadership. Although some rightist women did join her pro-Pinochet women's group, most did not. And many of those who did had hoped that they would win the support of the women Hiriart had organized through her volunteer movement for their own parties. Both parties competed for the allegiance of these women and of those who had remained outside the volunteer movement but were loyal to the Pinochet regime.

As the battle over the plebiscite approached, it was only natural that both the Pinochet regime and the rightist parties would emphasize the importance of the female vote. After all, conservative women had projected themselves as the vanguard of the anti-Allende struggle and as the most committed backers of the military dictatorship. Conservative women did respond to the calls of the dictatorship and of the rightist parties, but in doing so, they also asserted their role as political actors. They defined themselves as citizens, not as apolitical mothers.

Rightist women exhibited a fluidity of identity that challenges many scholars' assumptions about them. As this chapter illustrates, these women were both willing and able to adapt their identities to meet the needs of the moment—and in a relatively short amount of time. Conservative women who had defined themselves as apolitical for the past fourteen years began, in 1987, to re-create their identities: they became the public-spirited citizens and political actors that the struggle to win the plebiscite demanded. Their capacity to do so indicates that it is a mistake to consider right-wing women as either changeless or tradition-bound.

Although conservative women rejected feminism as an ideology, feminist ideas and demands permeated their discourse, especially that of younger women. Even as they upheld the ideal of motherhood, they complained about male dominance in the parties, the workplace, and occasionally the home. And as so often happens with conservative female activists, they railed against feminism because it supposedly undermined the family—even as their political activity meant that they spent much of their time away from their homes and their families.[74]

---

74. For a discussion of this phenomenon among conservative women in the United States, see Susan Faludi, *Backlash: The Undeclared War Against American Women* (New York: Crown Publishers, 1991), 239–56.

BIBLIOGRAPHY

PRIMARY SOURCES

Journals and Newspapers

Amiga (Santiago, 1973–83)
Cosas (Santiago)
El Mercurio (Santiago)
La Época (Santiago)
La Tercera de la Hora (Santiago)

Interviews

Armanet, Victoria. Interview by author. Santiago, 17 March 1994.
Braun, Olga. Interview by author. Santiago, 11 April 1994.
Correa Morandé, María. Interview by author. Santiago, 4 January 1994.
Cousiño, Marta. Interview by author. Santiago, 10 March 1994.
Flores, Juanita. Interview by author. Santiago, 3 March 1994.
Guzmán, María Pía. Interview by author. Santiago, 4 November 1993.
Infante, María Teresa. Interview by author. Santiago, 15 December 1993.
Larraín, Elena. Interview by author. Santiago, 30 June 1994.
Rosa. Interview by author. Santiago, 26 November 1993.

SECONDARY SOURCES

Anderson, Jon Lee. "The Dictator." *The New Yorker,* 19 October 1998.
Berrier, Karina. *Derecha regimental y coyuntura plebiscitaria: Los casos de Renovación Nacional y la UDI.* Santiago: Servicio Universitario Mundial, 1989.
Boeninger, Edgardo. "The Chilean Road to Democracy." *Foreign Affairs* 64, no. 4 (1986): 812–34.
Bunster, Ximena. "Watch Out for the Little Nazi Man that All of Us Have Inside: The Mobilization and Demobilization of Women in Militarized Chile." *Women's Studies International Forum* 11, no. 5 (1988): 485–91.
Cavallo, Antonio, Manuel Salazar, and Oscar Sepúlveda. *La historia oculta del regimen militar: Chile 1973–1988.* Santiago: Editorial Antártica, 1990.
Constable, Pamela, and Arturo Valenzuela. *A Nation of Enemies: Chile Under Pinochet.* New York: W. W. Norton and Company, 1991.
Drake, Paul W., and Ivan Jaksic, eds. *The Struggle for Democracy in Chile, 1982–1990.* Lincoln: University of Nebraska Press, 1991.
Faludi, Susan. *Backlash: The Undeclared War Against American Women.* New York: Crown Publishers, 1991.
Fundación CEMA Chile. "La artesanía de un país es la más fiel exponente de su cultura." Santiago: Fundación CEMA Chile, n.d.
Hipsher, Patricia. "The New Electoral Right in Chile and the Poor: Strange Bedfellows." *Southeastern Latin Americanist* 39, no. 3/4 (1986): 17–34.
Hiriart, Lucía. *La mujer chilena y su compromiso político.* Santiago: Editorial Renacimiento, 1984.
International Commission of the Latin American Studies Association to Observe the

Chilean Plebiscite. "The Chilean Plebiscite: A First Step Toward Redemocratization." Pittsburgh: LASA Secretariat, 1989.

Lechner, Norbert, and Susana Levy. *Notas sobre la vida cotidiana III: El disciplinamiento de la mujer.* Santiago: FLACSO, 1984.

Munizaga, Giselle. *El discurso público de Pinochet: Un análisis semiológico.* Santiago: CESOC/CENECA, 1983.

O'Brien, Phil, and Jackie Roddick. *Chile: The Pinochet Decade.* London: Latin American Bureau, 1983.

Pinochet, Augusto. "Un año de construcción." *Mensaje Presidencial 11 de septiembre 1973–11 de septiembre 1974.* Santiago: n.p., 1974.

Power, Margaret. *Right-Wing Women and Chilean Politics, 1964–1973.* University Park: The Pennsylvania State University Press, forthcoming.

Renovacíon Nacional. "Declaración de Principios de Renovacíon Nacional." Santiago: El Mercurio, 1987.

República de Chile. "Resumen votación por regiones de plebiscito 5 octubre 1988." Santiago: Servicio Electoral, 1988.

Valdés, Teresa, and Marisa Weinstein. *Mujeres que sueñan: Las organizaciones de pobladoras en Chile, 1973–1989.* Santiago: FLACSO, 1993.

Valenzuela, María Elena. *La mujer en el Chile militar: Todas íbamos a ser reinas.* Santiago: Ediciones Chile y América/CESOC, 1987.

Conclusion

The very idea of comparing the experiences of right- and left-wing women activists makes many people uncomfortable. Some even see it as heretical. For if "our" women fight for values like truth, justice, and motherhood, then "those" women must favor something else or they must have been manipulated by male politicians. (We think it is worth finding out why there is so much resistance to even asking such comparative questions, resistance that is extremely common among activists—and to a lesser but still significant extent among academics.)

However, even in the face of resistance, we should not stop asking comparative questions. By analyzing four interrelated themes—maternalism, feminism, autonomy, and coalitions between left- and right-wing women—in six Central and South American countries, we have come closer to understanding the roles that women have played in Latin American politics in the twentieth century.

Throughout this volume, the language of motherhood has been used by activists to explain and perhaps justify their decision to become politically active. For example, one woman who supported the fascist Nationalist movement in Argentina in the early 1930s used the language of maternalism: the "Argentine and Nationalist woman . . . [knew how] to be the light of a home, to coo to a child, . . . to love with the saintly love of a mother" (quoted in Deutsch, this volume). In the 1970s, members of Poder Femenino in Chile called upon the military to overthrow the elected government of Salvador Allende "because there is no meat to make soup for our babies and as a result, they get sick from diarrhea" (quoted in Baldez, this volume). As Power and Kampwirth have shown here, other right-wing activists, including members of the Pinochet dictatorship's Mothers' Centers in Chile and the

Contra guerrillas in Nicaragua, also utilized the language of maternalism, even in cases when they themselves had no children.

But left-wing radicals may also be mothers, and they too sometimes justify their activism through the language of maternalism. Contrary to what one might expect, in Nicaragua maternalism was utilized more frequently by the political left than by the right during the years of the Somoza dictatorship (1936–79) and the Sandinista revolution (1979–90) that followed it. A leader of the opposition to Somoza was disgusted by the dictator's tactics "when he paid a large number of prostitutes to throw themselves at the mothers and wives of those who were imprisoned at the time" (quoted in González, this volume). In countries like El Salvador and Chile, Ready and Baldez have argued here, even left-wing feminists have frequently organized women as mothers, though they have also tried to challenge the gender inequality that is often intertwined with maternalism.

But if activists on the left and the right can promote sometimes diametrically opposed projects by using the same discourse, does maternalism have any inherent political content? Or is it so malleable that it can be all things to all people? Perhaps it is really a way for women to justify their decision to become activists, rather than the major motivation for that decision. Organizing as mothers may facilitate radical activism that would not be socially acceptable otherwise.

Yet justifying political activism through the language of maternalism may carry a cost. To what extent does the choice to take on the identity of "mother"—as opposed to alternative identities, such as "citizen" or "worker"—shape and limit women's ability to act? Under what circumstances have women chosen to mobilize as mothers, and when have they chosen other identities? How do the movements they join differ, depending on the identities they embrace?

Maternalism, with its claim that women should be self-denying *(abnegadas)*, would seem to preclude the rise of feminism, with its claim that women should demand equality. Yet feminist organizing is also a theme that runs throughout the chapters in this volume. Interestingly, many feminist activists first became politicized through maternalistic mobilization (see Kampwirth, this volume). Like maternalism, feminism is a theme that sometimes crosses the right/left divide. Under what circumstances have successful women's coalitions been forged across partisan lines?

The contributors to this volume who analyzed the (still rare) cases in which women from the left and right managed to unite around a shared interest in ending gender inequality showed that the women's groups that joined such coalitions all enjoyed a certain degree of autonomy; these groups were somewhat independent of the male-dominated organizations, such as the guerrilla groups, church groups, and political parties through which the women first mobilized. Autonomy allowed them to challenge the idea that they had nothing in common with women from the other side of the political divide.

But what sort of autonomy is necessary for effective coalition building? Is control over income and budgeting the key? Is it decision-making power? Or does a women's group need to cut all ties to the original organization before it may build even temporary coalitions with women from the other side? And if complete independence is necessary, to what extent is autonomy a euphemism for isolation and weakness?

A real danger is that the same autonomy that allows for coalitions between left- and right-wing women around shared gender concerns may diminish the influence of those women in national politics. Both Blandón and Luciak (this volume) note that the autonomous feminist movement in Nicaragua, which by the 1990s was by far the largest and most influential feminist movement in Central America, has nonetheless had trouble influencing the left-wing FSLN, the very party through which it initially emerged. Similarly, Haas (this volume) argues that despite many common goals and historical ties, Brazilian feminists have had difficulty promoting feminism within the Workers' Party (or PT).

When autonomy facilitates the formation of left/right women's coalitions, what are the issues that motivate their members? While such coalitions are never easy to build, certain issues lend themselves more to coalition building. For instance, opposition to domestic violence is probably the easiest gender issue around which to generate agreement; however, if that agreement is to be put into practice through things like state-supported battered women's shelters or public education programs, inherently fragile coalitions may break apart. Another demand that often unites women across the political spectrum is for responsible paternity—specifically, the demand that men not abandon their children, and that they at least pay child support if they should leave them. A third issue that is often supported by women across the political spectrum in Latin America is quotas for women within parties or as candidates for office, though that issue tends to be fought out within each party, limiting its usefulness as a coalition-building issue. In contrast, building a broad-based political coalition around demands such as providing access to safe contraception and abortion or ending discrimination against gays, lesbians, and bisexuals has been impossible so far.

Why is it possible to form coalitions around some issues but not others? As Hipsher and Ready suggest here, one explanation is that anything that relates to economics or the neoliberal agenda—i.e., the trend for the state to cut social spending—is hard, if not impossible, to sell to political elites of the right. Interestingly, though, coalitions between non-elite women of the right and left have been forged around economics in a different sense (i.e., daily survival tactics such as pooling resources to build housing, neighborhood gardens, or economic cooperatives [see Kampwirth, this volume]).

How can we explain the near-impossibility of one sort of economic alliance and the effectiveness of the other sort? First, the second sort of economic alliance, an alliance around grassroots projects, does not directly challenge neoliberalism and may even facilitate the implementation of a neoliberal agenda, as the state is relieved of its responsibilities to its poorest citizens. Second, the extreme poverty that originally fueled the guerrilla wars also may bring the antagonists in those wars together out of desperation. Poor right- and left-wing women may be more willing to ally with each other than elite women are simply because the stakes are higher for them.

Another framework that might be helpful in explaining which issues cut across partisan lines is that of *practical* and *strategic* gender interests (see the introduction to this volume). But while that framework offers insights into women's participation in social movements, it does not take us very far in the analysis of cross-politics coalitions. All four of the issues we mentioned above—domestic violence, responsible paternity, reproductive rights, and respect for sexual orientation—are strategic gender issues; that is, addressing them would directly affect power dynamics between men and women. Yet two of these issues lend themselves to left/right women's coalitions, and two of them do not.

Answering the question of why certain gender demands lend themselves to coalition building and why others do not will help us understand the nature of political divisions within Latin America and the ways in which women understand their own interests. The role of the Catholic Church may be the key: where the hierarchy of the Church opposes gender reforms (on reproductive rights, for example, or respect for sexual minorities), the political right, including right-wing women, also opposes such changes. This is the case even though right-wing women, like left-wing women, sometimes wish to limit pregnancies and even though some of them are lesbians or bisexuals. However, in the cases when the Church agrees with gender reformers—opposing domestic violence and irresponsible paternity—then right-wing women are more free to forge coalitions with left-wing women around their common interests.

In the twentieth century, the Latin American countries we have studied have undergone military coups, dictatorships, guerrilla challenges, revolutionary experiments, and periods of political democracy. The radical women who have appeared in these pages have helped to make those political changes possible, for better or worse. As the century came to a close, all six countries analyzed in this volume were characterized by democratic regimes, albeit with many limitations.[1]

Is the restoration or establishment of democracy good news for radical women? On the one hand, the return to democracy has all too often been a return to gender inequality as usual. The principle of "one person, one vote" means that people are free to vote their old prejudices, and so it often solidifies social inequalities. This was clear in the cases of the left-wing guerrilla groups considered here: once the wars were over, female leaders found themselves marginalized within the new parties, though in the case of El Salvador's FMLN, that marginalization was later successfully challenged through quotas (see Luciak, this volume). Also, to the extent that money buys access to democratic politics, the vast majority of women have less access than men.

On the other hand, the divisions generated by the civil wars and dictatorships often kept women from recognizing that they sometimes shared common interests with women on the other side. That some of them have started challenging their male allies by questioning maternalism, seeking autonomy, exploring feminism, and forging coalitions with women from the other side means that democracy has presented them with new opportunities along with new challenges.

---

1. On the limits of the latest wave of democratization, see John Peeler, *Building Democracy in Latin America* (Boulder, Colo.: Lynne Rienner, 1998), 154–55; Kenneth Roberts, *Deepening Democracy? The Modern Left and Social Movements in Chile and Peru* (Stanford: Stanford University Press, 1998), 1; and Richard Stahler-Sholk, "El Salvador's Negotiated Transition: From Low Intensity Conflict to Low Intensity Democracy," *Journal of Interamerican Studies and World Affairs* 36, no. 4 (1994): 1–59.

BIBLIOGRAPHY

Peeler, John. *Building Democracy in Latin America.* Boulder, Colo.: Lynne Rienner, 1998.

Roberts, Kenneth. *Deepening Democracy? The Modern Left and Social Movements in Chile and Peru.* Stanford: Stanford University Press, 1998.

Stahler-Sholk, Richard. "El Salvador's Negotiated Transition: From Low Intensity Conflict to Low Intensity Democracy." *Journal of Interamerican Studies and World Affairs* 36, no. 4 (1994): 1–59.

CONTRIBUTORS

LISA BALDEZ is Assistant Professor of Political Science and Harbinson Faculty Fellow at Washington University in St. Louis. She received her Ph.D. in Political Science from the University of California, San Diego, in 1997. She is currently completing a book tentatively entitled *Why Women Protest* that explains women's mobilization in terms of the intersection of political institutions and cultural norms.

MARÍA TERESA BLANDÓN is Director of the Central American Current (Programa Centroamericano La Corriente) and a member of the Malinche Feminist Collective (Colectivo Feminista La Malinche). She has written on feminism and the women's movement in Central America, gender and public policy, and women's role in Nicaragua's democratization process.

VICTORIA GONZÁLEZ is a Ph.D. candidate in Latin American History at Indiana University. Her dissertation documents the transition from early-twentieth-century feminism in Nicaragua to the Somocista women's movement. She also addresses the reasons women had for supporting the Somoza dictatorship (1936–79).

LIESL HAAS is Assistant Professor of Political Science at Western Michigan University. Her most recent publication is "The Catholic Church in Chile: New Political Alliances," in Smith and Prokopy, eds., *Latin American Religion in Motion* (Routledge, 1999). She is currently working on a book manuscript examining the effects of institutional politics on efforts to expand women's legal rights in Chile.

PATRICIA HIPSHER is Assistant Professor of Political Science at Oklahoma State University. Her published research has focused on urban social movements and democratization in Chile and on the Salvadoran women's movement. She is currently conducting research on identity politics and social movement organizations in the United States.

KAREN KAMPWIRTH is Assistant Professor of Political Science and Chair of the Latin American Studies Program at Knox College. She has published articles on women's movements, gender and elections, and guerrillas in *Latin American Perspectives, Political Science Quarterly, Women's Studies International Forum, Social Politics,* and the *Bulletin of Latin American Research.* She is also the author of *Revolution in the Real World: Women and Guerrilla Movements in Latin America* (Penn State University Press, forthcoming).

ILJA A. LUCIAK is Associate Professor of Political Science at Virginia Polytechnic Institute and State University. His research on revolution, democratization, grassroots movements, gender politics, and reproductive health has been published in Austrian, Swedish, British, Mexican, Nicaraguan, Salvadoran, and North American journals. His latest book is entitled *Gender Equality and Democratization in Central America* (The Johns Hopkins University Press, 2001). He has been a post-doctoral fellow at Cornell University and a guest professor at Stockholm University, Innsbruck University, and the Central American University in Managua, Nicaragua.

SANDRA McGEE DEUTSCH teaches history at the University of Texas at El Paso. She is the author of *Counterrevolution in Argentina, 1900–1932: The Argentine Patriotic League* (University of Nebraska Press, 1986) and *Las Derechas: The Extreme Right in Argentina, Brazil, and Chile, 1890–1939* (Stanford University Press, 1999). She is also the co-editor of *The Argentine Right: Its History and Intellectual Origins, 1910 to the Present* (Scholarly Resources, 1993).

MARGARET POWER is Assistant Professor of History in the Humanities Department at the Illinois Institute of Technology. Her book, *Right-Wing Women in Chilean Politics, 1964–1973,* is forthcoming from The Pennsylvania State University Press. Her research interests include rightist women, democratic forces within the Chilean military, and modernity, technology, and gender in Chile.

KELLEY READY is Visiting Assistant Professor of Anthropology at Northeastern University. She is a solidarity activist turned academic, and in 1999 she completed her dissertation, "Between Transnational Feminism, Political Parties, and Popular Movements: Mujeres por la Dignidad y la Vida in Postwar El Salvador." She continues to study feminism and sexuality in El Salvador.

INDEX